Mountain at a Center of the World

Mountain at a Center of the World

Pilgrimage and Pluralism in Sri Lanka

ALEXANDER McKINLEY

Columbia University Press
New York

Columbia University Press
Publishers Since 1893
New York Chichester, West Sussex
cup.columbia.edu

Library of Congress Cataloging-in-Publication Data
Names: McKinley, Alexander, author.
Title: Mountain at a center of the world : pilgrimage and pluralism in Sri Lanka / Alexander McKinley.
Description: New York : Columbia University Press, 2024. | Includes bibliographical references and index.
Identifiers: LCCN 2023032153 (print) | LCCN 2023032154 (ebook) | ISBN 9780231210607 (hardback) | ISBN 9780231210614 (trade paperback) | ISBN 9780231558501 (ebook)
Subjects: LCSH: Pilgrims and pilgrimages—Sri Lanka—Adam's Peak. | Religious pluralism—Sri Lanka. | Adam's Peak (Sri Lanka)—History.
Classification: LCC DS490.A2 M35 2024 (print) | LCC DS490.A2 (ebook) | DDC 305.80095493—dc23/eng/20230811
LC record available at https://lccn.loc.gov/2023032153
LC ebook record available at https://lccn.loc.gov/2023032154

Cover design: Milenda Nan Ok Lee
Cover art: Johnston, Harry Hamilton, Sir, 1858-1927, Public domain, via Wikimedia Commons

FOR MY LIGHTS, ROSHNI AND RISHI

Contents

PART III

Being Like a Mountain

A Note on Translation, Transliteration, Terminology, and Teaching

When translating poetry from Sinhala and Tamil, I strive to render the original verses into English as literally as possible while still preserving intelligibility. In many instances, I have added punctuation to clarify meaning. In others, I have minimized these interventions in the imagistic interest of the poetics. Foreign terms in italics are transliterated with diacritical marks. Names of interviewees are rendered phonetically into English. For place names or major landmarks like mountains or rivers, as well as names of gods and other famous personages, I use conventional English spellings, allowing readers to better cross-reference these. Many names for the mountain appear in the pages that follow, including Sumanakuta or Samantakuta from Pali, Sri Pada or Samanala from Sinhala, Samanai or Sivanolipadamalai from Tamil, al-Rahun from Arabic, Adam's Peak from English, etc. In my own prose, I mostly use the term "the Peak." This is not only the pithiest option, but is also meant to avoid endorsement of any one sectarian affiliation at this plural site. For those interested in teaching with this book, I have designed an accompanying module of course content, which is hosted by the American Institute for Sri Lankan Studies: https://www.aisls.org/resources/teaching-about-sri-lanka/teaching-about-adams-peak/. This includes a virtual pilgrimage comprising photographs from my fieldwork, which serves as a good introduction to the Peak. It is an especially useful way to orient students when only teaching selections from the book.

Acknowledgments

Thanks are first and foremost due to all the Sri Lankans at the mountain who facilitated my research. Those whose voices appear most often, including Aryapala, Chandra, and Ranjit, showed me great hospitality, introduced me to others, and shared a wide range of their own thoughts. Those who also offered essential aid, but whose voices appear less or are absent here, include Nimal, Siva, Bandara, Prakash, and the rest of the staff at the White House Hotel, Rajah, Sunil, and their family in Nallathanni, Rukmal, Kelum, and the whole family of the Matara Kade, the staff of the Aehela Kanuwa Kade, the Indikatupana and Udamaluwa police officers, and all the monks and employees of the Sripadasthanaya temple on the summit.

Elsewhere in Sri Lanka, I owe thanks to staff of the Colombo National Museum Library, the Sri Lanka National Archives, and the Ratnapura National Museum. The librarians at the University of Peradeniya, especially Buddhika Konara, were of great help. Other University of Peradeniya faculty who lent aid include Mangala Keshawa, Godwin Kodituwakku, Nimal Wijesiri, and especially W. Amarakirthi Liyanage, who tutored me in the art of translating Sinhala poetics. Thanks are also due to Premakumara De Silva of the University of Colombo, for conversations about our mutual site of study. Additionally, I am grateful to the Faculty of Humanities and Social Sciences at the Open University of Sri Lanka for providing forums in which to discuss my research, and to Sanmugeswaran Pathmanesan for his friendship. Many other friends and families in Sri Lanka have opened their homes to me and facilitated my stays in innumerable ways for years. They include the Kodituwakku family of Aniwatta, Singha and Mala Weerasekera of Kurunduwatta, Subodha Angammana, Patrick and the extended Vanhoff/Webster family, as well as Sunil Nanayakkara, Dhanuka, Prabath, Ganesh, and all my other friends from Malwatta Road in the Pettah.

Deep thanks are due to my first and most long-standing Sinhala guru, Bandara Herath, with whom I was blessed to work for two rounds of the South Asian Summer Language Institute in Madison, Wisconsin. Without his instruction in spoken and poetic Sinhala, all this would have been impossible. Herath's coteacher on the ISLE program in 2006, where we first met, was the legendary P. B. Meegaskumbura, from whom I learned the sagest advice that a good song can get you out of a tight spot in Sri Lanka. Herath also introduced me to Chandini Tilakaratna, with whom I studied literary Sinhala prose for a summer in Colombo. Thanks also to Richard Frasca for all the Tamil tutelage at Harvard.

Many generous sources of funding have made this book possible. Two FLAS grants in 2011 and 2015 provided tuition for the SASLI Sinhala program. Additional language training and archival work in Sri Lanka was facilitated by summer research grants from the Kearns endowment of the Duke University Graduate Program in Religion from 2013 to 2017. My fieldwork at the Peak in 2015–2016 was sponsored by a research grant from the United States–Sri Lanka Fulbright Commission. More time for writing was thereafter afforded by a Charlotte W. Newcombe Doctoral Dissertation Fellowship in 2017.

Stateside, I owe thanks to the staff of Duke University Libraries, the Newberry Library in Chicago, the New York Public Library Manuscripts and Archives Division, and the Asian Reading Room at the Library of Congress. I must offer heartfelt gratitude to my advisor, Leela Prasad, whose guidance has always been apt, insightful, and encouraging. Advice from Anne Blackburn, Richard Jaffe, Hwansoo Kim, and Laurie Patton guided me toward shaping this book. Many other faculty mentors at Duke and beyond recommended sources, provided forums for discussion, or carefully read and commented on chapters or proposals related to this project, including Charles Hallisey, Engseng Ho, Janice Leoshko, Sumathi Ramaswamy, John Rogers, Sujit Sivasundaram, Sharika Thiranagama, Mark Whitaker, and Michael Woost. A hearty thanks are also due to my scholar friends in Sri Lankan studies and beyond who have been valuable conversation partners, offered important sources, or otherwise lent their skills to aid this project. They include Mark Balmforth, Hunter Bandy, Phil Friedrich, Justin Henry, Tyler Lehrer, Roshni Patel, Nethra Samarawickrema, Ben Schonthal, Tom Soderholm, Ven. Upali Sraman, Don Stadtner, and Shobhana Xavier. I am also grateful to the Institute for Religion, Culture, and Public Life at Columbia University for inviting me to workshop my research and eventually opening a pathway to publication. Thanks to the editors and reviewers at Columbia University Press for all their help. Finally, I must thank those closest to me for keeping me whole: my parents, sisters, wife, and son.

Introduction

Making the Most of a Mountain

A white-haired, white-clothed couple shuffled along with their arms around one another. The sunlight was intense atop the mountain summit, but the wind was chilling. They stayed close for warmth, moving tentatively, legs surely sore. They had climbed without shoes, carefully placing calloused soles on one cement step after another. When they reached the top, they first worshiped the large footprint set in stone. They then walked around the summit area. There was a crowd that afternoon, but not so thick as to inhibit movement, like on the opening day of the worship season. Some pilgrims waited in line to see the footprint, some rang the summit bell, marking their number of ascents, some made offerings to the god Saman's shrine, some lit incense or oil lamps in a designated area. Children giggled, chased one another, and hid behind adult legs. Young men and women with slim jeans and coiffed hairstyles were casting glances and jokes, huddling to take selfies. Mostly paved with concrete, little of the original mountain was visible on the summit, but the elderly couple moved past one piece of old rock face. As they ambled alongside it, the man trailed his hand over the rough granite. "This is the rock that Lord Buddha has placed his foot upon," he whispered with some awe in his voice. He paused to touch his forehead against the stone, closing his eyes in quiet reverence.

I saw this on a sunny March day, midway through the six-month worship season at Adam's Peak, also known as Sri Pada, or Samanala, in Sri Lanka. For the entirety of the 2015–2016 season, I lived in the trailhead village of Nallathanni at the mountain's base on the "Hatton side," the shorter, more accessible, and far more popular route. I climbed to the summit several times a week, interviewing pilgrims and employees along the way.[1] Over the course of the season, I ascended fifty times, a lifetime of pilgrimages for most Sri Lankans, but less than two months' work for an average professional courier at the Peak. During the season, pilgrims continually come and go in all manner of relations and group sizes, from solo travelers on public transit, to friends or families in private vans, to schoolmates or village neighbors aboard rented buses. Once in Nallathanni, many climb at night to avoid the heat of the day and to watch the sunrise the next morning. All spend several hours ascending the mountain's thousands of steps toward their goal, and then hours more back down again, their bodies all the sorer for it.

The six-month length of the pilgrimage season is dictated by the weather, with the summit lost in rainclouds the rest of the year. During these rainy months when the mountain is mostly left alone, I explored libraries and archives in Sri Lanka, finding a wealth of Sinhala pilgrimage literature in palm-leaf manuscripts (*puskoḷa pot*) and early-print pamphlets (*kavi koḷa*). Meanwhile, over several years before and after my fieldwork, I mined digital repositories and library loans for references to the Peak. My span of sources became staggering, with ethnographic data alongside hundreds of texts over the past thousand years that linguistically included Sinhala, Tamil, Sanskrit, Pali, Thai, Tibetan, Chinese, Arabic, Persian, Latin, French, German, Dutch, Italian, Spanish, Portuguese, and English. In this way, it became clear to me that the Peak was a mountain at a center of the world, noticed by generations of visitors to Lanka, and bearing a footprint on its summit variously identified as belonging to the Buddha, Siva, or Adam. In light of its incredibly diverse heritage, the Peak has understandably become famous as a site of religious pluralism. The central question of this book therefore asks how pluralism is best conceptually understood and practically managed at the Peak.

The answers I pursue are meant to counter a popular refrain, in Sri Lanka and beyond, that the Peak is an apolitical space where easy coexistence, or even harmony, is automatic among different religions. Aside from being unrealistic, this narrative presumes "religions" are separate and discrete categories, and that they occupy and interact with an inert space, the same sort of boxed-in modern thought that distorts many of our perceptions about how the world works.[2] A more useful account of pluralism refuses to make religion an exception out of the constancy of everyday life, instead examining its instantiations everywhere, with interactions that exceed official forums or shrine walls. Still, some stable point of orientation around which to track these pluralities remains helpful. As few things are more constant than mountains, I position the Peak itself as the main character of this book, the common denominator under every foot. Its range of pilgrims, human and otherwise, is only a piece of its history, as contingent and conditional actors moving in malleable formations among one another and a host of other planetary forces. With such an ecological view of pluralism, this book departs from conventional expectations about what constitutes the content of pilgrimage and religion, inquiring instead from the higher ground of the Peak. This is not meant to flatten all difference into a singular humanity beneath the mountain. Rather, a mountain's point of view, physically and temporally, is precisely the vantage point from which to relay more realistic accounts of pluralism, as the Peak's environment is a touchstone that reveals recurrent patterns across diverse pilgrim accounts, past and present.

Yet an expanded definition of religious pluralism, or a more holistic edition of its history at the Peak, means little if it serves only to edify academics or translate the pilgrimage into English. I therefore follow Qadri Ismail's advice to "abide by Sri Lanka," which "means to display a commitment to attending to its concerns, to intervening within its debates, to taking a stand," seeing "the stakes . . . [as] ethical and political as much as epistemological."[3] The Peak must be acknowledged as actively political, and a theory of pluralism must point to practicalities in this realm. I therefore overlay empirical and ethical lines of argumentation in this account of the Peak. Empirically, I pursue evidence of past and present pilgrimage motivations, infrastructure, and literature across multiple religious traditions, shown in both cooperation and conflict with each other and the natural forces of the mountain. Ethically, I advocate for this cultural and ecological diversity of the Peak to be acknowledged and sustained. In the process, the empirical and ethical inform each other. This is partly because empirical history is part of Sri Lankan politics, often invoked as a discourse of control.[4] The plural history I relay is thus meant as evidence against proliferating modern-box histories of a pure Sinhala Buddhist land where others are always alien. Such discourses have increasingly crept up the slopes of the Peak, displacing even the simplified ideal of religious harmony there. Through this book, I therefore seek what Leela Prasad calls "truth in history . . . tied to narrative justice, a form of equity that is possible only through a many-sided narration."[5] While my opening image of elderly Buddhists devoutly worshiping at the summit is idyllic, to present the Peak as only a place of Buddhist piety would be both empirically insufficient and ethically unjust, even if representative of the majority of pilgrims who attend today. The multifaceted account that unfolds over the following pages instead shows the mountain to have long been shared, made sacred by Muslims and Hindus well before more recent Buddhist myths made it an anti-Muslim and anti-Hindu space.

As the divisiveness of religious politics has intensified over the past century, it has coincided with unprecedented levels of environmental degradation, making conscientious intervention necessary for both cultural and ecological pluralities to continue flourishing on the Peak. To emphasize how its religious and environmental issues are intertwined, I suggest the mountain itself can make an ethical demand upon human actors, as its temporal dominance instills humility in our own ambitions toward control, and its ecology attunes us to the diverse assemblages of nature. The mountain was already full of agendas before humans found it, including its own geological habits, and those of the life that grew upon it. From our place as modern addendums to montane assemblies, humans are positioned to reflect on this deep history and rhetorically use the mountain as an inspiration for political action to maintain the best conditions of possibility for pluralism. The Peak thus precedes us in many ways, as a theoretical anchor for this book, and a precondition for religious life in Sri Lanka.

Centering Ourselves

If the Peak occupies a center of the world, the indefinite article is important, for the mountain itself proves the rule that all centers are relative. It makes this point not only with its varied significations across different religious traditions, but also because it temporarily becomes the center of the world for pilgrims as they climb it. This is just as true for the young visitors who take advantage of the summit's sweeping backdrop to frame their selfies as for the whispering old couple who tenderly touched the rock beneath the footprint shrine. At these moments, the Peak is the center of what matters. Another pair of visiting pilgrims made this clear to me at the start of my stay, when I was surprised to find large groups of Tibetan monks and nuns using the preseason weeks of December for their pilgrimages. On his own more singular journey was Ösel Dorje Rinpoche, son of Terchen Dorje Tsegyal, a Tibetan treasure-text revealer, or *terton*. After emigrating to India, Ösel Dorje Rinpoche settled in Dharamsala, where he met Tenzin Sherab, an employee of the Dalai Lama's office. The Rinpoche and Tenzin were sent by that office in 2015 to perform a special ritual at the Peak: a *lama chöpa*, or *guru pūja*. They arrived in Nallathanni only a few days after I did, and coincidentally stayed at the same guesthouse. I noticed them at dinner one night and wordlessly met the Rinpoche in the buffet line. A large man with a hulking gait, his huge palms completely enveloped mine when he shook my hand and smiled with a soft growl. Yet Tenzin came to dinner alone the following night and asked if he could join my table. I assumed the Rinpoche was resting from the climb, but Tenzin explained, with some exasperation, that the Rinpoche had no intention of descending from the mountain before week's end. The Rinpoche had told Tenzin to continue the rest of their tour of Sri Lanka alone, having received permission from the resident officials atop the Peak to stay in a stark cell on the summit for a week in meditation leading up to the *guru pūja*, fulfilling a longtime aspiration. The Peak is ritually potent among the Nyingma sect as a site where Padmasambhava, the legendary monk who transmitted Buddhism to Tibet, buried hidden treasure texts. The Rinpoche told Tenzin that seven days of meditation atop it are equal to seven years of practice.

Over the next week, as I climbed up and down the Peak for research, I also acted as a courier for notes between the Rinpoche and Tenzin and brought the monk tastier food than was available on the summit. Tenzin also sent a chair up via a professional courier to make his teacher more comfortable. The Rinpoche's daily practices included meditation and quietly reciting mantras, counting off beads with his fingers. Slowing walking back and forth across the summit, he would point out surrounding summits to me and signal that he wanted to meditate there, too, though there was no easy way to reach them. As centered as he seemed at the Peak, this was only one center among many where spiritual treasures could be pursued.

Meanwhile, on lower ground, Tenzin spoke of the mountain's centrality in a different way. Happy to meet an American academic, he told me he studied for a master's degree at the University of California, Santa Barbara, many years ago. One theorist he read stood out in his mind after climbing the Peak. As we sat eating dinner together, he remarked on the extent to which the Hatton trail was built up with lights, stairs, and far more shops and snack stalls than he expected. It reminded him strongly of what the French author Henri Lefebvre wrote about spaces. Our conversation deepened as Tenzin lost interest in the bland tourist-buffet fare on his plate and reminisced about the Lefebvre he had read: "He talks about mountains specifically in one of his books, and the way that people build on them. That is one idea that may be helpful for your research." Enchanted by this chance encounter, I took Tenzin's words to heart, and procured a copy of Lefebvre's *The Production of Space* to read on days when I rested my legs. Lefebvre does indeed mention mountains, placing them among previously remote areas now subject to the expanding reach of capitalism, as "the space of nature remains open on every side, and thanks to technology we can 'construct' whatever we want, at the bottom of the ocean, in deserts or on mountaintops." This made all centers relative for Lefebvre, dependent on flows of capital so that "centrality is moveable," and "centrality is therefore a *form*, empty in itself but calling for contents—for objects, natural or artificial beings, things, products and works, signs and symbols, people, acts, situations, practical relationships." The Peak thus takes the form of a center due to its varied contents—the many types of pilgrims, the ritual actions that occur there, the money to be gained, and the workings of the entire environment. After all, Lefebvre did not want to isolate capital or economics in a separate sphere, but sought a more unitary theory of space, arguing that "centrality as a form implies simultaneity, and it is a result thereof: the simultaneity of 'everything' that is susceptible of coming together—and thus accumulating—in an act of thinking or in a social act, at a point or around that point."[6] At and around the point of the Peak, the act of pilgrimage is an event of immense simultaneity. Crowds of people meet each other and the mountain, surrounded by tea plantations that give way to a cloud rainforest where gods dwell, all the while flanked on the trail by commodities. Conveying the detail of this active assembly is one challenge this book undertakes, explaining interactions among the multiplicity of its components.

The day before I met Tenzin, I encountered a group of Sri Lankan pilgrims at the summit, an older man with three younger companions in their late teens and early twenties, two of them monks. We descended the trail together for a stretch, treading carefully down the steps on an overcast day with intermittent showers, pausing at intervals to look back at the summit shrouded in clouds. I chatted with one of the young monks, asking for stories about the place. He confidently told me that the Buddha's words would reveal all I needed to know about this mountain. The stories locals told were one thing, but the truth lay in the Pali canon. I nodded politely in response but, having just spent the previous months immersed in Sinhala literature about the Peak and having come to the mountain for ethnographic corroboration, I was not initially receptive to his advice about canonical texts, chalking it up to the orthodox devotion of a novice monk. Yet his words never left my memory, and, as time passed, I began to wonder why I should take this endorsement of the Pali canon any less seriously than Tenzin's recommendation of a French Marxist.[7] To abide by Sri Lanka, my argument must also engage Sri Lankan terms of political discourse, which often use an overtly Buddhist tenor. I therefore complement critical theory and political ecology with Buddhist philosophy, especially ideas of expansive temporality and interdependence, which are also helpful in describing the nature of mountains. This is partly meant as an antidote to the divisive brand of Sinhala nationalism that thrives in Sri Lanka, making plural sites like the Peak exclusively Buddhist in aesthetic and ritual.[8] Lefebvre would cite this as further proof of modern state centers replicating themselves at every level, as "centrality now aspires to be *total*," spreading the abstract space of the nation that has "homogeneity as its goal, its orientation, its 'lens.' "[9] The young monk with whom I spoke may very well approve of such homogenous trends, but as I searched for theoretical insights from the Pali canon, I instead found encouragement toward ever more expansive understandings of a heterogeneous yet fundamentally connected world. It is through such philosophies, and similar insights of local mountain residents, that avenues emerge for the Peak to assert its own unique centrality. My approach therefore builds on Lefebvre like Nihal Perera's does, furnishing examples of "people's spaces," which "defy homogeneity assumed in abstract spaces and larger categories."[10] My granular reading of the Peak and its people attests to the singularity of the place, unclassifiable according to conventional dichotomies of urban versus rural, nature versus culture, or Buddhist versus non-Buddhist. The Peak requires its own mountainous perspective.

To idealize expansive awareness, the *Dhammapada* uses a metaphor about centering oneself on a mountain, where "the wise one by awareness dispels unawareness, and having ascended the palace of wisdom . . . observes the sorrowing folk . . . as one standing on a mountain [observes] those standing on the ground below."[11] These heights of perception refer to the enlightened Buddha, though such attainment is made relatable with the image of standing on a mountain, presaging Sinhala poetry that likewise compares ascent of the Peak to attaining nirvana. Greater awareness is therefore a real possibility if the right effort is expended to gain a better vantage point. Centering us on higher ground, this book begins from the premise that the Peak itself provides the best perspective for an awareness of pluralism in all its potentialities. Surveying past and present around the point of the Peak shows not only a diverse parade of humans sharing its slopes, but also the pluralities inherent in its ecology and geology. In the process, the Peak is recognized as an actor, exerting its agency into human and planetary affairs.

Mountainous Agency

The idea that mountains can wield power over people is not new in scholarly circles. In 1859, colonial official James Tennent suggested that the Peak first became significant "amongst aborigines of Ceylon, whom the sublimities of nature, awaking the instinct of worship, impelled to do homage to the mountains and the sun . . . to convert awe into adoration."[12] This argument was rephrased a century later by the Sri Lankan professor E. F. C. Ludowyk, who wrote that "the peak stands for something . . . older than civilization, something anterior to the Buddha, which is still a living force. It belongs to the old gods who are not dead yet."[13] At the time, such sentiments about mountains pervaded general scholarship on religion, as Gerardus van der Leeuw wrote: "The oldest heaven is the mountain-top,"[14] while Mircea Eliade mused: "Mountains . . . share in the spatial symbolism of transcendence—they are 'high,' 'vertical,' 'supreme' . . . the dwelling of the gods . . . where sky and earth meet . . . a region impregnated with the sacred, a spot where one can pass from one cosmic zone to another."[15] Mountains are massive, hard-to-reach, and touch the sky; how could they not be special? The sacredness of such locales was presumed.

Although older theories about the inherent holiness of nature are now seen as stereotypes, something does remain unique about the Peak's landscape. As Ludowyk wrote: "Geologists have noted its difference from the rest of the mountains in Ceylon. . . . Few have the conical configuration which distinguishes this. . . . The peak stands out."[16] As the Peak's relief rises sharply above the surrounding terrain, it is clearly visible from many miles away in several directions, even out to sea. Sight of the Peak made people write of it, orienting worldviews across cultures, whether as a political boundary or soteriological goal. In this way, the Peak helped create pilgrimage to it. As one Sinhala poet put it: "Although a rock, it brought about this journey."[17] Ludowyk likewise called the Peak's power "a living force," an animation of nature akin to recent theoretical trends that pluralize agency in an effort to be less anthropocentric.[18] Jane Bennett, for example, writes of "the capacity of things . . . not only to impede or block the will and designs of humans but also to act as quasi agents or forces with trajectories, propensities, and tendencies of their own."[19] Such sentiments have framed new projects in religious studies, considering material objects, affective responses, and ecology over textual exegesis.[20] Following these trends, this study of the Peak takes seriously the mountain's agentive role in human history. Unlike other sacred South Asian mountains, however, the agency of the Peak does not mean the rock is equated with divinity, as with Vishnu's presence in the rocks of Govardhan or Siva in the summit of Kedarnath.[21] Instead, pilgrims to the Peak understand it as a physical platform that has hosted visits by divinities and other great beings. As it takes a special sort of summit to qualify for such an honor, the mountain as a mountain is the powerful agent under examination here.

Yet care must be taken not to let this yield simplistic or fantastical explanations for pilgrimage. Attributing agency to a mountain is not meant to presume that the Peak has a magical magnetic pull on those who climb its slopes. Critiquing similarly simplistic explanations of pilgrimage that assume some inherent ineffable sacred power, Russell McCutcheon argues that "human beings involved in routine, mass, or coordinated movements from place to place are not inherently 'pilgrims'—they're just people on the move," and calls for greater sociopolitical investigations into why this is the case for any given locale.[22] In the chapters that follow, the agency of the mountain is therefore examined in tandem with the human politics, commerce, and conquest that also fuel motivations to visit. Chapter 1 and chapter 2, for example, are two sides of the same coin. The first focuses on the Peak as the main actor, showing how its long temporal presence allows a variety of cultures to be compared, as its same natural features are described by different visitors. In this way, chapter 1 has the Peak structuring life as long as there have been beings to scale its slopes. Chapter 2, however, turns to human structures upon the mountain, outlining the infrastructural interventions people make into the environment to explain how the Peak also shoulders local economies and political platforms. This interplay of mountain and human actors then continues through the final three chapters, as gods, devotees, merchants, political leaders, and natural creatures share the same stony space, influencing each other's behavior. A full picture of this plural pilgrimage therefore unfolds over the course of the book, on a composite Peak with space for many actors, expressed through the varied stories they tell.

Speaking Through Myth

In some ways, the Peak transcends storytelling altogether, its deep-time history giving it a power wholly apart from human concerns. As Eliade put it: "Above all, stone *is*. Rock . . . transcends the precariousness of . . . humanity: an absolute mode of being."[23] Yet this seemingly transcendent geohistory also creates conditions for the Peak's fame among humans, in its relief, watershed, and gemstone geochemistry. As people enter the picture, the Peak becomes a vantage point from which to compare past and present interfaces with its landscape, a most stable object for narrating history in the vast archive of stories it has inspired. If one stacks these stories up, as I attempted to do on a spreadsheet during my research, the data quickly becomes difficult to interpret at a glance if organized by chronology alone. For patterns to emerge, I color-coded sources by language, and found the lines of citations came to look more like geological sediment—a visual representation of what Sri Lankan anthropologist Gananath Obeyesekere would call the Peak's "mythic stratigraphy."[24] As more stories were added, I worked to fit them together like a mountain, per the geometric theory of fractals that argues "a mountain is not a cone,"[25] but rather a conglomerate pattern of smaller mountains, capable of being broken into versions of itself—a larger whole made of many different wholes (fig. Int.1). In texts across varied languages, diverse pilgrims wrote similar things about the Peak's

FIGURE INT.1. The fractal nature of the Peak summit

gems, forest, rivers, rain, and famous footprinted stone. Interpretations varied, but the commensurability across accounts remains remarkable. In this way, the Peak helps make its own myth, with humans sometimes seeming to be mere mouthpieces for tales the mountain is already telling.

The few modern histories of the Peak, however, tend to divide the story by religious denomination rather than letting the mountain lead. William Skeen's colonial monograph separated "the origin of Buddhist, Hindu, and Mohammadan Pilgrimages," followed by another chapter designated for "notices of the Peak and foot-print by early Christian writers."[26] Eschewing such divisions, chapters 1 and 2 of this book look at engagements with the Peak that precede and exceed the religious, while chapters 3 and 4 focus on Muslim and Hindu movements to the mountain by showing their myths to be in mutual evolution with Buddhist neighbors. This method has more in common with the later chapters of Skeen's book that follow a pilgrimage route. His anecdotes there are more attuned to landmarks, stories springing from sites with entangled historical actors. Skeen thereby glimpses a mode of thinking through the Peak, rather than only about human claims to it. As several historians have argued, "if deep time is to figure into our histories, we need narratives that can triangulate between agents and materials. . . . Thinking *through* objects rather than thinking *about* objects."[27] Thinking through the Peak means not only recognizing how it structures storytelling, but also using its materiality to organize the analysis of those tales.[28]

To call these sources "myth" is not to marginalize them as false. I instead refer to myth in Eliade's sense of "a *true history*: it relates how things came into being."[29] Leszek Kołakowski likewise saw myth as defining parameters of reality, setting discursive terms with "information regarding what is or is not a value in the first place. . . . The mythical consciousness is . . . present in every understanding of the world as endowed with values . . . in every understanding of history as meaningful."[30] Myth in this sense is not only a narrative but also an accompanying framework of thought, making facts cohere into significant existence through valuation. "Myths therefore announce dense, powerful truths."[31] Judgments of good and bad, or true and false could not occur without a consensus of shared myth. What makes a summit beautiful, sacred, or even a mountain at all is based on collective understandings of beauty, sacrality, and mountains in general, given voice through stories. Not all who come to the Peak see it within the same mythic frame, and no collection of myths could ever be comprehensive. Even my stratified spreadsheet, the privileged perspective of a scholar, is not a *complete* myth of the Peak. As Claude Lévi-Strauss notes: "We are dealing with a shifting reality, perpetually exposed to the attacks of a past that destroys it and of a future that changes it . . . analysis of myths is an endless task."[32] The myths pilgrims retell are therefore variable, so the same mountain can be seen as an inert rock, a sacred space, or a living being by different accounts.[33] Mountainous agency does not therefore supersede and simplify the diversity of human engagements, but the similarities across stories show the mountain at work, encouraging commonalities in myths of otherwise dissimilar worldviews.

To facilitate these cross-cultural comparisons, the mountain's mythic stratigraphy must be interpreted with some flexibility. It is not immutably "set in stone," just as the literal stone of the Peak has never been entirely stationary. Made of metamorphic rock repeatedly folded by heat and pressure over billions of years, the Peak is streaked with curving lines, not neat layers. In some places these lines even seem to fold around one another, leaving the impression of swirling rock waves frozen in motion, all the more so when rains make the granite shiny black, and rivulets run over the metamorphic stretch marks, crossing and deepening the lines in the stone. These geologic phenomena suggest a method for reading the Peak's mythic stratigraphy. Like metamorphic rock, the sources in the following chapters fold over one another, lines of analysis curving across them, often eschewing chronological linearity.[34] Human interaction with the Peak thus arises in polytemporal assemblages. As Michel

Serres describes it, "time is layered in local space."[35] Bruno Latour elaborates that "every cohort of contemporary elements may bring together elements from all times. In such a framework, our actions are recognized at last as polytemporal. I may use an electric drill, but I also use a hammer. The former is thirty-five years old, the latter hundreds of thousands."[36] This becomes still deeper when mountain elements are considered. Imagine a Lankan sapphire, crystallized hundreds of millions of years ago, embedded in parent rock formed thousands of millions of years ago, lying in a streambed where it washed down tens of thousands of years ago, picked up by a human who lives no more than a century. Layers of time in a material moment encourage a corresponding polytemporal perspective for the Peak's mythic stratigraphy, comparing recurring themes of its environment. Poetry on its rivers and rock circa 1216 can resonate with accounts in 2016, both referencing pieces of the mountain extant sixteen thousand or even sixteen million years ago. Using geological perspective as an interpretive lens keeps this range of mountain history in view, facilitating thematic groupings of sources around their common parent materials.

By reassembling myths to rewrite the history of the Peak, I also recognize pilgrims doing the same. Stories conglomerated around a particular subject are picked up, changed, and used as tools. I call these working narratives "mytholiths," after the lithic tools used by early humans of the Lankan highlands. When cataloging artifacts unearthed from gem pits, antiquarian P. E. P. Deraniyagala found "entire crystals of quartz and corundum, sometimes with the apex flaked into a sharp edge, and roughly chipped (and ground) to provide a secure grip. . . . For such an implement the name *Crystalith* is here suggested."[37] The crystalline material of this artifact pairs well with Lévi-Strauss's description of how "through the repetition process . . . myth grows spiral wise . . . it closely corresponds, in the realm of the spoken word, to the kind of being a crystal is in the realm of physical matter."[38] A mytholith therefore describes the formation of stories as a cumulative process apart from the intentionality of any one agent, while also showing stories as tools, picked up and modified by a particular person. Stories that have gradually grown are susceptible to sudden change, like crystals chipped to fashion hand axes. Deraniyagala noted *crystaliths* were often quartz "since this material readily provides cutting edges at the first cleavage."[39] Quartz is a predominate crystalline mineral at the Peak, inset in its gneiss rock, including the footprint,[40] around which stories are likewise modified because they are so cleavable, edges honed into various versions with unneeded pieces shorn away for different ends. The mountain's mythic stratigraphy thus breaks down in fractal fashion, into sections with their own thematic facets shaped by shaving certain details and fashioning others into blades or bludgeons for construction or destruction. Whether they become weapons reflects the ethical implications of mythmaking, determining who counts as a legitimate pilgrim, and who is cut out.

Pursuing Pluralism

There are some who claim the Peak as an exclusive domain of one party, cutting away a history of cultural diversity. Others proclaim the Peak's pluralism, but only with token nods to harmony among "religions"—a modern category that presumes a universally shared phenomenon of religion, yet speaks through a dualistic language of difference.[41] This definition of pluralism may actually be welcomed among those who seek exclusive control over the Peak, as the presumption of an automatic harmony can mask agendas of Buddhist hegemony, while the language of discrete religions marks Buddhists as expressly distinct from religious neighbors on the mountain. Yet this presumed pluralism maintains popular purchase in public discourse because of its tidy answers, ignoring the difficult truth that political theorist William Connolly summates: "Pluralism emerges as *a possibility to pursue* rather than the certain effect of determinate conditions."[42] I suggest that pursuing pluralism at the Peak requires a perspective that uncouples analysis from categorical divisions, including those present in the way pluralism itself is defined. Scholarly critiques of pluralism have shown that the word is applied to at least two phenomena: the basic fact of communal diversity with its relatively unreflective interactions that mix myths and rituals in mutually constitutive ways (i.e., "religious plurality"), and the intentional institution of initiatives to encourage healthy coexistence among different groups in modern shared spaces (i.e., "interreligious pluralism").[43] As Pamela Klassen and Courtney Bender describe it, "pluralism has retained both descriptive and prescriptive burdens and . . . it is not always easy to tell them apart."[44] Rather than jettison the word as unwieldly baggage or separate its meanings in my method, however, I carefully repack pluralism to consciously take up both descriptive and prescriptive agendas, and increase their weightiness by expanding these pluralities into the environment. If one problem with the genealogy of the term "pluralism" is its link to the inherently dualistic term "religion," resituating it in relation to the literal common ground on which religious actors walk may give it better footing to sidestep prior pitfalls and describe this pilgrimage.

A more planetary pluralism accounts for more of the mountain, including myriad natural forces that make the Peak its own center. Although now somewhat homogenized by Buddhist majoritarianism, the Peak retains powers that are a resource for resisting such trends. As Lefebvre advises, "the only possibility of so altering the operation of the centralized state as to introduce (or reintroduce) a measure of pluralism lies in a challenge to central power from the 'local powers,' in the capacity for action of . . . regional forces linked directly to the territory in question."[45] As the Peak has historically constituted a relatively autonomous territory in Sri Lanka, this book makes the mountain speak as the local representative for the plural life upon its land, using its deep view of the past to present a case for sustaining future diversity. The many myths of the mountain recounted herein capture the fact that "plurality is formative,"[46] with shared spaces generating unique stories and rituals, some freely exchanged and some exclusive. By combining them as I do, my own mytholith of this book, with its edges of prescriptive arguments, is meant to be a tool for the conscientious pursuit of equitable diversity.

Yet I do not wish to make my argument easily dismissible by imposing foreign standards of a purportedly universal pluralism "as a model for export" to the Peak.[47] Local understandings of pluralism can also be identified, existing "genealogically independent of European magnanimity," as Elaine Fisher has shown for South India.[48] In the case of Sri Lanka, Benjamin Schonthal notes, "some forms of Buddhist toleration conform to notions of toleration celebrated in European philosophical liberalism; some do not."[49] Yet even by Buddhist models of rule, where inclusion is "exercised and enforced from the top-down," and "toleration appears less as a mode of egalitarian politics and more as a kindness extended to non-Buddhists by Buddhists,"[50] I argue that those in control of the Peak fall short of their own standards, and I consult Pali and Sinhala Buddhist texts alongside the thoughts of modern workers at the Peak in support of this claim. While Schonthal notes that "the Buddha advocates a posture of epistemological discrimination (the jettisoning of wrong views and the adopting of right views)," he also explains how this right view provides "an understanding of reality that is so accurate that it permits adherents to engage the world without grasping, dogmatism, or defensiveness."[51] In this spirit, many Buddhist sources I consult challenge the boundaries of almost every discriminating category, by virtue of teachings about the interdependence that undergirds the workings of the world around the Peak.

The pluralism to be pursued therefore runs deeper than religious identity. The Peak puts the many mobile strangers who meet there into interdependent perspective. Seen in this way, the mountain cannot be claimed, but rather claims those who climb it by incorporating them into its environment. The Peak is thus a composite, fitting Bennett's point that "agency always depends on collaboration, cooperation, or interactive interface of many bodies and forces."[52]

The plural agents of the mountain include rock bodies, water bodies, forest bodies, and human bodies together, interwoven with other forces like climate and planetary positioning in a trajectory of geohistory. So the mountain is neither a cone, nor only stone, as its nature inspires narrative and puts pilgrims on the move. To reflect this dynamism, most sources I use to tell the Peak's story are poetic, as poetry is a special sort of speech, public in performance yet able to subvert common significances and assumptions. Lefebvre agrees that "poets struggle against the iciness of words and refuse to fall into the traps set by signs."[53] For this reason, poetry provides a counterbalance to my own empirical prose, exemplifying how to think outside of categorical language and static arguments, to instead represent in imagistic detail a plural world with multiple meanings.

In turn, the fluid understanding of pluralism sought here refashions the study of "religion and ecology" by not treating its two categories as bounded entities that only occasionally overlap. Instead of limiting questions to how religious actors impact ecology or vice versa, I cast the mountain's ecology as the theoretical foundation of my analysis. I thereby depart from earlier works organized by denominational designations, or focused mostly on the ironic harms religion inflicts on environments.[54] It is not that such works are incorrect in their content, but their approach is confined by expectations of preformed categories. I instead follow those anthropologists of South Asia who address both religious and ecological questions without being limited by either concept as a dominant frame, their work instead structured around singular places, species, or practices.[55] Religion is then not artificially made into an isolatable object of analysis apart from existence, "removed and *separated* from life, into some aspect or category *of* life."[56] This book therefore strives to present a picture of the Peak that does justice to its life in full. The frame of planetary pluralism places humanity within the rest of nature, thereby showing the idea of pure harmony or effortless unity on the Peak to be misleading. What actually exists is more nuanced and suggests that the cultivation of a robustly multireligious space now requires active attention and maintenance, just like the modern health of the highland rainforest. Rather than harmony springing from a simplistic sacredness, coexistence must be forged with conscientious intentions.

In my intentional mytholith of this book, each chapter represents a facet of the mountain's pluralism. They are not organized by linear chronology, nor denominationally divided into separate religions, but instead interwoven in historic evolution and modern cohabitation. The book unfolds over three parts. Part 1, "A Mountain and Its People," describes the Peak's origins and agency, while also showing a wide spectrum of human engagements with and modifications of the mountain, thereby outlining the many elements that constitute a planetary pluralism. Chapter 1, "Rock, Water, and Montane Agency," focuses on the Peak as the main actor, explaining how its deep temporal presence allows it to anchor comparison, as its same natural features are described by diverse visitors, illuminating long-standing links among humanity and planetary forces. Chapter 2, "The Workaday Mountain," then turns to human habitats built upon the Peak, outlining the infrastructural interventions that people make into the environment for economic, political, and religious gain. Humans are still influenced by the mountain, which sets physical limits, and conditions bodies of those who work upon it, including kings, colonizers, merchants, mendicants, vacationers, and laborers. Motivations for building have included the performance of military displays or improvement of karma, while more modern agendas include public health, corporate advertising, and international tourism.

The movements of people with such varied motivations show the friction inherent in plural existence. Part 2, "A Mountain of Myth," therefore explains both positive and negative religious interactions at the Peak, refuting popular presumptions of easy unity there. Buddhist, Hindu, and Muslim stories are shown to be in mutual evolution with one another, creating mytholiths that can cut—either to carve out a space on the island for new visitors, or excise unwelcome interlopers from Lankan history. Chapter 3, "Adam's Peak and Buddhist Visions of Mecca," examines Muslim stories that grew around the mountain as the site of Adam's descent into the world, told to interpret new landscapes encountered by Islam. These are compared to a corresponding reaction in Sinhala poetry that mentions the Buddha leaving his footprint in Mecca. As Muslims have been increasingly discouraged from performing pilgrimages to the Peak, some Sinhala nationalists have redeployed this Buddhist Mecca mytholith as another type of triumphalist tool. Likewise, chapter 4, "Admitting and Forbidding Siva at the Peak," explains some sharper edges of storytelling between Buddhists and Hindus. While some Sinhala and Tamil sources reflect common interests, especially in the Peak's rivers and other natural features, another mytholith that grew in Pali and Sinhala texts, spanning royal chronicles to modern pilgrim tales, has made evicting Hindus a lasting trope of Buddhist success.

In light of these past and present contestations, I return to the environment to seek future common ground. Part 3, "Being Like a Mountain," details the lessons that can be learned from the Peak's planetary pluralism. Chapter 5, "Pilgrimage Ethics from Pluralism," considers not only conservation practices by people, but also how the environment intervenes to encourage proper action toward it. Modern residents of the mountain explain how pilgrim behavior shifted with environmental history: as the forest diminishes, so do its miraculous powers and physical challenges; in turn, pilgrim behavior degrades, causing further forest damage. Disrupting this cycle of natural and moral decay thus depends on conservation, but even this can engender further Buddhist dominance. In response, the ethic of planetary pluralism uses Buddhist philosophy to recognize the mountain's multiplicity of beings, and encourage an equitably sustainable mix of pilgrims, plants, animals, and divinities. While acknowledging the likelihood of some continued friction, this ethic advances an attitude of inclusive stewardship over the Peak instead of hegemonic monocultures. Finally, the conclusion, "Deep Stakes," considers the Peak's lessons in terms of the Anthropocene. Learning what it means to be a mountain encourages humanity to explore its own geological status within the deeper patterns of our species—always on the move, gathering, building, niche making, and worshiping. The history of the Peak is a microcosm of how modern technology sped these processes, and its mytholiths can now be used to make them more sustainable by promoting an ethic of mutualism, where treating one another well in a plural world is a means to treating the planet in a way that we may all remain pilgrims upon it.

Resting at Chandra's Tea Stall

An average trip up and down the Peak via the Hatton side goes something like this. Most pilgrims arrive at the trailhead settlement of Nallathanni in the late afternoon or evening. Some will rent a room at one of the small hotels to serve as a base camp. Others will decamp from the private vans or buses they have rented, or alight from the public bus that runs from the Hatton train station, and immediately start their walk up the mountain. The goal for many pilgrims is to time the climb so that they are at the summit when the sun rises, just before six in the morning. Depending on fitness level, this might require beginning a climb just after sundown, or around midnight, or a few hours thereafter. Some, like myself, prefer to climb during the daylight hours instead, although the hot sun can make this more tiring. On the other hand, the chill of the night often causes Sri Lankans to don winter hats or wrap towels around their heads for warmth. There is no expectation of being fully comfortable on the mountain. As later chapters discuss, the discomfort is part of the pilgrimage's purpose.

From the trailhead, one begins a six-kilometer hike with an elevation change of around a thousand meters. The second half of the trail is much steeper than the first. Except for the dirt path near the start, most of the trail is now paved with cement, including over five thousand steps of varying height and breadth, with railings near the steepest portions just below the summit. The steps make the trail smoother, decreasing chances of tripping or turning an ankle, but are nevertheless grueling on the legs. Despite the cool temperatures at night, it is easy to work up a sweat before reaching the mountaintop, making it feel all the colder as the summit winds whip over damp clothes. At the summit of the Peak, the first stop is to worship the sacred footprint, sheltered in a small shrine at the absolute apex of the rock, with one final stairway to climb to reach it. After touching one's head to the imprinted stone and placing an offering of money or flowers, pilgrims mill about the summit compound doing different things. Some chat while huddled for warmth, some pray, some light oil lamps, some make offerings to the Saman shrine, some simply wait for the sun to rise, smartphone cameras pointed at the eastern horizon in anticipation. Once the sun appears, or when people have simply had enough of the biting breeze, pilgrims will start their journey back down, grateful to be descending instead of ascending, but tentative with each tender move down the uneven steps, as muscles have already cooled and begun to stiffen in the interim.

Even when climbing at night, the mountain trail is never terribly dark during the worship season. All along the pathway, fluorescent tube lights are strung up every few meters, facilitating the overnight ascents. There are also the lightbulbs hanging from the many trailside shops, which are ubiquitous on this side of the mountain. One rarely encounters a stretch of trail where the next tea stall cannot be seen. While shops nearer Nallathanni sell all manner of goods that they hope pilgrims will buy on their way home, the stalls on higher stretches of the trail specialize in the necessities of the moment: hot tea or coffee and snacks for the weary climber. These stalls are small, even perched on precipices in higher places, and are only temporary constructions that must be rebuilt every season, requiring purchase of a permit from tea plantations in the lower stretches of the trail or the Wildlife Conservation Department that manages the upper wilderness reserve. Yet for six months of the year, these stalls are homes for the shopkeepers, who partition off small sections that act as personal quarters, places where pillows and blankets over raised wooden pallets keep them dry and warm enough to catch sleep whenever the crowds thin enough to warrant it.

While I lived in Nallathanni and climbed the Peak several days a week, the shopkeepers were the folks with whom I spoke the most. The ethnographic portions of this book consequently represent more employees of the Peak than visiting pilgrims. Some workers became good friends whom I met almost daily, developing a rapport that encouraged longer conversations. I was also able to arrange multiple interviews with them, offering new questions as my research developed. We seemed to develop a comradery like coworkers, all part of the mountain's seasonal contingent of laborers. Moreover, their shops were good places to meet pilgrims, as many avail themselves of these stalls up and down the Peak to rest legs and lungs. Not all pilgrims stopped in such stalls. Some were afraid of resting their legs for too long. Others could not afford the inflated prices of foodstuffs at higher elevations. But many pilgrims stopped to rest at least once or twice along the way, and whichever shop was closest to their breaking point of exhaustion benefitted from their business.

I benefitted from these shops, too, needing time to rest and research. Some became more regular stops, either because they lay at a convenient point in the trail, or because their personnel never changed throughout the season, allowing me to befriend them. One shop was an example of both: the stall owned by Chandra and Mathu, just below the Sitagangula stream crossing. Chandra and Mathu were forty-year veterans of the Peak pilgrimage shop business and had many stories to share. Their shop was built into a small cutout in the hillside just adjacent to the trail, its tin roof and walls of tarpaulined wood keeping out the rainforest for a few months. On a landing between two stretches of steps, a space large enough to for several wooden benches to be posted in the shade across from the shop, their location relied on the weariness of pilgrims too tired to make that final push up to Sitagangula—a traditional stopping place for pilgrims, where devout Buddhist visitors follow rituals of sharing a meal, bathing in the cool mountain stream, taking the precepts, cutting a lime and tying a tribute coin for Saman's shrine, before donning white clothes for the harder half of the climb. But the crowds at the crossing are larger and the shops more impersonal, with the din of the waterfall making it especially hard to converse. I therefore preferred to take my own break with Chandra and Mathu, having a cup of tea and conversing with them and their customers.

Chandra and Mathu were a charming pair, fairly toothless but eloquently loquacious. The portly Mathu spoke with ebullience in the face of age, his gray horseshoe moustache dancing down his chin. The shop bore his name, although not a sign. Most stalls were like this: publicly unmarked but named among mountain veterans. In my mind, however, I always thought of the stall as Chandra's. She seemed to be the real force anchoring customers in conversation. She had a talent for storytelling, and skills as a conversationalist that also included patience with my foreign Sinhala. She was a font of information about the pilgrimage and its history, and a friendly face when I grew weary of climbing and talking with strangers. Only once did I pass their stall without stopping for a hello, after which Chandra scolded me so soundly I never did it again. When we parted at the end of the season, we both got a bit misty-eyed.

Just as it did for me on the mountain, Chandra's stall acts as a waystation throughout this book. It is not the only shop that is visited, but the one returned to most often. Stopping there provides opportunities to hear unique stories, meet diverse pilgrims, and ground theory in practice. Sometimes ideas encountered at Chandra's stall complement other sources I present, and at other times contradict them. Like the polysemous poetry in the pages that follow, these ethnographic interludes are a counterbalance against the slippage of academic prose into positivism. It is therefore fitting that Chandra's shop was one of the few on the trail that still sold pamphlets of poetry meant for singing on pilgrimage, including the text known as *Purāṇa Himagata Varṇanāva,* or *The Ancient Praise of Himagata* (fig. Int.2). For this reason, her stall is also a portal into the past, as this compilation was a creation of the early twentieth-century print boom, cobbling together several styles of earlier pilgrimage verse. Its title reflects an intent by its editors to preserve verses that would otherwise fall out of use. It is rare to find groups of pilgrims singing these old songs, but their persistent presence on the trail via shops like Chandra's preserves the possibility of their recitation and the continuation of their

FIGURE INT.2. Gloves, fruit, and poetry for sale at Chandra's stall

messages. In this indefatigable spirit of pilgrimage, I leaf again through the thin white pages with magenta lettering in the *Purāṇa Himagata Varṇanāva* copy Chandra gifted me, and I am drawn to one of its concluding aspirational verses as I conclude this introduction. Ultimately, my hopes for what follows are not all that different from those of the original poet and the generations of pilgrims who voiced these wishes:

> For my voice to be heard for seven leagues like a celestial
> musician
> For my form to become light for the three worlds when born
> To take the gold stylus in hand and write the gold book of
> Buddha virtues.[57]

PART I

A Mountain and Its People

1

Rock, Water, and Montane Agency

nidos vemin dasa diga sura räsi nā
salas ulela häli mudunen vähe nā
ahas gañgin sädi isuruse soba nā
vilas däru ehi hima kula niti nā

Being flawless, the gods of the ten directions gather.
The mountain's waving waterfall drops from the summit.
Beautiful like Siva adorned with the celestial river,
the form is borne there on the mountain summit always.

This verse was composed by an anonymous poet around the start of the sixteenth century.[1] The poem, called *Saman Sirita*, or *Acts of Saman*, describes the miracles of the Peak's guardian deity Sumana Saman, including his invitation to the Buddha to donate the summit footprint. This verse appears as the mountain is elegized to this end. Structured like most Sinhala quatrains, its initial rhyming syllables are offset in front, while the final rhyming syllables stand apart at the end of each line. Together the four lines create an image, if not always grammatically complete sentences, with the links among them sometimes not fully apparent until the final line lands. Like many styles of South Asian verse, the last word of Sinhala quatrains often carries extra weight. In this case, that word is "always."

Permanence thus anchors this poet's picture of the Peak and its watershed. Although infinite time phrases like "always," "continually," or "in every age" are syllabic filler in many poetic verses, their usage here is especially sensible due to the enduring nature of stone. Yet if the mountain's agency is seen within the frame of planetary pluralism, we must also acknowledge its deeper histories, with a timeline that shows human perceptions of what counts as "always" are really only "momentarily" on a geologic scale. The mountain may still be considered continual, but only if this is recognized as continuous change. This perspective into the past highlights the evolving relativity of all natural forms and our myths about them, including stories about the deepest reaches of temporality itself. This chapter therefore presents a range of tales about the Peak's natural powers, to show it as both a prehuman force in the world, and an agent structuring human history.

Orogen Myths

Where does the biography of a mountain begin? With formation of rock, or uplift of cliffs? In the case of the Peak, pinpointing either proves challenging, though a greater amount of research has been devoted to rock formation. A succinct recounting of the Peak's geological birth goes something like this: Sri Lankan bedrock first formed the Precambrian epoch, the four-and-a-half-billion years comprising most of the planet's history. The rock that would become the swath of crust stretching across the center of Lanka, known to geologists as the Highland Complex, likely formed through sedimentation and volcanic intrusions about 3,000 million years ago (Ma), and was significantly metamorphosed by 2,000 Ma.[2] This Precambrian crust underwent many more changes by intense heat and pressure into different grades of rock over a time span from 1,900 to 900 Ma.[3] These metamorphic events formed and reformed granulite, charnockite, and pegmatite parent rocks that would eventually generate Lanka's famous gemstones.[4] A more recent metamorphic event provided a necessary infusion of rare elements to make those gemstones unique. The apex of this occurrence, sometimes called the Pan-African orogeny, or simply the Pan-African event, is dated to the range of 600–550 Ma, and included the final supercontinental fusion of southern Pangea. The position of Lanka at the center of this continental collision and uplift became its claim to fame among geologists. Lanka was wedged between Madagascar, South India, and East Antarctica during this period, creating a mineral belt that, after the breakup of Pangea, now spans the ocean.[5] The heat and pressure of meeting landmasses molded rock, deforming and reforming the gneissic backbone of future highlands.

Concurrent magmatic events left the granulitic terrain rich in elements like zirconium, which, when bonded with silicate of the earth's crust, became the mineral zircon, acting as a sink for many different elements, generating a unique geochemistry evident in names of Lanka's gemstones that mimic the island's toponyms: serendibite, sinhalite, ceylonite, taprobanite.[6]

Around the time of the Pan-African event, another shelf of future southeastern Lankan rock, known to geologists as the Vijayan Complex, fused with the Highland Complex by thrusting beneath it.[7] Uplifts from both tectonic activities are estimated as the birth of the Lankan highlands, but the Peak did not exist in its present form. Lanka still had thousands of miles and millions of years to travel before it became the teardrop island recognized on modern maps, with many cycles of uplift and erosion affecting its relief. The Highland Complex continued to morph all the while, "too complex in detail as to be amenable to an analysis of its genesis."[8] Seafloor spreading in Jurassic and Cretaceous periods further fractured the highland's "network of megalineaments into a mosaic of wedge and rectangular blocks," leading to modern neotectonic shifts.[9] A seismic profile of the island shows a subtle movement to its mountains, with frequent microearthquakes along highland lineaments.[10] Contrary to the picture of perpetuity presented by the poet of *Saman Sirita*, rock and falling water ensured an impermanent face for the highlands, evident in the steep falls encircling the third and highest peneplain of Lanka, walled in by lines of escarpments that include the Peak.[11]

Although the above story is a simplified summation of scientific literature, it remains incomprehensible in a number of ways, and not only for the geojargon adorning the sentences. The most glaring obstacle to understanding is time, although many other large integers are also difficult to grasp.[12] As if the oldest estimates of original Lankan rock formation were not deep enough at 3,000 Ma,[13] that is still a billion years after the creation of the planet. And while the 70 Ma of the Cretaceous period seems more relatable, with continents close to present positions and dinosaurs roaming rainforests, is the actual difference between 3,000 Ma and 70 Ma intelligible to a human living only a century? John McPhee, geopoet and ethnographer of geologists, credited with coining the term "deep time," wrote of our geologic temporal disconnect with his first use of the phrase: "Numbers do not seem to work well with regard to deep time. Any number above a couple of thousand years—fifty thousand, fifty million—will with nearly equal effect awe the imagination to the point of paralysis. . . . The human mind may not have evolved enough to be able to comprehend deep time. It may only be able to measure it."[14] Yet McPhee's book shows that some sense *can* be made of millions of years, that its presentation is possible to curious audiences who may not know what to make of the numbers, but who still relate to stories. The vivid metaphors that animate geohistory, refashioning distant sediments before the mind's eye, allow us to glimpse wonders of former worlds that sustain the passions of actual geologists. The human ability to think in this way is born from our unique trait of mythmaking. Deep time is its own sort of myth, not simply in the sense of a single narrative with beginning and end, but as the expansive structure of consciousness and consensus comprising a worldview.

In rendering reality visible, myth makes pictures. McPhee reported shorthand among geologists for the history of the planet to be "the Picture."[15] Mythic images of "the way things are" become largely subconscious backdrops to our thought. As Ludwig Wittgenstein put it: "I did not get my picture of the world by satisfying myself of its correctness.... It is the inherited background against which I distinguish true and false. The propositions describing this *world-picture* might be part of *a kind of mythology* ... learned purely practically, without learning any explicit rules."[16] Language and life training convey implicit certainties about the world, the basis of our mythic picture. To this end, the antiquity of mountains is intuitive, absorbed automatically in how we speak of them: "I am told, for example, that someone climbed this mountain many years ago. Do I always inquire into ... whether the mountain did exist years ago? ... The question whether it is so doesn't arise at all."[17] Mountains are old because they are mountains. That is implicit background in the mythic pictures framing stories about them. Yet early earth scientists did not always grant immense depth to geologic temporality, as myths are always mutable. Using a geologically appropriate metaphor, Wittgenstein noted: "The mythology may change back into a state of flux, the riverbed of thoughts may shift ... And the bank of that river consists partly of hard rock, subject to no alteration or only an imperceptible one, partly of sand, which now in one place now in another gets washed away, or deposited."[18] This sort of gradual yet relentless eroding and reforming of ideas and truths, at times dramatically shifting the picture altogether, represents the sort of changes occurring throughout the history of science. Thomas Kuhn, who coined the concept of shifting scientific paradigms, made a telling reference to myth in the opening pages of his seminal book: "Once current views of nature were, as a whole, neither less scientific nor more the product of human idiosyncrasy than those current today. If these out-of-date beliefs are to be called myths, then myths can be produced by the same sorts of methods and held for the same sorts of reasons that now lead to scientific knowledge."[19]

The conceptual riverbed of geohistorical paradigms underwent a major shift that made possible the narrative of the Peak's orogenesis opening this chapter: the development of a dramatically deep temporal framework. This shift was steeped in Judeo-Christian myth, as historians of science have recognized the influence of cosmology and clergy on scientific theory and method.[20] Deep time itself was not shocking; the main obstacle was thinking in a grand enough scale. Imagination was stretched through mythology. Geohistorians used mythic monikers, like "the argument between '*Neptunists*' and '*Vulcanists*,' between champions of water and fire as causal agents."[21] Some also found geological evidence in Hindu mythology, expressed in Purana texts.[22] Judeo-Christian myths likewise appeared in fusions of Genesis and geohistoric timescales, where a "sequence of epochs was broadly compatible with the events of the successive 'days' of Creation . . . bound to suggest a concordance with the Genesis story, if not a sly parody of it."[23] The geologic naming of Lanka was no less legendary. The aforementioned Vijayan Complex of Lankan bedrock evoked Prince Vijaya, the mythic founder of the Sinhalas in Lanka. The name came in the 1940s, when that rock was still believed to be older than the Highland Complex.[24] A change in scientific chronology left the Vijayan moniker as sedimentary evidence of fluctuations in the mytholiths of geology.

Early geohistorians did not overlook the Peak either. Mythic tales guided scientific gazes. Thus the nineteenth-century scientists of the Austrian frigate Novara recorded "the geology of the isolated pinnacle of Adam's Peak . . . a granulitic gneiss of varying texture from coarse to fine, and abounding in garnets,"[25] but also took note of the stories swirling on its summit: "There is the scene of a story, here is the starting point of a myth."[26] Myths were recorded alongside geology, while geology wrote the new myth of the Peak. Scientists sought to supplant its old stories with novel theories, suggesting "rocks may have once been in a fluid or soft state . . . and become petrified in the course of time. . . . This hypothesis might also explain the phenomenon of the impressions of two large feet on the summit of Adam's Peak"[27] Yet even as science reframed the picture of the Peak with supposedly nonsuperstitious assessments, the mountain's fame allowed it to remain the main actor in new stories. Tennent, for example, conjectured: "At whatever period the mountains of Ceylon may have been raised, the centre of maximum energy must have been in the vicinity of Adam's Peak, the group immediately surrounding which has thus acquired an elevation of from six to eight thousand feet above the sea."[28] As a center of maximum mythic energy, the Peak was a conceptual anchor in the uncertainties of deep time. Of course, stories of the Peak's deep time also antedate geologists, as Buddhist myths have likewise served as a means to contemplate the relativity of humanity embedded in unknowable time.

Buddhist Deep Time

The *Aggañña Sutta* is often characterized as the Buddhist creation myth. Steven Collins translates it as "The Discourse on What Is Primary," using temporal and evaluative connotations of "primary" to describe the *sutta* as origin story and sermon.[29] It tells of an evolution of humans, from foraging clans to landed agricultural societies, split by caste and occupation, eventually joining to settle disputes by electing a king—a mythic charter of social-contract governance that attracted structural anthropologists.[30] By comparison, deep time aspects of *Aggañña Sutta* were brief, in two verses where the Buddha explained a cycling universe:

> Eventually, after a long time, monks, it comes to pass that the world contracts. As it contracts, usually beings devolve. . . . Eventually, after a long time, monks, it comes to pass that the world evolves. . . .
>
> At that time there is nothing but water, (all) is darkness, deep darkness. It is not possible to discern the moon or sun, the twinkling stars, night or day, month or half-months, seasons or years.[31]

Scholars have noted Vedic influences on this cosmology, especially the primordial waters and darkness, likely a reference to the *Ṛg Veda*. Such allusions are cause to read the *sutta* as part satire, as is the fact that the discourse is addressed to two young Brahmins accepting Buddhism.[32] Important to a deep time perspective, however, is the notion of contracting and expanding worlds over a period so long it is difficult to articulate.[33] Collins described the temporal markers in the above verses as a "profusion of imprecise time-words" (i.e., eventually, after a long time, usually), which "might suggest that there is a studied vagueness to the cosmology here."[34] As satire, parodic cosmology could work with such vague stereotypes, yet these also capture a cyclical notion of temporality seriously elaborated by later Buddhists.[35] Such a continually contracting and expanding world over innumerable eons coincidentally resonates with geohistorian James Hutton (1726–1797), who concluded his *Theory of the Earth* thusly: "If the succession of worlds is established in the system of nature, it is vain to look for anything higher in the origin of the earth. The result, therefore, of our present inquiry is, that we find no vestige of a beginning,—no prospect of an end."[36]

As for the Peak specifically, there is no Buddhist narrative of its orogenesis. Those I asked simply said it formed by natural processes. In past pilgrimage literature, however, I found stories of footprints also left by Buddhas before Gautama, placing the Peak in another layer of Buddhist deep time. The canonical *Buddhavaṃsa* narrates the lives of prior Buddhas, using the idea of "unfathomable" (*acintiya*) time to describe great temporal expanses between Buddhas, some in numbered eons, but for many, "the eons between them are incalculable by number."[37] In a history measured by Buddhas, the Peak, demonstrative of its mountainous past, hosted several of them. King Vijayabāhu's twelfth-century donative inscription recorded "offerings of various adornments studded with seven types of beautiful gems to the Sacred Footprint impressed on the summit of Samanoḷa rock, which sustained the sacred lotus-like feet of the four Buddhas that attained Buddhahood in the present cycle, namely, Kakusandha, Koṇāgama, Kassapa, and Gotama."[38] Later Sinhala poetry sung on pilgrimage often mentioned one or more of these Buddhas, and the practice proliferated with the profusion of printed literature.[39] Past Buddhas became so present they were near non sequiturs, used for rhymes in verses otherwise describing the pilgrimage route:

> Our Konāgama Buddha became enlightened
> World leader setting jurisdiction over the world
> The crowd of us all going to Samanala
> Turn at Nonāgama junction.[40]

Other texts indicate the recitation of former Buddhas was itself a pilgrimage practice. H. G. K. Ratnasēkara noted that his 1923 poem about the twenty-four prophecies by former Buddhas was meant for Sri Pada pilgrims to use. He devoted a quatrain to each Buddha, including the name of Gautama's incarnation in every era, along with the prophesies (*vivaraṇa*) bestowed on him to become our Buddha, matching *Buddhavaṃsa* in detail. The final line of each quatrain—"I bow to the sacred foot atop Samanala"[41]—preserved the practicum of this poem as a worship manual.

Many similar examples exist.[42] W. Ātar Ähäliyagoḍa Baṇḍāra included even more *Buddhavaṃsa* detail in 1928, mentioning each Buddha's parents, the tree species under which he reached enlightenment, and how many weeks or months of effort it took. The last line of the quatrains included the same injunction to bow one's head, linking pilgrims on the Peak to every prior Buddha:

> Happy father Sāgara and mother Sudasana.
> The time of eight months was passed with great effort.
> The Bō experiencing buddha rays was named Sapu, beautiful.
> Let us bow to the Atadas Buddha foot devoutly.[43]

Other Samanala poems simply summarized multiple Buddhas in one verse, mentioning "prophesies regularly received from the twenty-four Sages."[44] It is possible these former Buddhas found easy mention in the context of the Peak because of an aura of ancientness associated with mountains. In turn, the longstanding material agency of the Peak allowed these pilgrim authors to connect themselves to the deep past:

> In this *kalpa*, first was the Sage Lord named Kakusan̆da who
> proceeded to our Lanka here and preached the famous dharma.
> Those marks of the lotus-foot well made on the mountain king,
> this we go to worship on that same mountain lord.[45]

This ability to connect with the past through the physical landscape is especially important in a Buddhist mythic picture where each pilgrim is part of a greater chain of karmic agents constituting the Buddhist *sāsana*.[46] The 1922 *Buduguṇa Kav Nohot Śrīpāda Vandanāva* (Buddha-virtue poetry or Sri Pada worship), which also began by naming prior Buddhas, contains a cover illustration connoting such communal cooperation in worship, with a couple about to queue in a coterie of pilgrims, the Peak destination shining with the sun on the horizon (fig. 1.1).[47] The twenty-four Buddhas are also mentioned in manuscript pilgrimage literature, but the proliferation of entire works dedicated to them in the print era might have been due to an overall revival in the worship of prior Buddhas around 1912, with the institution of "*sūvisi pinkama*" dances in temples commemorating the twenty-four.[48] Yet the myth has seemingly eroded away in the modern day. When I asked Chandra about it while resting at her tea stall one cloudy afternoon, gesturing up toward the misty summit, she was certain that only Gautama Buddha had left his footprint atop the Peak.

Although Buddhist and geologic visions of deep time exist within their own shifting mytholiths, they have intriguing similarities, as both recognize prehuman planetary processes over massive time spans. A verse from the tradition of pilgrimage songs called *Samanala Hälla*, for example, turns to planetary metaphors to convey the permanence of the footprint on the mountain, using a superfluity of infinite time words:

> During the beautiful full moon, people and gods always worship
> continually in all ages.
> The sacred sole has graced the summit for a long time like the
> moon's continual beauty.
> With the beauty of heaven where the retinue resides is
> the always given sacred sole.
> Group gone, faults removed, worship the sacred sole of the
> supramundane Sage.[49]

FIGURE 1.1. Detail of cover for Dehigama Paṇḍita Samarasiṅha Puṅcibaṇḍāra's *Buduguṇa Kav Nohot Śrīpāda Vandanāva*
National Museum Library, Colombo

"Continually in all ages," "always for a long time," and "always given,"[50] the mountain and its footprint have only the moon for temporal comparison. Such sentiments are reminders of the transience of humanity, and the relative instantaneousness of any one existence. As the Peak backdrops varied human histories, it anchors comparisons across generations and cultures. The remainder of this chapter details commonalities recorded by diverse authors about the Peak's environment, cataloguing recurring observations about rock, water, and forest life that make the mountain manifest its own myth over time.

General *Gebirge* and Unique Peak

One antecedent branch of geology was the mining science of geognosy. Concerned with interiors, geognosts strove to know the total mountain—the *gebirge*, not merely as a feature of terrain appearing above ground, but the whole rock mass above and below the surface. Thinking in three dimensions demanded a fourth: "Geognosts were well aware that this structural order was likely to reflect a corresponding *temporal* order of deposition."[51] In fact, the story of deep time that opened this chapter was more a narrative of *gebirge* than single summit, the Peak considered in a massive massif of highland peneplain—a full range that allows access to its geohistory.

Considering the Peak as part of the larger Highland Complex finds justification beyond geology. The range around the summit is part of its attraction for tourists, providing spectacular views from the top where the entire highlands became an ocean of clouds or trees. On her 1833 climb, Anna Walker observed "the appearance of dense masses of cloud greatly below us, through which the rugged tops of some of the highest mountains appeared like islands in a tempestuous ocean."[52] In 1875, John Capper recorded a similar oceanic impression: "To the tourist . . . the great attraction will be the unrivalled view obtained from the summit . . . Farther away, from the dim obscurity of many miles of forest, arise peak after peak, ridge after ridge, of mountain tops, towering high above the ocean of jungle, like islands in an ocean of forest."[53] Even off the summit, the highlands sparked seascape imagery. William Howard Russell observed in 1858: "The blue mountains struck up towards heaven from a sea of vegetation. Adam's Peak looked some volcanic island rising from a fairy ocean."[54] Some Sinhala poets wove similar visions of an oceanically undulating montane landscape with Samanala at its center:

Samanala is the light of the great royal milk sea.
Water taken, the well-made of colorful gem surface looks like
charms.
Super extensive waves of jungle give sounds at once.[55]

Like the legendary milk ocean of Indic myth studded with gems at its bottom, if the "water" of the forest waves is removed, the bejeweled grounds of the highlands will be revealed around the Peak.

Samanala is also conceptually linked to specific surrounding summits such as Bāna Samanala and Dharmaraja Kanda. These mountains make a perimeter around the western side of the Peak. They are mentioned in standard invocations for Saman, the god of the mountain who requested the Buddha's footprint.[56] The *kapurāla* priests who serve Saman's summit shrine told me these encircling mountains are mentioned because they function as guardians, echoing the landscape's depiction in Vimalakīrti's 1415 *Saddharmaratnākaraya*, where surrounding hills are "deep-blue fortresses . . . forming the entourage for the Saman Mountain King like an elephant herd."[57]

Although the Peak is geologically and culturally indissoluble from the surrounding highlands, it still stands apart, a mountain among mountains. Lawrie called it "the most conspicuous mountain in Ceylon," and devoted a lengthy section to it at the start of his gazetteer, set outside the alphabetical order arranging the rest of the book.[58] Were the mountain positioned differently, it would likely not have become so famous. The Peak predominates. Taller than surrounding summits, and conically narrowing at the top, it seems to rise into the sky much higher than its 7,359 ft (2,243 m). It was cited for centuries as the highest summit on the island until trigonometry proved three taller farther inland, though their relative relief was less dramatic. Indeed, British poet Benjamin Bailey (1791–1853), composer of several sonnets to Adam's Peak, even when writing lines about the highest summit of the island, Pidurutalagala, knew the true landmark lay elsewhere:

This mountain-brow ascended . . .
I have seen the distant map of hill and plain,
As I descended, beautifully spread
Before the eye: and at one sudden break
Stood visibly the cone of ADAM'S PEAK![59]

The Peak's agency therefore arose from its sheer visibility, overruling other mountains.

The Peak had long been considered kingly. As Vedeha Thera described it in the Pali verse of his thirteenth-century *Samantakūṭavaṇṇanā* (The elegy of Samantakūṭa):

> With rivers for wives, wearing the summit crown,
> with surrounding mountain-lord generals,
> this great king of mountains
> shines in the court of the city of Lanka.[60]

The Peak also presided over a humbler Sinhala verse of *päl kavi*, or field-shed poetry, call-and-response songs that those perched as lookouts guarding crops in the night would shout to one another across fields to combat drowsiness:

> Alagallē mountain unable to eat yams [*ala*]
> Batalē Gala mountain unable to eat rice [*bat*]
> Hunnas Giri mountain unable to eat bamboo [*huṇa*]
> For these three mountains, the leader is Samanala mountain.[61]

As Samanala was considered a ruler among mountains, the Peak understandably became an organizing device for boundaries of polities, used as a starting point to draw divisions of the island's three main territories in different Sinhala *kaḍaim pot* (boundary books). The first sentence of the fourteenth-century *Tri Siṃhalē Kaḍaim* was: "In Sri Lanka from Samantakūṭa mountain, the abode of god Saman, to Vālukāntāraganga (Mahavali river) fourteen leagues away, is the confluence of the Pingā-oya. From this point is reckoned the beginning of the boundaries of Ruhuṇu, Māyā and Pihiṭi of the Tri Siṃhalē."[62] The mountain thereby became the primary sign by which the whole island was organized. As *Śrī Laṅkādvīpayē Kadaim* recorded: "The Mahavali river and Samanala mountain are common to all three divisions or kingdoms."[63] In other folk poetry, Samanala was even named as its own direction, somewhere between north and south,[64] and the Peak was a symbol that could be carved into stone as a boundary marker.[65] Summating the Peak's centrality in the Lankan landscape, one poem simply named over forty settlements and landmarks in every direction that could be seen on the summit.[66] Not only was the Peak visible from these places, but they were visible *to* the Peak according to the dative case used by the poet. Whether it presided or stood watch, the mountain's dominant presence shaped the landscapes of Lankan authors.

As the Peak oriented territory and became a direction, it also guided travel. Sinhala poetry prolifically adopted the Sanskrit style of *sandeśa*, or "messenger" poems, describing a journey along a route of named places.[67] *Säḷalihiṇi*

Sandeśaya, written in the fifteenth century by the decorated poet Toṭagamuvē Śrī Rāhula, "the most prominent monk of the day,"[68] described the coastal capital of Kotte and its surroundings, including the most prominent mountain of the day, before instructing the *säḷalihiṇi* bird to take flight. The Peak rose in the direction of the rising sun, attended by divine devotees:

> God king Saman with heavenly maidens at that time
> spread *maňdārā* and *parijat* flowers wrapped in colors,
> offering and worshiping the remaining sacred foot-lotus.
> Noble friend, Samanala mountain is visible in the East.[69]

Visibility was the Peak's claim to fame, useful as a terrestrial landmark, and even extending its agency all the way out to sea, stretching mountain renown around the world. The Peak guided travelers farther flung than *sandeśa* birds, as explained in the next section, which commences a series of reflections on the links between rock and water.

Summit from Surf

McPhee describes a geologist's eye: "They look at mud and see mountains, in mountains oceans, in oceans mountains to be."[70] Coincidentally, approaches to Lanka by ship were often painted with such a perspective, albeit accelerated, the mountain seeming to arise from the sea in mere moments: "The height of the mountain, and its looming form, at first produces the effect of a mountain rising abruptly from out of the perfect level of the waves . . . abruptly from the very bottom of the sea."[71] Likewise, "like a queen on her throne, with the sea as her kingdom, Ceylon presented the appearance of a mountain in the sea."[72] Even when steamship travel became passé, this phenomenon still dazzled: "Landfall is now an outworn thrill, but there is promise of romance in the first far-off glimpse of Ceylon, when the voyager sees Adam's Peak emerge out of the ocean like the spiked boss of a mighty shield, to lift up a roseate dawn."[73] As the early steamship period was also a heyday of geologic theories of rising and sinking mountains, perhaps these travelers were already primed by myths of their day, ready to see a summit emerge from the sea in an enchanting acceleration of deep time processes.[74]

Yet the Peak's famous trick of planetary physics, cresting on the arc of the horizon as if slicing the surf, made it a navigation sign well before steamships, as "one solitary cone, towering . . . stood an excellent landmark for ships

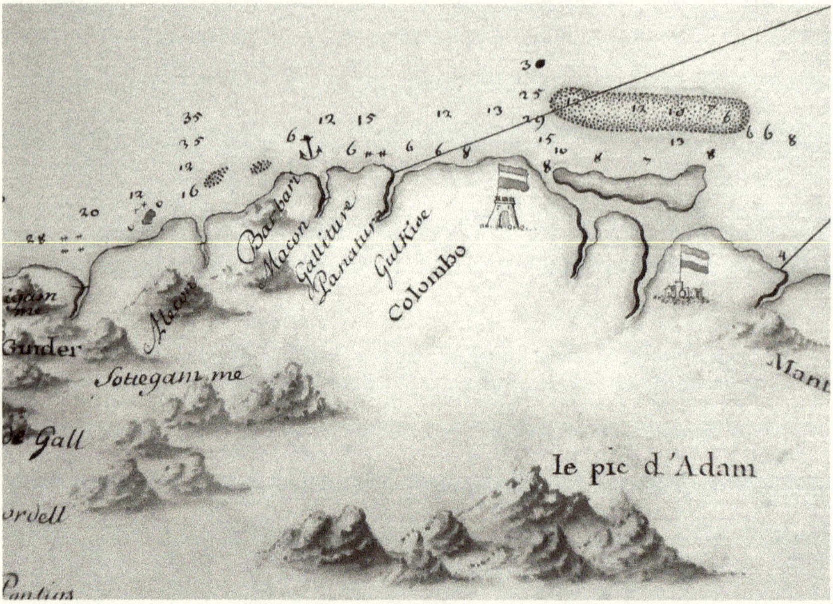

FIGURE 1.2. The Peak as navigational reference on an eighteenth-century French map: *Carte de l'Jsle Ceylon et parte de la coste de Coromandel*
Newberry Library, Chicago

approaching the roads."[75] The mountain thus made its way onto many marine maps of Europeans, often the only piece of an otherwise unknown blank interior of the island (fig. 1.2).[76] Even local Lankans writing from the island's interior captured the image of the Peak rising from the ocean. The idea first appeared in Vedeha's *Samantakūṭavaṇṇanā*, as Saman tells the Buddha how the mountain split the sea:

> Its chest having cleft the ocean waters,
> and come to your feet in obeisance,
> shining like the discus-carrying one [Vishnu],
> is the great mountain lord with supremely high summit.[77]

Later, an eighteenth-century Tamil temple history of Koneswaram called *Tirikoṇācala Purāṇam* described people going to worship Siva's presence on the Peak, manifest in a pillar of light coming from within the mountain that cleaves the ocean:

> The residents of the Lankan region go and surround the Lord of this earth.

> Conquered and cleaved, the billowing ocean in the west does not oppose,
> as his cast grace is like a pillar placed where it shines
> through the inside of the illustrious ancient mountain called Samanai.[78]

The Peak's ability to conquer the vast seas in this way was part of its prowess, making it a suitable site for hosting the presence of Buddha relics or divine grace.

Seeing the Peak from the sea even encouraged a mobile ritual for some. Munshi Abdullah (1796–1854), who lived in Singapore, made the long ocean crossing to Mecca for hajj in 1854, and recorded the behavior of his shipmates on the way:

> we arrived opposite Mount Ceylon. At that precise moment all the sailors broke out in a jubilant roar while beating trays and drums. They immediately dressed up one of the Abyssinians on board to look like an old man complete with a walking-stick in his hand and a long beard. He was then followed by a motley crew who danced before the *Nakhoda* [captain] . . . and they bowed and paid their respects to us. Each of us then gave them some money according to our due. I queried the coxswain . . . and he replied, "It is the usual custom for ships sailing past here, to merrily seek alms to buy food for the recitation of the *Fatihah* for our father Adam, upon whom may there be peace."[79]

Seeing the mountain went beyond navigation, uniting a mixed group of Muslim sailors in devotion toward the first man. The religious significance of the mountain was therefore not limited to pilgrims who scaled its summit. The Peak's fame as a landmark gave it a guiding role even for those in the midst of a different pilgrimage. Glimpsing the mountain from the ocean was enough to initiate a float-by ceremony from afar.

Uttering a prayer upon seeing the Peak was probably common, considering the latitude on which it stood was treacherous with typhoons.[80] One struck Munshi Abdullah's vessel moments after leaving Lanka: " 'Oh God! Oh God! Oh God!' I can't even begin to describe how horrendous it was and how tremendous the waves were."[81] As the last landmark before the vast southern Indian Ocean, the Peak's navigational function was also salvational, preventing ships from being lost at sea, and heartening sailors whose hulls groaned from wind-buffeted waves. Glimpsing the Peak just as a storm blew in on March 25, 1663, was surely comforting to the Germans in employ of the Dutch East India Company trying to arrive safely at their posts: "The next day saw two high Hills of the Island of *Ceylon*, the one nam'd *Pico de Adam* or Adam's Hill . . . This day and also the same night we had much gusty Weather, with loud Thunder and strong Winds."[82] When J. Drew Gay (1846–1890) sailed with the Prince of Wales, his journey was similarly beset by bad weather that made seeing the Peak all the more satisfying: "It is a great privilege to see Adam's Peak. When I first looked at it we were fifty miles from Ceylon, in half a gale, on our beam-ends. Still, trying as was the tossing of the ship, and doleful as looked the inky sky, with its afterward fulfilled promise of storm and lightning, there was the summit bearing the footprint of Buddha."[83]

Storms aside, there was also the prospect of provision depletion. Another German in Dutch employ recalled sighting the mountain on two occasions, the first routine, on October 20, 1676: "In the afternoon we got sight of the high and steep Mountain, call'd *Adam's Pick*, and by that we knew that this was the place we wanted to be at, *viz.*, the Island *Ceylon*." When he saw the Peak again on March 8, 1679, he and the crew were in dire straits, returning from a short trip to a Malabar-coast pearl fishery: "The Steersman had us all look out sharp for *Columbo*, where we earnestly desired to be, especially because our Water Vessel was every drop drunk out because of the great Heat. The 7th, By break of day, we found that we were carry'd wide off it by the strength of the Current . . . For we could see no *Columbo* nor Land neither." The officers and soldiers thought to cast their steersman into the sea, but he beat a retreat up the mast. Another took charge: "Our Ensign inquired for the Map of the Island *Ceylon*, and he directed us on our course; and about night we got in sight of the *Pico d'Adam*, or Adam's Hill . . . and at about five of the Clock next morning we got happily to the Water-Pass at *Columbo*. But what sort of a Hunger, and even more Thirst, we suffered these two days, is easy to imagine."[84] It is also easy to imagine the awesome wave of relief that would have washed over the crew at the sight of the Peak, having awoken that morning lost at sea, by evening parched to the tune of two sunbeaten days without fresh water. Two centuries later, history repeated itself as farce when, all out of mutton, pork, and roast duck on the Duke of Sutherland's yacht, Florence Caddy feigned hunger for a portly crewmate: "I sharpened the paper-knife ominously, and drew the blade across my finger. No, fat Joe must be eaten first, I reflected, and refrained. The look-out men reported the sight of Adam's Peak—and none too soon; it saved Joe's life."[85]

Lankan authors were also familiar with the navigation salvation of the Peak. This function was preserved in the seventeenth-century *Rājāvaliya*, when Prince Vijaya, as punishment for killing his father's subjects, was put on "a ship and sent adrift. . . . The seafarers, in the middle of the sea, saw the rock *Samantakūṭa*. Considering it to be a suitable island for them to live in . . . they landed at the port."[86] In other Sinhala settlement myths, poems about the goddess Pattini preserve the history of her cult's migration from South India through stories of her arrival in Lanka.[87] In one telling, Samanala guides her to shore after no sight of land:

> The work of both eyes having seen almost a thousand things
> without seeing land
> Shaking ships adorned and fixed to go in the northern direction
> Pattini with great majesty displaying virtues of divine words to
> the three worlds
> With her eye saw Samanala mountain, having looked to come
> ashore exactly.[88]

Divine eyes thus fixed upon a sacred mountain, with the land signaling that the goddess's long search for land had finished. Similarly, in a village drama tradition with seafaring themes like shipbuilding and ocean travel, one verse described the arrival of the main character in Lanka due to sighting the Peak:

> The coming ship of Madurāpura that beheld and beheld
> This one having come to the country, saw Samanaḷa mountain
> Drawing ashore various beings like the sacred Sage foot
> Having seen, praying so as to come to worship.[89]

After a lengthy journey in which many sights were seen, the final view of Samanala signaled settlement. The Peak drew boats like the sacred footprint on its summit drew beings to nirvana from the ocean of samsara, the poet using an idiom of double meaning in the third line to express physical and metaphysical senses of drawing ashore (*goḍalana*). The footprint thereby imbued the mountain with the Buddha's soteriological agency, while geology made the Peak a navigational actor. Meanwhile, the final line implied that the vision of the mountain from the ocean inspired worship once the boat landed. The verse thus captured the planetary agency that made Samanala a site of pilgrimage traffic, interest in the Peak piqued by its visibility. A landmark of ocean roads, it was essential for global travelers, raising spirits and even saving lives, or afterlives.

Incidentally, this experience of approaching the Peak that made it world famous is no longer available to the casual traveler. With the rise of air connectivity, a tourist's view from the deck of a ship or steamer is extinct. People approaching Lanka see no mountain crown cresting, only a distant glimpse of ocean and earth interrupted by airport concrete. Consequently, Skeen's suggestion is no longer accurate that "there is perhaps no mountain in the world of which so wide-spread a knowledge exists, as Adam's Peak. Almost every traveler to, or writer on, India and the East, has alluded to, noticed, or more or less described it."[90] Geological positioning of the Peak vis-à-vis the sea can only affect humans situated to see it. As the oceanic perspective diminishes, no one now writes of a mountain surfacing from surf, and the Peak is therefore less famous. Nevertheless, links between ocean and mountain continue unabated via the water cycle.

Falling Rain, Flowing Rivers, Finding Rubies

The ocean comes to the mountain through the air. Water, vaporized into clouds, travels on the same prevailing winds that brought ships across the sea. As clouds burst, rocky slopes break their fall. McPhee notes how "mountains are not somehow created whole and subsequently worn away. They wear down as they come up . . . rising and shedding steadily through time, always the same, never the same, like row upon row of fountains."[91] His fluid metaphor is especially apt in the case of the Lankan highlands, their rising-and-shedding tectonics capturing rainwater, as "fractured zones along the lineaments are the most potential aquifers."[92] The motion of rock thus formed reservoirs for fresh water cleansed of sea salt through its aerial journey, stored underground for future generations to tap as the highlands simultaneously arose and eroded.

The deep history of rainwater also played a particularly important role at the Peak, likely being the geologic reason for the summit indentation identified by so many as a footprint. Some might find this reading overly disenchanted, not unlike colonial propaganda using the same argument in an 1871 book of Sinhala verse meant to disabuse pilgrims of belief in the footprint:

> At the low spot atop a rock, water remained—having soaked,
> it bore into that place more and more continuously.
> If not being like that from the ages passed, how then—
>   was the rock leveled?
> Look and answer, friend, at this time.[93]

Yet, polemics aside, if attuned to the myth of deep time, the print's aqueous origin is no less impressive than buddhas, prophets, or gods intentionally imprinting feet. The mark on the Peak took millennia of monsoons to make, indented by continual crashing of rain on rock. It is the footprint of the water cycle itself, a fossil of prehistoric deluges.

Rains appear in many accounts of the Peak. In *Samantakūṭavaṇṇanā*, Vedeha mentioned the regular work of wondrous deluges: "Beings gather and pay homage and, as soon as they have departed, rain-clouds gather to purify the enclosure with streams of water—this constant wonder is there, too!"[94] Likewise, in his list of significant mountains around the world, Persian scholar Hamdallah Mustawfi Qazvini (1281–1349) held the "Mountain in Sarandīb" as "one of the most famous of mountains. . . . The footprint of Adam may be seen on a rock here. . . . Every day here, without there being a storm or thunder-clouds, the rain falls and washes clean from all dust this footprint, and the people consider this a mark of great blessedness."[95] This sentiment was echoed by a later Persian author, Āzād, in his 1764 *Coral Rosary of Indian Antiquities*: "The Master 'Alī al-Rūmi said in his *Discourses*: 'The first place where Adam descended was the mountain called Rāhūn on an Indian island, in the kingdom of Serendip . . . upon which is his footprint. . . . There is no doubt that it rains there every day and washes his footprint.'" Likewise, when Āzād used a phrase of praise after the name Serendip in his writing, he chose "May God water it with downpours of rain!"[96] It is fitting for devotees to view frequent rains as blessings, as these very waters, with each washing, continued a geologic agenda of erosion that formed the print of their devotion.

As the receptacle for so much rain, the Peak also became known as a source of rivers. In Sinhala texts, the number of rivers flowing from the Peak was often set at four, and some poets stylized them as *nāgas*—serpentine beings thought to be older gods of rain and subterranean fertility converted by the Buddha, assimilation of their territory often marked by the placement of a relic, frequently a footprint.[97] The 1788 *Käṭakirilli Sandeśaya* includes a verse recounting how, as the Buddha left his footprint on the Peak, the *nāgas* in the mountain were so eager to see it they burst forth from their home in different directions:

> Loving Sage Lord decided to bestow the foot
> Four divine *nāgas* breaking the Himagiri anthill
> Coming this direction, happily journeying ahead
> Four rivers issuing from the Himagiri grounds.[98]

The mountain was compared to an anthill not only for its conical shape, but also because anthills are considered homes for serpents, especially divine ones.[99] Also around the eighteenth century, an author styling himself Kaviraja ("poet king") composed a work called *Laṅkā Vistaraya* (Lanka description), which equated description of the island with praise for the Peak and its rivers.[100] To this end, the anthill-mountain/snake-river theme was used in two verses:

> Samaṇola is an anthill made of gold.
> Like serpents in the forest going in four directions,
> running on the summit, the four with four hoods,
> all the valuable four rivers are like this.
>
> In the known forest, the eggs are protected well.
> As though the female serpent has gone out,
> taking out the small babies beautifully,
> the river water is as if having gone like this.[101]

Fertility ideals were expressed in these verses, with *nāga* babies protected in the forest, nurtured and hatched into yet more alluvial affluence.[102] Kaviraja names each of the four rivers, some of the most significant on the island: the Kalu Ganga, Kelani Ganga, Walawe Ganga, and the longest and most geologically stable, Mahaweli Ganga. Kaviraja then connects these rivers with the ocean through rainwater:

> Lines and lines of great rains clouds are elephants in description
> Waves and waves like the ocean body's waves
> The body of water issuing from the Kaḷu river became full.[103]

Comparing rain-fed rivers to the sea represents the water cycle, precipitation literally bringing ocean to land, expressed even more directly in another manuscript of this poem, where the second line of the above verse read: "Waves and waves, the great ocean going on the earth."[104] In hydrological terms, however, none of these four rivers begins exactly at the Peak summit, but rather from surrounding hills, the Kalu being closest, a cement sign on the Ratnapura trail marking its trickling beginnings. In this way, pilgrims and workers remain familiar with the Peak's reputation as a watershed, even if they acknowledge that older stories embellished this attribute.

Birthing rivers thus became another myth of the mountain, which was personified through local gods. The minor deity Gange Bandara, or the River Chief (*gaṅgē baṇḍāra*), is another piece of Lankan religiosity that may have been absorbed by Buddhists, originating among Vädda clans.[105] While the Väddas were reputed to be "wild men" or "aboriginals" by modern colonial observers, Gananath Obeyesekere has convincingly argued that they were not a primitive tribe, but a group of non-Buddhists who held various political affiliations with Buddhist kings in Lanka. Some were likely forest dwellers, but many others were landed nobles. As Obeyesekere notes, however, old myths of wildness persist, especially after most landed Väddas were absorbed into Sinhala lineages, casting remaining forest Väddas as tribal in the minds of modern Lankans. There is thus a certain mystique that accompanies Väddas, as I witnessed one afternoon resting in Chandra's tea stall on my way up the mountain. A group of three men with thick black beards and long hair, wearing simple checkered sarongs and white shirts, walked by at a much swifter clip than the average pilgrim. Chandra stepped out of her stall to watch them ascend the steps in double time despite their bare feet. She turned to me and explained who they were in a half whisper: "Väddas. They have walked the whole way here from their villages," she guessed. "It would be good to talk to them for your research." I was intrigued, but too slow in following. By the time I reached the summit, they were long gone, descended via another trail without doubling back. Whether or not these alleged Väddas were Buddhists, their pilgrimage is understandable. Vädda territory is traditionally associated with the Peak and its surrounding range, and many Vädda religious practices are centered on sites where God Saman holds sway. Such religious overlap between Buddhists and Väddas extends to chieftain gods like Gange Bandara, who represents the Mahaweli River itself. Most poems to this god double as elegies of the waterway, charting a course that begins at Samanala.[106] Some verses even allude to the deep temporality of this hydrology:

> Moving amid the forest, the river origin thundering
> Taking control of *yakkas*, too, through all good dharma
> Swords striking as long as the sun and moon exist
> Displaying jurisdiction, majesty not leaving an age.[107]

The line about dharma controlling *yakkas* matches belief that these spirits often reside in waterfalls, and that the Peak and its footprint relic could help subdue them.[108] The swords striking then add a clattering to complement the thundering of the river origin, this sound lasting "as long as the sun and moon exist." This is a ubiquitous phrase in Indic writing, most often applied to land grants or royal elegies, symbolized by suns and moons imprinted on stones, palm leaves, copper plates, and doorways, including those on the Peak footprint shrine. The Peak waters, like the mountain itself, therefore represent immortal royalty, with their "majesty not leaving an age," needing a planetary scale to express their temporal permanence, like that of the mountain.

Samanala references also abound in river poetry that lauds the Mahaweli by mapping its route from highlands to sea.[109] One manuscript labeled *Mahaväli*

Gaṅga Väṇīma (Praising the Mahaweli River) alludes to the deep time of the river by claiming that "these waters are of the same nature that the Brahma gods saw in past ages when creating" the world. Although this incomplete manuscript is only three leaves long, its author fit in five quatrains about the Peak, including a verse about the river issuing from the mountain like *nāga*s, another comparing the mountain to an elephant and the river to its trunk, another about the river as Lady Lanka's outstretched arm holding hands with the ocean, and another that seems to imbue the summit waters with the powers of the Buddha by originating at the site of his footprint:

> Like four refuges, when Saman Mountain gives
> gems to the four guardian gods from the four directions,
> four jasmine flower garlands are offered likewise, as
> four rivers in this way are well-made amid this Lanka.[110]

The four rivers are described as refuges (*saraṇa*)—a term usually used in triplicate for the Buddha, Dharma, and Sangha, but here quadrupled into generous rivers that make offerings in all directions, whether to the gods or the island itself.

Other rivers beyond the famous four also became associated with the Peak. Some Gange Bandara poems also source the Hulu River from Samanala, although this Mahaweli tributary actually begins in the Knuckles range farther east.[111] Meanwhile, Tamil works mentioning the Peak also added rivers to its mythic watershed. Tamil authors shared a special reverence for the Mahaweli River, which meets the sea near the Koneswaram temple at Trincomalee in the northeast. The temple history *Tirikoṇācala Purāṇam*, for example, includes a lush description of the Peak in its chapter on the sacred *tīrtha* confluence of Mahaweli and the ocean. Tracing the river's origin back to the summit, *Tirikoṇācala Purāṇam* explains how its waters, having begun at Siva's footprint, continue to convey the presence of the god even in his absence:

> Even without the divine form being there, everybody worships, praising
> the *tīrtha* after demerit is destroyed by the water that eliminates their sins.
> Those ones who stay and worship are sages and celestials who receive
> the great merit of Siva's river by its coming into being at Siva's foot.[112]

In the next two verses, the author lauds other rivers that also carry these blessings, including the Kelani (Tamil: Kaḻaṉi; Sinhala: Käḷaṇi), also connected to the Peak in Sinhala compositions, as well as the unique addition of the Menik (Tamil: Māṇikka; Sinhala: Mänik), a river that flows southeast to Kataragama, and technically begins far from the Peak.[113] Likewise, a later temple history of Koneswaram added yet another river to the Peak's mythic watershed, even more distant from the mountain, using deep time notes of perpetual waters springing from mountain caverns: "The joyful meetings of the three streams, Māvali Ganga, Māṇikka Ganga, and Kāvēri Ganga, on Sivanolipadamalai on Siva's foot on the auspicious day, in the auspicious hour, became the eternal flooding abundance. . . . Having come by way of the mountain cavern and converged, in the mountain cavern's interior always residing . . . from our foot this river began in the core of the earth."[114] In addition to the Mahaweli and Menik, here appears the "Kāvēri," which the author says flows northwest to the temple of Ketheeswaram. This suggests it is actually the Aruvi Aṟu in Tamil, or Malvatu Oya in Sinhala, here renamed for the famous Kaveri River of Tamil Nadu. In these Tamil texts, the Peak's rivers thereby unite important Saiva temples on different coasts, connected via the crisscrossing island waterways born of the highlands. Overall, the varied river associations across Sinhala and Tamil literature show how the Peak became a synecdoche for the whole Highland Complex in terms of its role as the island's chief watershed.

The four rivers of four directions was a trope that also played upon the minds of European Christians, consecrating their conceptions of landscape. In Genesis 2:10, "a river flowed out of Eden to water the garden, and there it divided and became four rivers." This scriptural priming conditioned Christians who settled Lankan shores. In 1723, some believed "Ceylon is so rich and fertile . . . that God placed in it the earthly paradise, but this opinion is not based on any solid reasons." Still, the author of this Portuguese mission report, despite his skepticism, managed to muster several solid reasons: "But the mistake can be excused because apparently it is due to a spring found there, called Adam's Peak, and to the precious things that abound there." The author praised spices and gems, but ultimately returned to water as most precious: "The Island is watered by fresh water rivers. With the water of these rivers and with the rain that never fails to fall every month, the trees grow better than in any other part of India."[115] This watershed also captured practical colonial attention, as "from this mountain the principal rivers of the island derive their source."[116] On early British maps without much in the island interior, blank space left ample room for the Peak, its four rivers of paradise squiggling away as thin black lines (fig. 1.3).

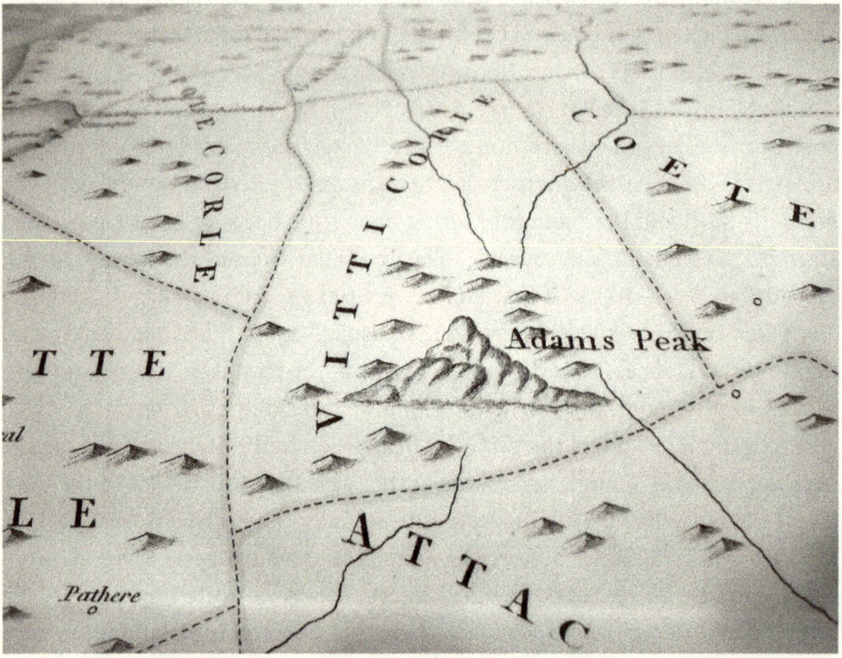

FIGURE 1.3. Detail of the Peak from an 1803 map by A. Allen and William Gent, based on Jean-François Duperron's 1789 map. Newberry Library, Chicago

Water also conditions the movement of pilgrims, sometimes preventing ascent, other times facilitating it. In 1860, a party of Germans met the onset of the southwestern monsoon. Water blocking their way, they ultimately failed to summit the Peak: "From the rocks which had been dry yesterday we could see waterfalls everywhere speaking volumes for the amount of rain which must have fallen in the upper regions. Before long it started to rain heavily and the water began to gush down the hollow path; darkness fell and I didn't think it wise to proceed." The next day, the situation only worsened: "The path which looked like stairs yesterday had turned into a river, making me slip and fall. I had prepared myself to climb a mountain and not a waterfall."[117] But rainwater moving from the highlands, filling rivers and reservoirs across the island, had a purpose when pilgrimage began for Lankans in post-monsoon months. In one late nineteenth-century poem, pilgrims set out from the southern coast of Matara, the Peak lying to the northwest. Initially, however, the group moved east along the coast, away from the Peak for several miles, before turning inland and winding back up. This maneuver is explained by two geographic factors: the elevation change directly from Matara to the Peak is much steeper, and the pathway father east is comparatively flush with water, this latter point poetically preserved:

> Now having taken water, its purity
> as we have never seen before this.
> Becoming happy, we go to Samanala,
> passing the marketplace at Hungama.
> . . .
> Here there are always great trees.
> See the beautiful lake water to drink.
> The venerable bodhi king flutters here.
> Saying here is beautiful Tunkama.
>
> Taking bundled bunches of flowers and going,
> ponds and lakes are seen in a state of beauty,
> with paddy fields in clusters at Ketarana.
> Pass Ämbilipiṭiya here and go.
>
> The bridge on the road is seen to be huge.
> Past the flourishing waterfall,
> with the drumming noise, the mill is visible,
> having passed the Tibolkäṭiya workshops.[118]

Ample freshwater at each village on the way allowed a group of pilgrims proceeding on foot to travel lightly, confident that they would be provided for at their rest stops. They enjoyed pure ponds and lakes for both drinking and gazing, filled by falls that powered workshops and worshipers, not to mention fertilizing flowers plucked for *puja*.

Another power of rivers over pilgrims is erosion. Aqueous agency washed gemstones into collectable deposits, engendering legends of mountainous wealth, and encouraging traders to venture to the highlands seeking fortune. In his book on gemology, al-Biruni (973–1048), citing a Chinese text, describes the rich gemstones near the Peak: "Water brings them from hollows, caves, and flooded places."[119] Two centuries later, Arab gemologist Ahmad al-Tifashi (1184–1253) affirmed: "There is a formidable mountain . . . from which winds and rains carry the corundum stones, which are picked as pebbles from this place, also as alluvial deposits. . . . This mountain is the one where Adam—may God bless him—descended from paradise and onto the earth."[120] A century later, the Chinese sailor Wang Dayuan (fl. 1311–1350), although associating the mountain with the Buddha instead of Adam, concurred: "The two kinds of stones . . . are found in the sand brought down by the water which falls on the slopes of the mountain and rushes down."[121] Wind and rain are what revealed the highland's gem wealth to visitors. These erosive agents are still studied by geologists, whose "GIS databases show a very significant spatial overlap and direct causal linkage between several hundred landslide occurrences and the innumerable gem pits and mines in the catchments," as "mountains, monsoons, mass movements and gemstones are all parts of a complex web of processes."[122] Similar knowledge was also expressed in Sinhala poetry. Kaviraja's *Laṅkā Vistaraya* described the production of gemstones through the erosive power of Peak waters in several verses:

> Having threshed bushes, the water body that comes is ocean
> shaped
> The path flowing with various crushed stone mountain . . .
>
> The mountain summit forest made like the Himalayas
> Having shaken, branches breaking and falling
> Thus the nine gems are driven out from the water
> The Walawē river goes with the hue of rainbows.[123]

As waters fall, they crush vegetation and rock to kick up jewels. The mountain's mythic rivers that coursed through compositions of so many authors positioned the Peak as the source of a dynamic chain of planetary forces that led to rainbows below.

The fact that these landscape descriptions repeat across religious traditions, ceaselessly assuming new metaphorical forms, demonstrates the influence of the planet on pluralistic cultural expression. It suggests that what drew people to the Peak was not only of human invention. Myths motivating pilgrimage grew from the geology and geography of the island, with a summit orienting travelers in space and deepening their relationship to time. The resonance of descriptions from disparate periods, places, and languages—spanning Chinese and Arabic lapidaries, Sinhala, Tamil, and Pali poetry, and scientific terminology—show that, for all the human trade in tales, in many ways the mountain made its own myth. Stone, water, wind, flora, and fauna are all bundled agencies of a complex mountain assemblage.

All Together in a Peak Assembly

Imagine living fifteen thousand years ago in the highlands near or on the Peak. Your home, which changed occasionally, was a cave or rock-shelter, its precipitous placement and distant view a defense against animal or human enemies. There you lived with immediate family, part of a colony of several other families who moved in areas nearby up to a quarter mile. You kept your home tidy, sleeping on palm mats, and removing waste and trash to separate spaces. Simple pottery was used for storing water from nearby falls and streams. Your tools of stone, animal bone, and plant material were small and light, ideal for carrying while climbing through rugged terrain. Sometimes a sunlit glint in a waterway or rock-face caught your eye, and you plucked out a gemstone, often a chunk of glass-like quartz that proved useful for boring or cutting. Other rocks and minerals were used for ornamentation, like triangular mica pieces, while feldspar and hematite could be ground into colored pastes and smeared on stone or bodies as part of ritual life. You stalked or trapped deer, monkeys, mongooses, boars, buffalos, birds, porcupines, civets, or squirrels, and foraged jungle flora like arboreal fruits and nuts, and fauna like terrestrial and freshwater mollusks. The diet was tough on the teeth, but they were bigger then. You lit fires at night, seeking shelter from weather and predators in the cave, making sure it was not already housing other beasts. There were many ways to die, mammalian threats alone including cats, gaurs, bears, hippopotami, rhinoceri, elephants, and other humans.

The above is a picture of early human habitation in Lanka as conceived by archeologists and paleontologists, with many ideas coming from P. E. P. Deraniyagala.[124] Paules Edward Pieris Deraniyagala (1900–1976) was a visionary of deep time, supporting McPhee's claim that geology is "a fountain of metaphor" with "more than a little of the humanities in this subject."[125] Deraniyagala was a poet, artist, and archeologist, talents that facilitated vivid depictions of prehistoric cave culture, sometimes expressed in sketches and watercolors of extinct environments and animals. Beginning in the late 1930s, Deraniyagala and his teams reconstructed lost worlds from uncovered cave sediments. Evidence of anatomically modern humans went back some thirty-six thousand years in the cave richest in artifacts—Batadombalena, "a small (c. 10 × 15 m), northeast-facing rockshelter on the banks of a stream in the foothills of Sri Pada ('Adam's Peak')."[126] The above account of life fifteen thousand years ago represents a period of increased use of the cave, climatically correlating with an intensification of the monsoon system, the weather making mobile open-air habitation less practical. Static habitation was also more feasible because of the abundance of sustenance facilitated by more rainwater. In the Pleistocene epoch, humans were not always the most impactful environmental force. People in caves were coeval cogs in the complex Peak and its *gebirge* of foothills, filled with interactive living, material, and climatic agencies.

A precursor to Deraniyagala when it came to imagining the deep time of caverns around the Peak was colonial tea planter turned archeologist John Still (1880–1941), who explored the slopes of Samanala at the start of the twentieth century. Seeing elephant trails in the Peak forests, he said they indicated the animal's ancient ascendancy: "Probably they are of enormous antiquity . . . the standardization of all such roads in their general system of avoiding valleys and pursuing ridges, and the similarity of their gradients, seem to reveal a very ancient craft now fixed in principles as scientific as elephants are likely to attain before man imprisons or slays the last of them. Doubtless man learned road-making from the elephants or from other great beasts."[127] A Sinhala poet in 1890 agreed with Still's picture of elephants as road builders, writing that "the road was cleared open by the tusker king."[128] Even today, those familiar with the more remote Kuruwita trail can still point out the elephant tunnels, their tracks and droppings crisscrossing the human pathway. Elephants adapted to highland terrain climb with ease, and Still guessed they were the original pilgrims to the summit: "One is tempted to think that wherever a man may climb so may an elephant, for their immense footprints, smaller only than that on the mountain's top, are to be found upon the highest ridges, and on the summits of peaks hard to scale. It is only the encircling wall that holds them from measuring their feet with Buddha's, and I have little doubt that elephants stood there before ever man did."[129] The Lankatilaka Vihara near Kandy, in one of its eighteenth-century frescoes, depicted just such a scenario, though far more than elephants were shown at the summit (fig. 1.4). The full painted wall shows the sixteen sacred places in Lanka touched by the Buddha. The other locales are represented by generic stupa images, nearly identical, but a special summit stood instead of a stupa for Sumanakuta. Here, birds, squirrels, deer, sambar, macaques, monkeys, and wild boar all join the scene, although the elephant is the one actually climbing the steps.

Depictions of elephants climbing to worship the footprint were also present in manuscript illuminations and at other temples. They likewise became common cover illustrations in the early twentieth-century boom of printed pilgrimage poems (fig. 1.5). Describing another temple fresco, Florence Caddy opined that a "picture of elephants cantering up Adam's Peak, with offering to the footprint, is very comical,"[130] but those like Still who were poetically taken with the Peak jungles would have affirmed its sentiment, as would the average Lankan. The myth still prevails of animals climbing during the rainy season, when most humans refrain. Elephants are the animals to whom Lankans most

FIGURE 1.4. Animal pilgrims to the Peak painted at the Lankatilaka Vihara

often attribute this capacity for worship at the Peak, as in a manuscript praising the Mahaweli:

> The off season having come, the mountain road fully bad
> Elephants seem to be spread endlessly
> Now going to the King who sows awareness
> Having proceeded here, the stream goes on.[131]

FIGURE 1.5. Detail of cover for *Śrīpādapatmaya Vandanāgātha saha Abhinava Himagatavarṇanāva*
National Museum Library, Colombo

The importance of elephants was also cause for their comparison to the Peak. Per *Samantakūṭavaṇṇanā*: "This mountain, which has shoots for tusks, heaped up peaks for frontal lobes, many natural tanks for eyes, a river for a trunk, and a cascade for a rushing stream of rut-fluid, shines like the elephant of the king of the gods."[132] A Sinhala version of this concept appeared in Śrī Rāhula's *Parevi Sandeśa*, the elephant-mountain's river-trunk grabbing the sea, with rumbling waterfalls for rut-fluid:

> The chief-elephant Samanaḷa mountain grasped the waters of
> the sea.
> Outstretched with vibrations, the long rut-fluid always shows
> beauty,
> as the Kalu Ganga shines by rows and folds of waves.[133]

As keystone animals of jungle environments, elephants were a worthy comparison for the island's keystone of mountains.

Yet in the Lankatilaka painting, the elephant climbing the steps is dwarfed by the number of other animals around, not to mention the massive waving trees. How was one to capture in words all these natural agents conveyed together in a mythic picture? Some opted for lists, like Vedeha Thera, who made plain his familiarity with the Peak wilderness in *Samantakūṭavaṇṇanā*. One can imagine him climbing on pilgrimage, distinguishing bird songs, gazing into mountain streams, and rubbing textures of different leaves between his thumb and forefinger, as his poem lists eight fish species, four birds, five lotuses, fifty-one trees, and thirty-three other types of flora, many left in the original Pali by the English translator for lack of equivalents of such specificity.[134] Two centuries after Vedeha, a student from his monastic lineage composed a Sinhala prose narrative around excerpts from *Samantakūṭavaṇṇanā*, with equally lengthy lists of species inhabiting the mountain.[135]

Another modality of description emphasized interconnection of sounds within a symphony of mountain signs. For John Still, these included "the song of the streams . . . the roar of the leopards, the horn-like challenge of sambhur stags, the scream of eagles, the deep tones of the great black monkeys of the hills, and, more tremendous than any, the trumpeting of elephants. For the forest is full of life."[136] In a similar fashion, Sinhala poets sewed sound as a single strand in quatrains with differently themed lines, as ascending pilgrims distinguished bees buzzing, wind whirling, and water rushing, coolly moving through the aural atmosphere to climb cliffs unconcerned:

> Having seen various bloomed flower nectar, the desirous bee
> springs to pollen
> While the sound of wind whips, without the ear being confused
> looking at cliffs
> Having fallen, flowing through rocks, pure streams come flowing
> making noise
> Gone quickly to clouds and become happy, forever worship the
> Samanala sacred sole.[137]

This bit of pilgrimage song exemplifies how well Sinhala quatrains animate the rich rosters of life in the Samanala wilderness, going beyond lists to show the dynamic interactions among living and nonliving forces at the Peak.

To conclude with a meditation on these bundles of agencies, we return to the poem that opened this chapter: *Saman Sirita*. Deraniyagala edited the print edition during his tenure as director of the National Museum of Ceylon, using an eighteenth-century manuscript his father donated in 1905, and estimated that *Saman Sirita* was composed in the early sixteenth century.[138] Its author was likely connected to the main Saman *dēvāle* in Sabaragamuwa, as the latter part of the poem gives a history of this temple's endowments. Despite being written long after the days of rainforest dwellers, when human political organization had expanded from quarter-mile cave colonies to kingdoms with imperial ambitions, the forest in *Saman Sirita* retains a primordial quality where humans are minor actors in a jungle panoply. Deraniyagala even used *Saman Sirita* to gauge previous habitats by references to extinct animals like spotted deer and gaur, corroborating literary records with antler relics excavated from highland caves.[139]

Forest descriptions in *Saman Sirita* are indebted to predecessors like *Samantakuṭāvaṇṇanā* and *sandeśa* poetry.[140] *Saman Sirita* also repeats many general tropes of the Peak discussed above, including the myth of four rivers, and comparison of the landscape to Lady Lanka.[141] Yet *Saman Sirita* also has its own unique effects, making great use of the imagistic potential in a Sinhala quatrain. Like *Samantakuṭāvaṇṇanā*, a vivid wilderness description precedes the Buddha impressing his footprint on the Peak. In this forest, some creatures receive detailed individual verses, but the poet especially excels at expressing interaction, depicting a landscape abounding with crisscrossing lines of agency, with actions often dictated by lines of sight.

The poet shows a particular penchant for portraying leopards' foiled pounces, with the big cat rethinking its prey choice after gauging the size of it in one verse:

> The prey was greatly desired without stopping
> Digging boars enter the wild forest area
> Leopards are afraid having seen their bodies
> They go having thoughtfully given up the hunt.[142]

One can imagine a stalking leopard crouched low, watching wild boar lumbering, muscles tensed in anticipation of attack, then slackened with a split-second switched decision. *Saman Sirita* showed a jungle world governed by such interrelationships of fear, a reminder that forests were excellent for elegizing, but also fraught with danger. Of course, some forest predation was mundane, like fowl foraging:

> There are wild chickens without hesitations
> Having brushed dry leaves, there are long worms

For sweet prey, their greed not dropped
Having dug, they heap up gem clusters.[143]

By rooting through leaves and topsoil looking for worms, these chickens stirred another agent from the ground, kicking up gemstones that had eroded off rock. These crystalline characters affected jungle life variously. For one, they foiled another leopard leap:

Edible honey mangos are properly in lofty treetops
Yet not only reflections of leaf monkeys are there
Rays of a gem wall are also seen on forest canopy branches
Cheating bounding leopards always.[144]

Gems on the ground reflected sunlight upward, dancing across the forest canopy in a way that made leopards mistake the rays for monkeys and bound up at the empty air.

Forest-floor gems catching the light also resemble flames, appearing like this in a verse that has Väddas and deer fleeing the sight and sound of stampeding elephants smashing through the trees:

From the sight of wild tuskers with sounds of tusks
From the sight of various deer herds coming
Väddas leave from atop the gems
Like exorcists trampling fire.[145]

Vädda feet trample the precious stones as quickly as fire walkers step over coals, unconcerned with their value in this dangerous moment. Other animals are afraid of the gems, illuminated by both sun and moon, because of their resemblance to previously felt fires:

Gold gems seen shining in the manner of
fearful forest fire flames like before.
As far as the eye sees, the group of deer ran quickly
Equally at night and noon in the forest region.[146]

The deer of *Saman Sirita* are easily spooked. In another instance, it is not the gemstones that send them running, but buzzing bees and flame-colored leaves:

The deer herd enters amid lotuses and looks around
Intoxicated bees are visible to the herd in the forest

The beautiful deer herd runs without staying
Becoming fearful again at the copper color tender leaf.[147]

Plants also have other agency in the poem, their shaking and shimmering interactions with wind animating the entire mountain:

Mountain summits are seen like rain clouds happily.
Desirously engaged in dancing like peacocks,
shimmering *giritil* flower bunches decorate the summit.
Yellow flower groves always shine in that forest.[148]

With mountain summits soliloquized as clouds, the flowers are dancing peacocks praising precipitation. Peacocks dancing on mountains in the rain, rejoicing in the monsoon marking their mating season, is a trope of Indic poetry. In this case, however, the peacocks are actually flowers, so dense they decorate the summit. The Peak thereby touches every metaphor in the verse—rain cloud, flower, and bird—embodying the agencies of water, vegetation, and animal life shouldered upon its stone.

Mountains are thus much more than the geology of their bedrock. Considered as complex assemblages, they include hydrological, biological, and climatological systems, with all these logics in dialogue. Of course, the forest surrounding the Peak today is less lush than in the sixteenth century, diminished by tea plantations and millions of pilgrims. Yet the landscape remains important to visitors, and environmental experiences are often cited as a reason for climbing the Peak. Sinhala books about Sri Pada continually emphasize its forested "range" (*aḍaviya*), whether with biodiversity catalogues, accounts of cave-dwelling monks, or folktales about the divine power of these hills.[149] To this end, the wilderness plays both ecological and theological roles in human reasoning, elaborated in chapter 5. Next, however, we turn to human infrastructure encroaching upon slopes of the Peak, explaining motivations behind increasing interventions into its wilderness.

2

The Workaday Mountain

While prehistoric peoples populated Peak forests, their niche-making activities were low impact. Over the past millennium, however, humans have carved increasingly wider roads into the environment for pilgrimage, culminating in the modern mountain's urban-esque infrastructure of cement, sewers, and electricity. While most of its slopes remain wilderness, the mountain has seen "scattered urbanization," implemented in part because infrastructure itself carries potent symbolism for those in pursuit of political power.[1] As Victor Turner put it, "pilgrimages sometimes generate cities and consolidate regions."[2] Even before the modern period, the mountain was modified by royal improvement projects and referred to as a "city" (*pura*) in Sinhala poetics, fitting Lefebvre's "first definition of the city as a projection of society on the ground."[3] The Peak's centrality makes it an excellent canvas for this projection, as "there is no urban reality without a centre, without a gathering together."[4] This is because "the signs of the urban are the signs of assembly: the things that promote assembly (the street and its surface, stone, asphalt, sidewalks) and the requirements for assembly (seats, lights)."[5] To create a central pilgrimage gathering, human activities on the mountain therefore constitute infrastructure as Brian Larkin defines it, namely "built networks that facilitate the flow of goods, people, or ideas and allow for their exchange . . . [to] generate the ambient environment of everyday life."[6] This chapter explains a subset of such systems I call *pilgrimage infrastructure*. This shares traits with infrastructures involving state sponsors and capitalism, but also extends to the cooperative work of devotees, whose motivations include merit making and other soteriological goals. Jobs can be devotional, described as both religious vocations and practical occupations. Employees include everyone from electricians to shopkeepers to road builders to garbage pickers to monks and priests performing rituals. Their whirl of activity, "the pilgrimage assembly line,"[7] makes possible the annual six-month worship season, facilitating visits from millions.

This chapter has three main parts. The first focuses on infrastructure installed by Lankan kings, showing the mountain as a symbol of rule. The second describes expansion of infrastructure during the British colonial period, where motivations for building still contained soteriological considerations for Buddhists, but were also fueled by medical and economic projects of the state, standardizing control and funding of new works. Third, the workaday mountain where I lived in 2015–2016 is presented. In all three cases, it is difficult to demarcate devotees from workers, as manual labor, karmic debt, corporate advertisement, royal legend, family business, and religious ritual whirl into pilgrimage infrastructure. Although such a history shows humanity exerting its will over the natural world, the mountain's agency also prevails, as "the earth, its rocks, soil and water . . . [are] the infrastructure on which infrastructures are constructed."[8] The Peak itself thus limits how and when people can labor, provides shoulders on which structures are hoisted, and serves as a slate where inscriptional records of work are carved.

Royal Pilgrimage Infrastructure

It is impossible to determine when exactly regular pilgrimage to the Peak began, but it was significant enough by the twelfth century to draw royal patronage. The first king to record a grant was Vijayabāhu (r. 1055–1110), who left inscribed stone slabs at both main approaches toward the mountain, at Ambagamuwa in the northeast and Gilimale in the southwest. This patronage precedent became a model for subsequent rulers to replicate, the Peak now a piece of political rule.[9] The inscription praises Vijayabāhu for his bodhisattva compassion, veneration of the Buddhist order, and war-hero status. It then lists his offerings to the summit footprint, upon which the king "raised also various canopies, flags, banners made of silk cloth, and, anointing it with four kinds of unguents, decked it with his own bejeweled crown." The king's coronation of the footprint relic fit the many royal titles and rituals with which the Buddha was praised. In turn, crowning this particular summit may have reinforced the idea that the Peak is a king among mountains, and thus an ideal site for royalty to display prowess. Vijayabāhu did so by making it easier for pilgrims to reach this mountainous instantiation of the Buddha, as "he instituted the maintenance of repairs, offerings, paintings, lighting of lamps on Samanoḷa rock which bears the sacred footprint; and for providing . . . suitable food and other necessary things . . . he had almonries [*dāna śālā*] established in his name . . . and in the area all around it he caused formation of paddy fields."[10] Pilgrim numbers by this time apparently required major infrastructure, with rest halls and fields to supply provisions. Beyond the summit, a whole range of territory was modified to facilitate visits.

Subsequent Buddhist rulers likewise performed Peak pilgrimages. The second extension of the *Mahāvaṃsa* chronicle compiled in the fourteenth century mentions the journey of Nissankamalla (r. 1187–1196): "With the four-membered army, the Ruler full of pious devotion went forth to Samantakūṭa and performed there his devotions."[11] Nissankamalla is famous for his many inscriptions, several outlining his island tours, when the king "toured the three kingdoms and inspected inaccessible places such as Samanoḷa."[12] Inscriptions said his pilgrimage came after consolidating power in Lanka and invading South India to collect tribute. The fact that the Peak was described as inaccessible emphasized Nissankamalla's strength, and climbing with his army was significant, too. It was specified in every record of his ascent, like *Pūjāvaliya*, completed around 1266, in which the king "went with the army to Samanola and worshiped the Buddha's sacred foot"[13]—a military-mountain link explored further below.

Nissankamalla also left the Peak's best-preserved inscription, sheltered beneath a small outcrop about a hundred feet below the summit on the Hatton side. As the trail runs beside this cave, some pilgrims leave small offerings and call it Bhagavalena—where the Buddha rested after imprinting his foot.[14] It was known to nineteenth-century archeologist John Still: "In a cave near the summit I found a little picture chiseled upon the rock wall with a few words cut beside it in twelfth century script. It showed a man in an attitude of veneration with a rosary held in his joined hands, and the words read 'King Nissanka Malla worships the footprint on the rock.' "[15] To the right of the image are fourteen more lines of inscription, some effaced. These contain content similar to Nissankamalla's pillar inscriptions, noting he united Sri Lanka ("sirilaka eksat koṭä"), went to India ("dambadiva väḍi kalhi"), and received tribute from the Chola country ("soḷi raṭin evū pañḍuru"). He then went to Samanoḷa, where he decorated the summit with a silver garland, nine gems, and a royally ornamented crown, worshiping the footprint ("samanoḷa väḍä . . . rajata mālāyen da navaratnayen da maḷuva sadā saha voṭunu raja baraṇin sädī vända"). Finally, Nissankamalla rededicated villages to the Peak that Vijayabāhu had bestowed, including Ambagamuwa.[16]

Despite Vijayabāhu's well-documented donations, and Nissankamalla crediting these earlier endowments as inspirational, in popular memory only the latter king is remembered as the primogenitor of pilgrimage infrastructure. Mountain workers and pilgrims frequently cite Nissankamalla as the one who rediscovered the pathway to the Peak and covered the Buddha's original sapphire footprint with stone for safekeeping. My friend Nimal, manager of the White House Guest House in Nallathanni, added an enchanted twist, saying the king planted pillars around the footprint to erect a canopy and, from the four holes he bore into the rock, the four famous rivers of the Peak flowed forth. In other stories, Nissankamalla is credited with everything from burying treasure to constructing a platform for low-caste people, which Vijayabāhu actually did.[17]

To describe Nissankamalla rediscovering the footprint, many used a folktale in which a crippled dwarf caught goddesses plucking royal-garden flowers to lay on the footprint. So the king could follow, the goddesses dropped flowers along the path to the Peak. Nissankamalla was not always part of this story. Nineteenth-century manuscripts had a Vädda, not a cripple, catch the goddesses in an unnamed king's garden.[18] A 1920 poetic retelling had a king named Bhātiya hire the cripple.[19] In a 1924 poem, however, Nissankamalla was the king who set it in motion.[20] He eventually absorbed the myth altogether, perhaps a historical exemplar of choice because his name and likeness are carved into the mountain itself. There are also other caves associated with the king. He is said to have rested under an outcrop near the foot of the Peak, now a shrine called Nissankamalla Cave. Inside stands a recently crafted statue of Nissankamalla holding a signboard with his own name, as well as a small diorama of the cripple sitting in the flower garden hut, ready to catch the goddesses who reveal the Peak pathway.

These emplaced memories of Nissankamalla allow the king to dominate historical imagination at the Peak, his legend extending to other sites off-trail only rumored to exist. One day I walked with Brenda, ninety-two years old, who worked in Nallathanni guest houses. Her climb on opening day in 2015 brought her total count to eighty-nine lifetime ascents. Brenda remembered when Sri Lanka was British Ceylon with nostalgia, telling me how "the white gentlemen" helped develop the country with tea plantations, where she worked as a nanny in the superintendent bungalows. She gave these same estates credit for developing the pathway to the Peak on the Hatton side. However, she believed remnants of older infrastructure lay hidden off the trail. Having stopped for a prayer to God Saman at Nissankamalla Cave, Brenda took me into the woods to seek the ruins of a small palace she said Nissankamalla built after his pilgrimage (fig. 2.1). Other shopkeepers smirked at Brenda's claims, but her

FIGURE 2.1. Looking for ruins of Nissankamalla's palace off the Hatton trail

conviction did not waver. She was sure we would find it if we had more time to go farther into the forest, but rain would be coming that afternoon, and the leeches were a nuisance.

Although Nissankamalla is most remembered for pilgrimage infrastructure, his actual endowments were relatively minor compared to Parakramabāhu II (r. 1224–1269), who bestowed more than any other king, as recorded in the second *Mahāvaṃsa* extension. He, too, went on pilgrimage with his army: "The best of kings betook himself with his fourfold forces to Samantakūṭa, this forehead jewel of stone mountains. . . . All around the mountain king [*girinda*], he granted in religious devotion to the sacred footprint . . . the land rich in various precious stones and thickly peopled with men and women."[21] Again the Peak was called a king, drawing parallels with a human ruler who allowed the grandeur and permanence of the stone to be shared. Meanwhile, granting gemming lands endowed the temple with wealth that increased its political importance. Parakramabāhu even endowed the footprint with people, the first indication of indentured labor for the Peak, making it even more kingly.

Nor did Parakramabāhu stop there. Later in his reign, power consolidated, he increased his pilgrimages and meritorious donations. He instructed his minister Devapattirāja: "By swamp, mountain and wilderness . . . the road leading to the Sumana mountain is at many places obstructed, inaccessible, and causes difficulties to the people . . . who make a pilgrimage there to accumulate blessings by venerating the footprint. . . . Do thus make it accessible."[22] Devapattirāja joyfully agreed "to build bridges . . . very strong and good so that elephants, horses, cattle and buffaloes could pass over them. And above each . . . he had fair houses built, adorned with lofty pillars . . . and had invitations sent to numbers of *bhikkhus*, gathered them together . . . distributed among them abundant alms and celebrated a great sacrificial festival. He built rest-houses . . . laid down . . . frequent stepping-stones, had the wilderness cleared, and thus built a great road."[23] This was the first endowment record showing significant alteration of wilderness, with jungle cleared, and attempts to pave at least the most difficult trail sections with stone. Devapattirāja's infrastructural agenda matched his Buddhist religiosity, with a gathering of monks connected to the construction. Holding an almsgiving ceremony and facilitating monastic pilgrimage to the Peak was a double act of merit atop the already meritorious trail building. Devapattirāja's work was thus presented not only for royal glory but the entire *sangha*. It seemed to fulfill a command Vedeha Thera gave in *Samantakūṭavaṇṇanā*, composed around the same time: "The Great Priceless Jewel, the King of Conquerors, adorned the crest of Samantakūṭa, which is the crown of the bride Laṅkā. Now, sirs, love and serve always that peak, which grants the heart's desires, which gives happiness, and is matchless in the three worlds!"[24] Roads served the Peak by channeling people and wealth to its slopes, the love of a king expressed in infrastructure facilitating the love of many others, showing the interdependency of karmic action among Buddhists.

Parakramabāhu's endowments certainly had other functions, too. Development on the northeast side of the mountain focused on river-port villages of the greater Mahaweli watershed. Bridges in these places linked inland pathways with riverine networks. The mythic importance of Peak rivers discussed in chapter 1 was also political, their development required to link the country. *Pūjāvaliya*, begun late in Parakramabāhu's reign, also recorded his endowments, described to Devapattirāja as necessary because the path to Peak was "*jaladurga—vanadurga—giridurgayen atidurga ya*,"[25] or water inaccessible, forest inaccessible, mountain inaccessible, most inaccessible. Everything was *durga*, or difficult to approach. This may have been true of much territory Parakramabāhu sought to govern from a relatively new highland capital in Dambadeniya. Clearing roads to the Peak, and creating bridges and rest houses at key river crossings, made a better connected polity in general. Bridges built for heavy traffic of pack animals functioned year-round regardless of pilgrimage season. Moreover, roadside rest halls have been described as public places of intellectual exchange.[26] Politics were likely discussed there, and a ruler theoretically gave cause for praise of his reign by their construction. Moreover, one cannot discount the impact that the physical presence of important political figures like kings, ministers, or powerful monks walking these jungle paths might have had on the average Lankan. As a Sinhala proverb notes: "Poor men, too, travel on the same road as kings."[27] Of course, they traveled in quite different styles, the poor with humble packs and provisions, kings with pomp and palanquins, enacting piety and power. Devapattirāja's road-building excursion had doubled as a giant religious procession, and he had a golden bejeweled image of Saman cast to be carried alongside the workers, infrastructure inaugurating the first recorded procession of a Saman statue up the mountain. Overall, these medieval endowments shared some modern "enchantments of infrastructure," including a desire for political integration and economic connectivity.[28] Yet pilgrimage infrastructure is draped in an extra layer of enchantment when sponsors are also motivated by what is soteriologically meritorious. Devapattirāja, for his own part, aspired to be more than a political minister, having taken a vow to become a bodhisattva, which was why the king chose him to lead the project.[29]

Endowments of several kings after Parakramabāhu II are recorded, but none on the same scale. The second *Mahāvaṃsa* extension and *Pūjāvaliya* both mention the visit of his son and successor Vijayabāhu IV (r. 1270–1272), though without further description.[30] *Saman Sirita* also states that Parakramabāhu's brother, the sub-king Bhuvanekabāhu, brought offerings and granted villages to the Peak after Saman visited his dreams.[31] Overall, however, records of Peak endowments are sparse in subsequent centuries, interrupted in part by local and foreign political discord. When the capital of Kandy stabilized in the seventeenth century, literary records emerged anew, and the intervening history of the Peak was back-written. These texts are discussed in chapter 4, where Buddhist-Hindu relations at the Peak are addressed.

Beyond being an ideal recipient of royal endowments, the Peak also possessed symbolic potency for kings through the poetic animation of its landscape as a powerful female. As noted in chapter 1, the Peak was routinely described as part of "Lady Lanka." The earliest extant application of this metaphor appears in the tenth-century *Mahāvaṃsa* commentary, *Vaṃsatthappakāsinī*. This describes the summit as Lady Lanka's head, a standard trope in later descriptions, but also makes a unique comparison of the Peak to Lady Lanka's waist and vaginal river: "she [wears] a jeweled girdle, completely beautiful, that is adorned by gems . . . which originate on the side of Sumanakuta and become garlands for her genitalia—the River that flows from its source on that peak"; the Peak was sexualized even further: "she became the chief queen to be enjoyed by four fully enlightened Buddhas." Wedded to the Peak, the Buddha displays his sovereignty via the conquest, as his "excellent signet ring is his foot, in order to point out the fact that he himself came here . . . and that this island is its own boss because of the establishment of the Buddha-*sāsana*."[32] With passages like this, Lankan kings were staking claims in a wider Indic imperial realm, in competition with South Indian rulers and their models of divine kingship. The Buddha's footprint was an imprimatur, not only commemorating his visit, but also acting as a political signature, granting Lanka independence by Buddhist status. Royal pilgrimages to the Peak acknowledged this. Their armied ascents displayed strength, while the mountain itself represented what kings had to protect. The Peak was mother and wife, standing for the fertile potential of Lanka, encouraging guarding rulers to mimic its steadfast strength.

This portrayal persisted in the Sītāvaka court of Rajasinha I (r. 1581–1593), whose kingdom was born of fraternal strife, and who became famous for resisting Portuguese incursions. In this martial milieu, *Sītāvaka Haṭana* (The Sītāvaka war) was written around 1585 in Sinhala verse by Alahapperuma Vijayavardhana, who claimed to be a former officer in campaigns of Rajasinha. Using the Peak as a ruling symbol and territorial landmark, *Sītāvaka Haṭana* promotes a new capital, giving heroic ancestries to its rulers as the last bastion against the dissolution of Lanka. Alahapperuma feminizes the land erotically and maternally, casting Rajasinha and his father Mayadunne (r. 1521–1581) as sustainers of Lanka who are also sustained by it.[33] The Peak therefore becomes a gentlewoman of the island:

> A noble woman of correct caste, supreme
> is the manner of the Samanala crest's appearance.
> Placing shining flowers with soft tips,
> removing troubles by her hand, is the shining river.[34]

This personification captures the Peak's agency to direct other natural elements, bestowing waters that distribute flowers and remove troubles. After several verses describing the mountain as a mother goddess full of milk, Alahapperuma links Samanala and Sītāvaka through the Buddha's regal footprint:

> The Sage beheld that suffering,
> and went so as to stop it.
> He preached words in this age,
> and placed the sacred foot lotus.
>
> Our illustrious king
> in Sītāvaka City [*pura*]

resides governing and
beholds Samanala City [*pura*].

Like Mount Meru in bearing,
the king beholds it on both sides.
Having beheld, mind happy
worshiping Samanala like this.

The king declared:
"The victory mark of the lord of the land
for Lanka Island is the sacred footprint."
The city was then brought into existence.[35]

These quatrains establish Sītāvaka and Samanala as two poles of a kingdom, with Mayadunne able to gaze upon the Peak from his palace. Capital and summit are classed as *pura* "cities," and the sanction of the Buddha extends to both. Mayadunne therefore makes a pilgrimage, apparently traversing both sides of the mountain.[36] The Peak is thereby established as the grounded palladium of highland courts, its Buddha footprint authorizing the creation of the new capital of Sītāvaka.

Thereafter, the devotion of Mayadunne's son, Rajasinha, emerges in his own countrywide circuits, as he makes offerings to the Saman shrine near Ratnapura and builds a new one elsewhere in Sabaragamuwa.[37] Although no pilgrimage to the Peak is recorded for Rajasinha, the mountain reappears from afar in feminized fashion, remaining conceptually important to his royal tour.

From the pure goddess's chest flowing
Pure milk in four directions shining going
Children of impure caste are living
Purely causing their improvement always
. . .
Divine woman crying there, having been horrified
Immortals mindful of the tears that cover the four directions
The gods continually saying, "Who angers the mother,
guarding infants of four directions and improving all beings?"

Noblewoman-like Samanala shining from face and neck
Having seen the sight, troubles are pleasantly removed
From forest tree flowers, woven flower garlands shake
Behold the way that the hill looks like its blue trees.[38]

These verses elaborate the maternal mountain theme, as Alahapperuma adapts the myth of four rivers from Samanala's summit and transforms them into streams of milk from the abundant breast of Lady Lanka. The beings reaping the wealth of these fluids are the children downstream, and Alahapperuma mentions erasure of their imperfect caste by the lineage of the land, as the mountain and its embedded relic improve the population, raising people alongside the Peak. Attacks on the land upset the maternal lifeline, and the four rivers of milk turn to tears, meaning that Samanala, the heart and soul of Lanka, must be guarded for posterity. Kings lead the charge to protect it, but the larger populace ultimately benefits. Imperiled yet autonomous, with delicate beauty but maternal strength, made of flowers and trees but thoroughly human, the Peak that Alahapperuma constructs is a plural amalgamation of positive traits, blurring literal and figural description. In the preceding centuries of courtly verse, including a *sandeśa* poem written for Rajasinha only a few years prior, conventional tropes of powerful handsome kings watching seductive dancing women prevailed.[39] In verses of comparatively colloquial Sinhala, Alahapperuma innovates within these paradigms by expressing them through the Peak, which becomes not only an alluring woman, but also a nursing mother, both needing the protection of a masculine king.

As much as Alahapperuma glorifies royal lineages, his description of Samanala cedes a certain amount of power to the Lankan landscape and its inhabitants. The references to a mother and her children imply the populace cared as deeply for the Peak as it did for them, a natural precondition for its efficacy as a ruling symbol. In addition to its draw as a pilgrimage place, the mountain's associations with alluvial affluence and fertility in later farming rituals also suggest a widespread appeal across class and caste.[40] In this case, royal endowments only capped a pilgrimage infrastructure that developed from the ground up. Regardless of who sat in which capital and whether they endowed the Peak, pilgrims presumably continued climbing season to season. Kings may have granted villages, but locals were responsible for long-term maintenance, repairing road stands and clearing footpaths.

Such histories of subaltern infrastructure are difficult to document beyond scattered clues. A folktale of the god Ranvala, for example, describes his prior life as a royal-granary thief who escaped to a remote village and later aided Peak pilgrims by giving torches to those walking an old path on his land.[41] One can imagine various networks of similar supply lines. Sinhala poems printed between 1890 and 1940 often describe poor pilgrims stopping at the homes of wealthy men who donated goods, offered advice, or cleared trails.[42] Most inscriptions of private donations, however, are too weathered to read, like the one at Dharmarajagala, hewn with a hundred steps into a granite outcrop on the Ratnapura trail.[43] Other inscriptions have been demolished by heavy monsoon rains causing rockslides.[44] I saw firsthand how even inscriptions a few decades old soon succumb to moss. Records of the British period, however, do preserve a wealth of infrastructural details, many departing from standards set by Lankan kings. Colonial motivations were more often medical or commercial, without the Buddhist soteriological framing of Lankan royal grants. Yet the colonial expansion of the urban mercantile class also led to private Buddhist societies engaging in their own sponsorship for religious ends. In both cases, we find Sinhala poets and British officials focused on the same landmarks of the Peak.

Colonial and Cooperative Pilgrimage Infrastructure

After the British conquered Kandy in 1815, a military attachment was sent to the Peak.[45] It was an act befitting patterns of Lankan rulers, similar to Nissankamalla's army ascending after consolidation of his island-wide claims. It did not take long for the British to intervene into the administration of the Peak, too, appointing a successor of Väliviṭa Saraṇankara as head monk in 1820.[46] The British continued appointments throughout the decade, but soon began to retreat from the issue. This was due in part to Christian lobbyists arguing it was untoward for the government to legislate heathen affairs, and British appointments were abolished in 1853. Thereafter, certificates of government recognition were presented to winners of monastic elections convened by local headmen. As one official described it, "the Government Agent has no legal status in the matter; he merely acts as 'amicus curiae' and repels the onus which is continually sought to be put on him, assuming some sort of responsibility for the election."[47] Even this much involvement, however, was a headache for government agents in Ratnapura, who found themselves referees in repeated monastic and chieftain conflicts. As a new government agent (GA) lamented, "evening in reading the multitudinous files with regard to the High Priest of Adam's Peak. Not pleasant reading at all and they provide more food for cynic than the optimist."[48]

The history of the head monk position at the Peak is far too lengthy and complex to recount here.[49] Instead, other moments of British intervention in infrastructural administration are detailed, with glimpses of local laborers and cooperative construction by devotees. Official records of pilgrimage infrastructure were sparse in the nineteenth century. In the annual *Administration Reports* that government agents from each province submitted, not until 1904 was a section for "civil" issues added, everything otherwise being about revenue. In 1906, the subheading "pilgrimages" appeared as a category in the civil section, included in R. B. Hellings's report for the Province of Sabaragamuwa: "The number of pilgrims to Adam's Peak during the year was estimated at 7,700. The usual precautionary measures were taken, including the appointment of a dispensary, a Sanitary Inspector, and four patrol coolies, at a cost to Government of Rs. 439.98. Considering the exposure, the hard climb, and the distance many of these people travel, there was wonderfully little sickness among them."[50] Hellings referred to these measures as "usual," but evidence for their advent is absent.

As with religious gatherings elsewhere in the British Empire, health and sanitation were central concerns at the Peak due to the influx of population from all quarters.[51] The earliest recorded pilgrimage health initiative came during the 1837 ascent of Governor Robert Wilmot Horton. He and his entourage used the journey to promote smallpox vaccination. After they arrived in Ratnapura, they "remained here the whole of the next day, and his excellency took the opportunity, as he did at all stations where we halted, to summon the chiefs and head men, and to explain to them his hopes that they had their children vaccinated to prevent the fatal propagation of the dreadful small-pox."[52] Still, health intervention at the Peak was minor compared to regulations instituted at Kataragama, which entailed a two-week encampment suited to an entry-ticket system.[53] The entire Kataragama pilgrimage was even canceled once for fear of a plague. The Peak season, however, lasting for months with waves of crowds, made cancelation impossible. In 1914, Ratnapura Government Agent R. N. Thaine reported: "At the outbreak of plague in Colombo considerable apprehension was felt that the Colombo pilgrims might introduce the disease into the Province. It was not practicable, as in the Kataragama festival, to restrict the number of pilgrims. Eventually it was decided to subject the pilgrims to medical examination at various points."[54]

While government expenditure on pilgrimage infrastructure was relatively minor, reports suggest substantial civilian investment. Thaine relayed: "The pilgrims are remarkably well looked after by the Buddhist societies. At every important halting place there are large iron or brick ambalams and a pipe water service."[55] The Sinhala term *ambalam* became current among many British travelers, who also utilized these open-air shelters. Records of ambalams were also preserved in Sinhala pilgrimage poetry that described routes to the Peak. An early example was a Sinhala Christian propaganda poem that discouraged belief in the footprint, which recounted its author's 1853 ascent:

> For the pilgrims who go and come there in the future,
> considering the means of their lodging and staying,

leaf-covered halls and huts have been built around there.
We see that they're filled at the time we went there.

He also described the structure sheltering the footprint, noting the name of its donor:

Behind that *vehera* on a long piece of timber in good style
"Mamitura Kehelgamuvē Ārachchine"
had been carved in Sinhala letters.[56]

This was not the only poem to record specific names of infrastructure sponsors.[57] *Abhivana Himagata Varṇanāva* (Modern praise of Himagata), published in 1902, gave the initials for the donor of the rest hall at Heramitipana, the key junction where the Ratnapura and Kuruwita trails meet, and where many eat and sleep before a final push to the summit. Heramitipana was mentioned as early as the 1788 *Käṭakirilli Sandeśaya*, which described pilgrims gathering there, and Buddhist lessons being delivered:

Place to place are great crowds, bringing offerings and alms.
Leaping speaking pundits are elucidating knowledge.
Mind thinking, composed in the mode of this truth the Victor
gave,
comforted for a bit of time, friend, at Heramitipana.[58]

Modern poems like *Abhinava Himagata Varṇanāva* began describing buildings there, turning this infrastructure into another Buddhist lesson:

For the people coming without a limit,
a place for accommodation at Heramitipana
was leveled and decorated like a town.
A place was made and constructed in the past.

The person named D.M.P.
working diligently to build the hall,
desiring to give merit to all beings,
by that merit, is a going-to-*moksha* being.[59]

Such construction was done for merit, as helping devotees ascend the mountain helped donors ascend to *moksha*, endowments bound in a larger soteriology. Even if not quite reaching nirvana, such acts could create better rebirths. An 1857 manuscript of Sinhala pilgrimage songs proclaimed that building an ambalam with the right intention was meritorious enough for one to be born in a heavenly realm:

> If an ambalam is made with committed heart and clear mind,
> you go with eyes that are love adorned and are born in that heaven,
> where, like the full moon shining in the sky, golden mansions are received,
> and divine armies adorned in lotuses and gems arrive as entourage.[60]

Opportunities for making merit like this abounded, as the ambalam network was not limited to the Peak trail. Poems of journeys from Colombo, Galle, Matara, and Hambantota are filled with mentions of the marketplaces and rest halls where pilgrims could sleep and resupply. Consider, for example, *Siri Pāda Gaman Vistaraya* (Sri Pada journey description) of 1891 by Disānayaka Don Lavarenti, who had gone on pilgrimage annually for the previous thirty-one years. He wrote his book to transmit accumulated wisdom about proper rituals to perform and routes to take. The towns and villages named therein represent the larger system that supported traveling pilgrims:

> In Kaduwala having halted, cooking rice then.
> Having eagerly descended to the river and bathed heads,
> at the shop everyone ate rice and relaxed,
> and departed at that time when the sun entered the west.[61]

As his pilgrimage group approached the summit, Lavarenti also devoted several verses to the Heramitipana rest stop, describing ambalam activities and infrastructure:

> People coming from each region stopping at the spot
> Without even a little bit of sleep when it is becoming light
> Each time getting up, they sit, drink, and eat shop food
> With wild animals around, they guard near the ambalam
> . . .
> In the previously dug well, the water became muddy and bad.
> Because of karma, our nation descended and dissolved.
> Having put on white clothes and stood up in pain,
> from the Heramitipana ambalam we departed.[62]

With the poor state of water service at Heramitipana attributed to the country's collective karma, infrastructure was again interwoven with soteriological reasoning, this time to express failure. The original well that fell into disrepair was likely dug as a meritorious act, but Lavarenti was disappointed that no one maintained it, and the suffering of the nation was thus mirrored by the dehydrated pilgrim's aching body. His sentiments were shared by others. With new Buddhist societies forming at this time, it was not long before the next generation of meritorious sponsors refreshed the waters for the benefit of pilgrims at this central rest stop.

The water supply at Heramitipana also caught British interest, as it was where they stationed a government-sponsored apothecary every year, even becoming a field clinic on occasion.[63] The first reference to a new water system there appeared in 1907, when R. B. Hellings noted: "at Heramitipana, the last resting place, a ram forces water from a stream to the plateau on which the pilgrims camp."[64] This system was described several times thereafter in administration reports and government agent diaries, when official inspection circuits through Sabaragamuwa Province began to include more frequent visits to the Peak. In R. N. Thaine's 1914 survey, he wrote:

> Heramitipana is the last big halting place before the actual ascent. It is a flat piece of land about an acre in extent. There are two large ambalams here—one quite a fine structure of iron frame work and galvanized zinc roof. A row of about 5 or 6 boutiques on one side, a dispensary, a pipe laid water service and a public latrine are all placed on this small area. The water service and the latrine were put up by a Colombo Buddhist Society. The water is pumped up by an automatic pump from the stream about ¼ mile below. It is good pure water and very cold.[65]

With all these structures and services at the site, situated at the crossroads of two trails, Heramitipana began to take on characteristics of street junctions, or *handiya*, commonly found in urban neighborhoods of Sri Lanka, defined by Nihal Perera and Nirmani Liyanage as "a social space created . . . where a road confluence is developed into a square of sorts through small interventions," creating "a place of opportunity" and "a people's laboratory to try out small-scale ventures."[66] Although perched on the side of a mountain, such scattered urbanization was possible due to the sheer number of people passing through. A small public square, complete with marketplace, medicine, and outhouse, arose from pilgrim demand and cooperation, a reminder that "infrastructure is a fundamentally relational concept, becoming real infrastructure in relation to organized practices."[67] The health and wealth at stake in these practices certainly drew the eyes of colonial officials, but it was once again the poets who best captured the multiplicity of gatherings here. Lefebvre notes how "the City appeared as a second nature of stone and metal, built on an initial, fundamental nature made of earth, air, water, and fire. This second nature acquired its paradigm . . . in and through the poets."[68] Something similar happened on the Peak when poet pilgrims were drawn to observe the infrastructure for how it stood out or modified the environment. But rather than posit the mechanical as unnatural, the poets depicted it as an appropriate manifestation of meritorious aspirations. Elegizing Heramitipana in 1912, for example, John de Silva blends water pumps with waterfalls, suggesting their complementary nature:

> near Heramitipana there is greatly cool water.
> It is distributed from the river by the water machine a gentleman
> built, very meritorious.
> People gathering and going are seen, told to also descend into
> the falls to fetch that water.
> That cold is great when bathing; there is not another place in the
> country with such pure water.[69]

De Silva distills the hustle and bustle of this trail junction into a quatrain where the natural and mechanical mingle meritoriously, where human interventions into an already superior environment can make the pilgrim experience even better, and cosmically benefit the material sponsors. Poets thereby account for these micro-engineering initiatives by naturalizing mechanical interventions into the land as part of the landscape.

Water pumps appear this way in many poetic verses. A 1929 work by W. A. G. Juvānis enchants such infrastructure by blending the mechanical sounds at the Sitagangula stream crossing with the recitations of Pali prayers there:

> At Sitagangula that bund was bound and,
> not far away, the water machine was installed, too,
> to resoundingly raise the stream from below.
> Reciting the *gāthā*, worship the sacred foot.[70]

This was the second time in his poem that Juvānis animated the Peak's infrastructure through sound. At an earlier trail stop, he noted, "A lodging house and pipes were installed, and sounds are heard of rumbling water, ice cold."[71] Juvānis's contemporaries were equally poetic: T. H. Udāris in 1923 sang of "the water pump giving off the sound of songs."[72] The dams and hydraulic rams that supplied pilgrims with water thus had their novel noises represented in verses that also inserted new sounds into Sinhala poetry itself, through English words like machine (*mäsima*), pipe (*payippa*), and pump (*pompa*). When he arrived at Heramitipana, however, Juvānis recorded problems with the water supply:

> Having placed aquatic flowers at Heramitipana,
> one thinks to compose poetry to recite at the time.
> The water is not there sometimes.
> Behold this thievery, oh Lord God Saman!
>
> The water had been there in the shops
> One-hundred-fifty take it at each time
> Hands, feet, and face are washed very pure
> Mind gratifying, worship the sacred foot eagerly.[73]

The stock of water at this important trail wayside was evidently exhausted at times by surges of pilgrims eager to cleanse themselves before a final ascent. A poet inspired to versify the collective beauties of this gathering place was thus left to elegize an absence.

Several years after Juvānis's verses, Government Agent N. J. Luddington reported pump problems when he inspected the site: "A scarcity of good drinking water was occasionally experienced by pilgrims at Heramitipana, an important halting place, where the Kuruwita and Ratnapura routes meet. Heramitipana has been provided with a pipe-bourne water supply, the water being raised by an hydraulic ram which not infrequently broke down. Efforts are being made to put the management and maintenance of this essential water supply on a sound basis."[74] He revealed more about the affair in his journal: "A late lunch at Heramitipana and in afternoon enquiring about the water supply here. This is secured from a large hydraulic ram erected with subscriptions. The promoter a Colombo man spends nothing on it and it is in the most ramshackle condition and the dam is leaking like a sieve. Tried to secure his agreement to its being handed over to the Trustee of Adam's Peak."[75] Luddington tried to transfer infrastructure maintenance from a private layperson to official administration from Peak temple funds. His implication was that this man was not using pilgrim donations for proper upkeep. The colonial archive thereby records an early instance of "pipe politics" at play, what Lisa Björkman calls "the multiple and dispersed forms of authority and expertise that are so crucial in mitigating the everyday risks of infrastructural breakdown."[76] While private Buddhist societies were able to quickly raise funds to install services like water pumps, pipes, and latrines, the money for regular maintenance was seemingly less flush, perhaps because upkeep lacked the flash of initial endowments that bore nameplates of donors marking their merits. When the issue remained unresolved a year later, in 1937, Luddington hinted that a final settlement would necessitate some sort of prestige-based bribe: "Trying to settle the matter of the ram used for pumping water to Heramitipana on the route to Adam's Peak. Begin now to see a hope of doing so but, alas, it is by playing on that deadly sin, a man's vanity."[77] The colonial authority of the government agent thereby needed to meditate between other authorities—from private citizen to public administrators of religious properties—to keep even modest infrastructural installations on the mountain serviceable.

However, the official trustee position that Luddington hoped would adopt the dam and ram was just as beset by vanity as any private donor, and this office had a history of accomplishing very little toward advancement of pilgrimage infrastructure. The position was a byproduct of the Buddhist Temporalities Ordinance, first passed in 1889, which underwent many revisions over time, with a version still operative today. Meant to ensure temple funds were used for temple upkeep and that temple landlord disputes had a forum for resolution before courts, the law took decades to implement, beset by squabbling over trustee elections and wholesale noncompliance by some temple officials. Archived correspondence of the Sabaragamuwa Buddhist Temporalities Committee shows the Peak was of less pressing concern than sites like the Maha Saman Devale in Ratnapura, which held far more land, and from which petitions were filed against government interference.[78] Among temples in Sabaragamuwa, the Peak lands were fourth in size (3,992 acres) and third in resident labor value (Rs. 1,825 per annum).[79]

When the ordinance was first being implemented, reports on landholdings in 1890 remarked how the Peak already had a system closer to the ordinance's intention than other temples: "The incumbent to Sripadastane is also elected and I believe a committee of lay men manage the revenues."[80] This stood in contrast to monasteries where head monks inherited through lineage, and temples like the Maha Saman Devale, where the landlord, or *basnāyaka nilamē*, reigned supreme. A Sinhala "commissaries book" (*komasāris pot*) written around 1870, regarding Peak funds and administration, shows the extent of its organization, with nineteen titles of employment, including the head monk, secretaries from various regions, farmers, builders, masons, smiths, alms takers, fire makers, clothes washers, and ritual specialists, the majority of whom had entered into land-for-labor arrangements with the Sri Pada temple. Duties for many included building or repairing residences on the summit or at Palabaddala, and traveling with the head monk or making preparations where he would stay. One rank was the "mountain headman" (*kandedurayā*), a post held by someone who lived in the hills and supplied the temple annually with fifty pieces of *hakuru*, or jaggery, hardened sugar chunks made from the sap of *kitul* trees.[81] The Peak temple thus assimilated easily into the Buddhist Temporalities system, and its trustee position was instituted in 1889.

The first trustee seems to have been one Punchi Bandara, who resigned in 1890 and was replaced by a J. M. Loka "Patakada" Banda that year. [82] Things went smoothly at first. In a letter of April 11, 1892, W. Ellawala, chair of the Sabaragamuwa Buddhist Temporalities Committee, wrote to the government agent: "The trustee of Adam's Peak is doing his work fairly well and he has undertaken the collection of the offerings and land revenues of the shrine. The High Priest Sumangala I am glad to say is giving every assistance to the trustee in the performance of his duties." The chair compared him with other trustees of the province: "on the whole the trustee of Adam's Peak is the only one who seems to take any interest in the work."[83] Several months later, however, Patakada Banda was accused of malfeasance: "As regards to the accounts of Adam's Peak it appears . . . that the Trustee Patakada Banda has collected the offerings without a priest. . . . No reliance could be placed on those collections because the expenses incurred . . . were very exorbitant."[84] An inquest was held at the Maha Saman Devale of Ratnapura. Witnesses were called, and Patakada Banda spoke in his defense, saying he did not know how costs were kept so low before. Regardless of whether he had embezzled, however, the trustee was dismissed on account of general incompetence, for he freely admitted: "I have no daily accounts of the expenses incurred for Priests and laymen and stranger Priests at the two places, neither have I any accounts kept weekly."[85] Moreover, the little he had recorded was useless, as the Ratnapura District Court told the Buddhist Temporalities Committee in 1893: "I regret to have to state that in the absence of vouchers and receipt foils there can be no satisfactory audit of these accounts, and that in my opinion they do not realize the intention of the Buddhist Temporalities Ordinance. The District Committee should exercise greater vigilance in controlling the accounts."[86]

This was only one of many snags.[87] Laymen and monks quarreled over offerings, and revenue was often stingily doled out by tightfisted trustees. Disputes over collections even raised the specter of violence. A government agent advised his successor "to keep a careful watch on events at the Peak itself, as . . . the priests . . . may try to secure the offerings themselves. Last year the President District Buddhist Committee had to apply to the Police Magistrate to bind over certain priests to keep the peace, as they were threatening to make a raid upon the collection."[88] Despite the warning, it was not the last time the head monk seized collections: "I am informed that in view of the absence of a

Trustee at the Peak, the priests have told the pilgrims to hand them their offerings instead of placing them on the Sripada—a clever way of keeping within the law!"[89] There is also evidence the Peak trustee or the Buddhist Temporalities Committee clashed with private patrons gathering funds for projects. An announcement on English and Sinhala leaflets circulated in 1922 warned against scams:

NOTICE TO PILGRIMS
TO ADAM'S PEAK.
Pilgrims are kindly requested to see that they
do "not" subscribe
anything to collectors of
BOGUS SUBSCRIPTIONS
who are to be found on the routes.

P.B. Muttettuwegama
President B.T. District Committee, Ratnapura[90]

With trustees and committees overly occupied with themselves, however, it was precisely the subscriptions of Colombo Buddhist Societies that filled maintenance gaps: "As it is, they have spent thousands of rupees on ambalams and water services."[91]

Meanwhile, the British continued tinkering with ordinance rules, trying to make trustees be transparent. P. B. Muttettuwegama advised in 1922: "No system of auditing can verify collections of Sripadasthane. The appointment of a man of the highest character and integrity as Trustee and close supervision can only bring about proper accounting. . . . The place will be veritable mine of fraudulent personal income to unscrupulous Trustees."[92] Stricter ordinance provisions were added in 1926 for the wealthiest temples of Sabaragamuwa: "*Adam's Peak and Mahasaman Dewale.* Offerings of money during the pilgrimage and perahera seasons shall be daily verified, currency notes being counted and specie weighed, and the trustees shall send a daily return of the amount of such offerings to the District Court, Ratnapura."[93] The first fully approved rendering of collections and accounts was accomplished in 1922, after the replacement of a retiring Trustee who had a reputation for nepotism and cronyism: "The collections at the peak under the administration of the Buddhist Temporalities Committee amounted to Rs. 12,326.75, a sum very considerably in excess of previous sums brought to account. This is an example of what may be expected under more efficient supervision."[94] The government agent elaborated in his journal:

The following figures of the gross amounts (cash, metal, offerings, cloth etc.) accounted for by the previous trustees are interesting:

1918. . . . . Rs.6167.00
1919. . . . . Rs.6279.25
1920. . . . . Rs.7677.14
1921. . . . . Rs.6833.28

This year . . . Rs.9667,76 received in cash alone. With cash offerings to end of season, receipts should come to about Rs.11,000. A fitting commentary on the work of previous trustees.[95]

All this cash on hand, but the Buddhist Temporalities Committee still only contributed one hundred or two hundred rupees annually to offset the cost of an apothecary and sweepers stationed at Heramitipana. Once the financial largess was realized, however, government agents of the 1930s urged the Peak trustee toward larger infrastructure-upkeep projects, like fixing water pumps, erecting ambalams, and installing latrines.

Roadbuilding was also essential to pilgrimage, just as in the days of royal endowments. Unlike kings, however, colonial men of business were not interested in meritorious donations, and attempted to offload some financial liabilities onto the temple. A government agent wrote in 1907: "It is hoped that the District Committee elected under the Buddhist Temporalities Ordinance will be able to divert some of the offerings to the improvement of the roads." Pilgrimage-road upkeep mostly fell to other government sectors: "I inspected the approach roads. So far as they are in charge of local bodies (the District Road Committee or the Village Committee) they were in excellent order, but the last 10 miles of the journey is performed over rough precipitous paths, which the temple authorities only pretend to keep clear of jungle growth."[96] Though many British were quick to criticize the state of Peak trails, most failed to realize their own conquest of the island was partly responsible for this infrastructural decline, which had disrupted not only royal patronage, but also local maintenance cycles that had accompanied pilgrimage under native rule. Two early British observers recognized this on an 1819 ascent:

During the native government, it was customary for a number of inhabitants . . . to go every year . . . on a pilgrimage to the Peak. The chiefs were particularly attentive to this act of devotion; and as they always traveled with a great retinue, it was the business of part of their attendants to clear the pathway of the jungle and young trees. These pilgrimages have nearly ceased,

> since the English occupied the country. In the month of February 1817, two chiefs, with about two hundred followers, went from Kandy by this way to the Peak; but since that period it was supposed not a human being had passed by this road. Hence the extremely overgrown condition of the pathway.[97]

Pilgrimage was a forum for displaying power that worked just as well for a regional chief as for the king in the capital. In a system where larger and more diverse retinues (*pirivara*) meant powerful lords, bringing an army of workers to make the journey easier for others was good publicity. This auspicious act generated merit for everyone—chiefs, workers, and many more pilgrims able to use the cleared path afterward.

For the British, however, building roads on both sides of the mountain was motivated mainly by industry. In the 1870s, plantations were booming, transitioning from coffee to tea. Significant portions of Crown forest in the Peak Wilderness were sold and deforested for agro-industry growth to offset losses from the airborne fungus decimating monoculture coffee plantations.[98] Areas closest to the Peak were prime for tea cultivation, already too high for coffee. Arthur Morice, owner of the most private Peak Wilderness lands, first petitioned the government in 1865 to open these upper highlands to tea, even offering to take a trip to India to learn about the business.[99] This meant that trails to the Peak began to merge with footpaths past tea bushes, via, for example, the Warnagala and Carney Estates in the southwest, or the Maskeliya and Delhousie Estates in the northeast. As one government agent noted of Warnagala, "the estate people help the pilgrims here. They have a fine ambalam, and a water supply by pipes."[100] Southwest plantations like Warnagala moved product via the village of Erathna, spurring government expenditure on roads there to connect it with the nearest town of Kuruwita; "the works done included clearing jungle and side drains, filling washaways, and leveling roadway, and building two culverts and repairing bridge."[101] Pilgrims benefitted in turn: "New swing-bridge put up by the District Road Committee over the Kaluganga at Eratne. The previous bridge erected in 1913 was washed away by floods last year . . . This is on one of the main pilgrim routes to the Peak.[102] Later GAs further linked pilgrimage infrastructure with development of the polity on this road: "to Kuruwita to discuss the arrangements at the station where the new Pilgrims' Rest is to be built. There was a question of the diversion of the road, which . . . serves the foodshed. . . . bringing this road into the Main road."[103] Transporting goods and people in and out of food, tea, and timber production centers via Kuruwita was only the first step. Subsequent wider circuits were made by rail.

Like bridges and cart paths, railroads were essential for the plantation industry, as "tea remained for a long time the single most important commercial article transported on the railways."[104] But pilgrims moved along these lines, too, as "the new railway to Kuruwita brought up a number of pilgrims from Colombo."[105] Railroads increased concentrations of annual visitor influxes, new patterns of movement bringing bursts of wealth: "Pilgrims swarm in the town. There was a special train last night which brought in many hundreds."[106] Likewise: "I was glad to see the trains passing the bungalow full to overflowing with travelers for Adam's Peak."[107] Similarly: "Pilgrim Rush. It was pleasant to see the trains full to overflowing but this prosperity will be fleeting."[108] Travel to the Peak around the Mädin full-moon day in March, when the Buddha left his footprint, was facilitated by special railway schedules and occasionally discounted passes for pilgrims. In 1934, the Peak trustee wrote to the public trustee in Colombo: "For the issue of cheap tickets on these dates from all Stations to Hatton, Kuruwita and Ratnapura . . . it would be a great relief to the pilgrims during a time of depression like the present."[109] Rail travel thus changed pilgrim arrivals, from scattered groups gradually passing on foot to crowds alighting in stations simultaneously, which incidentally made Ratnapura and Hatton ideal sites for health initiatives, with third-class passengers undergoing inspection there in plague years.[110]

Trains and tea created what is now the main Peak pilgrimage transit junction of Hatton. The railway reached there in 1884, and a town rapidly grew. In the censuses of 1871 and 1881, it was not even populated enough to register, but by 1891, it boasted over one thousand residents.[111] In the next twenty years, that number tripled.[112] Hatton provided a hub by which many surrounding plantations could ship their product. As on the Kuruwita-Erathna side, this necessitated a network of roads, which ultimately served pilgrims as well as planters. As J. P. Lewis, Central Province government agent, noted in 1908, "the opening of the road from Laxapana to Dalhousies (the Pilgrims' road), the construction of which was begun during the year, will help to make this pilgrimage easier."[113] This road passed the settlement of Maskeliya: "What is now the planting district of Maskeliya was of old the remotest part of the Wilderness of the Peak, an unbroken forest traversed only by pilgrims . . . There is now a resthouse for travellers to the Peak."[114] Plantation infrastructure doubled as pilgrimage infrastructure, and Hatton became the main thoroughfare to the Peak, with its tea-funded rails and roads making pilgrimage from Colombo or Kandy possible in a day or two. Already in 1888, an American tourist called the Ratnapura trail "the wrong side."[115] Although statistics were irregularly recorded, the different attendance reports of government agents in Sabaragamuwa and the Central Province suggest Hatton had many more pilgrims than Ratnapura in the early twentieth century, despite most pilgrimage poetry of this era continuing to focus on the Ratnapura route.[116] Attendance was often only summarized, with reports of "large numbers" visiting the Peak, or remarks that it was more or less than the previous year, but occasionally numerical estimates appeared. For the Kuruwita and Ratnapura routes together, these were:

1906: 7,700	1908: 10,000	1909: 17,000	1913: 40,000
1919: 10,000	1920: 9,500	1921: 13,650[117]	

Attendance figures from the Hatton route in the Central Province were less frequent, but each year they appeared, in 1906, 1907, 1908, and 1913, the number was reckoned at fifty thousand.[118] By comparison, in 1911, the city of Colombo had a population of 211,274.[119] Such citizen concentration in one spot shows the Peak's potential for forging collective imagination, understandably a favorite landmark among early nationalist poets publishing in twentieth-century literary magazines.[120]

The Peak's place in statecraft thereby shifted with the accessibility of modern infrastructure. What was once a remote site, visited precisely because its rarefied air was hard to reach, became a center of the nation, one all good Sri Lankans hoped to visit. Annual attendance only multiplied: "By 1968 it was 600,000–700,000. . . . According to police estimates, during the 2000–2001 events, the number of pilgrims attending Sri Pada was 2.2 million, a figure that, if true, would indicate that one eighth of the total population visited."[121] The estimates I was given for the 2015–2016 season were around 1.2 million for the Hatton side alone, and most workers on the mountain agreed it was an off year, with crowds below the usual levels. Due to this density of visitors, and the ability to get up and down the trail in one laborious day, I based my ethnographic research on the Hatton side, witnessing its workaday life. To work our way over there, let us proceed via a vignette that traverses the Peak's least developed trail, but nevertheless reflects the indelible imprint of infrastructure on the mountain.

The train no longer comes to Kuruwita or Ratnapura, and these trails have consequently become the least used. The Kuruwita trail also never received elaborate paving with steps like the Hatton and Ratnapura trails, so it's mostly still a forest with a few rusted railings or carved footholds in places where the climb is tricky. The Kuruwita trail had only six empty ambalams when I walked it with a friend from Erathna named Rukmal, just as the season began in December 2015. He had hiked this trail since childhood and had even built a shop along the path years before. He was knowledgeable about signs of the forest, pointing out various plant species that only grow at certain elevations, indicating elephant tracks, and naming lookout points on the trail. Rukmal said he learned all this from older workers, having listened to their stories from a young age. His notion of time, however, was unusual. Every mark of somewhat old human impact he called *kristu purva*, or "before Christ." Rukmal did not have an academic notion of a Common Era. Perhaps for him *kristu purva* meant before Christians came to Lanka, or maybe it simply meant a long time ago, an abstract temporality given depth by association with the mountain. Indeed, in some cases it seemed almost plausible, as with the footholds hewn into the stone. Yet Rukmal also pointed at relics not much older than a century, including rusted chains, ladders, water pumps, and the ruins of an ambalam. These, too, were *kristu purva*. The unconventionality of his time scale may have come from another convention—characterizing the Hatton side as new and the other side of the mountain as having the "real" (*niyama*) and "old" (*parana*) paths. As Rukmal knew the Hatton trail was recent, perhaps everything else was automatically ancient.

Rukmal chose to work on the Hatton side that season, the obvious place to do business now. I met him there the first time I climbed to the summit. It was a rainy day with heavy clouds enshrouding the Peak, but I was too eager to begin my fieldwork to stay away. During my descent, I stopped at a shop not far below the summit, known among mountain workers as the Matara Kade, the original owners of the spot having hailed from that southern coastal city. The shop was being run that year by the Dissanayaka family of Sabaragamuwa, their son Kelum having worked with Rukmal and other friends to build the structure in which they sat chatting when I met them. We talked for some time beneath the tin roof and tarpaulin walls, atop a hard earthen floor that was supplemented by a wooden platform on stilts, allowing the shop to half perch beside a steep stretch of the trail (fig. 2.2). Rukmal smiled when he was identified as the "chief engineer" by the others, having a skill for building temporary shelters that he attributed to his time in the army. The shop certainly held up well over the course of the season at this wind-whipped altitude. A few days after our meeting, Rukmal invited me back to his home in Erathna, promising that we would return in time for opening day, as he was set to work at the shop anyway. He kept his word, although not in the way I had imagined. After touring around Erathna and Ratnapura during my visit, we were sitting with some of Rukmal's friends when one informed him that the Kuruwita/Erathna trail had opened. Rukmal lit up with excitement, not expecting the jungle would have been cut back in time for opening day. "It's really open?" he said in disbelief. He turned to me, beaming. "Shall we climb back by the Erathna trail?" I thought he meant the next day, but that lengthy trek meant we had to leave

FIGURE 2.2. The Matara Kade

that afternoon. By the time we finished readying ourselves and found a ride up to the trailhead, it was dusk. "No problem," Rukmal assured me. "We don't have to climb the whole thing tonight. We can stay with friends." He pointed at a tiny light far in the distance. "We only need to go as far as the electric board."

The Kuruwita trailhead is near a small hydroelectricity plant—the Erathna Mini Hydro Power Project. Begun in 2001 and operational by 2004, it is definitely not *kristu purva*, but rather a testament to the ingenuity of modern Sri Lankan engineers, according to Rukmal. The pipeline (or more precisely penstock) that feeds this power station runs alongside the trail for the first few kilometers. As part of an agreement with community stakeholders to fund local development works in exchange for building the plant, the Vallibel power company added steps, footbridges, and handrails to this stretch of the trail to aid pilgrims.[122] I trudged behind Rukmal's swift pace up this steep and still mostly unpaved path, wondering what I had gotten myself into, hiking an unknown trail into the dark. Although the sun had set, I sweat profusely. After a few kilometers that felt like many more, Rukmal gestured toward a fluorescent glow ahead. "The electric board." He grinned. The camp for electricity board workers who maintain the water intake consists of a few concrete bungalows painted green. The property is a well-manicured oasis in the mountain forest, with cut grass and a small flower garden. Most of the workers had gathered that evening to drum, sing, play cards, and converse together in the pilgrim ambalam that is also onsite. Rukmal bartered with them using the supplies he had brought, which consisted of several polythene bags of moonshine that I had puzzled over when we bought them. It proved to be an effective currency that secured us not only a spot on the dormitory floor that night, but also a couple of plates of rice and coconut sambol from the lone person we met with cooking supplies the next day on the trail. Of course, it also eased the prospect of sleeping on cement.

Before we left the next morning, Rukmal talked his way past the workers and walked with me over the intake channel for the hydropower plant (fig. 2.3). He enjoyed referring to the Kuruwita trail with the English phrase "full natural," but he tempered that sentiment when discussing these pumps and pipes. "Well, it's not actually full natural, because the electric board has changed it." Rukmal again praised the engineering, especially the sedimentation tank, yet he also marveled at the natural conditions that made the human infrastructure possible. When we reached the end of the line and stood atop the weir, a small half dam that rerouted a waterfall into the penstock, he gestured toward the tall falls that ceaselessly filled the deep mountain pool that

FIGURE 2.3. Walking over hydropower infrastructure near the Kuruwita trail

overflowed into the waiting cement mouth of the intake. "Not even the engineers could measure the actual depth in the middle of this pool. That's how much miraculous power it has."[123] For the only time on our hike, Rukmal took a picture on his phone, aiming the lens at the water and rocks and omitting the infrastructure.

After another full day of hiking, we reached the junction at Heramitipana, joining with the Ratnapura trail. I was relieved at the familiarity. We continued upward and then wound our way to the Matara Kade via the shortcut around the base of the summit that workers often use to move between the Ratnapura and Hatton trails. Rukmal got right to work in the Matara Kade, frying snacks for pilgrims on a small gas range, and I was offered the quarters below, two cubbies suspended between the wooden stilts supporting the shop, with just enough room to sit and be plenty cozy for sleep. After dozing for a couple hours, I awoke to increasing numbers of pilgrim feet treading up the cement steps beside me, as well as the sound of melodious pilgrimage poetry being sung in a recording that came through speakers plugged into Kelum's laptop. I recognized the words as *Samanala Hälla* verses. I climbed back up into the main shop and asked Kelum whether they played such songs regularly. He replied that they used them only for special occasions, like opening night. "You arrived just in time."

The Worker-Pilgrim and Mountain Life

My journey with Rukmal reinforced the reality of the worker-pilgrim, as both he and I were workers on the move in a special place and time, with motivations for our labor that exceeded monetary compensation. This phenomenon first struck me after my arrival at the Peak when I met a group of electricity board employees singing the traditional call-and-response chants that pilgrims use, snickering somewhat at themselves, but enthusiastic nonetheless (fig. 2.4). Were these men at work? Certainly, and hard work at that, lugging lights, poles, cables, and tools up to the Ceylon Electricity Board quarters on the Hatton trail. Yet there was also a lightheartedness to this job that came from its unique nature. The Peak was only wired for pilgrimage once a year, so hiking in a wilderness reserve was not in the daily routine of these electricians. This was a special sort of pilgrimage work. I soon realized that many such ordinary jobs took on elevated significance when occurring at the Peak. Old work was imbued with new excitement, enchanted because it contributed to a larger cause. As facilitating pilgrimage is meritorious, both laborers and

FIGURE 2.4. Ceylon Electricity Board workers climbing the Hatton trail

capital investors adjust comportment accordingly. An excellent example is the case of powering the Peak. The electricians I met singing like pilgrims were only the latest in a long line of devotees donating resources and labor to light the trail.

On March 4, 1950, a massive stone arch on the Hatton trail was completed, a monument to pilgrimage infrastructure. It is known as Makara Torana, or the *makara* gateway, named for the *makara* creatures flanking the top—part porpoise, part pachyderm, part dragon.[124] God Saman sits between the *makara* with elephant attendants, and every pilgrim on the Hatton trail passes beneath. The arch bears an inscription recording the installation of lights on the trail, powered by the Laxapana hydroelectric dam. Coming just two years after independence, the lighting of the Peak consecrated a larger scheme of hydro-development projects that prevailed throughout the twentieth century and beyond, often explicitly interwoven with nationalist rhetoric and Buddhist ritual.[125] Before this source of energy, lighting the Peak summit was done by private donors. Inspired on a 1930 ascent, M. V. Elias Appuhamy founded a society for summit illumination, the Sri Samantakuta Electric Lamp Light

Brotherhood. Elias pawned his bus to finish funding the first petrol generator. Lights went on in 1933 and every year thereafter, save during World War II, when security forbade illumination.[126] In 1949, the project was taken over by the government, and the chief electrical engineer was careful to write for advice on how to best preserve old dedication plaques on "outdoor lamps . . . donated by certain devotees," which had to be replaced.[127] The Brotherhood recommended all old plaques be put on a special new lamppost that would also bear the name of the society, adding, "this Society will be very happy to place at the disposal of the Government all or any of the dismantled material should they be of any use in order that it may acquire further merit in the cause which has been so close to its heart and in which it has devoutly laboured."[128] The society wanted to maximize merit, and the state was conscientious about maintaining merit-making records as it assumed the structural and soteriological responsibilities of pilgrimage infrastructure.

The Makara Torana also records the importance of individual vows made by state actors who controlled infrastructure. On the right leg of the arch is a trilingual inscription in English, Sinhala, and Tamil: "Built to mark the occasion of the lighting of Sri Pada in fulfillment of a vow made to Saman Deviyo by Col. the Hon. Sir John Kotelawala, K.B.E., Minister for Transport & Works, for the successful completion of the Laxapana Hydroelectric Works." The inscription on the left leg is only Sinhala, reproducing the original vow made to Saman in 1947 for successful completion of the hydroelectric plant.[129] This inscription, titled "invocation" (*ayädīmayi*), noted several *puja*s made by officers of the hydroelectric board, namely J. L. Kotelawala, Chandra D. S. Gunaratna, and S. S. Prananda, out of paramount devotion (*pramukha bhaktimat*). These were presented to the Norton Bridge *vihāra*, and included lamps, flowers, incense, and food for monks (*gilanpasa*), with the resultant merit to be shared by Saman and all the gods. The inscription continues: "In that same joyful sharing, we respectfully and dutifully beseech the group of gods entrusted with this area of God King Sri Sumana to always protect and prevent all dangers from occurring to the population living in the region and the group of workers and officers there at the hydroelectric plant at Norton Bridge, which is a national treasure of the great populace [*mahā janatāvagē jātika vastuvak*]." The national asset of hydropower is invoked alongside the gods of the mountain to bless the populace, and the merit of such infrastructure and almsgiving was meant to be spread among everyone, as indicated by the term for "joyful sharing" (*anumōdan*), derived from *anumodana* in Sanskrit and Pali, which Maria Heim defines as "a feeling of jubilation and rejoicing upon witnessing others perform good deeds or acts of worship." Thus, "giving is not a zero-sum game with a limited amount of merit redounding to the donor. Rather, it multiplies by the number of people who rejoice in it, just as a flame can be taken from one lamp to light many."[130] Or, in this case, just as the electricity from one hydropower plant can be taken to light the many lamps of the Peak. The next line of the inscription highlights how widely this good deed will be shared by specifying the benefits of hydropower for pilgrims: "When this electricity plant is completed without misfortune, we promise and vow by this to illuminate with electric lights, as aid for the great populace, the great path for journeying there to the Sri Pada *caitya*, protected by the God King Sri Sumana." Power produced by distant waterfalls, sanctioned by human and divine officials, thereby lit the journeys of many aspiring to enlightenment, spreading merit among all these happy parties as a result.

The dedication of Makara Torana and illumination of the Peak were prominently covered in newsprint.[131] Poets also commemorated the event. The Himalayan monk turned Sinhala author Sikkim Mahinda was asked by the Ministry of Transport and Public Works to compose a poem. His resultant *Samanoḷa Kava* had 113 verses on the Buddha's visits to Lanka, Saman's invitation to leave the footprint, the nature of mountain and forest, and the Buddha making the print.[132] Sikkim Mahinda did not mention government patrons or infrastructure, but this monk being chosen as the author was significant. Nearing the end of his life in 1950, he had lived to see the Lankan independence for which he so strongly campaigned as a poet over previous decades; he was a living symbol of the nationalism that the Makara Torana buttressed.[133] Other poets recorded specifics. In an eight-verse poem on the back cover of a 1950 pilgrimage pamphlet, a poet named D.G.J. commemorated the Peak illumination:

> For Lord God Sumana guarding the Sambuddha sacred sole,
> a solemn vow was made to offer light.
> Laborers and noble ministers were inclined, worked and
> lighted noble Samanala for the sacred foot lotus.
> . . .
> By courageous lineage victory, behold enemy strength was
> subdued.
> To guard the sacred foot is the Trustee Ellawala.
> Having suffered, the whole group of people goes to worship the
> sacred foot.
> Together with them, protect, Lord God, the Minister Kotelawala.
>
> So as to supply Samanala Mountain with electric light
> appropriately,

much fatigue was experienced, day and night, having suffered
and worked.
The character of the good people shone, great ones, all the
workers who
Lord God Sumana protects always, compassionately and
reverently.[134]

These verses show the blend of royal precedent and new populism shaping the ideals of the nation. The Peak trustee and government minister were singled out in classic elegiac manner, lauding their lineage (*parapura*) and subduing of enemies, presumably the British. As with the archway inscription, the general population was praised alongside elites, with repeated mention of laborers or workers, the *kamkaru*. Rather than a king taking all the credit, here the actual workers, however anonymously collective, were recognized as integral to the state as a nation of cooperative citizens.

Nowadays, though they are proud citizens of the Peak, most *kamkaru* are not counted as Sinhala, however well they speak the Sinhala language, belonging instead to the highland Tamil community. The lives of many of these mountain workers are infused with a sense of special responsibility and acknowledgment that the Peak is a uniquely privileged place to work. Becoming part of its infrastructure, workers meld with the mountain, and the lines between labor and devotion are never starkly drawn.

Concrete Couriers

After the government assumed illumination responsibility, the Sri Samantakuta Electric Lamp Light Brotherhood needed a new project. They decided to install a pump that would take water up to the summit, "and distribute water by pipes, within a radius of ½ a mile."[135] The Peak trustee eventually acquired all the Brotherhood's designs and estimates in 1957.[136] Dates on the small concrete dam and five pump houses on the Ratnapura trail indicate completion in 1961. The next year, a large tank was installed on the summit, allowing water to be transferred to shops and rest halls near the top of the Hatton trail. These waterworks projects along the Ratnapura trail mark the beginnings of large-scale concrete constructions being built at the Peak. They now require careful maintenance to keep running. In 2016, the rattling pumps often malfunctioned, sending resident mechanics bounding up and down the mountain stairs.

Shops farther down the Hatton trail source their water from the streams that are equally plentiful on that side of the mountain. The name of the village at the trailhead on the Hatton side is Nallathanni, Tamil for "good water." Nallathanni as it appears today is a relatively recent settlement. Since the Sri Lankan civil war concluded in 2009, Nallathanni has seen a rash of investment in small hotels, many built atop an embankment overlooking the stream running through the village. While construction continues, the village risks a lodging glut with far more rooms than visitors, reliant on fickle foreign tourism to pay prices too steep for most Lankans. Lodging is a risky industry, given Nallathanni's seasonality. From late December to May, visitors crowd its streets. The rest of the time, however, when rains fall hard, it is a ghost town. Many shops are boarded up, others dismantled entirely.

Those who live along the main hotel road in the village explained to me that they once resided in an "original" or "root" village (*mulgama*) which lay slightly downstream, near the junction serving roads to Maskeliya and surrounding plantations. Before the recent hotel boom, the only residents of Nallathanni lived in the small line-house settlement on the plantation through which the first two kilometers of the trail climb. Many split work between the plantation and the Peak. During the pilgrimage season, line-house kitchens become production centers for *dodol*, a sweetmeat sold in dozens of shops. In the offseason, finding regular Peak work depends on whether pilgrimage infrastructure is being built. A Nallathanni native named Naganada was a veteran of such projects. He was sixty-three years old when I met him, with a large mustache stretching across his cheeks. Having seen each other on the trail, we chatted in his house one day, which he shared with son, daughter-in-law, and five grandchildren. I guessed at the number of times he had climbed the Peak: "About five hundred?" "No, more than that," he immediately responded. He explained that Tamil people like himself had built the many structures on the summit. "Before, in our grandfather's grandfather's time, there was nothing on top except the footprint. No covering, nothing. We indeed built the buildings there. Without us, there would be no buildings." Although age meant his trips were not usually to the summit now, he explained that he looked young and could still work as a mountain courier because of divine favor. "God gives me the strength, in my heart, to climb almost every day." He used the generic word *deviyo* for god, which can also be plural, so I asked if he meant Saman. Yes. And Shiva? Yes, and Goddess Pattini; all gods were in his heart.

Although Naganada remembered only the footprint being present in his great-great-grandfather's day, nineteenth-century sketches show small structures, albeit rudimentary compared to what exists now. An 1833 sketch had a small shrine for the footprint, secured with ropes, an even smaller shrine for Saman, and a retaining wall around the summit.[137] Rough summit weather likely necessitated the repeated rebuilding of structures. A nineteenth-century visitor claimed: "The temple has been more than once blown away."[138] A 1929 photograph showed only minor shrine expansion over a century.[139] The full paving of the Peak was a project of Naganada's day. Massive concrete buildings now hang off the side of the summit, including two long halls to shelter pilgrims. Other buildings have rooms for monks or workers, and, in another, a narrow staircase leads down to a small dining area, and then further down to a kitchen. During the season, different groups, usually families, volunteer to cook for the two dozen monks, priests, musicians, laborers, and police officers who live on the summit.

In 2013, the paved area around the pinnacle was retiled with stone, giving the floor a more mountainous look and feel, however artificial, compared with the smoothed cement previously there (fig. 2.5). Most original rock is now covered, along with many of its inscriptions, much to the dismay of an archeology student I met on pilgrimage. At the end of the nineteenth century, John Still noted: "The rock on which the shrine is placed has a number of short inscriptions on it, some in Sinhalese, a few in Tamil, and some in Chinese."[140] As the footprint shrine and the Saman shrine evolved into large block structures with full staircases and high cement walls, few rock faces were left unpaved and unpainted. Only one modern Sinhala inscription remains on the shrine

FIGURE 2.5. Original rock between tile and cement on the summit

rock, the imprinted history of the Peak's pluralism otherwise effaced in favor of homogenous cement, a manufactured conversion of rock's natural agency into a human tool.

Naganada was proud of his involvement with this development of the summit into its own small settlement. He seemed to disapprove of the fact that so much Tamil labor came from Maskeliya now, but it was clear that demand had outgrown the population of Nallathanni. Naganada's son, thirty-two-year-old Rasi, recognized this, and explained that, in terms of the overall hill country, Tamils who lived close enough to the Peak to work there during the season were lucky. Without shops to sell sweets, toys, coats, and other knick-knacks to tourists and pilgrims, Tamils elsewhere often worked in the tea plantations year-round. He described it as lousy, full of leeches, with extremes of rain and sunlight, and low pay. Pilgrimage infrastructure thus provides one outlet for Tamil entrepreneurs who, although living in line houses, forge community and financial solvency off the plantation.[141] Their Peak labor was a tradition the British began, from placing "coolies" as garbage collectors on the Peak trail, to their use of this same labor for European holiday excursions up the mountain, forcing all manner of frivolous equipment to be hoisted behind them. The Tamil mountain couriers now provide almost all the essential services that keep pilgrimage functioning, like delivering shop and temple provisions, devotee offerings, or old and infirm devotees themselves, carrying them atop cloth stretchers on bamboo poles. Chandra's shop, for example, relied on a young man named Suresh to come once a fortnight to ferry up supplies when food and gas shipments arrived in Nallathanni. Profit margins were modest, and both shopkeepers needed to be present to keep turning customers over. As Chandra remarked a few weeks into the season, "We are trying to have our business quickly ticking along [*ṭak ṭak gālā yana*], so we can say it has done well. Somehow this year we'll try to bring it in." Chandra and Mathu also admitted they were getting too old to make supply runs so frequently and were happy to outsource this work. When Suresh suddenly stopped coming, they had to take turns hiking down to grab the bus from Nallathanni to Maskeliya and procure their own provisions. I had hiked a trail with Suresh after meeting him in Chandra's shop, so she and Mathu often asked if I had heard from him, but I had not; after all, he was a young man with two babies at home and only one day off a week from his job on a tea plantation, which was a bumpy bus ride away.

When I arrived in Nallathanni in December 2015, such mountain couriers were in high demand, as the final touches were being put on another large waterworks project on the Ratnapura side: the Peak's first water reclamation plant. The project began a year prior, undertaken by the National Water Supply and Drainage Board, under the auspices of the Ministry of Urban Development,

Water Supply and Drainage, for around 220 million rupees. Aside from the engineering experts needed to install a vertical sewer line running down the summit, the project also required many hearty couriers, those called in Sinhala *bara usana kaṭṭiya*, or "the heavy-lifting group." Naganada was one in his heyday. Now a younger generation of twenty- to forty-year-olds had the big bags on their backs. At the start and end of the project, huge machinery went up and down, requiring dozen-man teams. During construction, daily concrete deliveries were required, with cement mix delivered in rice sacks. All traffic went up the shorter Hatton trail, then through the unpaved shortcut around the summit to reach the Ratnapura trail, where the sewage plant stood.

I met a Tamil heavy lifter named Satyasilan from a plantation near Maskeliya, who came to work with some companions, each carrying a forty-kilogram bag of cement. Satyasilan led in pace and spirit, and, as we kept breaking ahead, spoke with me in Sinhala instead of chatting with the others in Tamil. When we crossed the Sitagangula stream, he noted that, from here onward, "if we tell lies or have bad words in our mouths we cannot come along the road. That's how much power (*shakti*) the god has." Does that mean Shiva? "Yes." And also Saman? "Yes, both." The gods helped the couriers reach the site, where bags were weighed and pay slips issued (fig. 2.6). One trip with a heavy load could earn a courier a full day's wages compared to tea work. Some took advantage and climbed three times a day, tripling the usual salaries.

Mountain Bodies

Stress on the body was explained away using not only gods, but also training from plantation childhoods. Some heavy lifters told me their bodies were accustomed (*purudu velā*), since they had hiked amid tea bushes for as long as they could remember. It is fitting that Tamil communities living in the Lankan highlands call themselves *malaiyaka makkal*, "mountain people," for their bodies have grown with the land. Cardiovascular conditioning is a point of pride in estate work that otherwise takes a grueling toll on the body. Work at the Peak, with its paved trail, plentiful shade, and toilets, was more comfortable than work in plantations, while still making positive use of highland Tamil skills. Signs of terrain adaptation are obvious on heavy lifters, with their large calves crisscrossed by extra veins raised under taught skin. They sweat little, and their muscle memory climbs with a special gait, cutting small switchbacks across the staircases. With flip-flops for footwear, many have mastered a running descent, reaching Nallathanni from the summit in under an hour, to turn around and head back up.

FIGURE 2.6. Weighing the worth of a climb

Physical ability to climb the Peak quickly was also boasted about by past Lankans, like the highland king Vīravikrama, coronated in 1543 according to a Sinhala chronicle called *Rājaratnākaraya*: "This king displaying heroic power of his body in keeping with his valor climbed Samanala in one day."[142] Conditioning was even a job requirement for British Peak positions. When Thomas Skinner took triangulation measurements from the summit to create the first minute map of Ceylon in 1833, the job "brought me into such splendid working condition that I could outrun anyone," including "one very active headman [who] begged me to give him an opportunity of racing me up the cone of Adam's Peak."[143] When Government Agent E. B. Alexander assigned the Peak sanitary inspector job in 1912, he traded traditional interviews for a feat of strength: "A lot of young applicants for the post of Sanitary Inspector for the pilgrims route to Adam's Peak appeared: very little to choose between them. Arranged for a Marathon race for them to Carney estate and back, 26 miles."[144] This narrowed the field, but two tied for first, and so other measures of competency were used: "Two competitors made a dead heat of the marathon race. . . . Mr. Woodman will examine them in arithmetic, dictation and English composition tomorrow."[145] Intellectual evaluation was secondary to physical fitness, the Peak dictating the qualifications needed to work on it.

But British obsession with bodies had a darker side: they used the darkness of skin for racial hierarchies, branding Tamil plantation workers as dull pack animals.[146] This racism extended to the Peak, as reflected in tourist travelogues. Mrs. Col. Walker had choice words for those who carried her palanquin in 1833: "I believe Capt. Mundy's Sketches . . .'that coolies are small horses.' He would have been nearer the mark if he had called them '*black cattle:*'—but mine have rested long enough, and I must proceed on my journey."[147] Likewise, *New York Times* writer David Ker's "Tamil retainers" did all the work for him in 1888, cooking, making coffee, carrying supplies, pitching and breaking camp, but Ker characterized them as animals, another species of the jungle:

> Around the fitful blaze sit crouching a group of swarthy, turbaned, black-haired, wild-looking Tamils—gaunt and wiry and supple as the leopards of their native jungles—who lift their small glittering rat-like eyes with a look of wondering amusement as Mrs. Ker comes forth from the doorless entrance of the tiny mud hut in which we have burrowed for the night, separated only by a hanging cloth from the greasy congress of bare-limbed citizens outside. . . . The wild faces and black elflocks and bare brown limbs and white shroud-like dress of our native followers outside looked quite unearthly in the fitful glare of the firelight, and when we did at length fall asleep these ghostly sights and sounds continued to haunt our dreams.[148]

As useful as he found these citizens, their dark skin literally terrified Ker.

Despite this legacy of negatively racialized mountain bodies, laborers at the Peak have forged their own discourse of honor for their work, describing it as a service to the gods, who in turn provide assistance, making heavy lifters their own class of pilgrims. Climbing hundreds or thousands of times over the course of their careers, mountain workers ascend more in a week than most Lankans do in a lifetime. For workers like Naganada and Satyasilan, this work had a direct devotional component, being otherwise impossible without divine aid. The physicality of mountain work makes it a sort of ritual, following Talal Asad's reminder that "ritual" refers not only to symbolic events, but also to ongoing disciplines, offering Marcel Mauss as an anthropologist who understood this.[149] In Mauss's 1934 "Techniques of the Body," both "climbing" and "descending" were examples of practices one must be trained to master: "I can tell you that I'm very bad at climbing trees, though reasonable on mountains and rocks. A difference of education and hence of method."[150] Nallathanni mountain workers have been specially educated in ascending and descending the Peak. Their method strives for efficiency, and their muscle tone and steady pace exhibit expertise. One anguished colonial tourist made no pretensions about his physical inferiority compared to better-adapted locals: "With the perspiration streaming from every pore, and with feet swollen and enflamed, we hobbled and stumbled on our way, objects of compassion to many who passed us. . . . I was obliged to seek the assistance of a coolie, in addition to that of that alpenstock."[151] Less seasoned climbers required help from mountain people more wholly devoted to the physical ritual of the Peak, as some still do today. The climb is certainly difficult for many Lankans. Soft bodies from Colombo cubicles hobble badly down the steps in the morning, and local mountain workers turn a profit by cutting and selling walking sticks that they themselves would never use.

The difficulty of the pilgrimage is, of course, part of the point. The effort expended is a reason ascent is meritorious. As noted of the pilgrimage of Vimaladharmasuriya II (r. 1687–1707): "Thinking of the great merit that lies in the use of the feet, he betook himself to Samantakūṭa."[152] Anthropologist Val Daniel explained that the Peak and similar sites "are meaningless without participation. . . . The body must be involved in the climb. . . . The myths that energize these places are not stories about their pasts, but rather ritual enactments of their pasts."[153] For all the storytelling about the Peak, it still must be climbed. Its myths would never be born without actual bodies meeting land.

Lifting specialists can therefore be ritual specialists even if only bearing offerings of cement. The bodily devotion required of their discipline is most apparent when novice workers attempt similar labor. The physical conditioning of mountain veterans comes into stark relief against newcomers' failings. The pilgrimage season brings a cadre of these temporary employees, often from the Civil Security Department (CSD), which has undertaken paving and other improvements on the Hatton side for several years.

A Military Mountain

The Sinhala name for the CSD makes its military evocations more apparent: Sivil Ārakṣaka Balakāya, Civil Security *Force*. Although technically a branch of the police, not the army as many assume, the CSD does fall under the Ministry of Defense. CSD workers often wear camouflage or fatigue-green clothes, and the sign at their post on the Hatton trail is camo-colored, with a crest of two crossed rifles. Military presence at the Peak has precedent in premodern kings who climbed with their armies, but the modern installation of military workers has made state presence at the Peak more permanent, perpetuating a postwar atmosphere there.

Mahinda Rajapaksa (r. 2005–2015) will forever be remembered as the president who ended the civil war. He was also the president most involved with the Peak. Without government intervention, the Peak had already seen reorganization that fostered Buddhist hegemony, beginning in 1954 with the head monk Morontuduvē Dhammānanda (1890–1970), who retooled administration, appointed allies who backed his election, and marginalized involvement of non-Buddhists.[154] The Rajapaksa family accelerated such Buddhist hegemony by lending powers of the state to the Peak. Their involvement in pilgrimage infrastructure began in 2007, when several regiments of the Corps of Sri Lanka Engineers, a branch of the Sri Lankan Army, paved the entire Ratnapura trail with a neat narrow staircase, bypassing the carved steps of older endowments in some places. Plaques commemorating the paving of this trail called it the *rāja māvata*, or royal avenue, crediting Nissankamalla with its origin per folkloric tradition.

After the war ended in 2009, the Rajapaksa family turned even greater attention to Peak endowments, part of their Buddhist victory-building scheme across the island. The largest event was the February 2014 donation of a new *dolosmahapahana*, or "twelve-month lamp," where pilgrims burn oil offerings, along with a second lamp for pilgrims to burn coconut husks, as well as a massive new bell for pilgrims to ring according to their number of ascents. The previous *dolosmahapahana* had been a modestly sized brass lamp, a donation from a Dr. A. Simon Silva in 1935, to make merit for his parents. When state replaced private donor, a colossal granite lamp was added, weighing 8,613 kilograms.[155] The sheer mass of these objects meant mountain couriers had to be supplemented by military helicopters, which, over the course of twenty-six trips, often delayed by fog, wind, and rain, brought the items up in pieces to be assembled on the summit.[156]

Increased presence of military men on the mountain coincided with the monastic election of the current head monk, Ven. Beṅgamuvē Dhammadinna, on November 25, 2011, a vote dogged by allegations of Rajapaksa-affiliated bribery and threats.[157] Thereafter, Ven. Dhammadinna made his own reorganizations that marginalized non-Buddhists at the Peak, including the use of soldiers to carry palanquins holding Saman statues in procession at season's end, edging out the Nallathanni Tamils who had shared the honor for generations. As head monk, it is Ven. Dhammadinna's prerogative to make such changes, as he holds the final say on who is allowed to donate ritual supplies and labor, or undertake new constructions on the summit. Ven. Dhammadinna does not spend the season on the Peak himself, but selects the summit staff who do, whether police officer, bookkeeper, janitorial sweeper, deity priest, resident monk, or ritual musician, and many military personnel have also been stationed in summit dormitories during his tenure. These martial developments crescendoed with the

2014 military helicopter-assisted endowments that concluded in a grand ceremony, with Defense Secretary Gothabaya Rajapaksa, Mahinda's brother, as a guest of honor worshiping the footprint alongside Ven. Dhammadinna. Mahinda himself did not climb the Peak that day, but he made an appearance via helicopter, showering the summit with flowers. The event made an impact, and it was still talked about among workers and pilgrims two years on. It was commemorated by poets, too, as in Sumanā Vīratuṅga's *Siri Pā Maḷuvē Mahā Piṅkama*—"The Great Merit-Making on the Sri Pada Summit:"

> Filled with noble government ministers and officials,
> the threefold army and noble police who guard the law
> assisted while distributing labor and resources,
> everyone having united in meritorious groups.
> . . .
> The noble President arriving in a helicopter vehicle,
> from inside the vehicle, directed the lowering of the *puja*.
> All the united devotees filled the summit,
> the meritorious ones there witnessing with both eyes.
> . . .
> In prior royal days, to raise the Ranväli stupa, the king
> proceeded to finish it with ten great giants.
> Today to do this noble honor,
> soldiers with giant power reside meritoriously.
>
> Offering for a full year for this merit making,
> taking as many heavy stones as needed on their shoulders,
> with desirous minds they climbed to the forested summit
> and received the majestic god's blessing.[158]

Here classic Buddhist and royal themes are blended with modern military and nation-state ideals. The word for government, to describe the ministers and officials, is *raja,* which means royal, too. *Raja* is also the word used to describe the days of prior kings, *pera rajadavas*, thereby linking legendary giants with national soldiers, and the president with the king who erected the Ruvanveli *stupa* in Anuradhapura. The poet also praises the labor of soldiers, with Saman blessing their concrete carrying. Yet this labor is for more than just service of state, as the poet emphasizes its soteriological value for the soldiers through the generation of merit (*pinkamaṭa*).

The drama of 2014 was only the most prominent display of a wholesale increase in military presence at the Peak. The Civil Security Department continued carrying concrete long after the helicopters departed. Gothabaya Rajapaksa instructed the CSD to begin repaving steps on the Hatton trail after the war, as recounted by Lieutenant R. Aśōka A. Dharmasēna in a short book he wrote about the Peak in 2012. The lieutenant described CSD work at the Peak as part of the "second war" that Mahinda Rajapaksa began after concluding the first, these new economic and social wars (*ārthika hā sāmājīya yuddhayayi*) necessitating the same military involvement. The lieutenant believed it was a great fortune (*mahat bhāgyak*) to perform government work with devout mind (*bäti sitin*) at Sri Pada after serving twenty-six years in actual war.[159] The lieutenant elaborated on the devotional aspect of his work after inviting me into the CSD headquarters. We had passed on the trail several times before, and his men told him I was a researcher. He wanted to share a copy of his book with me, and chat. When I asked what inspired him to write it, he said: "I am from the war time. From a young age it was there, and for over thirty years the war continued. So I fought in the war and, because of that, accumulated a lot of demerit [*pav*]. Demerit means the things that we shouldn't do." He listed the five main Buddhist transgressions, including killing living beings. He said some made arguments about the justification of war, but, in the end, many people still died, and responsibility must be taken. "So to reduce this demerit a bit, out of devotion I came and started this special government service, building paths, steps, and facilities. I did this for the country, out of devotion. While working here, others would ask me for the facts about Sri Pada, so I thought I should investigate a bit, and, having researched, I wrote this book." The soteriological thrust of his infrastructural work was clear, as he labored to offset the sin of war and settle some of an old soldier's karmic balance.

The number of CSD workers stationed long-term was small, but larger crews rotated month to month. When I arrived at the Peak, most were busy finishing a new ambalam and a set of toilets high up the mountain, less than a kilometer from the summit. Others were paving steps, installing railings, and constructing the Kalpavrukṣa Vihāra in Nallathanni. These jobs required CSD workers to become concrete couriers, and the ambalam project meant some had to carry loads quite far. Compared with the local mountain workers and their ritually disciplined bodies, some CSD members were overwhelmed by the difficulty of the job, especially on their first few days at the Peak. They erred in their method of ascent, huffing, puffing, and resting too often, letting their muscles cool and increasing their struggles. This made it difficult to always see a karmic upside to their work. When I posed a question to one worker about links between his labor and merit making, he was too fatigued to humor me, only snorting and half rolling his eyes. To be fair, it was also raining on us. Such struggles are perhaps one reason little camaraderie was displayed between the

CSD and Tamil couriers. The relative speed and ease of Tamil ascents may have irritated winded CSD workers. One griped to me that Tamil climbers were not good people because they only cared about money, perhaps a reflection of frustration with the fact that local workers making three ascents a day could earn more than CSD workers, as the latter were bound to a modest monthly salary no matter where they were stationed. Or perhaps the rift between Tamils and the CSD was a war wound, CSD members being predominately Sinhala and proudly nationalist.[160]

Although the sweat of CSD laborers mixed with the cement they laid, they won only minor official recognition. After stretches of steps on the Hatton trail were repaved, plaques were erected in commemoration. Three from 2015 and 2016 follow the same format, beginning with mention of the head monk Ven. Dhammadinna, by whose advice the project was undertaken, and then noting it was carried out by coordination of Sunil Śānta Vīrasēkara, former *basnāyaka nilamē* of the Maha Saman Devale. The inscriptions also describe the repaving as a noble *puja* to the sacred foot lotus and God Saman. Among the smallest letters on the monuments, however, are those mentioning the "labor contribution" (*śrama dāyakatvaya*) of the CSD. Everyday workers are anonymous in comparison with the Buddhist elites who sanctioned the project. Yet even the latter have their inscription size rivaled by the real monetary sponsor, with its large letters and laser-engraved logo: Commercial Bank.

And Now a Word from Our Sponsors

Commercial Bank was already sponsoring pilgrimage infrastructure before the CSD provided labor for paving. A 2008 inscription commemorates Commercial Bank's work repaving a stretch of the Hatton trail near Sitagangula, and does not specify any government agency backing the project. Other banks joined in earlier infrastructure investments, too. Standard Charter Bank paid 5.9 million rupees to fund a repaving project under the Ministry of Construction, Engineering Works, Housing and Public Facilities. These are only the most expensive examples of corporate presence in the twenty-first century. From season to season, a plethora of businesses descend on the Peak, joining advertisement with pilgrimage infrastructure.[161] Bank of Ceylon, National Savings Bank, and People's Leasing Company all posted eco-conservation signs, and the seasonal work of many companies went well beyond posters.

Nestlé built booths for free tea on busy weekends. Similarly, the Axe Oil company marketed menthol-laden rubbing oil for aches and pains, setting up a free-sample stall for a few weeks mid-season. These giveaways are more than just product placement. They are pitched as a form of *dansala*, a merit-making act of donation, free samples becoming soteriological. This is not to say that employees dwell on the philosophy. For most, it is just another short-term job. The companies hire locals to build and run stands, and this off-plantation labor is something the women of Nallathanni participate in, too. With building and heavy lifting dominated by men, women can be tea dispensers, shopkeepers, and free-sample distributers. Big brands give them new shirts to wear, and the jobs are a respite from tea leaves and domestic work, even if only for a few weeks. Two women I knew from the Nallathanni line-house community joked about what a cushy job they had, sitting, chatting, snacking, and occasionally pouring oil samples into hands.

Another medicinal balm company established more permanent quarters on the Hatton trail. The Siddhalepa Ayurvedic pharmaceutical company built a rest hall and guesthouse a third of the way up the mountain in 1979. It stands in Gangulathenna, a plateau that also houses the CSD, Electricity Board, Public Health Department, a police post, the Nissankamalla Cave Temple monk's residence, Buddha and Saman shrines, and a number of seasonal shops and tea stalls. Pilgrims who stop at Siddhalepa meet young men in bright orange coats who hand out free coriander tea and ginger lozenges. Bottles of oil are on sale, and one can purchase a head or foot massage. Siddhalepa also contributes to sanitation infrastructure by supplying dozens of trash barrels—with brand logos, of course—strapped to lampposts up and down the Peak.

Appropriately, the soap company Lifebuoy is another proponent of sanitation. In 2016, they set up a line of public showers beside the river running in Nallathanni. Taking a page from colonial health initiatives of old, Lifebuoy connected pilgrimage and disease control. The slogan on the giant red sign above the showers read: "This worship season let us develop devout minds. Let us prevent illness and disease." Nor was this the first time Lifebuoy had entered pilgrimage marketing. It sponsored Hatton-trail signs naming stops near the summit, providing descriptions in English, Sinhala, and Tamil, along with an ad for Lifebuoy "Nature" soap, perfect for pitching in the Peak Wilderness Reserve. Likewise, an older Lifebuoy advertisement, which had been reappropriated as a temporary shop wall by 2016, included a photo of the Peak, weaving familiar tropes into its mythic picture (fig. 2.7). The summit is photoshopped against a river, evoking watershed themes of purity, as well as fertility, for an image of motherhood dominates the foreground, conjuring old poetics of the mountain as part of Lady Lanka. Meanwhile, the slogan pitched its product as integral to pilgrimage: "Let us purify body and mind / The pure pilgrimage / Lifebuoy / 'Herbal' / With botanically rich traits of margosa and aloe vera." Soap purified bodies to complement pure minds, yielding a "pure pilgrimage,"

FIGURE 2.7. Lifebuoy advertisement in Nallathanni

literally "very pure worship" (*supirisiduyi vandanāva*), which was certainly meritorious.

Some admen even come in person to worship, another sort of worker-pilgrim. They are sent by companies with stakes in the stocks of trailside stalls. While these small shops usually make their own tea, coffee, and roti from wholesale ingredients, they rely on corporate supply chains for other items, like bottled drinks or biscuits. Shopkeepers enter into deals with brokers from whom they buy in bulk, often deferring most of the payment until after the product has had time to sell. I met one such group of corporate representatives resting in the Matara Kade on the season's opening night. They were seven men from Munchee, proud to be Sri Lanka's number one biscuit company. They went shop to shop on the Peak making sure owners' supplies of Munchee products were flowing smoothly, so everyone's wares read Munchee, and not their main competitor Maliban. These men made rounds at other pilgrimage sites, too—they told me they had been twice to the Catholic St. Anne's festival in Thalawila. They said they would visit the Peak again some months later. As the season progressed, they explained, competing brands edged their way in. Products flew off shelves and shopkeepers turned to whatever supply chains were available. These Munchee men were mostly Buddhist, with two Muslims, who said in front of their colleagues that they did not really believe the Adam story. Yet all ultimately went to the summit to pay their respects to the footprint.

There is no doubt that trade and pilgrimage have long gone hand in hand, from the bridge building of Parakramabāhu II to the roads and rails of tea plantations. The Peak's transition to corporate branding was only the most recent piece of this trend. Lefebvre describes how capital modifies places like mountains, "fragments of nature located at sites chosen for their intrinsic qualities (cave, mountaintop, spring, river), but whose very consecration ended up by stripping them of their natural characteristics and uniqueness. Thus natural space was soon populated by political forces."[162] Many political forces were outlined above, from kings to colonists to executive presidents. All impacted infrastructure and encouraged investment by private pilgrims. The mountain thereby grew a market, a new niche in its forest that made it more like a city where "urban centrality welcomes produce and people."[163] In the process, however, branding uniformity and Buddhist hegemony have crept up the Peak, too. This is not limited to corporate advertisements, but extends to gods, rituals, and stories, as some groups wield mytholiths in ways that deconstruct rather than build up the pluralism of the Peak.

PART II

A Mountain of Myth

3

Adam's Peak and Buddhist Visions of Mecca

Unique to stories of Buddhist-Muslim interaction, the case of Adam's Peak was only indirectly about commerce or conquest. Unlike in Persia, Bactria, India, or Tibet, Muslim presence in Lanka never involved military invasion.[1] Similarly, commerce alone cannot explain the impetus for Muslims climbing the Peak. While settlement in Lanka had mercantile motivations, one did not have to ascend the summit to find the gems that glittered in riverbeds below. Risking one's health and wealth to climb required a special reason. The first part of this chapter considers the creation of the Peak as al-Rahun—a sacred Islamic space predicated on the ancient presence of the Prophet Adam there. This was accomplished by Muslim authors outside Lanka as the island was settled by merchants, a mytholith grown simultaneously with a search for literal gemstones.

The Peak is also unlike sites such as Bamiyan, where Muslims reinterpreted a mythic landscape after Buddhists left.[2] The Peak never ceased to be a Buddhist pilgrimage site as Muslims arrived. Such close quarters produced textual reactions, and so the second part of this chapter considers the emergence of Mecca (Makkama) in Sinhala Buddhist verse. Some of these Mecca myths persist, some have worn away, and others are intentionally reshaped as the mytholith is shorn into a tool. The third part of this chapter considers the rhetorical role of the Makkama footprint in twenty-first century Sinhala historiography, nationalism, and interreligious dialogue, showing the stakes for Buddhists or Muslims who support or deny its translation as "Mecca."

Along the way, I use the terms "figural space" and "literal place" to analyze how descriptions of locales alternate across Buddhist and Muslim accounts. A figural space refers to locales in abstract, metaphorical, and imagistic ways. Conversely, a literal place is specified in detail to make it into a single point, mappable and touchable, "right here." One can morph into another, as "what begins as undifferentiated space becomes place as we get to know it better and endow it with value."[3] Conversely, firsthand travelogues can speak of places in a literal fashion, but an accumulation of accounts, often embellished for readers at home, may also create figural spaces for foreign imaginations to map dreamlike monks and monsters.[4] Even something as grounded as a name, where "by the act of place-naming, space is transformed symbolically into a place, that is, a space with a history," can be riddled with ambiguity in possible significations and reasons for the moniker.[5] This occurred with the Arabic word that came to signify the Peak—al-Rahun. Some say this was from the Lankan kingdom of Rohana.[6] But the Muslim writers who propagated the name al-Rahun were unclear. One guessed, "I should believe Rāhūn to be the Arabic form of Rūnk."[7] Another said, "more likely it is the mountain Rāhūm . . . because the rain [*rihām*] hardly leaves it."[8] The origin of the name "Serendib" was even more uncertain, as discussed below. A name, though it grants a place history, cannot guarantee its preservation. Locales become disconnected, place-names fading into imagined spaces.

An excellent example is the tale of Balavhar and Būdāsf, which moved from a Sanskrit story about the life of the Buddha, to Arabic, Georgian, Greek, Latin, and myriad European languages, its heroes Buddhist, Muslim, and Christian in turn, becoming the medieval Catholic saints Barlaam and Josaphat by the end.[9] The Arabic version alone made a remarkable loop, translated from Sanskrit in Baghdad and then returned to India.[10] In the Arabic, Balavhar identified himself: "I am a merchant from Sarandīb."[11] Yet in the tenth-century Georgian Christian adaptation, Balavhar was not a merchant, and "he dwelt in the land of Sarnadib."[12] The English translator explained "Sarnadib" is "a corruption of the Arabic Sarandīb. The transposition of the vowel 'a' and consonant 'n' is . . . characteristic of a misreading of Arabic."[13] "Sarnadīb" became a figural space, its place-name persisting in misread form. When the story jumped to Greek, Balavhar became Barlaam, Būdāsf became Ioasaph, and Sarandīb was dropped altogether in favor of "a waste howling wilderness in the land of Senaar,"[14] the Hebrew term for Mesopotamia. In most European vernacular versions, names vanished altogether into the figural—"Barlaam lived in the wilderness."[15] Yet this was not the end of the Serendib link, and the Peak became the catalyst for the mythic reassembly. In his 1666 *Ásia Portugueza*, Manuel de Faria e Sousa noted of the footprint creator: "Some believe this Saint was *Josaphat*."[16] This is an accidentally apt attribution as Josaphat really *was* the Buddha, transposed several times across languages and religions. The sage thus returned in a new form to where he had trod before, showing the mythic serendipity of this globally connected mountain.

Mapping a Muslim World

We begin with the collection of stories that form the latticed facets of the Muslim mytholith of the Peak. References to a mountain of Adam began early in Islamic traditions, and the fame of this landmark expanded through the labors of geographers and cartographers from around the world. The wide range of Muslims who wrote of the Peak is a testament to its mythic power, used for myriad rhetorical ends. From sailors' tales, to lapidaries, to global encyclopedias and maps, the Peak evolved from a vague space to an anchoring place for Muslims in South Asia.

Finding Adam in Early Islam

Whoever first forged the Adam-Serendib link, it is clear that a longstanding cult of Adam in the pre-Islamic world—where Jewish, Zoroastrian, Gnostic Christian, and Manichean texts crossed Greece, North Africa, Arabia, Persia, and India—formed the basis for Muslim myths on the primogenitor.[17] The Muslim literary tradition of Adam's mountain began during the Abbasid Caliphate. Baghdad, on the banks of the Tigris and Euphrates rivers, said to run with the tears of Adam, became an emporium of culture and capital in the eighth century, with translation teams, bureaucratic agents stationed around the empire, and commissioned explorers and cartographers reporting on wonders of the world.[18] The world drew closer via connections to Persia, which had already absorbed much Indic material, including Buddhist branches, adding to Baghdad's bricolage.[19]

Fittingly, an analysis of how Adam's mytholith grew in Serendib is best begun with a historian who hailed from Persia: al-Tabari (839–923). Tabari spent much of his career in Baghdad, but also traveled in Egypt, Syria, and Persia for study. His history therefore has a range of Adamic myth, citing Jewish, Greek Christian, and Zoroastrian opinions to compare with Islam.[20] The topic meant Tabari dealt with extremely figural spaces, like the world before creation, although they were made factual by the evidentiary mechanics of his historiography, which used transmission chains (*isnād*) by witnesses of original teachings to compile an early Muslim mytholith of Adam. To locate the site of exile, Tabari cited six chains of transmission that all placed Adam in India, providing a total of thirty-one individuals attesting to the fact.[21] Four of these chains involved Ibn Abbas, a young companion of the Prophet Muhammad, only twelve when Muhammad died in 632. Ibn Abbas was the originator of three *isnād* about Adam; in another, he heard it from Muhammad's uncle Abu Talib.[22] The latter was a mercantile clan leader, someone likely familiar with fables of India. As for Ibn Abbas, he served as governor of the port city of Basra in the caliphate of Ali (r. 656–661), a position that likely came with exposure to seafaring stories. India in most of Tabari, however, is vaguely figural, an abstract distant land connoting paradise.

Only one *isnād* on the location of Adam's fall gave multiple specific place-names to orient the site. This came from the historian Ibn Ishaq (d. 761 or 767), grandson of a Christian, who became a tutor in a Baghdad court. He recorded: "The people of the Torah on their part said: Adam was cast down in India upon a mountain called Wāsim on a river called Buhayl between two places in the land of India, al-Dahnaj and al-Mandal."[23] This is intriguing evidence for how Jewish mercantile communities, with settled connections in India dating from the first century of the Common Era, may have used place names to sacralize a foreign landscape, the figural Adamic exile made more literal to the exilic lives of a merchant diaspora.[24] But this version of Adam's India had little staying power compared with the next one. With no chain of transmission, Tabari only noted: "Others said: Rather, Adam was cast down in Sarandīb upon a mountain called Nūdh." While the name here matches a mount Nūdh in an Ibn Abbas transmission, Tabari remained fairly skeptical of the Serendib opinion because it lacked an official *isnād*, but he ultimately deferred to the general consensus: "Its soundness is rejected neither by the Muslim scholars nor by the people of the Torah and the Gospel. Proof is firmly established by reports from some of them."[25] By Tabari's time, Serendib was a believable site of the fall for Jews, Christians, and Muslims alike.

Tabari also included several transmissions regarding what Adam brought from Paradise. Ibn Abbas and Ibn Ishaq were again the *isnād* originators, the former relaying: "The perfumes brought from India come from what Adam took out of Paradise." Ibn Abbas also reported: "When Adam came down, the smell of Paradise was with him. It clung to India's trees rivers and valleys, and everything there was filled with perfume." Ibn Ishaq was more specific about a mountain: "Adam fell down upon it—meaning upon that mountain—having with him the leaves of Paradise. He scattered them on that mountain. This was the origin of all perfumes and fruits that are found only in India."[26] By including this mythic link of Paradise and trade goods, Tabari kept with other ninth-century writers enchanting commercial goals of an expanding Islam.

For other authors, more than just perfumes marked the Peak. Another Baghdad scholar from Kufa, al-Kalbi (737–819), wrote of Adam's grave in the mountain: "When Adam died, the children of Seth (Shīth), the son of Adam, buried him in a cave in the mountain whereon Adam alighted to the land of India. The name of the mountain is Nawdh and is the most fertile mountain in all the world. Hence the saying, 'More fertile than Nawdh and more arid than Barahūt.' . . . a valley in the Ḥadramawt [South Yemen]."[27] The name of the mountain here is essentially the same as the Nūdh reference by Tabari. It was apparently known well enough to have become a local idiom that juxtaposed the different topographies of India and Yemen—lands long linked by oceanic trade.[28] Nūdh was a more figural space than Barahūt, but by comparison to Yemen, even as its opposite, the Adamic mountain was drawn that much closer to home.

Stabilizing the Peak in Serendib

Geographers, merchants, and other travelers of the ninth and tenth centuries were less concerned with *isnād*.[29] Their reports came not through scholarly chains, but as sights seen on personal travels and via interviews with those who journeyed even further. These authors were key agents in shifting the Peak from a figural space to a literal destination. Yet they also supplied elements for further figuration with tropes that enchanted future writers, conglomerated into a mytholith through generational repetition.

The merchant Sulaiman al-Tajir returned from his second journey to India and China around 850. The following year, the written account of his travels began to circulate in Baghdad. In the incomplete manuscript that remains, the narrative begins abruptly in the area of the Lakdives and Maldives. Serendib was described as

> the chief of all these islands they call the *diva*. In its coast there are pearl fisheries, and it is completely surrounded by the sea. On its soil is a mountain called al-Rahun on which Adam fell.—salvation be upon him!—The trace of his foot on the rock is seen on the summit of this mountain, the imprinted hollow in stone. At the top of that mountain we see only the one foot marked because it is said that, Adam—salvation be upon him!—put the other in the sea; it is said that the footprint at the top of this mountain is about seventy cubits. Around this mountain abound stones: ruby, topaz and sapphires.[30]

Sulaiman made an important place-name distinction. Rather than Nūdh, the mountain was al-Rahun, the usual appellation of the Peak among subsequent writers. And rather than an abstract India, this mountain was on a specific island, near other specific islands, on the way to farther-flung locales. Sulaiman's was the first of the still-extant accounts to mention the footprint—a critical specification suggesting that the transposition of Adam's exile onto a literal place in Serendib resulted in absorption of the local footprint myth, a maneuver matching other Islamic footprints.[31] Although Sulaiman turned from the figural to the literal in his specificity of geography, the inclusion of the footprint and the mountain's boundless gem wealth helped forge a Peak still steeped in the fabulous, establishing tropes repeated in later reports.

Sailors enjoyed fabulous sea stories, as "without trade in anecdote there would be no trade at all, for story is integral to commerce. . . . A kind of seafaring song line, a marker for cosmopolitanism, the trading in stories stitched the world together."[32] The world was sewn in most marvelous ways in the compilation of stories called *The Book of Wonders of India* (c. 953), with tales collected by merchant captain Buzurg Ibn Shahriyar. These stories included figural islands for Islamic parables, fabulous wealth, or fantastic bestiaries, as well as literal facts on trade routes, products, and taxes, with details of navigation techniques and the special vocabulary for designating lands, waters, winds, and weather.[33] The book mentions "Sirandib, called Ceylon" several times, as well as the Peak: "Among celebrated islands, there is not one in the sea like Sirandib. . . . There is a mountain of rubies and diamonds that is hard to climb. They say it was here that Adam fell, and his footprint can be seen, seventy cubits long. The islanders say it is Adam's footprint, and that he put one of his feet here, and the other in the sea."[34] Compared to some of his other stories, this myth is one of the less fantastic. The author expresses no incredulity about it, as he had with other tales. The story also deals in Serendib tropes from at least a century before, its literal description figurally enhanced by the entire mountain being made of gems.

Many ninth- and tenth-century writers were not strictly merchants. Most were not any one thing. Geographers were also scientists, historians, musicians, and Quran exegetes. Ibn Khordadbeh was such a savant. As a geographer, he completed at least two versions of his *Book of Routes and Realms* (*Al-masālik wa-al-mamālik*), circa 846 and 885.[35] He hailed from a Tabaristan Zoroastrian family that converted to Islam under the Barmakids, who were themselves once Buddhist.[36] Ibn Khordadbeh's work as an Abbasid postmaster helped him gather geographic information. He became an official caliphate mythmaker, textually reproducing imperial extent, implying Abbasid rulers replicated divine order on Earth.[37] In this world emanating from Baghdad,

> we see there the mountain on which Adam was cast out (after being driven from Paradise). The summit is lost in the clouds, and it is surveyed by

> navigators at a distance of about twenty days. Brahmins, who are the devotees of India, exhibit on this mountain the footprint of one of Adam's feet; another imprint is in India, at a distance of two or three days from the first. Collected on this mountain are aloe, pepper, various varieties of spices, and perfumes. Found in the area are different varieties of rubies and other precious stones; finally, in the valley, a diamond mine and musk goats. The people of India say the foot of Adam has left only a single footprint on the rock, and that a flame shot incessantly, like a flash, from the summit of the mountain.[38]

Ibn Khordadbeh apparently acquired seafaring reports describing a summit seen from the ocean, estimating distance by days out to sea. He expands sacred geography with another footprint in India, moving the figural space of Adam to a measurable landscape. He is also the first to mention locals with interest in the mountain. It is a figural snippet, "Brahmins" being an imagistic catchall, but the reference acknowledges a local significance to the Peak. Figural Brahmins were part of a literally emplaced geography where others lived, which removed the Peak from a purely exegetical realm.

Ibn Khordadbeh's geography was widely cited, and its title, *Al-masālik wa-al-mamālik*, became a genre unto itself.[39] The scholar al-Masudi was born into this atmosphere of Serendib stories in Baghdad in 896. He became the most famous geographer since Ibn Khordadbeh, whose work he admired.[40] Before his death in 956, al-Masudi made voyages around the known world, putting his accumulated knowledge in a book. Serendib had an important empirical role, orienting distances to other islands, and he was cited as the best coconut exporter.[41] Yet the stories al-Masudi told of "mount er-Rahūn in Serendib" remain steeped in prior tropes, like Indian perfumes from paradise, and descriptions like "in this mountain sparkle diamonds and other precious stones."[42] So the al-Rahun name helped stabilize the Peak as a literal place, but without forfeiting its oft repeated figural qualities. The later geographer al-Muqadassi, however, tried to empty the Peak of some of these imaginations. Around 987, he completed his geography, compiled from personal travels, previous works, royal archives, and interviews with merchants and sailors. In his opening account of seas and rivers, al-Muqaddasi located Serendib: "In it is situated the mountain on which Adam was thrown: it is called al-Rahūn, and may be seen from a distance of a journey of several days. On it is the impress of a foot sunk to the depth of about seventy cubits; the other footprint is distant the journey of a day and a night, and is on the floor of the sea. A light is seen on it every night. Here also are found rubies."[43] This account is very similar to Ibn Khordadbeh, but some original points are tempered. The light atop the Peak is less fabulous, its visibility from shore more vague, and the Brahmins vanished entirely. Since al-Muqaddasi was obsessed with accuracy, it is possible he amended the earlier stories because some had branded Ibn Khordadbeh as a charlatan.[44] Lacking further detail, al-Muqaddasi improved the work by making it less specific, and thus less likely to be incorrect. His devotion to accuracy implies he held Adam's mountain to be a literal place, but he could say this only vaguely, as the Peak was still highly figural. To further fix island and summit in place, mapping was needed.

The Peak in Cartographic Circles

Serendib goes unmentioned in the *Tarikh al-Hind* (History of India) of al-Biruni (973–1048), but does appear in his treatise on gemstones, where he cites authors like al-Masudi, who "has mentioned the mountains of Rāhūn and has said that it was here that Adam was made to descend." Yet al-Biruni was skeptical of the Adamic link: "Some authors have presented the following argument in support of Adam's descent upon this island: 'The plants that grow upon this island at first grow to a certain height and then recline toward the earth a little. . . . This is because of the prostration performed by the angels to Adam.' But these people forget to note that the place where the prostrations were made was situated elsewhere and the place to which Adam was brought is elsewhere." This passage reveals a contested discourse on Adam's place of exile. Serendib was not the only candidate, nor did al-Biruni consider such stories essential to the island's identity. It was rather gems, especially rubies, that were of real concern. He also provided a realist interpretation of the summit light others had described fabulously: "This light guides boats and ships at night just as . . . the Alexandrian lighthouse serves as a beacon."[45] For al-Biruni, the Peak was important as a navigable place—a guide to sailors and a source of gemstones—rather than a space where flora reflected angels bowing to Adam.

Yet the location of Serendib was itself contested. The name was used variously for (1) the island Sīlān or Sāylan (Ceylon), (2) a specific area containing Adam's Peak on the island, (3) a gulf region including the south coast of India and its island attachment, (4) a larger littoral region including smaller islands around Sīlān, or (5) another side of the Indian Ocean, usually Sumatra. Taking option four (though he also used option three), al-Biruni wrote: "In the Indian language, Serandīb is Sankladīp. Dīp is the generic name for an island. When I ponder upon the name it appears to me that the name designates a cluster of islands, that is, a mother of islands surrounded by several isles."[46] There was confusion even among experienced seafarers like Ahmad Ibn Majid. His navigational treatise, completed circa 1490, was infused with knowledge from Tamil maritime traditions, calculating the latitude of Sīlān more precisely than the Sanskrit astronomy figures used by al-Biruni that put Lanka on the equator.[47] Yet Ibn Majid notes: "Opinion differs as to the name Sirandīb. Some say it is a name of the island of Sīlān and some say of Sumatra." Although Serendib had become vague from variegated usage, Adam remained fixed on his familiar island: "It is said that Adam is in the island [of Sīlān], but it is not correct that he has a built-up tomb like the tomb of our prophet Muhammad in Medina."[48] Ibn Majid cites neither mountain nor footprint, only mentioning Adam to debunk tales of special sepulchers. Yet even with this literal approach, Ibn Majid makes Adam's presence figural by omitting location and even a verb.[49] Adam was *in* the island, part of the land, permeating its stories.

The Peak of Serendib (Ǵebel Sarandīb) appeared on maps of the "Persian Sea" (Ṣurāt baḥr fārs), which helped to stabilize its placement. These came from the cartographic school of Abu Zayd al-Balkhi (d. 934). In some manuscripts, the mountain was moderately sized, but still stood out against an otherwise blank landscape. And just as the legends of the Peak grew, so did its cartographic prominence, sometimes so elaborately illustrated as to dominate all Serendib. Two Persian recensions show markedly different "mountains of Serendib" (Koh Sarandīb), one an elaborate series of summits, the other simply a white triangle. In an elaborate recension by al-Istakhri, the mountain grew large enough to be dotted with caves.[50]

When another Muslim scholar drew his own circle of the world, the Adamic footprint was marked emphatically in the whole of the hemisphere. Around 1074, Mahmud al-Kashgari, the father of Turkish linguistics, finished his massive lexicon, accompanied by a world map to create "a dialect atlas."[51] With less than a hundred names on the map, al-Kashgari reserved three labels for Serendib on the right edge of the circle: "Sarandīb," "Mountain of Sarandīb," and "Footprint of Adam," increasingly specifying mythic terrain (fig. 3.1).[52] It may be that al-Kashgari wrote three labels to emphasize how important Serendib and its footprint had become in Islamic geography. It is surprising that Serendib and Adam are triply emphasized on the map, but Mecca and Medina are absent, perhaps due to local contestations. In the eleventh century, Buddhism expanded across the Tarim Basin, with translations of Tokharian and Chinese texts to Uyghur.[53] Meanwhile, the rest of Turkic Central Asia underwent Islamization, including al-Kashgari's region, and polemics ensued. The *Insadi Sūtra*, for example, a thirteenth-century Uyghur anthology of Buddhist teachings, describes religious rivals squeezed out by the salvific suzerainty of the future Buddha: "My Maitreya, when you descend at that time, you will be at the foot of the Mahabodhi Tree. . . . The Lord Messiah, Mother Mary, and Muhammad

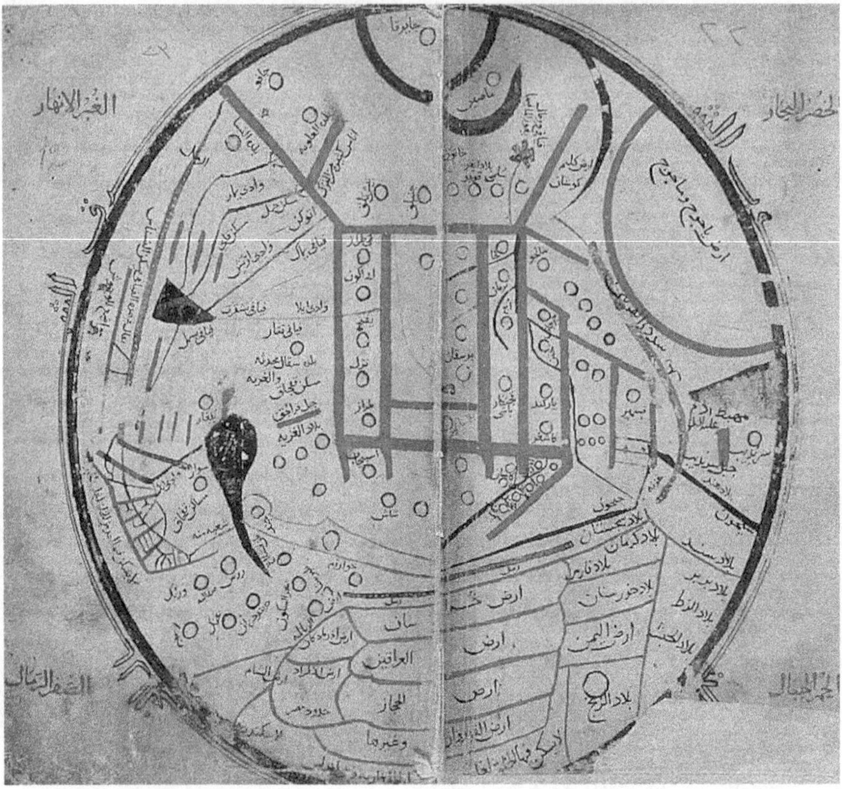

FIGURE 3.1. Mountain at an edge of the world on the world map by Mahmud al-Kashgari

the Prophet . . . will find their places cramped, and, my Maitreya, they will rely on you!"[54] In turn, al-Kashgari expressed no sympathies for the Buddha. In his lexicon section on nouns, under the entry for *känd*, or "city," he included a sample verse:

> We came down on them like a flood
> We went out among their cities
> We tore down the idol temples
> We shat on the Buddha's head.[55]

Considering such traces of competition, al-Kashgari emphasizing Adam's footprint on his map was likely a strategic mythic maneuver. Turkish scholar Emel Esin describes cosmographic takeovers that match the geographic: "Holy places, such as Uyghur Buddhist Tantric temples . . . became the seat of Qalandar *dervīshes*, who considered the caves as abodes of the 'Seven Sleepers' of Islamic hagiography. Mount Budh, in Ceylon, was also associated with Adam."[56] The Peak thus became a tool of competition far from its literal slopes, mytholith modified so al-Kashgari could claim the entire mountain of Serendib for Muslims on his map, specified down to the footprint.

Meanwhile, on the Mediterranean side of the world circle, Andalusian intellectuals made their own maps. Muhammad al-Idrisi (1100–1165) was invited to the court of Roger II in Sicily on a cartographic commission, resulting in one of the most advanced atlases yet produced in 1154.[57] Though al-Idrisi also drew a world map in the Balkhi-school tradition, Serendib played no major role. Regional maps were al-Idrisi's more substantial project, their combination creating a detailed vision of Mediterranean and Indian Ocean realms. In these regional rectangles, Serendib holds a prominent place across manuscripts, even when the Indian peninsula vanishes. Always holding a central spot in Serendib is the massive mountain labeled al-Rahūn. Using older geographies, al-Idrisi replicated Ibn Khordadbeh's account of the Peak verbatim.[58] He used Ptolemy, too, randomly transposing Taprobane place names across Serendib. The island's large size was not geographically accurate, but it was a fair representation of how great its mytholithic accumulation had grown. In turn, al-Idrisi's geography was important for transmitting Muslim myths about the Peak into Europe, especially after publication in Rome in 1592, and translation into Latin in 1619.[59] As part of this same transmission of the Adamic mytholith, one last author must be considered, shifting the story from cartographic circles to pilgrimage circuits.

The Peak in Muslim Pilgrimage Circuits

Despite all the discussion of the Peak in the above texts, Ibn Battuta's *Riḥla* (Journey) provides the only extant firsthand account of medieval pilgrimage ascent. From his description, however, it is clear he was far from the first Muslim to scale the summit. Ibn Battuta left his hometown of Tangier on pilgrimage to Mecca in 1325, and did not return for twenty-four years. After treks across Egypt, Syria, Persia, Baghdad, East Africa, and the Red Sea, with stops at important pilgrimage sites, Ibn Battuta worked for several years in Delhi as a jurist, and thereafter in the Maldives, the islands recently converted from Buddhism to Islam under another North African Muslim. His account suggests the Maldives were a stop for pilgrims in transit to and from the Peak. Such a group helped Ibn Battuta make a good impression: "a ship arrived from Saylāṇ bringing some poor brethren, Arabs and Persians, who recognized me and told the Wazīr's attendants who I was. This made him still more delighted to have me. . . . I asked his permission to give a banquet to the poor brethren who had come from visiting the Foot."[60] Considering all the talk of the Peak in Arabic and Persian literature, it is only natural that Ibn Battuta should encounter people coming to see it, and the exchange of stories that occurred over the banquet surely whetted his own appetite for pilgrimage.

It is unclear, however, whether the Peak had been on the intentional itinerary of those Arab and Persian pilgrims. Ibn Battuta's account implies that, unlike hajj to Mecca, trips to the Peak were less planned, generated instead by the randomness of the winds—a planetary agency that fits Donovan Schaefer's idea that "religion traffics in a network . . . better understood as a regime of accidents than an icon of rationally organized *logos*."[61] While still in the Maldives, for example, Ibn Battuta sent his companion Abu Muhammad Ibn Farhan to Bengal to sell cowrie shells. The cargo and riggings were lost in a storm, and the ship drifted. "At last they came to the island of Saylān after suffering from hunger, thirst and privations. Then came back to me my comrade Abū Muḥammad after a year. He had visited Adam's foot, and he visited it later again with me."[62] Lanka again proved the salvation of a shipwreck, and Abu Muhammad made the best of a bad situation by a pilgrimage to the Peak, likely inspiring Ibn Battuta's ascent during his own unintended detour on the island and thus offering a glimpse into how pilgrimage circuits arose in the shared stories and spontaneous sojourns of wind-powered travel.

When Ibn Battuta left the Maldives, chased out by locals who deemed him too strict a jurist, "we set sail though we had no able captain with us." A skilled navigator being imperative for this stretch of sea, the ship found itself lost in the Gulf of Mannar. Once more, the Peak served as a navigational aid: "We saw the mountain of Sarandīb there, rising up into the heavens like a column of smoke."[63] While his crew feared piracy in Lanka, Ibn Battuta trusted his own diplomatic skills, proclaiming himself a relative of a South Indian sultan by marriage. Admitted to see the king at Puttalam, Ibn Battuta recorded a wealth of timber and spices on the coasts, and noted armed fleets at the harbor, bound for Yemen. This king was from the Āriya Cakkaravartti dynasty ("Ayrī Shakarwatī" as spelled by Ibn Battuta) that had controlled the Jaffna peninsula since the thirteenth century. When Ibn Battuta landed, they were vying for power on the west coast with the southern Alakeśvara merchant ministers, especially over lucrative pearl fisheries.[64] The king presented Ibn Battuta with a luxurious spread of pearls, impressing the traveler with this marine wealth, as well as knowledge from maritime connections. "He understood Persian, and was delighted with the tales I told him of kings and countries." The king played a generous host to Ibn Battuta:

> "Do not be shy, but ask me for anything that you want." I replied: "Since reaching this island I have but one desire, to visit the blessed Foot, the sacred Foot of Adam . . ." "That is simple," he answered. "We shall send an escort with you to take you to it." . . . The Sultan then gave me a palanquin which was carried by his slaves on their shoulders. And he sent along with me four *jūgīs*, whose custom it is to make annual pilgrimage to the Foot, three Brahmins, ten other persons from his entourage, and fifteen men to carry provisions.[65]

There is a wealth of information on fourteenth-century pilgrimage and politics embedded in this short exchange. For one, the Peak was foremost on Ibn Battuta's mind as the sight to see. Pilgrimage infrastructure had also apparently advanced to the point where the journey was considered simple. Evidence of Hindu presence at the Peak is also presented, Ibn Battuta's courtly retinue including Brahmins and yogis with annual pilgrimage vows. This large retinue, including a slave-borne palanquin, was likely also a political display. Parading an honored foreigner across the island via Āriya Cakkaravartti largess could be read as a communication of this dynasty's cosmopolitan prowess.

This theory of political pilgrimage performance gains further traction considering that Ibn Battuta's guides cut a path through the inland city of Kurunegala, which contained a palace for Buddhist monarchs. The power of these kings in the fourteenth century was limited. Fractious successions, courtly subversions, and an opposing Jaffna kingdom were reasons the Kurunegala stronghold was needed, "built in a narrow valley between two hills."[66] The real financial power of this court was likely controlled by the aforementioned Alakeśvaras of the southwest. So although Ibn Battuta met "the principal Sultan of this country" and was impressed by his rubies and the only white elephant he had ever seen, the Kurunegala court was surely aware of a rival kingdom supporting this curious foreigner, flaunting wealth in the process—a more subtle form of invasion compared with the actual military campaigns that were waged.

Along the way, Ibn Battuta visited sites attesting to Muslim pilgrim predecessors. Outside Kurunegala, "there stands the mosque of Shaikh 'Uṣmān of Shīrāz . . . The Sultan and inhabitants of the town visit his grave and venerate him. He was the guide to the Foot."[67] The presence of a mosque and Persian guide from Shiraz suggests Kurunegala was a normal stop for rest and resupply on Muslim pilgrimage, and contemporaneous Sinhala descriptions of the city boasted much to entice travelers.[68] Ibn Battuta mentions another sheikh of Shiraz: Ibn Khafif (d. 982), who "occupies a high rank among the saints and is widely celebrated. It was he who revealed the track of the mountain of Sarandīb in the island of Saylān in the land of India."[69] Ibn Khafif had once guided pilgrims, who, suffering hunger, slaughtered a small elephant. The sheikh forbade it and refused to eat. He was spared by the elephants who came to exact revenge, winning the respect of the locals and access for Muslims to the Peak: "These infidels used formerly to prevent Muslims from making this pilgrimage and would maltreat them, and neither eat nor trade with them," but after the elephant event, "the infidels honor the Muslims, allow them to enter their houses, eat with them, and have no suspicions."[70] The basic plot of this story of elephants sparing a pious Muslim who refuses to eat their kin, resulting in the conversion of nonbelievers, had been in circulation in the Arabic and Persian literary worlds since at least the tenth century.[71] It is possible that Ibn Battuta added it as his own narrative flourish, or that he heard it from a Muslim informant on the island. In the latter case, the story would function as a charter myth of a longer process of Muslim assimilation in Lanka, using an animal common in Sinhala lore, especially near the Peak. The tale also conveniently resonates with stories of the Buddha calming wild elephants by meditating on loving-kindness. Ibn Khafif was likewise spared by his own virtuous ethics.

With Peak access, Muslim pilgrims mapped various sacred locales of the highland landscape. Ibn Battuta described many parts to the Peak pilgrimage circuit: "We continued our journey to a place called 'The Old Woman's Hut,' which is the end of the inhabited part, and went on to the cave of Bābā Ṭāhir, who was a devotee, and then to the cave of al-Sabīk. This al-Sabīk was a Sultan of the infidels who had retired there for devotion."[72] It is not clear if the cave of the infidel king had significance to Muslims, or if Ibn Battuta's party visited because of the Brahmins and yogis in his retinue. In any event, the caves were close enough to show overlapping styles of sacred land on this multireligious route. Ibn Battuta continued naming places: "We continued our journey to the seven caves, and then to the pass of Iskandar [Aqba-i-Iskandar], the al-Iṣfahānī cave, a water-spring and an uninhabited fortress, below which there is a hollow called the place of the mystics [*gāh-i-'ārifān*]. At the same place is the cave of the bitter orange and the cave of the sultan, and close by is the *darwāza*, that is, the gate [*bāb*] of the mountain."[73] Although Ibn Battuta wrote about these places literally as an eyewitness, to a reader today the names are extremely figural. It is impossible to say where these points were, but they were apparently obvious pilgrimage stops for the guides. Persian traditions were clearly rooted in Lanka, shown by the names of the saints, the cult of Iskandar, and the Persian word for "gate" that Ibn Battuta translated into Arabic for readers back home.[74]

From the *darwāza* gate of the mountain, the ascent began.

> This is one of the highest mountains in the world. We saw from the sea when we were nine days' journey away, and when we climbed it we saw the clouds below us, shutting out our view of its base. On it there are many trees whose leaves do not fall off, and flowers of various colors, including a red rose as big as the palm of a hand. They maintain that on these roses there is writing in which can be read the name of Allāh the exalted and that of His Prophet. May peace be on him! There are two tracks on the mountain leading to the Foot, one called Bābā track and the other Māmā track, meaning Adam and Eve. Peace be on them![75]

Devotion merged with the land. The name of God grew on the mountainside in the form of calligraphic rose petals, and the pathways were named for progenitors. Ibn Battuta said the harder Bābā pathway, likely the Ratnapura side, was considered more meritorious, a belief shared by Buddhists. He also noted the pilgrimage infrastructure: "Men of yore have hewn stairs in the mountain . . . and they have driven iron pegs from which chains are suspended." Ultimately, he hiked "to the summit of the mountain where the foot is. The blessed footprint, the foot of our father Adam . . . is on a lofty black rock in a wide plateau. The blessed Foot sank into the rock far enough to leave its impression hollowed out. It is eleven spans long." Ibn Battuta measured the footprint by the length of human hands, putting reports of earlier geographers in perspective. His literal report makes a previously repeated figure of seventy cubits fabulously figural. Regarding summit ritual, Ibn Battuta explained: "the custom is that the pilgrims remain three days at the Khiẓr cave and that all these days they walk up to the foot, morning as well as evening. We did the same. The three days being over, we returned by the way of the Māmā track. We encamped at the cave of Shaim, namely Shīṣ, the son of Adam."[76] As Ibn Battuta descended, he visited more of the Islamic landscape, proceeding past a number of villages, including one where Ibn Khafīf had stayed. The highlands were traversed by Muslim pilgrims who made story slates from its gneiss caves, the mytholith of al-Rahun solidified by literal emplacement and detailed information. While Ibn Battuta also reinforced figural tropes repeated by earlier Arabic authors, such as the wealth of trade products associated with the island, like gems, metals, and oils, these, too, were described with an eyewitness realism.[77] Dialogue and narrative in his travelogue made for more tangible realities than theological exegesis, and more relatable places than names in a geography. Ibn

Battuta's text is inhabited by people, and its circulation helped grow the Muslim mytholith of the Peak.

Living Shoulder to Shoulder—Muslim Neighbors and Figural Meccas

Many centuries after Muslims began to write of the Peak, evidence of a Buddhist counterreaction surfaced in Sinhala poetry, claiming the Buddha left a footprint in Mecca to match the Peak. The title of this second section, living shoulder to shoulder, is borrowed from a Sinhala phrase that has been used to describe Buddhist-Muslim relations—*uren ura gäṭī siṭi*.[78] What I find evocative about the idiom is its incorporation of the verb *gäṭenavā*, which can mean "touch" or "brush," but also "collide" or "conflict." So the shoulders do not stand passively, but are close enough to bump and jostle. When faced with the specter of ethnic nationalism and its dire toll on minorities, some scholars chose to tint the historical lens as rosy a shade as possible,[79] while others wrote Manichean histories of idealistic harmony or anomalistic violence, with colonizers being scapegoats for the latter.[80] Fuller histories of Buddhist-Muslim coexistence must acknowledge the deeper roots of prejudice and stereotyping, illustrated in part by Buddhist Mecca.[81] This approach avoids assumptions of an "implicit cosmopolitanism"[82] by virtue of Lanka's oceanic links, instead showing how communities negotiate varying anxiety and concord, rejection and acceptance.

The Buddhist Mecca in Peak Poetry

Historical evidence of early Muslim settlement in Lanka includes tenth-century tombstones, and family genealogies tracing port settlements to Arab ancestors.[83] The gem trade is often cited as a reason for Muslim habitation on the island, and *Saman Sirita* does describe locals (*medēhī*) and foreigners (*paradēhī*) happily gemming together.[84] After European coastal conquests, more Muslims moved to the highlands, integrating into reciprocal systems of landowning in the Kandyan kingdom. They provided a variety of products and services, like salt, buffalo, oil, sweeping, or thatching. Some accepted grants requiring a religious exchange. In these cases, Muslims were free to practice Islam on lands given for homes and mosques,[85] but they were expected to make a return investment in Buddhist ritual.[86] At large temple villages like Ämbäkke, for example, all tenants participated in the annual festival for the Kataragama shrine, including Buddhist monks, Vellala Hindus, and resident Muslims.[87]

It was also during the Kandyan period, likely in the seventeenth or eighteenth century, that Mecca began appearing in Sinhala pilgrimage poetry.[88] A manuscript with quatrains meant for singing, for example, includes the following verse:

> Atop the shining sandy plane of Mecca, he willed the sacred foot attractive
> He saw that the slab that the moon dearly worshiped was unattractive
> Walking meditating in the sky, his command shook, his caste attractive
> Having mindfully seen it, oh worship this Samangira sacred foot attractive.[89]

This basic outline of the Buddha leaving his footprint is perhaps the most detailed version of the story still extant, as most poems simply reference the Meccan footprint in passing. Another eighteenth-century Samanala poem with a Mecca mention was *Samanala Vistaraya* (Samanala description). Its quatrains varied in length and topic, describing stops on the mountain path, auspicious marks on the Buddha's foot, allusions to other myths, and invocations to gods, most often Saman. Its quatrain on Mecca also survived into the age of mass print, one of several *Samanala Vistarya* verses incorporated into *Purāṇa Himagata Varṇanāva* (Ancient praise of Himagata) in the early twentieth century. Pamphlets of this poem are still sold in trailside shops like Chandra's. Mecca appears rather randomly in these works, flanked by verses narrating the Buddha foiling Mara, or describing deities landing on the Peak to worship.

laksa gaṇan budu guṇa agavā	lā	Having signified Buddha virtues numbering 100,000
lakṣana äti siri patula obā	lā	Having imprinted the auspiciously marked sacred sole
sakraja deviṅdun deskara vā	lā	Having shown evidence to Lord God Sakra
makkama väḍiyē laksana pā	lā.[90]	He went to Mecca and displayed splendor.
laksa gaṇan budu guna vimasā	lā	Having examined Buddha virtues numbering 100,000

lakṣana äti siri patula obā	lā	Having imprinted the auspiciously marked sacred sole
sakraja deviṅduṭa desa pēnnā	lā	Having shown the area to Lord God Sakra
makkama väḍiyayi laka pēnnā	lā.[91]	He went to Mecca and displayed Lanka/splendor/skills.

The latter *Purāṇa Himagata Varṇanāva* verse carried greater valiance of interpretation in its last line, the use of *laka* over *laksana* allowing the multiple meanings of Lanka, splendor, or skills, suggesting the Buddha might represent the island itself on his Mecca journey. Sakra's presence as king of the gods is similarly significant for both verses, embodying world-conquering power that beholds the Buddha stretch suzerainty overseas.

Where did this myth of Buddha feet in Mecca originate? At first glance, it seems a simple countermove by Buddhist pilgrims who noticed Muslims making a claim on one of their most sacred spaces and returned the favor by sending the Buddha to Mecca. This is part of the story, but its roots may go deeper, grounded in the shifting meanings of the Sanskrit and Pali words *yavana* and *yonaka*, shortened to *yona* or *yon* in Sinhala (Tamil: *cōṉakar*). *Yon* has been a name used for Muslims for several centuries in Sri Lanka, but it was not always so. In the early days of Buddhism spreading into Central Asia and Persia, the term *yavana* denoted someone from the west.[92] Some historians romantically translate the term as "Greeks." More likely, *yavana* Buddhists belonged to emporia of Central Asia, like Balkh and Bamiyan in Afghanistan. B. E. Perērā, perhaps the first to reflect on the floating signifiers that led to the common poetic line about "the right sacred sole on the sands of Mecca" (*dakuṇu siripatula makkama välleya*), described the original *yona* as "the mountainous province between India and Afghanistan, the Syr Darya and Amu Darya river valleys of Afghanistan, and some parts of Persia belong to this Yona region."[93] The presence of a Buddha footprint in "Yonakapura" is commemorated through its mention in the Pali *gāthā* recited when a *śrīpāda* is worshiped in Lanka, words that are affixed to the Peak's summit on an inscribed plaque:

yaṃ nammadāya nadiyā pulineca tīre	On the sandy bank of the Narmada River,
yaṃ saccabaddha girike sumanācalagge	atop the Saccabaddha and Sumana mountains,
yaṃ tattha yonakapure muninoca pādaṃ	and in the city of Yonaka is the Sage's foot.

taṃ pādalāñchanamahaṃ sirasā namāmi.	I bow my head to those footprints.

Yet Yonakapura became a malleable figural space as those from the west changed. With merchant ships captained by Arabs, *yon* came to mean Muslim, *yonaka* Arabia, and *yonakapura* Mecca. This shift in signification surely went unrealized by pilgrims singing of the Buddha in Mecca, confident in the historical depth of their mytholith as it grew around a Pali *gāthā* inherited over generations. The story solidified until Mecca balanced Samanala like right does left:

> The right-side foot being established in Mecca
> In Lanka, the left foot going to Samanala
> The group of gods today having shown up worshiping
> Having gone through Pavanella, worshiping the sacred foot.[94]

Some Buddhist poets, however, more actively used the Meccan footprint against Muslims. For example, this 1902 pilgrimage poem, *Abhinava Himagata Varṇanāva* (Modern praise of Himagata):

> The right foot placed at Mecca is for the Tambi to go to worship.
> They go together every day without a teacher.
> God Saman bless the teachers who go observantly.
> God Saman bless those accompanying the teachers.[95]

The tone here is decisively derisive, the term for Muslims being the diminutive *tambi*, literally meaning "little brother" in Tamil, often used with the intent to offend.[96] The pronoun "they" in the second line is also the lowly *un*, and the overall message insults. The Buddha not only placed a footprint at Mecca, but Muslims also lack the religious instruction to properly revere it. The word for "teacher" in this instance, *guru*, also means a leader of a pilgrimage group, and, considering such poems were sung, there is a good chance this verse was meant to fall on Muslim ears at the Peak.

But not all Buddhist visions of Mecca were negative. Other mytholith facets used Mecca in a manner not necessarily meant to insult. It became part of world geography in Sinhala literature, and, by association with the Buddha's footprint, Mecca was imbued with ritual power, too. It remained a figural space in this sense, but one worthy of being invoked in poetry sung during rituals, especially ceremonies dedicated to various Buddhist deities.

Sorcerous Seafarers and Meccan Might

The traditional pilgrimage verses in *Purāṇa Himagata Varṇanāva* and the modern ones in *Abhinava Himagata Varṇanāva* share a coincidence aside from Mecca mentions: both invoke the god Devol Deviyo.[97] Although his main shrine is on the southwest coast at Sīnigama, his cultural range extends to the Sabaragamuwa hills. Some origin stories settle Devol in the Samanala forest, the Peak even sighted from sea to navigate to shore: "Having seen that Saman Siripā enthusiastically/Having beheld, the ship turned to go at the spot."[98] The appearance of Devol in *Himagata Varṇanāva* poems is likely related to this Samanala link, and Mecca also happens to be part of his mythic profile. When Obeyesekere studied the cult in the late twentieth century, the homeland of Devol Deviyo had become a figural space in India, ambiguously named, "impersonal and generalized."[99] Nineteenth-century manuscripts, however, record more details on Devol, showing several different origins amalgamated around a single deity. The most diverse crew to reach Lanka appeared in *Devel Alaṃkāraya* (Devel decoration), or *Devel Upata* (Devel origin), a poem extant in two palm-leaf versions.[100] These gave the longest background myth for Devol gods, describing seven princely merchants sailing seven ships with motley crews, including "Yon-pura foreigners," which implies Muslim settlers.[101] Even when Yon-pura was unmentioned, Devol poetry often invoked Mecca:

> Proceeding to the island of Lanka having seen every country
> Proceeding having worshiped Mecca and Kälaniya.[102]

> When proceeding amid the Lankan island Sinhala
> Worshiping Mecca and Samanala to come.[103]

Mecca worship continued in the Devol cult Obeyesekere studied. At commencement of a fire-trampling rite, the god announced: "I have looked toward Mecca, toward Kälaniya, toward the peak of the sacred footprint." Obeyesekere conjectured that "secondhand descriptions of minarets and domes in Arab cities must have led to the notion of the great *dagaba* of Mecca."[104] Obeyesekere also claimed some Buddhists began to pray facing the direction of Samanala after observing this habit of Muslims toward Mecca; both practices are preserved in the myths of Devol Deviyo.

Mecca thereby became a place of power in Sinhala imagination, suited to the ritual work of Devol: cursing, protecting, and healing of illnesses brought on by *yakka* influence. This broad range of literature had many more Mecca mentions, the site commemorated during poetic mantra recitations:

> The *yaku* from upon the rock of the universe challenged the
> Sage King.
> I burn the house where the *yakka* army dwells. The rice basket
> quickly dedicated
> for the footprint of Buddha, who pressed the sacred foot at
> Mecca and Samanala,
> by the command put forward by Kassapa Buddha, for this dance
> festival.[105]

Mecca and Samanala are positive here, both spaces of Buddha presence helping to control *yakkas*, sanctioned by a prior Buddha. Verses invoking Mecca and Samanala together appear in several manuscripts of *yakka* literature,[106] but Mecca alone is also powerful enough to open incantations.[107] The Buddha's visit there evoked defeat of *yakkas*: "On the day that the Sage proceeded to Mecca, the *yakku* in the outer universe were quaking."[108] Mecca thereby helped humans command *yakkas* by virtue of recalling the Buddha. Gods controlling *yakkas* likewise received power by following the Buddha's footsteps, visiting the same locales he did, including Mecca. This was the case with minor gods like Ilandāri Deviyo, who rode a white buffalo, tossed elephants, and broke necks in the forest, a fierce foe of *yakkas*. Ilandāri traveled to receive exorcistic authority:

> Mecca, Mahiyangaṇa, on the peak of the Samanala mountain
> summit
> All the gods residing, having looked after beings of the three
> worlds
> Subduing all *yakka* armies and proceeding
> Circumambulating dancing, going and coming on the journey.[109]

By dancing around a triad of Buddha-touched sites, Ilandāri gained the power to control *yakka* armies. Another foreign deity, a Malvara chief of western India, likewise traveled to Mecca before landing in Lanka.[110] Meanwhile, the god Upulvan had Mecca listed among his shrines, which also included Samanala and its nearby Divā Guhāva cave.[111] Mecca even worked its way into lists of the *solosmahasthana*, or sixteen sacred Buddhist sites.[112]

Occasionally, the positive or negative significance of the Mecca footprint was unclear. Consider its appearance in the corpus of God Kaḍavara:

> Take the beautiful gold-colored shining four-faced sword.
> Come and guard in the shade of the Mecca sacred foot lotus.
> Offerings laid in the mendicant bag as people look to bring
>   tribute,
> proceed, godling, with majesty for protecting all beings.
>
> Lacking everything, Kaḍavara shook the garment.
> Departing on the naughty journey, he caused mischief.
> Having bowed the head to the Mecca sacred foot,
> Kaḍavara blessed all spirits.[113]

The first verse imagined ritual in Mecca, Kaḍavara guarding the footprint while ascetics begged and people brought offerings. The second quatrain had a more mischievous Kaḍavara, still near the Meccan footprint, but worshiping it as a precursor to his power. Another double use of Mecca came in a *Bali Sanniya* poem, each *sanniya* demon representing an illness to banish:

> The Buddha who went to Mahiyangana and Mecca
> brought about glorious *moksha* comfort for beings.
> . . .
> Their gaze rumbling around the universe
> Issuing forth ferocious flames of fire
> Laying hands on the Mecca sacred foot
> Cackling *sanniya* takes away the offerings.[114]

The first verse makes the familiar move of linking Mecca positively in the network of sites the Buddha visited. The second verse, however, is more ambiguous. Like the other *sanni yaku* in this song, the cackling *sanniya* takes his offerings at the end of the verse. Yet why is the creature in Mecca first? Is laying hands on the Meccan footprint an act of worship or defilement? It is significant that this occurs at a footprint site outside Lanka, making Mecca more ominous as a figural nefarious space where hysterical *yakkas* dwell.[115]

The Buddhist-Mecca mytholith is therefore double-edged. In its lighter facets, some Mecca mentions are positive enough that they may have been appreciated by Muslims. Sinhala folktales describe Muslims attending *yaktovils*—a form of nighttime entertainment they could visit due to their familiarity with nocturnal travel for mercantile careers. In one story, a Muslim even apprenticed with a *yakaduru* exorcist.[116] Muslims still patronize divine healing shrines, sharing rituals in an "everyday pluralism, usually lived below the radar."[117] There is, however, more evidence for the darker side of the mytholith, its cutting edge deriding foreigners. Devol Deviyo as enacted in Obeyesekere's observations was a comic character of ribaldry through his foreignness:

DEVOL: Ah *gala gala* . . . [unintelligible gibberish] I have looked toward Mecca, to Kälaṇiya, to the Peak of the Sacred Footprint, I look at the whole country and *sitōsē renavā*.

DANCER: What's that, ha ha, what did you say? ha! ha!

DEVOL: I look at the whole country and *sitōsē renavā* ["I shit with pleasure"].

DANCER: No no, not *sitōsē renavā*, but *sri lanka dvīpete enava* ["I come to Sri Lanka"]

This type of verbal error goes on . . . Devol also feigns a Tamil accent.[118]

As Mecca appeared in poems about the fraught assimilation of foreigners, it developed Tamil associations. Muslims were conceptually linked in Tamil narratives to coastal populations like the Mukkuvar fisher caste,[119] and such identities were succinctly collapsed in Sinhala poems that portrayed riverside villages with "Muslims (*yon*), Mukkaru, and vile Tamils living."[120] Mecca is likewise linked with Tamil in the corpus of ritual texts for the goddess Pattini. One composition trades verses in Sinhala and Tamil, with one line in Tamil inquiring *makkama pō il*—"didn't you go to Mecca?"[121] Another piece of the Pattini corpus put this South Indian–Muslim–Mecca–Tamil–faceted mytholith to work. The poem called *Pataha* deals with the trope of the rotten king, using public labor for frivolity rather than welfare, with *Pataha* referring to royal ponds, but "which literally means 'pit.' The term itself is contemptuous and derogatory, signifying the public attitude to such works."[122] The story is set in South Indian Pandyan lands where workers from around the world are summoned, including Muslims:

> The rough and rugged Pandyans and Maruttu of the great Mecca country
> And which country, the great famous countries of Gauda and Licchavi under Muslims
> And to this country, the great group of Muslims of Mecca came from country to country
> The great being with massive tusks [brought] to serve for this pit.[123]

By this point in the poem, many Indian peoples have been named, from Bengal, Kalinga, Kashmir, Oddisa, Madura, as well as across the sea, from Burma (*aramaṇa*) and Malaysia (*javika*). Yet the Mecca mention is not necessarily because workers came from Arabia. Rather, it describes South Indians, Pandyans and Maruttu, whose Muslimness represents Mecca in India. Paranoid about multiplying Muslims, the poet mentions two old North Indian Buddhist realms: the Licchavi, Buddhist patrons and relic possessors, as well as Gauḍa, a region near Bengal that was a capital of the Buddhist Pala dynasty. Spaces famous from earlier Buddhists now fell under Muslim jurisdiction (*yon pahaḷa*), cause for consternation to the poet, who portrays it as part of a pattern around the world. Muslim hegemony is said to stretch from south to north, but at least they brought an elephant to help dig the pit.

Sharing Work Songs

While Sinhala stories present conceptual conglomerations of Tamils, Muslims, and Mecca, there are also Lankan Muslims who primarily speak Sinhala. They settled as small groups in the interior, separated from coasts where Muslim traded and literature flourished in Tamil. Highland Muslim farmers likely joined Buddhist neighbors in important agricultural events, singing similar sorts of Sinhala quatrains. In 1959, M. B. Mohamed Ghouse went hunting in the hills for vestiges of Sinhala Muslim folksongs. He met a farmer in his seventies in a village on the edge of Harispattuva, an area with 4,239 Muslims to 25,201 Buddhists in 1891.[124] According to Ghouse, the farmer learned the songs from his mother, dating them to at least the nineteenth century. The farmer admitted he had forgotten much over the decades, wistful for a fading tradition. The few verses Ghouse recorded were on a topic to which farmers of any religion could relate:

> God Allah, yours is the secret of the world.
> All that, the poor farmer will remember through verse.
> All assets will take cover in the shade and rain.
> If thou do not give that to the world, the *sangha* will wither in suffering.[125]

Ghouse tried to erase the Buddhist vocabulary in his own translation, rendering *saňga* as "mankind," and putting the Sinhala word in scare quotes within the original quatrain. There is no need for fear, though. Why should a Sinhala-speaking Muslim farmer, perhaps in a land-tenure agreement where he participated in annual Buddhist rituals, not consider himself part of a larger Lankan *sangha*, subject to the same suffering (*dukina*) as everyone else? This Muslim sang in an idiom Buddhist neighbors understood, sharing hopes for aqueous prosperity.

There are certainly instances when Buddhist and Muslim farmers were likely to have cooperated closely, especially during seasonal events like the plowing and repairing of fields, and their sowing, reaping, and threshing. As bullocks were essential, Muslim involvement was likely. During threshing, grain was heaped upon a chalk diagram with depictions of agricultural tools, which were elegized in verse like "the rake brought from Samanala."[126] The Peak's hydrological role made it suitable for invocation in a fertility circle's auspicious marks for high crop yields. In verses on such occasions, footprints also found mention, as in an incantation after all the grains were husked, sung atop the paddy pile:

makkama siripāda usaṭa	As high as the Mecca sacred foot
samanala siripāda usaṭa	As high as the Samanala sacred foot
ihala velē tibena bätat	The paddy in the upper fields
pahala velē tibena bätat	The paddy in the lower fields
aṭukoṭuvala tibena bätat	The paddy in lofts and barns
äda puravan mē kamataṭa.[127]	Drawn to fill this threshing floor.

Another variation of this song was recorded, encouraging grain to be stacked as high as the "great shrines" (*maha veherea*) of Samanala, Mecca, Kälaṇiya, and Ruvanväli, again drawing Mecca closer to Lankan pilgrimage sites with Buddha relics.[128]

Imagine a Muslim farmer who had just walked his bullock over the paddy straw, helping thresh grain for his village. When the song was sung, what did he make of Mecca? Buddhist vocabulary would not necessarily exclude Islamic resonances.[129] The *maha vehera* of Mecca may have made perfect sense to highland Muslims unlikely to leave the island for their own hajj pilgrimages, whose only basis of comparison for such a place was the large shrines of Buddhist neighbors. In threshing songs, as well as some *yakka*-ritual verses, the Buddha was not actually specified as the Meccan footprint author. Assuming it was the Buddha seems obvious in a Buddhist-majority context, but how would a Muslim threshing paddy have understood it? After all, there *are* footprints in Mecca allegedly left by Abraham. If the Muslim farmer knew this, perhaps Ibrahim's *pāda* came to mind when he heard Sinhala songs about Mecca.

For paddy patrons who never sailed the seas, Mecca was a figural space for Buddhist and Muslim farmers alike. This, however, should not romanticize farmers as harmonious in blissful ignorance. Sinhala farming verses could also use Mecca critically, as in a quatrain of *neḷum kav*, or "plucking poetry," sung during harvests:

> At all countries' ports having submitted, [they] will live by trading.
> Approaching boats, ships, sloops, and sampan paddling, they come having seen the port.
> Desiring to get ahead without merit guards were posted at both Mecca and Samanala.[130]

As in the *Pataha* poem, Muslims are cast as invasive. With Samanala and Mecca as opposite poles of the ocean that they jealously guard, Muslim merchants settle every point in-between to advance economically. These traders' aspirations are portrayed as lacking the same meritorious motivations of Buddhists, suggesting Muslims are poor caretakers of the sites they deem sacred. Therefore, the extent to which poetry could create communal unity certainly depended on the communities themselves, and what verses they chose to sing at work.

Comparisons can thus be drawn between Sinhala uses of Mecca, and Arabic and Persian depictions of the Peak. While the previous section showed a general trend of the Peak transforming into a literal place when firsthand reports and geographic precision improved, the same intellectual history did not shape the Sinhala literary tradition. Certain texts did have expansive visions of the world, like the seventeenth-century *Rājāvaliya*, which categorized countries of the world into Buddhists and non-Buddhist, "Yonaka" included among the latter.[131] Yet, without the travelogue genre in Sinhala that existed in Arabic and Persian, such places often remained only names of figural realms. A *pataha*-myth manuscript, for example, cited over thirty places around India from which workers were drawn to the pit/pond, but the two names of farther places—Makkama and Paraṅgi, Mecca and Portugal—were the only ones doubled in figural fashion, reappearing in the list as *mahā makkama* and *mahā paraṅgi*.[132] Mecca and other distant places overseas remained metaphorically malleable. This flexibility has continued, leading to a recent radical reinterpretation of Mecca mentions.

Shifting the Sands: Erasing Adam's Peak and Buddha's Mecca

In June 2014, I caught a bus from the Colombo Pettah neighborhood. As I boarded, I met a young Muslim man, dress shirt tucked in jeans, black beard neatly kept beneath black-rimmed glasses. He struck up a conversation in English, explaining he was an Islamic banker in the city for few days on business. We discussed Lankan Islam for twenty minutes or so as the bus inched down a packed road. I asked about Adam's Peak. He smiled nostalgically. He had been there once for fun, with classmates after his college degree. But do Muslims still go for religious reasons? No, he didn't think so, just for fun. If I met some Sufis, he suggested, I might find belief in Adam's footprint, but almost all Lankan Muslims are Sunni now, he said, and do not subscribe to such myths.

That August, I met a friend hanging out with old college buddies. About seven of us drank beer and ate *kottu roṭi* outside an electronics shop one owned. The group was a mix of Buddhist and Catholic men in their late twenties and early thirties. One Catholic said he climbed Sri Pada, and, although it was the Buddha's footprint there, he prayed up there, too, no problem. He told me that "generally, the people in Lanka get along, but sometimes a few people cause problems." His companions concurred that Muslims could not really be part of a Sinhala country because they never mixed to the extent where they would join us drinking and chatting on the roadside. Reflecting on these bookends to a summer that also brought the largest anti-Muslim pogrom since 1915, I wondered: How had Islamic significance of the Peak disintegrated, and how had Muslims de-integrated from Sinhala sociality?

Loving and Leaving Adamic Ancestry

A great unraveling of religious integration accompanied the British 1870 Service Tenures Ordinance, which attempted "abolition of predial serfdom in the Kandyan provinces."[133] It allowed the tenants of temple lands to commute services into a monetary fee based on acreage, cash now the organizing sign for all, down to one-hundredth of a rupee. This altered the logic of the religious landscape, as Muslims living on temple lands could forgo festival services for an annual fee.[134] Religious revivals in Colombo added concepts to validate this dismantling of reciprocal religious patronage. Muslim leaders adopted the label "Moor" in discourses of ethnology and race in the British empire.[135] By claiming their religion as an ethnicity, they dissociated from Tamils, who increasingly met with scorn from Sinhala political factions. Muslims tried to placate the Sinhala majority, especially after the pogrom of 1915, which crept even to the Peak: "Also tried a case against looters of a boutique at Eratne halfway up the Peak and in a most inaccessible spot. The fact that the idea of looting reached this out of the way spot shows the care with which the anti-moorish riots were organised. . . . evidence was sufficient to convict and the two accused local boutique-keepers—rivals to the moormen—were sentenced."[136] Economic discontents and mercantile rivalries began to bleed into identity discourse and political action that carried a specter of violence.[137] Muslims became accordingly cautious.

While Colombo elites modified Muslim identity for their own political ends, some mytholithic tools they used had wide appeal, including claims of Adamic ancestry. Stories of Adam reverberated around the world. The idea of Adam's exile in Serendib entered the mythos of Malay Islam, becoming a theme in writings of Malays living in Lanka.[138] The primordial man was also conceptually important for South Indian Muslim identity. Although many dated their arrival to the time of the Prophet Muhammad, the Sufi revivalist Sayyid Muhammad al-Kirkari (1816–1898) went even further by using Adamic deep time. In the ninth chapter of his Arabic *Minḥatu Sarandīb Fī Mawlidil Habīb*, he describes a journey to Lanka in 1878, where, beholding its beauty and prosperity, he became convinced it was blessed with the bounties of Allah. Sayyid Muhammad thus hypothesizes that Arabs made pilgrimage to the Peak for over a thousand years before the birth of the Prophet Muhammad on account of its association with the Prophet Adam.[139] This was echoed by Aptuṟ Ṟahīm in a 1957 book on Tamil Muslim literature:

> Cherished by those who research world books on legendary lands and by others, in the history of Islam in this Tamil country, my sacred motherland, is the golden footprint with which the first man Adam stepped from heaven into the human world. Called "Sarandip" [*carantīp*] by Arab historians, originally being a place in Tamil country, now in Lanka, is that great mountain where, for worship of the one Supreme God hereafter, the noble sacred prophet, that first man, first stepped. Today, with the beautiful name Adam's Mountain [*ātammalai*], the land provides a view of the cone pinnacle extending with great wonder and majesty.[140]

Ṟahīm uses the mythic fame of the Peak and its footprint to claim the Peak as an originally Tamil site, keeping with those who posited a wide swath of ancient territory to the Tamil homeland, including old ocean-swallowed continents.[141] Ṟahīm thereby participated in Tamil-language devotion in order to make Islam native to the Tamil country, transforming it from an adopted foreign practice into the original link Tamil people had with divinity and their mother tongue.[142]

Another appearance of Adam's Peak in Islamic revival came with Ahmad Arabi (1841–1911), an Egyptian revolutionary exiled to Ceylon in 1882, where he inspired local Muslim reform.[143] In 1887, a *Baltimore Sun* reporter met the exile:

"He and his fellow-exiles are said to find much consolation in their captivity in the old Mohammedan belief that Adam and Eve made this island their home after they were turned out of Paradise. He . . . seldom sees any of his own countrymen. . . . Those who do reach here are pilgrims on their way to Adam's Peak."[144] An American on his own pilgrimage, Moncure Daniel Conway (1832–1907), also emphasized the Adam idea in his meeting with Arabi:

> I alluded to the Moslem tradition that Ceylon was selected as the place of Adam's exile, its beauty being some compensation for the loss of Paradise, and expressed the hope that he, Arabi, also found its charms some mitigation of exile. I saw his face brighten. . . . He went on with rapidity to describe how . . . Adam had come to Ceylon. . . . I could not gather clearly whether he shared the notion that the huge oblong mark on Adam's Peak is Adam's footprint. He was willing, I think, to surrender that footprint to Buddha.[145]

Conway thereby documents Arabi's enthusiasm for the Adamic myth of the Peak. In Arabi's retelling, Adam eventually got to leave the island, perhaps reflecting his own hopes. The Arabi-Adam link was likewise drawn in a propaganda poem called *Arābi Haṭana* (Arabi's war), written in Sinhala to praise British victory in the Anglo-Egyptian War. The poet claimed Arabi accepted exile in Ceylon for its Adamic history:

> Amid this ancient world lived that teacher Ādam; good
> God's command disobeyed, it is said he came to this Lanka,
>   delightful.
> Facts about that put into words in that Muslim religious book the
>   Koran.
> Knowing that fact well—Ahamat Arābi Pāsātum.
>
> Without a single "*hāram*" thing in this Sinhala country in the
>   past, nothing
> about an account of Adam's living were we aware.
> Though it is in the Koran book, about that on this day, friend,
> let us not speak a single clarification of his way of truth.
>
> To live in this beautiful Lanka, Ahamat Arābi at that time
> desired with his friends, remembering Ādam always.[146]

This poet was ignorant of Islam, misattributing the Adam story to the Quran and rejecting its veracity, but he left a record of how Lanka's Adamic significance could inform not only the perspectives of the exile, but also the side that did the exiling. It is unknown if Arabi ever climbed on pilgrimage after arriving in Lanka, but his mere exilic presence there made locals and foreigners draw comparisons that Arabi himself encouraged. Adam's Peak in this sense was a globally pliant marker of Muslim identity.

Adam was also used in identity battles of Lankan Muslims. In his 1907 rejoinder to a claim that Muslims were Tamils, I. L. M. Abdul Azeez wrote of early Arab settlers: "This Island had many attractions for them. It is the place where their primitive father, Adam, was when he obtained the forgiveness of God for the sin of disobedience committed by him, and where the mountain, which bears his footprint, and which for that reason is visited by Muslims from time immemorial, stands."[147] By invoking the "primitive," along with "time immemorial," Azeez expanded Muslim claims on the island to creation. The myth of Adamic deep time lent Azeez a temporally broad argument, familiar to European colonial consciousness, and all classes of Muslims.

Adam's Peak was also linked with other Lankan Muslim landmarks, like the Dewatagaha mosque in Colombo. In 1820, when the area was covered with cinnamon trees, an oil trader was traveling in the forest; she tripped over a root and smashed her pot, spilling her wares. Awash in despair at losing her means of sustenance, she wept until she fell asleep. An old man dressed in green promised her new oil if she brought a new pot. His foot pressed the ground, causing new oil to bubble up, and he told the woman to spread the tale. A group returned and prayed to know the identity of the saint, but no revelation came until Sheikh Ali Jabbarooth Moulana arrived from Maghreb in 1847. Learning of the Dewatagaha miracle, he went after Friday prayers and knelt there, shrouding himself with his robe and communing with the saint's spirit until he emerged, face alit, and proclaimed: "Oh Almighty Allah, this is a most venerable saint. His name is Seyed Usman Siddiq Ibn Abdurahman, one who came to this island on a pilgrimage to Adam's Peak and after living in the vicinity for some time, died here."[148] The shrine soon grew into a mosque, patronized by Hindu and Muslim businessmen. Today in a tangled intersection of Colombo, Dewatagaha is still visited by passersby of all religions, who drop coins in the till or light lamps for the saint.

The mosque's story outlines the stages of nineteenth-century Lankan Muslim identity. The mosque was discovered in a manner similar to other Lankan folktales of forest revelation, where a period of unconsciousness precedes divine boon, at the foot of a tree, another divine trope. In fact, an etymology of Dewatagaha is *devata* meaning "godling," and *gaha* meaning "tree." Later, when the saint was named, the narrative became more aligned with exclusively

Muslim identities. Links to perceived authentic places of Islam were emphasized, with a Maghrebi visitor identifying the saint's point of origin as Arafat in Arabia. These global connections were then localized through prominent places of Lankan Muslim pilgrimage—Sheikh Usman came to see Adam's footprint on the famous Peak, and also visited the Dafther Jailani rock shrine.[149]

In the 1980s, Lankan Islamic reformist groups took harder lines against the shared signs of multireligious milieus like the Peak. A connectivity of airplanes, television, and the internet caused an influx of international reformist influence. As the number of Lankans laboring on the Arabian peninsula boomed, Muslim wealth and hajj pilgrimage increased. Mecca became less of a figural space, and the Arab identity many Muslims claimed in ethnic discourses was more tangible, reflected in sartorial and architectural changes in Lanka.[150] Reformist groups Jamaat-i-Islami and Tawhid Jamaat, drawing on a Wahhabi ethos, have opposed Sufis in the midst of their own revivals,[151] while Colombo piety movements discouraged common rituals like dropping coins in the tills of deities, instead using the exclusive term *kafir* to brand all non-Muslims as infidels.[152] Meanwhile, the postwar moment has freed reserves of Sinhala prejudice to be directed toward Muslims as the new enemy in place of defeated Tamils.[153]

These changes coincided with Lankan Muslims ritually delinking from the Peak, a relatively abrupt transformation considering the conceptual importance of the mountain and Adam just decades prior. Of course, Muslims have not stopped pilgrimage entirely. I met some during my fieldwork, but their numbers were small compared to Buddhist and Hindu visitors. Many Muslims were foreigners, indicating that the global purchase of the Adam myth persists. Pilgrims came from Tamil Nadu, Bengal, Pakistan, Bangladesh, and Egypt. I also met a fascinating pair from Iraq, devotees named Ali and Muhammad. Muhammad was half-Turkish, a large man with a long and straight black-and-gray beard; he was Ali's spiritual teacher. They were on a mission after a historian's heart. Having closely studied Ibn Battuta's travelogue, they came to find the places he mentioned. They even brought an Arabic copy. Ali and Muhammad were not the first to undertake this task. British visitors had come looking to retrace history, too, but quickly found it impossible to pinpoint most places.[154] Paths changed, as did names. Ali and Muhammad expressed some disappointment at being unable to find the "Gate of Iskandar," but they were pleased I was named Alexander. They were also disappointed by the photography prohibition at the footprint, but Ali took the time to utter a prayer, eyes closed, palms upturned. He said he was impressed with the feeling of power in the place. Accompanying them was a Lankan Muslim from Colombo named Faiz. They were introduced by a travel agency at the airport when the two visitors asked for a Muslim guide. Some Buddhists at the Peak found them curious, asking me where they were from and what they were doing.

In general, I encountered much ignorance about the Islamic history of the Peak. Many non-Muslims told me Muslims believe it is Allah's or the Prophet's footprint. Islamophobia is a product of similar ignorance, born of social isolation intensifying with acts of prejudice in a violent feedback loop of misinformation.[155] Thus, there were also people who would actively resist befriending Muslims. Rowdy boys roamed the trail at night, especially in weekend crowds, making outsiders uncomfortable with rude jokes, whispers, and laughter. Most Muslims I met climbed on weekdays during the daytime, when the crowds were at their lowest. Meanwhile, sartorially marked Muslims usually climbed in large groups of young men, often busloads of students from Colombo on a highland tour. Although he was middle-aged, it was Faiz's first time to the Peak. He said most Muslims preferred the offseason, when they were free to have a better look at things. As we sat chatting over tea in the Matara Kade near the summit, Rukmal came over to join us. His face was earnestly curious, but he was wearing an old army windbreaker, and I noticed Faiz suddenly became more reticent with his words. The conversation quickly shifted from Muslim religiosity toward a mundane chat over modes of employment.

Even when Muslims came in large groups, they did not always find the space comfortable. When I asked one young man what he did at the summit, he said he tried to pray, but felt uneasy about the "Sinhala people" watching. The Peak has become something of a panopticon lately. Installation of CCTV cameras, including over the footprint, with police and sometimes military guards, thickens summit surveillance. Buddhist hegemony also leaves little room for Muslim religious traditions on the mountain, whether they involve visiting the graves of saints, or rituals like those recorded in the nineteenth century: "The fakirs of the Mahomedan religion take impressions of the footstep on a piece of white cloth that has been previously covered with pulverized sander."[156] Any such activity on the footprint would now be forbidden. One modern Muslim author, Manippulavar Maruthur A. Majeed, opined on the loss of plural religious representation on the summit, which he remembered existing as recently as the mid-twentieth century:

> In 1954, when I was a student, I visited this mountain. On this mountain's summit, the mosque [*paḷḷi*] of Muslims, the shrine of Hindus, and the dagoba of Buddhists were seen. At that time, there was a threefold accord of equality [*camaracam*]. Even in 1959, this situation prevailed. In 1975, when I returned

> for a third and fourth time, I could not find the mosque and the Hindu shrine. Also, they had fenced off the footprint so that it could not be seen. The dagoba of the Buddhist people remained there. Muslims still call this mountain Bawa Adam Malai.[157]

This memory matches the timeline outlined by Premakumara De Silva of the transition toward Buddhist hegemony at the Peak, beginning with a key monastic election in 1954.[158] Majeed's account shows that changes were not instantaneous, but the gradual erosion of pluralism proved just as dangerous for religious representation. The solely Buddhist summit that remains still risks further erosion if it totally revokes its welcome to others.

Even Saman, a purported pinnacle of compassion as the bodhisattva god of the Peak, has seen his mytholith weaponized against Muslims. Saman has been adopted by Buddhist extremists who decry deity worship as ignorant and un-Buddhist, but exempt Saman from this. Unlike the foreign gods of Hindus and Muslims, they call Saman "Sinhala Deviyo," a racialized deity for a nationalist religion. Of course, nothing about Saman's mytholith is intrinsically built for anti-Muslim work. Some Muslims in a highland village even equated their saints with bodhisattvas, so "Mohideen Andawer is the same as the Buddhist god Saman Deviyo."[159] Furthermore, in a story recorded in 2013, a seventy-three-year-old Palabaddala villager, Malankandalāya Vijēsēna, recalled how the Saman statue was once being carried to the summit when its bearers became tired and placed the casket on the ground. A ferocious storm whipped up with thrashing winds, rains, and lightning. A local Muslim Berber immediately realized the cause, and, to stop the storm, bathed, donned white clothes, and ran to lift up the casket, although it had become burning hot and was too heavy for one man.[160] Yet some now use Saman to wash Muslims off the Peak with the same mythic mechanism of the Berber story: the god's control over rain. People often had stories of the Peak being purified with deluges. A young woman named Yamuna told me: "The god will cause it to rain. You know the Saman statues at the summit are brought in the procession every year. Well, one year, I saw a full curtain of rain going ahead of the procession. Really. It was washing away all the impurities. It was amazing how different the country looked after the rain." The tenor of most such purification tales is harmless, but, in one instance, the story was refitted for offense. A group of young Muslim men were descending the Peak one afternoon, visiting on a school trip from their *jamaat* in Colombo. They were a striking sight striding down the mountain one after another in matching white kurtas and skullcaps. I sat on the benches outside Chandra's shop as they passed. Some stopped for a break at the spot, and we had a chat. Meanwhile, Chandra continued greeting all the passersby with friendly "*as-salaam-alaikums*." After they left, however, she lowered her voice and said something I did not expect.

"You know whenever a Muslim visits the mountain, the god causes it to rain."

"Really? What's the reason for that?"

"To purify. Because Muslims eat beef, no? Every day they eat so much beef and kill cows. Sinful, no?" A bodhisattva's mytholith was thereby honed into a cutting edge by someone who was otherwise quite kind to everyone who entered her shop, and who told me early in the season that Sri Pada was open to every religion and every race. Such subtle religious prejudice reflects the persistent challenges of pursuing pluralism, for even when friendly accords are struck, human perception still traffics so heavily in stereotype.[161]

But Lankan Muslims continue to be intentional in their pursuit of the Peak. They have not altogether abandoned it despite disincentives for their attendance. Some continue to climb and encourage other Muslims to do so at least once in their lives, as "it is imperative to visit important sites of ethnic unity [*iṉa oṟṟumai*] and Muslim history in Lanka today."[162] The mountain has also been a rhetorical tool of modern authors writing books on Muslim identity in Lanka, who seek to reconcile their minority status on the island with the rich transoceanic history that is part of the greater Muslim community. Books with titles like *From the Middle East to Batticaloa* or *Some Observations on Minorities* contain chapters that cite a plethora of Muslim writers who mention Adam's Peak, including Quran commentators, hadith scholars, geographers, travelers, and more.[163] Like the parade of sources in the first part of this chapter, these are almost entirely Muslims who lived outside Lanka. Nevertheless, their writings on the presence of the first prophet on the mountain lent an important imprimatur of Islamic identity to the island. Such writings have continued into the twenty-first century. While I was busy climbing up and down the Peak in February 2016, a Tamil weekly newspaper called *Ceylon Muslim* published its first issue, connected to the news website with the same name. The publication included an article called "The First Print of the World in the Island of Ruby," once again running the gamut through Muslim testimonies about Adam in Serendib, with appearances by Ibn Abbas, Ibn Khordadbeh, Ibn Battuta, and more.[164] The Peak thus remains a landmark of Lankan Muslim selfhood, partly because it deepens their historical ties to the island, and partly because it places them at a center of the Muslim world.

An interesting visual example of this dual global and local identity was produced among the Muslim community living nearest the mountain in Maskeliya. It comes in the form of a devotional poster made by Kalibha M. Jalaludheen (fig. 3.2).[165] The Peak and its footprint stand prominently at the center of

FIGURE 3.2. Kalibha M. Jalaludheen's devotional poster of the Peak
Nationaal Museum van Wereldculturen, Leiden

the image, which functions as a novelty map of the pilgrimage route on the Hatton side of the mountain, not drawn to scale or concerned with precision in its placement of landmarks. Tea plantation buildings and other landscape features are labeled in English, but the image is bordered on all sides by Arabic calligraphy. Aside from the text in red ink on either side of the summit that mentions Adam, his footprint, and Serendib, the remaining textual fragments along the borders are not specifically about the Peak, but are instead expressions of Islamic piety intelligible to Muslims anywhere in the world. These include the names of the four caliphs, epithets for Allah, Quran quotations, prophetic hadith, lines from a famous benediction by the Persian poet Saadi, as well as mathematical magic squares with auspicious numerology.[166] The image is therefore centered on a definitive Lankan site, but bordered by Islamic elements born beyond the island. Even the very form of the image seems to straddle global and local influences. Is it an homage to the pilgrim certificates with illustrated diagrams of Mecca that had been common among Muslims for centuries?[167] Or is it a Muslim version of similar Buddhist diagrams of the Peak that also circulated in the latter half of the twentieth century, and which are still common on hotel murals and signboards in Nallathanni?[168] Such unknowns are a testament to the multifarious nature of Muslim identity in Lanka, with Muslims able to use the Peak's potency as both a Lankan landmark and a larger Islamic symbol.

Even those Lankan Muslims who have not climbed the Peak find the site important. My Muslim friends in the Colombo Pettah market, young and old, were as curious about and supportive of my research as any interested Buddhist. Some reminded me it was important to mention the Islamic history of the Peak, but they never went as far as those Buddhists who said I should *only* refer to the mountain as Sri Pada, never as Adam's Peak. Such anti-Muslim sentiments also thrive in internet spaces, where commentators complain about news like the world's largest sapphire, discovered in Lanka in 2015, being named the Tear of Adam. A petition to change the Google Maps name from Adam's Peak to Sripadasthanaya followed (it was eventually changed to "Sri Pada/Adam's Peak"). Such digital calls to action can also bleed into real life. In November 2016, fulfilling a call for vandalism on a Sinhala nationalist Facebook page, "Adam's Peak" was blacked out on the painted trilingual trailhead stone in Nallathanni. When the stone was repainted, Adam's Peak did not return. The name of the mountain in English was instead "Sri Pada," which remained the case when a new inscribed plaque replaced the older trailhead stone in 2018. Erasure remains a prerequisite for imposing hegemony.

Remaking Makkama

Buddhist redefinition of the Peak is one of many cases of Sinhala nationalists claiming places in Sri Lanka as exclusively Buddhist, their arguments supported with archeology inherited from Europeans, but charged by Buddhist myth. In cases where sites are shared with Muslims, citizens have been encouraged to produce the past as evidence, as courts arbitrate identity alongside land, opening space for Buddhists to claim identities *for* land and use figural spaces of the past to aid litigation over literal places.[169] As Glenn Bowman notes, "spaces are far more easily 'shared' than places, if sharing is the correct term to use when . . . entities can move past and around each other in space without effecting significant contact. Movement in shared places, however, entails negotiation, commensality, and at times conflict."[170] Even the highly figural space of Mecca in Sinhala literary imagination has continued to be claimed as a Buddhist place by modern monks and laymen, whose arguments are increasingly couched in "evidentiary" language when formulated during interviews, newspaper articles, and propaganda circulated online.[171]

Another camp of Sinhala nationalists, however, has taken an entirely different approach toward the Buddhist Mecca. This occurred among the school of historians who champion Ravana's kingdom as the first advanced civilization in Lanka, complete with airport and intercontinental ballistic missiles.[172] These are exaggerations of a Ravana myth previously promoted by nationalists like John De Silva, who took offense in a 1912 poem at the presence of "a huge flock of these Muslims uniting" at the Peak, decrying them as "not understanding good versus bad" and "ruining the country," showing "hubris with great force" by their presence in "the mansion made to behold God Saman."[173] He therefore sought to rhetorically displace them from Lanka by replacing the Adamic primogenitor with Ravana:

> In this earthly world, the Sage Lord had placed the sacred foot in four places.
> In the Moors' Mecca one foot-lotus form has been placed.
> They say that it is Adam's, the sacred foot hidden due to that error.
> Where in a hundred homes of this Lanka is there an awareness of that?
>
> It is not apparent that Adam was united with his wife on the island.
> If it were like that in this Lanka, it was Ravana who showed those skills,
> making Shem, Ham, and Japeth well, though not appearing in the Bible.
> The good wife does not bite that given fruit in that way.[174]

Although evicting Adam and his ill-mannered wife from Lanka, De Silva kept the Buddhist Mecca myth intact, suggesting Mecca was a foreign place where a Buddha footprint was hidden. In new Ravana myth, however, this Meccan footprint is relocated to Lanka.

A leading voice in the new Ravana field has been Ven. Mänāvē Vimalaratna, who claimed to have obtained a palm-leaf manuscript written in an ancient secret language of the *yakka* tribe. In a 2001 publication, the monk alleged that the Buddha left a footprint for this tribe in Lanka: "It is said in folklore that he placed a print of the sacred foot per request of the *yakka* clan that gathered there. . . . This important place not being directed to the attention of archeology . . . is a shame."[175] As the Ravana-school historiography mimics scholarship, footnoting and invoking archeology, it also makes broad, unsupported, disjointed claims. It prides itself on a counteracademic standard—the key book in the erasure of Buddhist Mecca proclaims on its back cover that the author offers a reading of inscriptions unobtainable from a university education in archeology. This book, *The Right Sacred Buddha Sole Set at Makkama, and King Ravana's Inscriptions*, was written in 2005 by Jayaratna Patiraāracci, who titled himself an "archeological researcher" (*purāvidyā gevişaka*). He picked up Vimalaratna's claim of the *yakka* tribe footprint and argued that "Makkama" in Sinhala texts did not refer to Mecca. If mentioned near a footprint or *vihāra*, Patiraāracci claims, Makkama was a settlement on the northwest coast, near Puttalam. He collected many poetic verses mentioning Makkama, and even constructed a Ptolemaic etymology to create even more evidence of a Puttalam-Makkama connection. He also treated verses about *yakkas* and Makkama as self-evident support of his argument due to Vimalaratna's secret *yakka* chronicle.

Some evidence is logical enough to warrant consideration, from sources outside secret manuscripts. One was *Kōkila Sandēśaya*; when the cuckoo heads north toward Jaffna, passing familiar sites on the coast, the poet mentions a place or places named Attāla Mukkama.[176] Although no present location corresponds to these names, Patiraāracci pressed on and read Mukkama as Makkama in light of another piece of evidence, the *Nam Pota* (Name book), traditionally used as a primer for children learning to write letters. The list of names therein is not fully random, but organized by spatial clusters. Here the names appear as Ättala and Makkama, mysterious toponyms wedged between two of the most familiar locales of the northwest coast: Munneswaram and Mannar.[177] That Attāla or Ättala and Mukkama or Makkama are now locally unknown did not dishearten Patiraāracci: "No one living in this region has heard of a Makkama in the area. That is because no one has studied the history."[178]

Yet no one *can* study history quite like Patiraāracci because so much of his analysis draws from personal fantasy. Citing Buddhist myths in both sensible and non-sequitur fashion, Patiraāracci's past is a figural space where the loss of the Makkama footprint is a national tragedy. In a morbid turn, he suggests that if the tsunami had hit the west coast, it would have unearthed ancient treasures and inscriptions, like the Makkama *vihāra* and footprint, previously buried by Europeans. If Patiraāracci were on Obeyesekere's couch, he would likely be diagnosed with postcolonial trauma, where "an attempt is made by Buddhists to regain their self esteem or self worth; in the process a kind of *reaction-formation* or *overcompensation* has occurred."[179] Overcompensation continued as Patiraāracci elaborated his theory in periodical articles. He made martial myths of Makkama in July 2008, when militarization was at an apex as

Mahinda Rajapaksa's regime began grinding the civil war to an end. Patiraāracci again left wide gaps in his logic when explaining missing Makkama heritage: "Today both these *vihāras* cannot be seen. But . . . the day the giant Dādhāsēna came to the seacoast along Colombo to leap to India, there was a . . . Bōdhi. . . . The Bōdhi met in the tale is the Bōdhi near the modern Kalpiṭiya naval camp. The Makkama Vihāra was a *vihāra* with caves. These caves were broken and smashed by the Dutch. Today, inside the naval camp, the caves that belong to Makkama Vihāra can be seen underground."[180] Patiraāracci leapt from the figural space of Dādhāsēna's seacoast to the literal place of a specific tree outside the Kalpiṭiya naval camp, his imagination the only conduit. The rest of his evidence lay buried beneath nationalist military might, cave remnants in naval-base basements being just as inaccessible to the public as secret *yakka* chronicles.

To support his cave claim, Patiraāracci cited two lines of another Makkama verse:

u ḍa ma uḍama väḍa makkama vä	llē	Going upward and upward on the Mecca sands
va si na vasina väsi ē gala pa	llē	Raining raining rain beneath that rock
du va na duvana näv samudura ē	llē	Running running ships straight on the sea
api t padimu dän ran onci	llē.[181]	We, too, row now on the gold swing.

Patiraāracci took the first two lines as referencing the Makkama footprint and *vihāra* rock caves, ignoring the context of the poem, an *oncillā* (swing) folksong. Swing games (*oncillā keḷi*) were performed at festivals such as new-year celebrations, with massive swings constructed so eight people were able to row together.[182] Mecca in this instance, sung while swinging, should be read with some levity, analogous to children today swinging themselves to the moon, a faraway figural space. It is also rhymes well, the syllables of *makkama* allowing a bouncy internal beat in the opening line—*ḍa ma ḍa ma vä, ḍa ma ka ma vä.* Patiraāracci, however, had no reticence about overdeterministic readings. Even if it was a swing song, that made no difference; everyone else simply did not study it correctly.

However baseless Patiraāracci's points, his Makkama mytholith grew. The book came with many endorsements, including eleven introductions by teachers, monks, and government education officials praising his research, and Ravana historians generally, as a triumph for Sinhala history and nation. With public approval comes mythic repetition. The internet provides a catalyst for replacing Mecca with Makkama at a speed much accelerated compared to the centuries it took the Buddhist Mecca mytholith to grow, "as freedom of access to information through the internet has given myth-makers an unprecedented capacity to disseminate augmented narratives and images."[183] Digital copies of Patiraāracci's books are shared, he repeats his points whenever he is given forums for publication, and his articles are copied on Facebook pages, forums, blogs, and Sinhala Wikipedia.[184]

Amid its repetition, Patiraāracci's theory found an unusual ally—the Muslim reformist group Sri Lanka Tawhid Jamaat (SLTJ). Countering the Islamophobic edges of a Buddhist-Mecca mytholith, SLTJ found Patiraāracci's argument to be a safer haven for Makkama interpretation, endorsing it at a meeting in Colombo.[185] The event was part of the SLTJ series of community talks titled *Islām hăňdinvīmak*—"An Introduction to Islam."[186] Its trilingual banner held descriptions for different audiences. In Sinhala, it read: "An Introduction to Islam: Question and Answer Session." In English: "Islam is an Excellent way of Life: Question and Answer." The Tamil title between the Sinhala and English, however, assumed its reader was Muslim, proclaiming "Islam is a sweet religion" (*islām or iṉiya mārkkam*). It is not clear how many non-Muslims attended. Over 150 men came, from teenagers to middle-age, and only a fraction were obviously Muslim by clothing or beards. At the far end of the hall, about two dozen women sat in full niqab dress, looking after children.

The main speaker at "Introduction to Islam" events, always held in Sinhala, has been Brother R. Abdur Rāsik, chief secretary of SLTJ and a prominent young face in the group, short beard neatly trimmed, hair parted in the middle, clothed in Western dress shirts. He is not a firebrand preacher, but a calm articulate intellectual. At the "Introduction to Islam" in 2013, where the Makkama issue was addressed, the question of whether *makkama vihāra* referred to Mecca seemed orchestrated, read off paper, and Rāsik's answer was clearly prepared, notes consulted throughout. Rāsik cited all major sources in the argument for relocating Makkama, including the *sandēśa* poem, Vimalaratna's secret *yakka* manuscript, the *Nam Pota*, and so on. Rāsik did mention Adam's descent to earth, but neither the Peak nor Lanka were included as part of this. Adam's function in the answer was to provide the correct Muslim history of Mecca, in which Adam originally built the Kaaba, later rebuilt by Abraham. The implied settlement of Rāsik's answer seemed "to each his own," where Muslims renounce association with the Peak, and Buddhists leave Mecca to Muslims, keeping Makkama as a Lankan site.

At first glance, it seems obvious why Muslims, facing continued claims on Mecca by Buddhist extremists, would be ready to endorse erasure of Buddhist

Mecca and abandon Adam's Peak. Forfeiting this history has little cost for SLTJ, which looks to a global *ummah* for religious standards. Yet Brother Rāsik might reconsider if he read Patiraāracci's book closely, as its darker agendas lie hidden in endnotes. Repositioning Mecca as Makkama is not only about nationalizing Sinhala literature; Patiraāracci also expresses interest in claiming literal land of the northwest. He tagged a note on his sentence about the people in the area being ignorant of history, making clear who they were—Muslim devotees, with a mosque on land Patiraāracci said was historically a Buddhist site. Another note had a picture of said mosque, making the target more visceral, a real threat in a country where dismantling Muslim shrines is done with expert efficiency.[187] With a new Makkama-edged mytholithic tool, Patiraāracci erased Mecca to vanish Muslims. This made his west-coast tsunami wish even more macabre: he was seemingly willing to sacrifice non-Buddhist residents for more Buddhist history.

Aside from warning people about endnotes, how else can conventional academics critique the Ravana school? Though seemingly absurd, it cannot be laughed away, and historicist arguments cannot defeat opponents who wish for nothing more than validation from a debate of "he said, she said."[188] If we are all ultimately mythmakers, then fighting over whose story is more factual, while effective for refutation in, say, a court case about the reality of Makkama, misses the point if seen as a final goal. The truly reflexive critique is to hold out the mytholith in my own hand and compare it with others. Whose tools are being used for construction or destruction? If Ravana historians cannot be met with fact, it is perhaps because they work in affect, Islamophobia feeding off emotion as fuel.[189] So a counter-affective response can be made to say they cleaved their mytholith into too sharp a blade, for its facets encase past violence and reflect it onto the present.

In turn, I turn my mytholith to see myself in it, crystalline structure growing as I write, cut and polished into a gem of mythic signifiers—Makkama, Mecca, Serendib, and al-Rahun in all their beautiful ambiguity overlapping around the Peak. Still, a historicist *yakka* has possessed me some nights, running Patiraāracci's argument through my head, as I wonder if he could be right about all those *makkamas*. To exorcise this, a quatrain from the *upahāsa sähäli* (farcical ballads) genre of Sinhala poetry drew me:

makkama siripā taṁbu	rū	Mecca sacred foot lotus.
okkoma hāmuduruva	rū	All the monks
dan kā̆maṭa itā su	rū	are very clever for eating the offerings.
niruvānē yā̆ma bo	rū.[190]	Entering nirvana is impossible.

The joke is seemingly in the last three lines, with monks being clever for gaming an impossible soteriological system to get free food. I was uncertain if *makkama* in the first line had any significance other than to rhyme with *okkoma*. The more I spoke it, however, the more I began to think the rhyme links the first line with the next three, the "all" of *okkoma* thereby extended to everything in the quatrain. This is anchored by the emphatic final word—*borū*, translated as "impossible," but most literally meaning "lies," a satirical subversion of the Buddhist teaching that nirvana is most true.[191] Did this poet find the Mecca footprint as big a joke as gluttonous monks pursuing enlightenment? Perhaps it was all lies to him, a grain of salt worth taking when facing such a mountain of myth, reminding us of the many manipulations of its stories, and the ethical stakes therein.

4

Admitting and Forbidding Siva at the Peak

Although Buddhist animosity toward Muslims at the Peak is a trend that has intensified over the past century, Saivas have been the more traditional "other" of the Peak in Buddhist narrative. The story of Buddhists and Saivas at the Peak is indeed laced with conflict on occasion, but it is important that sectarian rhetoric not obscure the material realities of coexistence. The physical landscape, for one, has been appreciated by Tamil observers as much as Sinhala ones. The shape of the Peak even inspired one scholar to compare it to the central icon of Saiva worship—the lingam: "Sivanolipadam was considered sacred by the Hindus because it is 'Linga' in shape. The sun worship at the Peak is the traditional sun-Siva worship of the Hindus."[1] Yet a Hindu history of pilgrimage at Civaṉoḷipātamalai, Siva's-Luminous-Foot Mountain, is not so simple to reconstruct. There are few extant texts, and Hindus at the Peak today do not have extensive storytelling traditions about the footprint.

This dearth of everyday stories can be explained without the need to assert a lack of myth. The Peak remains part of a larger mythic picture within highland Hindu religiosity, even among some who do not identify specifically as Saivas. In this chapter, we will also consider those who have addressed the lack of stories by crafting new ones, manufacturing mytholiths in scholarship. Several key Tamil sources about the Peak do exist, though they have been heretofore ignored by historians. These show a history of Saivas using the mountain's landscape and waters as theological devices. In comparison, Sinhala sources show another multi-edged mytholith of collaborative or combative Buddhist representations of Siva and Saivas. However, the ethnographic snapshot at the end of the chapter reveals how much the latter has won out.

When Myths Lack Stories

I first met Sivanasam before the pilgrimage season started in 2015. He was pulling a shirt over his head and tamping down his hair as he stepped out for a morning betel chew. Over the next six months, we passed one another almost every day. He was a Nallathanni native and part-owner of a small shop near the trailhead. Its stalls sold toys, kitchenware, vases, and religious paraphernalia, and its kitchen served one of the best breakfast deals on the trail. Beside the restaurant was a tree, beneath which a small roof had been built. Stone icons marked the spot as a mini *kōvil* (Tamil) or *kōvala* (Sinhala)—a shrine to "Hindu" gods, although often including deities Buddhists venerate, too. This one had a large poster of Saman, adorned with a forehead *tilaka* and turmeric paste. But there was something amiss: the images of the gods on the tiles at the shrine's base were defaced (fig. 4.1).

I asked Sivanasam about this one day and he explained how he and surrounding shop owners had pooled their money to build the small shrine for themselves. Not long after, however, it was vandalized. "Someone from the other religion [*anit āgama*] chiseled and destroyed the faces. It's been like that for two or three years now." Sivanasam did not elaborate on his accusation, but precedent and pilgrim demographics suggested to me that Buddhists were responsible.

This early observation colored the subsequent months I spent at the Peak, counting instances of prejudice over the course of a season. Some Sinhala Buddhists treated Tamil shopkeepers and couriers arrogantly, including once when the Tamil worker was in a position of authority as a summit staff member—a pilgrim responded to a directive by disdainfully badgering him with the question, "Are you Tamil?" Other Buddhists would tell me Tamil people were no good, and accuse them of stealing pieces of infrastructure, like lightbulbs and metal. Some judged the Tamils for being plantation workers. A 1932 Sinhala pilgrimage poem captured this still-present perception of Tamils as an animalistic herd known only for labor, "plucking tender leaves and carrying them on their heads in the tea plantation; behold with both eyes the coming Tamils in the flock."[2] I noticed how most Hindu shrines along the trail near Nallathanni were half-hidden, tucked amid tea bushes, or off-trail behind boulders, perhaps to avoid conflict.

FIGURE 4.1. Vandalized Siva and Parvati tile on the Hatton trail

Indeed, the only obvious Siva shrine on the mountain, just over a hundred meters from the Nallathanni trailhead, had its own history of friction with Buddhists (fig. 4.2).[3] This *kōvil*, originally built in 1998, managed by a priest from a larger *kōvil* in Maskeliya, had to be relocated after its trustees lost a court case in 2011 against Buddhists who wished to build the new Kalpa Vrukṣa

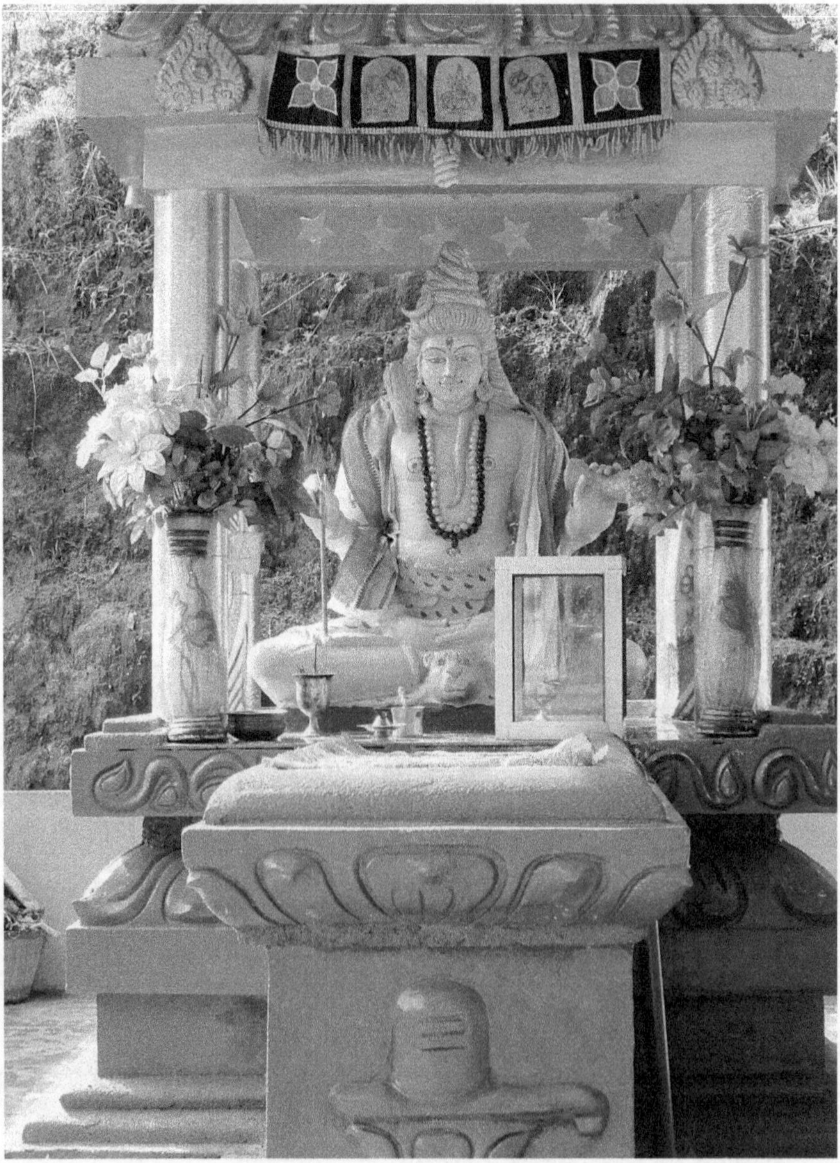

FIGURE 4.2. The trailside Siva shrine

Vihāra on the spot.[4] Land for the new *kōvil*, rebuilt in 2013, was donated by the Maskeliya plantation association. Why did some Buddhists feel they could so freely dismiss Saiva counterparts on the Peak? For some, the issue was one of stories. The Buddhists had the *Mahāvaṃsa*, I was told, which proved their claims were authentic. What book could say the same for Hindus or Muslims? Indeed, the more Tamil people I spoke with, the more I noticed the lack of a popular narrative about how, when, or why Siva had left his footprint.

This was true for Sivanasam, too. When I finally asked him in the last month of the season for a story of how Siva's footprint had wound up on the Peak, he puzzled over it: "Mmmhmm." He took a step back to spit betel juice over his shoulder, continuing: "So that sacred sole is there, no? God Siva's. That leg had been placed there. So we say when we're studying in school, that a leg is a thing like this, no?" he explained gesturing toward his own leg, "but his leg is much longer than this. Having placed the leg there, a red-colored stone appeared in that way. A gemstone. Then there are rocks like this that could have covered that one," Sivanasam said, pointing toward mundane trailside stones. "At that footprint, that is what we can look at freely." Sivanasam's story ended abruptly when a group of descending pilgrims passed and he tried to sell some of his sweetmeats.

Sivanasam had recycled a story that the original footprint, whether left by the Buddha or Siva, was a gemstone, subsequently covered with granite for protection. This showed a common Peak mytholith, available to be picked up and used regardless of religious affiliation. Yet Sivanasam had nothing to say about how, why, and when all this happened, details almost all Buddhist pilgrims told me, often citing a *Mahāvaṃsa* standard.[5] I noticed my own historiographic bias for narrative when I felt I had to draw a story from Sivanasm near the end of my stay, worried about a lack of Saiva accounts. When people actively try to erase Siva off the Peak, however, is it fair to expect robust storytelling with no room to grow? Must all myths make stories?

A man named Ananda Murugan helped me put the relative lack of Saiva stories in perspective. He was a traveling pilgrimage salesman, making the rounds at the Peak from January to March, the months with the heaviest traffic. He was peddling belts because they were easy to transport, but he sold all sorts of goods everywhere. He was originally from Jaffna, and visited home occasionally, but he also had a small flat in Colombo, where he bought his wares. Aside from the Peak, he enjoyed going to pilgrimage sites on the northwest coast, like St. Anne's church in Thalawila, St. Mary's in Madhu, and the Siva *kōvil* in Munneshwaram. Although Ananda Murugan had stories to tell about Saman, and the worldly manifestations of Siva called *muṉi*, who had similar roles as guardian gods, when I asked specifically for a story about Siva leaving a footprint, he came up empty. He only offered a fact that several others had given me, that the footprint from Siva's other leg was in India, in the Himalayas, but then he explained: "There isn't that much of a story. It hasn't been seen. It's indeed the *belief*."

Ananda Murugan's contrast of a story (*katāvak*) versus belief (*viśvāsaya*) is illuminative. While Lankan Tamils have a broad mythic picture of the Peak and Siva's footprint, the corresponding mytholithic tool of storytelling is smaller. There may be many reasons for this. Perhaps it is due to Val Daniels's theory that Tamil Hindu literature approaches the past in terms of general "heritage" instead of the text- and date-specific "history" of Sinhala Buddhists.[6] This would make Hindus at the Peak comparable to other cases where "we see the past manifest in ritual while being absent in narrative or 'historical consciousness.'"[7] Otherwise, a lack of Siva stories may be due to the relative importance of other deities. Although some Tamil families from Nallathanni visit the trailside Siva *kōvil* on occasions like children's birthdays, to daub foreheads with ash, an official priest usually only attends that shrine on pilgrimage-season weekends with more passersby, Buddhist and Hindu, who stop for blessings. Hidden off-trail, however, is a smaller shrine that a priest visited weekly. This is for Rotamuni, a manifestation of Siva's wrathful side, for whom shrines are built on the edges of new Tamil settlements. It seemed the site of greater ritual attention, and the *muṉi* deities overall had a richer storytelling tradition.[8]

It is also questionable how many highland Tamils would even call themselves "Saiva." The *kōvil* in the Nallathanni line-house village, where residents were spending hundreds of thousands of rupees on renovations, was dedicated to the goddess Kannaki, also known as Pattini in Sinhala. Meanwhile, the goddess Mariyamman is even more central to the religiosity of Tamil plantation workers, mythically refashioned to represent their migrations to Lanka and indentured labor there.[9] Additionally, other groups of highland Hindus have developed their own myths of the Peak footprint belonging to Vishnu, worshiping the footprint in a special annual ritual at the discretion of the head Buddhist monk of the Peak.[10] All these factors add up to a reasonable explanation for the absent Saiva mytholith, but other scholars have been left unsatisfied. Considering the importance of historical claims in the political arena of the Lankan nation-state, there is a certain urgency for beliefs to find expression as stories. To this end, some historians have engaged in academic mythmaking, either straining for more substantial Saiva histories of the Peak, or seeking to undermine Siva altogether.

Manufacturing Mytholiths

Mythologist Bruce Lincoln reserves a sphere for scholarship separate from myth, by "the passages that graphically differentiate scholarly prose from that of other genres: the footnotes . . . [which] mark the fact that a scholarly text is not a discourse of free invention, wherein ideological interests escape all controls."[11] It is precisely the footnotes, however, in which scholars become mythmakers par excellence, performing an expertise that legitimates the story being told, outlining the greater framework of thought against which their texts should be read.[12] Scholarly mythmaking in Lanka began in earnest in the British colonial period, when racial government taxonomies determined political groups, and Sinhala and Tamil parties invoked history to argue for rights and representation. A historicist style of scholarship was especially prevalent at the Peak, as the British enhanced the long-standing European fascination with the mountain by chronologically ordering its references, and categorizing classes of pilgrims into competing "claimants" of the footprint.[13]

So when William Skeen compiled his authoritative account of the Peak in 1870, he felt it necessary to craft some sort of narrative about Saiva claims, although a paucity of evidence led to speculative phrasings. Suggesting the story of Siva's footprint at the Peak coincided with South Indian kings invading Lanka, he wrote: "It is reasonable to suppose . . . the oldest probable period from which to date the legend, is that immediately following the invasion of the Solians, A.D. 1023 . . . for all that is known to the contrary." Skeen hypothesized a mythic contagion via shared landscape and similar stories of salvific feet:

> ascetics discovered upon [the Peak] medicinal trees and plants well known to them on the Himalayan ranges, the peaks of which are supposed to be Siva's favorite abodes. . . . As all those whom Siva destines to celestial bliss are said to receive upon their heads the impress of his sacred foot, by an easy process of transition the belief would become prevalent . . . that the footprint upon the mountain . . . was none other than Siva's own. When once such a belief obtained hold upon the Hindu mind, the legend to account for it would speedily be framed.

Despite Skeen's assumption that stories automatically follow belief, he actually had no Tamil sources to cite, and offered the caveat that "many of the most orthodox of the Hindus repudiate the legend and decline to accept the rockmark as a tangible memento of the presence of Siva on the spot."[14] As this was still a less than satisfactory conclusion, Skeen also included an appendix from a Tamil scholar, P. K. T. Kangeratina, which "should throw some additional light on the subject."[15] Kangeratina did in fact bring to light one of the few texts from Lankan Saiva literature to mention the Peak, *Taṭcaṇakayilāca Māṉmiyam*, discussed below. Yet he was ignored by subsequent scholars. The renowned historian Senarat Paranavitana, writing in 1958 as the nation increasingly turned to Sinhala majoritarianism, dismissed Kangeratina's citation as "obviously a work of recent origin. Though this *purāṇa* is claimed to have been written in Sanskrit, the names quoted from it are in Tamil form, and no actual extract from the work has been given so as to enable one to judge its age."[16] Portions of the Sanskrit were available in printed editions,[17] but Paranavitana chose not to pursue Kangeratina, arguing instead "that, in the fourteenth century, the Hindus venerated Adam's Peak as the abode of Agastya."[18]

Agastya, "the centre of multifarious mythic accretions,"[19] is a sage said to have traveled from northern to southern India and invented the Tamil alphabet. Placing him at the Peak was an intriguing move, as he was significant to Buddhists and Saivas. Agastya also fit the Peak with his riverine links. One of the first Tamil texts to include him was the Buddhist epic *Maṇimēkalai*, where he creates the South Indian Kaveri watershed as "the immortal sage Agastya's water vessel overturned, and the Lady Kāviri flowed exactly to the East."[20] Paranavitana translated passages from two ninth-century Sanskrit dramas that placed Agastya on Mount Rohaṇa. In Murāri's *Anargha-rāghava*, for example, Rāma points out to Sīta, " 'There appears to view the Siṃhala Island, a blue lotus arising from the Ocean, which is beauteous with the filament of the Mountain of Precious Stones.' Sīta adds: 'Where roams noble Agastya . . .' Rāma replies . . .'yes, the second shrine on the low-land of the Rohaṇa mountain here, indeed, is that of the Sage.' "[21] The Agastya mytholith was then used as a tool by Paranavitana to forge a Sanskrit legacy for the Peak over its Tamil history, despite his acknowledgement that "at Adam's Peak today, there is no evidence of Agastya."[22] The sage of multifarious mythic accretions thus received another layer of storytelling to suit a scholar's ideal Siva-less imagination.

Meanwhile, certain Tamil scholars wrote Saiva stories. One mythic maneuver was performed by J. R. Sinnatamby, who used Ptolemy's map of Taprobana to prove ancient Tamil presence at the Peak. According to Sinnatamby,

> this footprint is actually recorded by Ptolemy . . . he has described it as Ulipada (also Ulispada). This constitutes . . . the earliest authentic record of the footprint and dates back to at least 140 A.D. . . . Its relative position on Ptolemy's map is just where Adam's Peak is shown on modern maps and that it is

> the footprint is further confirmed by the fact that . . . Ulipada is phonetically and even in the spelling almost identical with Oli Padam (Radiant Foot Print in Tamil) and so is Malea with Malai (Mountain in Tamil). . . . The strongest argument that can be urged in favor of this . . . is that it is a unique topographical feature, which rises sharply . . . and can be seen many miles out to sea.[23]

Sinnatamby maneuvered to find a source even older than the oldest Buddhist reference, using the ancient Greeks, an unassailable classical pedigree, a metonym for history itself.[24] The names Sinnatamby cited did appear on Ptolemaic cartography. Yet his argument stretches. Ulipada is not always "just where Adam's Peak is shown on modern maps," but usually farther south and more centered. Some recensions of the map left it out entirely. Admittedly, Sinnatamby's best proof was the mountain's physical agency, its demand to be acknowledged by its visibility. As seafarers must have seen the Peak, Ptolemy's maritime charts could be a voice of Tamil history.[25]

The contrasting mythic agendas of Paranavitana and Sinnatamby demonstrate the varied assemblages of history among early scholars of the nation-state. When faced with meager evidence, mytholiths archived what history forgot. Contorted logic and gymnastic assumptions made unassailable sources, from esteemed Greek or Sanskrit traditions, legitimate or discredit the presence of Tamil Saivas at the Peak. Paranavitana, who likely inherited prejudices from the anti-Saiva rhetoric discussed below, made room for almost any god *except* Siva, and even dismissed the name Sivanolipadam, as "the word '*Sivaṉ-oḷi*' appears to have been based on the name of the mountain as given in the *Maṇimekalai*—'Samaṇoḷi'—and not a genuine, independent development."[26] However, rather than examine any other non-Buddhist Tamil texts, which, as seen below, would have actually advanced his Agastya thesis, Paranavitana left the above as an excuse to ignore a deeper Tamil past. Equitable treatment of extant sources in both Tamil and Sinhala reveals a more nuanced history of Buddhist-Saiva interaction at the Peak.

Pieces of the Peak in Tamil

The Peak appears twice in the sixth-century Tamil Buddhist epic *Maṇimēkalai*, the story of a woman named Maṇimēkalai, daughter of Kovalan and Mātavi, characters in another Tamil epic, *Cilappatikāram*. In this sequel, Maṇimēkalai becomes a Buddhist nun, and her tale maps a Buddhist world, centered on

Tamil-speaking South India and expanded to many sites by narratives of her prior lives, or those of bodhisattvas and deities she meets.[27] This Buddhist world includes Lanka and its famous mountain, the first mention of which comes from a goddess, Tīvatilakai, who recounts her pilgrimage:

> Near this place at the Gem Island [*irattiṉatīvam*],
> on the most-high great Samanta Summit,
> are the pair of feet of the Master of Dharma [*aṟam*],
> like the virtue-ship to cross the great ocean of our birth.
> There I worshiped, circumambulated, and came here.[28]

The footprints are the Buddha's, master of *aṟam*—a Tamil word meaning "virtue" and "good works," used for dharma.[29] Meanwhile, the Tamil name of the mountain, Samanta (Camanta), matches the Pali. The Peak is then mentioned again several chapters later, as a character describes how a king was once interrupted in his pleasure garden:

> When, returning from Lanka Island [*ilaṅkai tīvu*],
> having circumambulated the mountain named Samanoli
> [*camaṉoḷi*],
> a few dharma sages [*tarum cāraṇar*], guests to rest,
> moved in a heavy dark cloud mass.
> Due to the king's past merit in that way,
> the great ones descended into this flower garden . . .
> On the suffering of birth and the bliss of no-birth,
> they poured out the truth revealed by the Foremost in Dharma.[30]

The Peak is thus a landed manifestation of Buddhist teachings. Its significance is explained to Maṇimēkalai by spiritually advanced beings, and pilgrimage serves as a form of dharma credentials, granting authority to deliver Buddhist lessons. The Tamil name in the above passage (Camaṉoḷi) is close to the Sinhala (Samanoḷa). In fact, the Tamil may have preceded the Sinhala, which does not appear in written records until Vijayabāhu's twelfth-century inscription.

These references to the Peak in *Maṇimēkalai* do support the assumptions of certain Lankan historians, who, based only on its *Mahāvaṃsa* mention, extrapolated that the Peak was already a pilgrimage site in the middle of the first millennium CE.[31] Some nationalists have used such *Mahāvaṃsa* presumptions to anachronistically claim an unbroken heritage of "Sinhala Buddhists" throughout Sri Lankan history. But extant evidence suggests the Peak was significant to

Buddhists from the Tamil mainland, too, further corroborated by a passage from Buddhaghosa's fifth-century *Manorathapūraṇī*: "Then the Tamil named Dīghajantu was like the Dhamma shelter. So that Tamil offered fine crimson cloth to the 'Sky Stupa' of Sumanagiri Vihāra, and then at death was reborn in the highest realm."[32] While Buddhaghosa's association of a Mount Sumana with a Tamil Buddhist again suggests the Peak was known in South India, it is absent from contemporaneous non-Buddhist Tamil literature. The *nāyaṉmār* poet-saints of the *Tēvāram*, for example, Appar, Campantar, and Cuntarar, were immensely concerned with pilgrimage places in the seventh and eighth centuries. Although they wrote mostly of Kaveri river-basin settlements in India, Cuntarar and Campantar did compose poems on Saiva sites in Lanka, but only the coastal temples at Manthai and Trincomalee. The early Saiva theology of the *Tēvāram* poets, however, did show potential for future mythic overlap. One of the main objects of worship in the verses were Siva's feet: "The greatest affective value is attached to the Lord's feet, the supreme symbol of his power and grace. . . . The very act of reaching (*cēr-*) Siva's feet is both the means and the ultimate end. In that act of taking refuge (*caraṇ aṭai-*) devotees are 'released.' "[33] Although various Tamil words for "refuge" were used in *Tēvāram* poems, like *pukal* and *aṭaikkalam*, the fact that the Sanskrit-derived *caraṇ* (*saraṇa* in Sinhala) was also used shows a resonant vocabulary between Buddhists and Saivas.[34] Both took refuge beneath feet representing liberation from rebirth, making it possible to join a footprint pilgrimage tradition already in progress.

A literary lacuna also exists for Lankan Tamil works about the Peak, likely due to a lack of research and preservation. The Tamil writer Kalāpūcaṇam Cāralnāṭaṉ describes a tradition of pilgrimage literature that existed when South Indian visitors to the Peak were more common:

> In the last century, you can know it was called Civaṉaṭipātamalai by various travel-song compositions that arose in that time. In 1930, the Civaṉaṭipāta travel-song hymnal, published by M. P. R. Āṇṭiccāmi from Matale, is one example of this. . . . Up until 1939, sacred pilgrimage to Sivanolipadamalai was made; South Indian Tamil poets, scholars, and pundits were all coming in full scale. There were abundant songs sung by them on travel. Now all those have gone extinct. . . . No one has paid due regard to preserving them.[35]

Although many pilgrimage texts are lost, the significance of a Tamil Peak does come into focus in Lankan temple literature. The devotional drama *Kaṇṇaki Vaḻarkkurai*, for example, is sung at east-coast temples during festivals dedicated to the goddess Kannaki, who immigrated from South India. In a chapter where a ship sails around the island, surveying its landmarks, the Peak and its waters are used to express the prowess of a Chola king in southwest Lanka, who is described as "the powerful guardian of the Māvali Ganga and the guardian of sandalwooded Samanoli [*camaṉoḷi*]."[36] As in Sinhala literature, the mytholith linking this mountain and river became an important theme in Tamil texts, especially in the genre of *tala purāṇam*, or "place histories" of Tirikōṇamalai, also known as the Koneswaram temple, in Trincomalee, on the northeast coast. While it is far from the Peak, a hydrological connection comes via the Mahaweli River, which meets the sea beside Koneswaram.

The Tamil Mytholith of Peak Rivers

The oldest *tala purāṇam* of Koneswaram is *Takṣiṇakailāca Purāṇam* (Southern Kailash history), likely composed by a Jaffna royal, "Cekarācacēkaraṉ," in the early-sixteenth century.[37] While it has no reference to the Peak, the Mahaweli River's origin is described with the same mythic structure as the origin of the Ganga in India, falling from Siva's dreadlocks.[38] After its creation, the river bubbles up from underground to cover the god's feet in worship as he stands atop the rock of Koneswaram:

> Seeking out on the mountain, the great spring goes over the pure
> red-lotus foot,
> rising from the subterranean world, revering the standing Lord
> there, and here
> pursuing him over the surface of the earth, revering the
> Virtuous One, a sky-high
> extending light occurring where he stands meditating on
> mantras and exerting mercy.[39]

Such mentions of rivers and lotus feet atop mountains in *Takṣiṇakailāca Purāṇam* likely primed the mythic overlap with the Peak in later *tala purāṇam* of Koneswaram. These later texts, however, source the Mahaweli all the way back to the highlands, mirroring Sinhala poets.

A mountain named Samanai that birthes the Mahaweli enters temple records around the seventeenth century. *Kōṇēcar Kalveṭṭu* (Koneswaram inscription) was a work of prose and verse that recorded the history of the temple and its patrons. It was likely written shortly after the temple's Portuguese sacking in 1624, and later updated in Dutch and British periods, framing colonial conquest as predestined.[40] Its mention of Samanai, although brief, may reflect the general inland turn of religiosity following the coastal temple's loss.[41] The mountain is mentioned when Siva instructs Agastya to go south to Lanka, because gods gathered for the divine wedding on Kailash were causing the world to tip north:[42] "'You, Agastya, come to this place, and we will bestow on you the divine vision of us coming in this wedding-procession-crowd. You, in Ilaṅkāpuri, at the Māvali River flowing from Samanai Mountain, near Karacai, by thinking and divine *dyāna* meditation on our Lord, by the divinity blooming into view, will be within the full grace of Lord Siva and Kaliash Mountain.'"[43] *Kōṇēcar Kalveṭṭu* thus emplaces Siva's essence in Lanka by the deity's direct instruction. A spot beside the Mahaweli is Agastya's seat for the Kailash wedding, with Samanai as its source upstream. Although the footprint went unmentioned here, the Peak's associations with Siva began, elaborated in subsequent texts.

The lingam at Karacai planted by Agastya in *Kōṇēcar Kalveṭṭu* became its own temple named after Agastya—Akattiyattāpaṉam.[44] The specific *tala purāṇam* of this temple, *Tirukkaraicai Purāṇam*, also mentions Samanai Mountain. While its author and date are unknown, the poet claims to be a student of Umāpati Civācariyār's lineage in Chidambaram. He is clearly familiar with earlier Tamil Saiva literature and the *tala purāṇam* form, which means the text is likely to stem from the heyday of this genre in the seventeenth or eighteenth century, perhaps another part of the inland turn away from Koneswaram that resulted in more ritual attention at Karacai. The poet's use of Samanai also indicates an increased importance of the interior, intrinsically linking Siva to the highlands as well as Karacai and Koneswaram. The Peak first appears in the "River Chapter" of *Tirukkaraicai Purāṇam*, as Agastya heads south and beholds the landscape of Lanka, described in rich poetic detail with classic tropes of wealth and fertility common to Tamil literature. Samanai anchors the final verse in this description, referencing Siva, paired with Parvati, setting foot on the summit:

> With the partner whose black hair has new bloomed flowers, the Lord's foot
> is made to come atop lofty Samanai, joining with abundant water.
> Silver scabbardfish swim in the Māvali Ganga whose waters come to
> brighten and behold the foot of the Black-Necked One's mountain.[45]

The poet thus makes a parallel between the Peak and Koneswaram by means of feet, as the same waters that join Siva's feet at their origin on the summit also come to worship at the foot of the Koneswaram rock, where Siva stands on the northern coast of Lanka.

The link across these sites is activated by Agastya's *dyāna* meditation, which transports him from his bathing at the Mahaweli riverbank at Karacai into Siva's presence at Koneswaram. The god speaks to him through a disembodied voice, telling Agastya of the Mahaweli's greatness:

> Having taken first steps at Mount Samanai, slope shining with
> tree sap and gem luster,
> at strong-sea-surrounded Mount Kōṇai keeping great beauty at
> the end,
> lying with greatness, the northern mouth's swelling nature
> unconstrained in that place,
> branching out in the world, the Māvali Ganga's fruitful water is
> like the Bhagirathi.[46]

The Peak is linked with the Himalayas, as the Mahaweli is compared to the Bhagirathi headwaters of the Indian Ganga, Siva's foot making it equally sacred. A connection of foot and river is subtly created in the first line, via double meanings where mountain slope (*taṭam*) can also mean footstep, and the verb for the origin of the river (*aṭivaittu*) can mean not only "to begin," but also literally "to place one's foot" or "take one's first steps as a child." Siva then focuses on the summit to explain how his mountainous permanence there is due to the footprint:

> By that place in the sky where our impressed footprint can exist
> and we never end,
> by the sweet waters where gem rays cascade with the nature of
> our form,
> by the wealth of fragrant ash-white lingam trees of limitless
> perfume,
> long and full, there is not a water in the world that compares to
> Māvali Ganga water.[47]

The god is written into the landscape not only through his footprint, but also through the waters that touch it, and the river's gems whose ruby light resembles the redness of Siva as depicted in Tamil Saiva poetics, as do the lingam trees (*tavaḷam māviliṅkam*) that are colored white like the ash smeared on his body. All this makes Samanai special, marked out as sacred and consecrated by nature itself, sourcing a river of celestial character:

> Like foremost Brahma removing all darkness for sages to see,
> the light of gem lamps is held, making special Mount Samanai,

> which the beautiful dark clouds desire to consecrate; by the streaming
> water's excellent nature, the Māvali Ganga is like the heavenly river.[48]

Samanai is therefore a key reason why immersion in the Mahaweli becomes so meritorious, ameliorative of bad karma all along its course. Whether at the estuary of Koneswaram, Agastya's bathing place at Karacai, or "immersing at the *tīrttam* where the praised river first rises, the received merit is produced."[49] The later *tala purāṇam* of Koneswaram thus appeal to broad conceptions of sacred space, with the main temple under consideration set in a constellation of other powerful sites Siva touches in Lanka.

The most extended Saiva elegies of the Peak are found in *Tirikoṇācala Purāṇam*, composed in the late seventeenth or eighteenth century, ending with an account of displaced Koneswaram priests settling in Kandy. The Peak appears several times in this lengthy text, including in its opening chapter about rivers:

> Its form like the pouring out of clear white light from the moon
> that blends with the summit gold of the Ganga-wearing Kailash,
> the river water was widespread that day, flowing down all sides
> of Mount Samanai over the long-limbed trees standing there.[50]

The author then deepens his elegy of the mountain by playing with its name, beginning each line of the next quatrain with "Samanai." The word *camaṉ* in its sense of "sameness" is used in the first line, a reminder of the generational weight of karma. This is followed by a more technical meaning of *camaṉai* in the second line, referring to the supreme state attainable by a Saiva soul seeking liberation from cyclical karmic existence:

> camaṉai uṟṟiṭum iru viṉai taṉayaṉukku āka
> camaṉai vīṭṭiya caṅkaraṉ tāḷ malar tayaṅkum
> camaṉai amkiri taṉil viḻuntōṭu taṇṇīttam
> camaṉai āṟeṉum oru peyar koṇṭu cārntatuvē

> Existing karma will be comparatively the same for one's son.
> With the supreme state that removes it, Śaṅkara's foot-lotus shines
> in the place of Mount Samanai with the falling water,
> the Samanai River being one name associated with it.[51]

This technique of homonymic multimeaning makes the mountain synonymous with the physical world as well as the highest spiritual aspirations of Saiva devotees. *Tirikoṇācala Purāṇam* then uses the river's more common name to describe it springing from the divine footprint:

> The luminous foot of Siva, who red-eyed Vishnu and
> Brahma seek,
> stays, stands, and imprints for all things moveable and
> immoveable to thrive.
> Purified and adorned with the name of the Māvali [river],
> the grace of the One with the moon in matted locks is what
> spreads.[52]

As in other *tala purāṇam*, Siva's essence is attached to the physical land of the mountain, his grace (*aruḷ*) spread through its waterways.

The mountain is mentioned again in the second chapter of *Tirikoṇācala Purāṇam*, which describes the divine country of Lanka, with the summit of Siva's footprint cited alongside other sacred sites on the island. The Peak then receives another extended elegy in the seventh chapter on the sacred *tīrtha* waters of the Mahaweli. The poet again uses double meanings to intertwine the slopes with Saiva tropes, in one verse using a word that can mean both sandalwood and dewlap (*āram*) and a word that can mean both branches and horns (*kōṭṭu*) to compare the mountain to Siva's bull Nandi.[53] Other verses compare elements of the mountain to features of Siva and Parvati.[54] Due to its divine resemblances, the poet employs another name beyond Samanai; this is seemingly the first place in the Tamil literary record where the name Sivanolipadam appears:

> The Lord is gracious to anyone who passes there while
> meditating upon him.
> What greatness of grace grows, gaining sight of the divine form.
> The karma that is made is cleared away, showing salvation.
> Strong Samanai mountain is called Sivanolipadam.[55]

With the poet explicitly stating the equivalence of the names, it seems an attempt was made to link the older Samanai moniker to the newer designation of Sivanolipadam.

As Lankan Tamil literature transitioned to print, texts that mentioned the Peak usually replaced the name Samanai with Sivanolipadamalai. When

A. Kumāracuvāmi published a commentary to *Tirukkaraicai Purāṇam* in 1890, for example, he glossed Samanai as Sivanolipadamalai.[56] Likewise, when V. Akilēcapiḷḷai composed *Tirukkōṇācala Vaipavam* in 1889, a Koneswaram *tala purāṇam* in modern prose, he used the name Sivanolipadamalai in his retelling of the tri-river myth of *Tirikoṇācala Purāṇam*, with the "Māvali, Māṇikka, and Kāvēri" flowing off the Peak as Siva's hair, and Agastya planting a *liṅga* beside the Mahaweli.[57] Whatever the mountain was named, its rivers were the most important feature. The text that P. K. T. Kangeratina had recommended for Skeen's book on the Peak also increased its circulation during this period, further expanding the river mytholith in Tamil. *Taṭcaṇakayilāca Māṉmiyam*, or *The Glory of Southern Kailash*, was originally written in Sanskrit, although the authorship and era of the work are unknown. C. Nākaliṅkapiḷḷai translated a Tamil prose edition in 1928 from two manuscripts, claiming the work was part of the *Skanda Purāṇa*.[58] Most scholars, however, consider *Skanda Purāṇa* not as "a single, coherent text, but 'only a name to which extensive works . . . claim allegiance.' "[59] The Indian Sanskrit editions that yielded the twenty-volume *Skanda Purāṇa* English translation have none of the stories or geographic details found in *Taṭcaṇakayilāca Māṉmiyam*, instead presenting Lanka as a figural space full of *rākṣasa* demons.[60] Refashioned for actual Lankan places, *Taṭcaṇakayilāca Māṉmiyam* replicates the *Skanda Purāṇa* structure by listing and describing pilgrimage sites, primarily *tīrtha* waters where bathing removes karmic demerits. *Taṭcaṇakayilāca Māṉmiyam* therefore relies on the Peak in its familiar role as a symbolic watershed. Nākaliṅkapiḷḷai did not specify what Sanskrit term was used for the Peak, but he substituted the Sivanolipadamalai name seven times in his translation. After Parvati finds the rivers in Siva's hair, the waters are given voice to thank the god for their existence, situating their own geographic source atop Sivanolipadamalai, and asking the god to lay them well. The language of the text suggests the waters share an essence with Siva, dwelling in his footprint, present in his Indian abodes, and also spreading his divinity across Lankan land. To this end, where each river meets the sea is also sacred:

> By Siva's grace, the joyful meetings of the three streams, Māvali Ganga, Māṇikka Ganga, Kāvēri Ganga, on Sivanolipadamalai, on Siva's foot, on the auspicious day, in the auspicious hour, became the eternal flooding abundance. Among those three rivers, Māvali Ganga . . . reached Southern Kailash from its mountain cavern in the south. There, the Lord of the Universe vanishes into the ocean confluence. On the summit of Sivanolipadamalai are Siva's feet. . . . From Sivanolipadamalai to Southern Kailash became . . . among places, the foremost place. Among *tirthas*, the foremost *tirtha*.

> Moreover, the Māṇikka Ganga, very clearly going eastward, having reached Kataragama Mountain, confluences into the eastern sea beneath. And the Kāvēri Maha Ganga, going westward, having reached the great place of Ketheeswaram, goes in circumambulation and mixes in the ocean sea.[61]

The rivers of the Peak connect it to renowned Saiva sites with deeper histories than Sivanolipadamalai, temples like Koneswaram and Ketheeswaram, for which the Indian Tamil *Tēvāram* poet-saints had composed verses. Likewise, the Kaveri River that appeared in so many of their lines is transposed onto a Lankan waterway. The Peak waters are also linked to the original Himalayan Kailash and the Chidambaram temple in South India. In the process, Lankan sites are elevated as equal or even superior to their Indian counterparts. In turn, characters of Indian epics enter the Lankan landscape in *Taṭcaṇakayilāca Māṉmiyam*, including Rama, who journeys through the Lankan highlands after defeating Ravana and worships Siva at "Samanai Mountain."[62]

As texts like *Taṭcaṇakayilāca Māṉmiyam* included the Peak in a larger ambit of Saiva sites, the mountain remained a piece of the Lankan Tamil imaginary into the twentieth century. It can appear in unexpected spots in the literary record, such as a special annual edition of the Jaffna weekly newspaper and literary journal *Eelakesari* (*Īḻakēcari*) in 1935. This volume included an opening song to elegize the publication with "salutary advice" that began with a vision of the world it covered, including "the lofty mountain of Samanai whose extensive fame spreads all around heaven and earth, and the Ganga named Māvali that expands with fresh waters."[63] In the middle of the publication, an illustration of the Peak also appears. As the decades passed, however, the Peak began to lose its links to the northern and eastern coasts of the island. As ethnic categories hardened, and civil war separated the country, the riverine stories of Samanai dried up. In *Taṭcaṇakayilāca Māṉmiyam*, the term "Sinhala" was used as a regional designation, not an ethnicity, allowing its author to proclaim that "ten rivers are especially important. Of those, six rivers are in Sinhala Desa. . . . Accordingly, Sinhala Desa is the best."[64] By the end of the twentieth century, however, the "Sinhala Desa" imagined by majoritarian politicians was meant to be absent of Tamils.

The ensuing loss of history means the Tamil literary legacy of the Peak has been largely overlooked, despite its connection with a temple as renowned as Koneswaram. Even Cāralnāṭaṉ's recent Tamil book about the Peak appeared unaware of "Samanai."[65] Nevertheless, these *tala purāṇam*, part of a textual tradition meant to map powerful landscapes, show the Peak has been a significant component of Lankan Tamil Saiva imagination for several centuries. They also continue to demonstrate the Peak's agency over all its pilgrims, with its same material elements of footprint, waters, and gemstones being transferrable across traditions. In turn, the landscape provides grounds for further comparisons, as the emplacement of Saiva divinities at the Peak is also reflected in certain Sinhala compositions.

Siva in Sinhala as a Coexistent God of the Peak

Sinhala literature, as a bastion of Buddhist composition, occasionally slants against Siva, but other texts make him just another god incorporated into a common pantheon. A 1924 Peak poem claimed Lankan descendants of Vijaya were originally Saivas before the introduction of Buddhism: "As human settlement happened like that, those people believed in God Siva."[66] Some Buddhists who visited the Peak in 2016 were Siva devotees of a sort, too, as the god's shrine on the Hatton trail received a steady contingent of supplicants on busy weekends. Buddhist texts also provide some of the earliest evidence for Hindu interest in the mountain. Vedeha Thera's thirteenth-century *Samantakūṭavaṇṇanā* alludes to non-Buddhist ascetics on the Peak: "Living in that place pleasant with mountains and trees are outsider ascetics [*bahitāpasā*], minds concentrated in yoga."[67] This is echoed in the following century by Ibn Battuta's mention of yogis in his pilgrimage party. A century after that, a Sinhala poet depicted "Brahmins" as regular Peak pilgrims communing with Saman.[68]

Not until the reign of Rajasinha I, however, was a specifically Saiva sect associated with the Peak, when he dedicated temple income to them in the 1580s. This is perhaps why panegyrics for Rajasinha blended Saiva tropes with ideals of Buddhist kings. Alagiyavanna's *Sävul Sandēśa* is replete with Saiva metaphors, comparing the ramparts and moat of the capital with celestial Siva-hair cascades off Mount Kailash.[69] While these are fairly generic pan-Indic tropes, "idealized visions of a city that exists both nowhere and everywhere,"[70] Alagiyavanna takes Siva metaphors further. He applies them to Rajasinha—a king well trained in the *purāṇas*—the stature of his body compared to the god, the size of his fame to Kailash, and the brightness of his majesty to the light of Siva's third eye.[71] Moreover, similar to Tamil texts, Siva (Hara) and Parvati (Uma) are written into the landscape as a river flowing down the mountain:

> From Lady Lanka's Saman Mountain head, braids opened,
> shining like plaits of hair adorned with jasmine flowers,

amid that city, the spread Kalu River is visibly huge.
Noble friend, go and behold your fill as desired.

Spread wave eyebrows with ointment,
large whirlpool navel, with blue moss hair plaits,
with the sandbank as heavenly Hara remaining always,
that beautiful river takes the form of noble Lady Uma.[72]

Placing Siva and Parvati on the Peak through riverine metaphors, coupled with Rajasinha as a monarch modeled on Siva, made *Sävul Saṅdēśa* a novel Sinhala panegyric, suitable for a Saiva-sponsoring king.

Mentions of Siva (Isuru) and Uma on the mountain appear intermittently in other poems. The verse from *Saman Sirita* that opened chapter 1 of this book uses Siva's link to celestial rivers as poetic ornamentation to metaphorically describe the Peak's waters. Moreover, the poet calls the mountain *hima kula*—a term also applicable to Himalayan summits. I noticed an easy association between the Peak and the Himalayas in casual conversations, too. One day, when I arrived at Chandra's shop, she had just acquired a new decoration to add to her walls, to complement the posters of the Peak and famous monks with verses of their poetry. It was a long foldout photograph labeled "Annapurna Himalayan Range," a panorama of snowcapped summits labeled with names and elevations. Chandra laid it on the table and suggested I take a picture for my research. I readily obliged, having come to appreciate the conceptual connection between the Lankan and Himalayan mountain ranges in so much Sinhala poetry. This is especially common in poems about rivers. A nineteenth-century manuscript praising the Mahaweli Ganga had its opening verses show the Peak struck by rains, soaked summit replenishing the watershed beside familiar Himalayan gods:

One end of the river made high atop Samanala.
From that, the Maskeliya is made full; behold.
Going on a third-quarter *poya* day in the forest,
Speak a bit of that and fully behold it.

At the end near Uma and Isuru in the sky,
love increasing, *karunāva* is spoken as a sea.
Soaked, spraying, running wild by the rain,
head bowed, let us worship the sacred foot.[73]

Standing on the summit, with the usual Buddhist plea for compassion (*karunāva*) shouted nearby, the poet places Siva and Parvati alongside the sky river that sources the island's life-giving waters. Variations on these verses also appear in poems for Gange Bandara, who, as an apotheosis of the Mahaweli, also comes into being atop the Peak:

> From the Samanala forest, the river fell,
> going up to the sea, I say without concealing.
> It darkens and revolves at lofty heights.
> Whoever speaks is forced to stop by the Hima Ganga.
>
> The end coming from the sky like Uma and Isuru,
> lovingly increasing *karuṇāva* for us.
> Soaked, sprinkling like flowers with yearly rain,
> bowing the head, we worship the sacred foot.[74]

Siva and Parvati again source the Mahaweli, called "Hima Ganga" here, the verse directly applying the Saiva Himalayan watershed myth to the Peak's rivers. In turn, that mytholith is reshaped to Buddhist parameters, so that Siva and Parvati are present more metaphorically, as annual rainwater pilgrims to the sacred foot, sprinkling compassion and aqueous offerings as they create rivers.

Some Sinhala ritual poetry alludes to Hindu shrines on the Peak. The Devol Deviyo myths of foreign settlers discussed in chapter 3 mention *kōvils* constructed in the mountain forest:

> On the Kaḷu river, to Samanala forest,
> we received permission to go.
> Making a *kōvil* of good form,
> we received permission to stay.[75]
>
> To the dark thick wild Samanala forest,
> receiving permission to go at that time,
> and to take *kōvil* offerings at that time
> by that majestic power well displayed.[76]

Other gods who came from overseas also found their way to *kōvils* in forests near the Peak, like Vīramuṇḍa, whose South Indian origin and name suggest a Sinhala transplant of a Tamil *vīraṉ*, or "hero" guardian deity of sacred groves.[77]

In one manuscript, he is twice said to have hunted deer that is then "taken to the tiled *kōvil* at Sitagangula," the stream that crosses the Peak trail.[78] This incorporation of new deities by Sinhala authors into texts meant for Buddhist rituals exemplifies Schonthal's model of "cosmological toleration," which "does not preserve the boundaries between Buddhism and other traditions but rather enfolds into Buddhism the beliefs and practices of non-Buddhists."[79] Siva, Parvati, and others thereby join a Buddhist pantheon, which, although plural, often causes these deities to assume more Buddhist attributes.

Some Buddhists, however, sought to reinforce rather than expand boundaries around their identity, in one instance by also referring to Hindu activities at Sitagangula. In *Saman Sirita*, a group of monks processing the Saman statue down the mountain did not necessarily approve of everything they saw:

> Undivergently, Brahmins learn and incant mantras,
> having charmed serpents of extensive defilements,
> continually incanting to see *dhyāna* images.
> It is good if the noble sangha observes the pride.[80]

The religious techniques of mantra recitation and *dhyāna* meditation, mentioned positively in the Tamil sources cited earlier, are cast more negatively here. From a Buddhist perspective, such actions only charm rather than sever snake-like defilements (*keles*). This makes the Brahmins a good lesson for the monks in the specific defilement of pride, as the poet played with the end rhyme of these lines through the similar words for incant/charm (*dapanā*) and pride (*dapa*). Using mental faculties of discrimination to distinguish between right and wrong paths is a fundamental part of Buddhist thought, but it at least presumes that other views need to be present so one can practice careful philosophical discernment. This is more than certain hegemonic nationalist Buddhists would allow at the Peak. Of course, not all passersby would necessarily see the scene with such a polemical eye in the first place. For example, a nineteenth-century manuscript of miscellaneous quatrains contained a comedic verse that balanced Saman and Siva in the sort of good humor that accompanies many pilgrimages:

> Gods of the four universes atop my head.
> God Saman of Samanala in my right hand.
> God Īsvara in my left hand.
> What hand gives a chew of betel?[81]

Did most Buddhist and Hindu pilgrims at the Peak coexist as casually as right and left hands? The fact that polemics are absent from the pilgrimage songs in manuscript collections, as well as from most early printed pamphlets, seems to support this.

Ambivalence toward Hindus at the Peak, however, did increase with modern Sinhala Buddhist nationalism and its print dissemination. John De Silva (1857–1922), prolific poet and playwright, expressed his interest in the Peak in his 1912 poem *Śrīpāda Śataka*, cited for its anti-Muslim sentiments in chapter 4. The *śataka* was a style of composition with one hundred Sanskrit *ślokas*, but here the *ślokas* were called *silō*, one of the poem's many words from *eḷu*, the classical style of Sinhala that converted Sanskrit poetic terms into its own vocabulary. This style fit De Silva's agenda. He was committed to the idea that the Sinhala were an Aryan people, and he founded a society for revival of this in the arts, incorporating North Indian styles in his own work.[82] *Śrīpāda Śataka* places the Peak in this reimagined history, but De Silva never found a handle on how Siva, and "Hindus" generally, should fit into his mythic framework.

A verse of the poem's invocation praises Siva and Ganesh, requesting their aid with the temperance agenda that pervades *Śrīpāda Śataka*.[83] This verse uses Siva to promote the advancement of Buddhism, and a similar idea follows when De Silva notes Tamil people arriving from Kochi. He uses a lowly pronoun (*unnō*) to describe this group, but otherwise uses their pilgrimage to show the Peak's worldwide allure:

> Boys, girls, the great populace, even women who are pregnant,
> they worship the footmark on Sumanagiri, giving merit to the
> noble god.
> The Kochi Tamil crowd, too, this noble foot so as to worship,
> they go up on this Sumanagiri where all worldly beings' minds
> are ever brought.[84]

De Silva, however, turns firmly against Saivas only four verses later, clarifying:

> Though many people in the world say this noble footmark is God
> Siva's.
> That, too, cannot be said to be true; that is the three-world-
> ruling Buddha's
> left footmark, so I say truthfully, without a doubt whatsoever.
> *Sādū! Sādū!* Let us worship devoutly that noble lotus footprint.[85]

As De Silva seeks to remove doubts over who has legitimate claims to the Peak, his rejection of Siva bleeds into a more wholesale rejection of Hindus, who, like alcohol, are one of the factors supposedly leading Sinhala people astray:

> In both this worldly earth and sky is various hidden skillful knowledge.
> On the island without an awareness of that, the minds of people are like this.
> Not knowing the four arts in this Lanka, there are holes in that history [*purāṇa*].
> To that Hindu religion having turned, some beings are going astray.[86]

De Silva defines Hindu thought as a barrier to true knowledge, another odd antagonistic choice, considering that, two verses later, he mentions a myth of the mountain, citing his source: "Among Hindu books there is one named *Sri Parvata* that showed this."[87] This left De Silva juggling two realities. While Hindus are part of a Sanskritic tradition, they do not fit a Buddhist revival. He therefore incorporated as he excised, delimiting the mountain for Buddhists, but claiming any possibly positive heritage that Hindus left.

De Silva's use of the Peak for Sinhala triumphalism was repeated in a play he published in 1913, *Alakēśvara Carita*, a romance of courtly life in fifteenth-century Kotte. There is much talk of warring with Tamil armies in the drama, and one scene begins with a minister singing about the Sinhala king causing Tamils to tremble. The royal family then gazes at the Peak from their palace. The prince asks about it, and his parents promise to go on pilgrimage someday. The minister adds: "Because of that Sri Pada mountain, some people say that the name Heḷadiva fell upon this Lanka."[88] Heḷa is a moniker derived from *sihala*, or Sinhala, but can also mean hill or cliff. The Peak is thus the reason why Lanka was Sinhala, where defeating Tamils was encouraged by custom. It is fitting that De Silva expressed this in old royal voices, as the rhetoric of kings helped forge such lasting tropes at the Peak.

Saivas as Enemies of the State

Despite his devotion to the Peak (discussed in chapter 2), Rajasinha I was rewritten as the villain by some Kandyan historians, becoming the antagonist angering his mother mountain. While eighteenth-century records claim he transferred trusteeship of the Peak temple to a Saiva sect, there is no mention of this in the sixteenth-century *Alakeśvara Yuddhaya*, or the seventeenth-century *Rājāvaliya*. Those chronicles are more interested in lauding Rajasinha's war exploits. Mention of Rajasinha's rededication does not come until 1751, referred to in an endowment record of Kīrti Śrī Rajasinha (r. 1747–1782). This was inscribed on a copper-plate *sannasa* grant, one of his first major acts after gaining the crown. The grant tells the story of the Buddha's enlightenment and his footprint impression. It then details the magnificence of Kīrti Śrī and his endowments to other sacred sites on the island, after which the king "learned that religious services were not performed constantly at Samantakūṭa Mountain where the sacred footprint of Lord Buddha, who is toward heterodoxy like a lion who breaks the forehead of elephants, was impressed; and that in the time of his majesty King Rājasiṅha of Sītāvaka it had come into possession of *aňḍi*—who smear their bodies with ash, presaging their own complete cremation in the awful fiery furnace of hell." Thus Kīrti Śrī, "in order to attain *svarga* and *nirvāna*," "donated the village called Kuṭṭāpiṭiya of one-hundred-sixty-five *amunam* fields in full sowing extent, together with houses, gardens, plantations, high and low land, situated in the Navadun Kōralē of Sabaragamuwa District, until the *ṣāsana* becomes extinct . . . to ensure continuous maintenance for . . . religious services at the sites; and ordained that performance thereof be entrusted to the student and pupil successors of Väliviṭa Saraṇankara."[89] It is curious that the *sannasa* derides ash-smeared ascetics, but makes no mention of Kīrti Śrī actually expelling them. That was only recorded in later works. So either the *sannasa* assumed it, or Saiva control was still in place when it was written.

What were Kīrti Śrī's motivations for drawing up this grant? For one, it placed a new king in line with predecessors who also endowed the Peak. In this way, Kīrti Śrī may have sought to anchor the Nāyaka dynasty in Lanka. As the family hailed from Madurai, rival Kandyan aristocrats attempted to deride them as outsiders. Likewise, legitimating lineages also appeared in a later Kīrti Śrī *sannasa*, which appointed a successor to Väliviṭa Saraṇankara for Peak leadership, granting control to Vehällē Dhammadinna and his lineage at Maḍagammana. This grant also began by linking Kīrti Śrī with former rulers, particularly Narendrasiṅha (r. 1707–1739), whose death gave his Nāyaka in-laws the throne. The grant specified that the Maḍagammana Thera won this honor because his lineage had helped remove Tamils at the Peak since Narendrasiṅha's reign, replacing them with proper rituals, new buildings, and maintained pathways.[90] The grant thus aligned Kīrti Śrī with the king who invited his family to Kandy, depicting both as supporters of eliminating the truly unwelcome foreigners in the country.

Near the end of his reign, Kīrti Śrī's role in the eviction of Saivas was detailed in the third *Mahāvaṃsa* extension, written by Ven. Tibbotuvāve Sumangala at the king's request. Rajasinha's Saiva dedication is presented as an angry response to Buddhists who said redemption from patricide was impossible: "Filled with fury like some terrible poisonous snake which has been struck by a stick, he asked the Siva devotees. The answer they gave him, that it was possible, he received like ambrosia, smeared his body with ash and adopted Siva devotion [*sivabhattiṃ*]. . . . He placed miscreant ascetics of false view on Sumanakūṭa to take for themselves all the profit."[91] This Saiva "conversion" story, composed two centuries after Rajasinha's death, should be read critically. Considering patronage precedents of prior Kotte kings, there would have been no contradiction in Rajasinha supporting both Buddhists and Saivas.[92] Yet Siva devotion reached controversial heights with the transfer of Peak funds. While he also accused Rajasinha of killing monks and burning books, these Peak profits were the bottom line for Tibbotuvāve Sumangala, showing how the wealth accruing at the summit made its religious significance surpass mere symbolism.

Before recording Kīrti Śrī's Peak restoration, Tibbotuvāve Sumangala noted other rulers' pilgrimages and endowments, including Vīravikrama in the sixteenth century, who "had the impassable road put in order and provided for convenience of coming and going seven hundred and eighty stone steps." There was also Vimaladharmasuriya II (r. 1687–1707), who "stayed there seven days . . . and celebrated a great festival," and Narendrasiṅha (r. 1707–1739): "twice the Lord of men went in faith to Sumanakūṭa, sacrificed there and so laid up a store of merit."[93] These histories suggest that even if Saivas gained control of the Peak in the sixteenth century, it did not interrupt normal patterns of patronage. Kings still visited, endowed the footprint, and sponsored infrastructure, with no evidence that Buddhists were ever barred from pilgrimage. Ultimately, however, the Peak was portrayed as being rescued by Kīrti Śrī: "The adherents of the false view destroyed everything there. When the highly famed Great King [Kīrti Śrī] heard of these things, he realized, reverently devoted to the Enlightened One, that this was unseemly. He commanded the adherents of the false view not to do so from now on, and charged the sons of the Buddha to carry out in the right way the many sacrificial ceremonies . . . income accruing therefrom he assigned to the [Buddhist] Order."[94] The bottom line is again income, the most critical piece of the Peak being profit, a monetary angle that may have made Tibbotuvāve Sumangala speak in such a derogatory way toward Saivas.

The rhetoric from the reign of Kīrti Śrī has led some scholars to assume that its anti-Tamil stance reflected public opinion, so that Kīrti Śrī's Buddhist endowments were to distract from his Nāyaka family, or private Saiva practices.[95] Such assumptions stem from the substantial amount of anti-Tamil rhetoric in Sinhala literature of this period, but anti-Nāyaka and anti-Tamil rhetoric has likely been overremembered due to its promotion by the British, who used it to justify toppling the Lankan throne.[96] Judging from two centuries of Nāyaka-Kandyan interaction, Obeyesekere argues that, "both in mythic and practical terms, the Nāyakas of Madurai were hardly aliens."[97] Moreover, the theory that Kīrti Śrī was trying to obscure his own Saiva background can also be overdeterministic in attributing historical intentions solely to the king. The tropes in royal grants and chronicles could also be due to powerful monks, like Välivița Saraṇankara and his chief student Tibbotuvāve Sumangala, whose lineage stood to gain significantly by transition of Peak income control.[98] Making Saivas into an enemy of the Buddhist state was perhaps fueled by particular monastic politics as much as general prejudice, but, with all their anti-Saiva rhetoric, Kandyan authors left a legacy that continues to inform negative perceptions of non-Buddhists at the Peak.

Who Are the Āňḍi and How Did They Die?

As Saivas became an easy narrative enemy in Peak storytelling, this trope has persisted in part through the figure of the *āňḍi*. The word *āňḍi* in Sinhala is a general term for wandering ascetics, usually with connotations of South Indian origins. *Āňḍi* could also specifically denote Saiva ascetics smeared with ash, matching the Tamil term *āṇṭi*, for non-Brahmin Saiva mendicants. There are folktales of wandering *āňḍi* passing through the highlands and settling beside bodhi trees to found villages.[99] Collective immigrant tales were also preserved in gods like Āňḍi Kaḍavara, who came speaking several South Indian tongues—all types of "Tamil."[100] According to *Rājāvaliya*, the South Indian Ariṭṭa Kivenḍu Perumāl came to Lanka as an *āňḍi*, ingratiated himself to Rajasinha I, and encouraged Saiva patronage, becoming the court minister Manamperuma Mohoṭṭiyā.[101] After Rajasinha's death, Manamperuma murdered the prince and made himself king of Sītāvaka. Yet thanks to a poet saboteur, whenever he stepped out in public, he was allegedly mocked so viciously in subversive song for having been an *āňḍi* that he defected to the Portuguese and again changed his name. So connotations of the *āňḍi* come with some chicanery, and Sinhala and Portuguese sources both called *āňḍi* appearance a form of disguise.[102]

Later, *āňḍi* were mentioned in Sinhala pilgrimage poetry, present in two extant manuscripts from the *Samanala Hälla* tradition. The only consistent stylistic requirement of *Samanala Hälla* poems was to end the last line of each quatrain with the phrase "worship the sacred foot on Samanala" (*vaňdin siripā samanlē*), allowing the genre some flexibility in topic.[103] While some verses match across manuscripts, *Samanala Hälla* poems also contain many unique Peak observations, including mention of *āňḍi*:

Circled around as if to match the *cakra* weapon in hand at the time
All together, three-hundred-sixty having taken bags at the right time
Having clustered, the taste everyone compared and shared, eating all the time
Those ones having joined, an *āňḍī* group worships the sacred foot on Samanala.[104]

Strings taken and fresh talipot leaves stitched, there are umbrellas on that gold rock
Paḷu palms also made into laced halves, shining sides bound around the top in blue
Rough and tough words said, those who approached desired the end, too, then
The freshly smeared *āňḍī* group, too, worship the sacred foot on Samanala.[105]

These characterizations are not necessarily negative, as the first verse portrays a large circle of *āňḍi* coming together to share food. The second verse is more ambiguous, its first two lines seemingly describing handsewn umbrellas, while its third line does not specify who voiced the "rough and tough words," although these could presumably come from any tired pilgrim. The last line casts the *āňḍi* as Hindu ascetics by describing them as freshly smeared, surely with ash, but they were nevertheless told by the poet to worship, too. That *āňḍi* were mentioned in these nineteenth-century manuscripts suggests the acts of Kīrti Śrī had by no means exiled them from the mountain.[106]

While *Samanala Hälla* verses portrayed the *āňḍi* as just another piece of the Peak, their presence was decried as inappropriate by others. Anti-*āňḍi* prejudice was likely fueled in part by the rhetoric of British colonizers.[107] In the Christian missionary propaganda poem debunking the footprint, the *āňḍi* were mentioned negatively, as proof that the print could not have been gifted by the Buddha for Saman, as it fell to these nefarious *āňḍi*, who damaged it:

In a place without humans,
for the forest god named Sumana

alone to worship,
was that foot put in that place?

On that given footprint for the god,
by the *āňḍi* the conch was struck.
Having opened the spot to mar,
where did that god go?[108]

The *āňḍi* were thereby portrayed as especially illegitimate by an author, who thought the entire Peak pilgrimage was itself illegitimate. These stereotyped Saivas provided another mythic trope around which stories could be spun, still the case at the present Peak thanks to a place-name that preserved *āňḍi* in pilgrimage lore.

The final large rest stop on the Ratnapura trail, about two kilometers from the summit, is Āňḍiyamalatänna—"the place where the *āňḍi* died." This *āňḍi* is ambiguous, only known by a stereotyped term. Still, as the *āňḍi* of Āňḍiyamalatänna belonged to such a trafficked pilgrimage site, people have filled in details with their own stories. As the mytholith of this mysterious ascetic grew, its edges have been put to various uses by Buddhists, the site representing either a benign history of cohabitation with Saivas, or the triumphant ousting of interlopers from the Peak.

The monk of the Hatton-trail Nissankamalla Cave, Ven. Talgaskandē Sujāta, sold a Sri Pada handbook to passing pilgrims. His explanation of Āňḍiyamalatänna claimed that the *āňḍi* referred to a chief Siva devotee (*pradhāna siva bhaktikayaku*) who died there in the time of Rajasinha. Ven. Sujāta included a verse of explanatory folk poetry:

A great deal of *āňḍi* having come to this forest
Of those, one died because of prior karma
Thus became the name, for the *āňḍi* dying
To Āňḍiyamalatänna let us go quickly.[109]

The first Sinhala poems to name trail stops, including *Saman Sirita* (c. 1500) and *Käṭakirili Sandeśaya* (c. 1788), had no Āňḍiyamalatänna. In 1816, however, it was recorded in one of the first British records of the Peak trail.[110] In 1929, a government agent recorded an origin story similar to Ven. Sujāta's, but he was more interested in modern sanitation infrastructure at the site, rather than ancient history: "In the evening went up to Andiyamalatenna—about 6300 ft up—the place of death it is stated of one of the Hindu 'heretics' placed in charge of the Sacred Footprint by Rajasiha of Sitawaka—hence the name. This place stands on a shoulder of the mountain from which the Peak itself rises. It commands a grand view. . . . The sunset was magnificent. . . . This halting place contains good ambalams and a water supply by pipes from a small protected spring. It also has a good system of latrines."[111] Lavarenti's 1891 poem also noted Āňḍiyamalatänna's importance as a rest stop:

> The people going are as novice as if they were reciting the
>   alphabet
> The sweat-mopping manner of going is apparent for me
> To take camp and release that bodily fatigue
> Except for Āňḍiya Maḷa Tänna there is no other place.[112]

Poets often lauded the view of the summit cone from Āňḍiyamalatänna (fig. 4.3).

> Sweat streaming, mountain lines having climbed
> Taking a seat and releasing sweat and heat
> At Aňḍiyamalatänna having united
> Let us take a seat there, having seen the beauty.[113]
>
> The amount of that beauty is impossible to know, staggering.
> See with your eyes while having sat at that place.
> So as to do the duty, climb at daybreak
> as soon as you see Āňḍiya Maḷa Tänna, friend.[114]

This sight of the Peak from this vantage point inspired weary pilgrims, urging them on to their final goal looming above.

Apart from pilgrims, those who live and work on the mountain have mused more on the meaning of Āňḍiyamalatänna. Stories circulated at tea breaks for my benefit, or as I passed the Āňḍiyamalatänna sign with others. One of the first people to tell me about it was a man named J. S. Vijayasingha, who lived about a kilometer down the steps from Āňḍiyamalatänna, at the Ratnapura-trail Makara Torana.[115] Vijayasingha hailed from a village near Ratnapura, and he had been to the summit for worship forty-five times in his life. He also often lived on the mountain to work during the season. In 2016, he and another caretaker shared a cement house with a monk, soliciting donations to expand the Buddhist shrines at their trailside landing.

Vijayasingha translated *āňḍi* for me as *dravida demala kaṭṭiya*, or the Dravidian Tamil group, and said they had settled since their invasions (*ākramaṇa*) of

FIGURE 4.3. The summit from Āňḍiyamalatänna

Lanka: "Since that time indeed they have been here. That group has constructed this place. This one . . . this Torana. After that, among them a person died. So then it became called Āňḍiyamalatänna, the place where he died. After that, to the south, the monks . . . in Sabaragamuwa province were entrusted with this place." Vijayasingha's narrative was both positive and negative. He attributed Tamil presence in Lanka to arrival by force, making the *āňḍi* of the Peak invasive. The flow of his story also suggested that the *āňḍi*'s death preceded the Peak's rededication to Buddhists. On the other hand, Vijayasingha credited the *āňḍi* with building the first Makara Torana at the Peak. I asked when, and he said it was constructed in the 1930s by a Tamil *sāmi*, or Hindu priest. I asked why, and he said they, too, believed the "leader" (*nāyaka*) of their religion had his footprint at the Peak. Chronologically, however, whoever erected this Makara Torana could not have been the original *āňḍi* of Āňḍiyamalatänna, for the latter name was well-established by the 1930s.

Other employees offered older origins, but with equally specious historiography. Descending the Ratnapura trail before dawn one morning with two summit employees, Aryapala Kapumahatya, the primary *kapurāla* priest to

Saman, and Ven. Gnanasumana, a resident monk of the summit, I posed the question:

> "So how did Āňḍiyamalatänna get that name?"
>
> "Kapumahatyo!" Ven. Gnanasumana called to Aryapala, who had moved several paces ahead. "Why did it get the name Āňḍiyamalatänna?"
>
> "Huh? Did Alex ask?" Aryapala slowed his gait to tell a story:
>
> "Before the *āňḍi* were in charge. It was the *āňḍi*'s place—Sri Pada. . . . So at that time, here at Sri Pada, there had not been a leader. A monk named Hikkaduvē Sumaṅgala and another monk, the two of them came, became angry at the *āňḍi*, scolded them, and removed the *āňḍi* from around here. Having removed them, so after that, one *āňḍi*, while going, died at this place. So that indeed is called Āňḍiyamalatänna.
>
> [Aryapala paused for two paces, then continued.]
>
> "The Tamil people had a *rājakāriya* at that time. So he who rescued it from Tamil control was a monk at Potgala Rajamaha Vihara . . .
>
> [Aryapala broke into a coughing fit, pausing to expectorate.]
>
> ". . . in the southern province. Hikkaduwe Sumangala, as I've said. That monk became the leader of Sri Pada."

Aryapala explained that Hikkaduwe Sumangala was the one to base the Sri Pada head-monk lineage in Pelmadulla, linking this to the current head monk, Ven. Dhammadinna. Ven. Gnanasumana then muttered that Āňḍiyamalatänna meant just that—*āňḍiyā maḷa tänna*—as if memorizing a lesson. Aryapala then gave more details on the *āňḍiyā*'s death:

> So that *āňḍi* had been struck by those monks.
> [Ven. Gnanasumana chuckled softly.]
> So the *āňḍi* while running away fell and then died.
> [Aryapala fell silent for a few paces before offering a new thought.]
>
> Muslim people? The Muslim people believe their Muhammad's foot is there. . . . Now the sacred foot does not belong to whomever. It is Lord Gautama Buddha's Sri Pada. That is our belief, the Sinhala Buddhist people. We come to the Sri Pada of Samanala Mountain and worship the Buddha, do *pujas* and so on. But if a Christian person comes, if a Muslim person comes, if a Tamil person comes, they can worship without religious division.

Aryapala's winding interpretation of Āňḍiyamalatänna shared certain themes with the shorter story of Vijayasingha. The *āňḍi* had been in charge, appointed to work at the Peak by a king, as Aryapala's word choice of *rājakāraya* implied. Yet Aryapala did not recognize the *āňḍi* as legitimate leaders (*nāyaka*). These could only be Buddhist monks, and Aryapala's portrayal of the Peak as rescued (*bērā gattē*) was similar to Vijayasingha's description of Tamils as invaders. Likewise, Aryapala also made the Peak's rededication to Buddhists related to the *āňḍi*'s demise, although his chronology was long after the 1751 rededication by Kīrti Śrī. Yet Aryapala's selection of a hero to evict the *āňḍi* was fascinating in itself. Hikkaduvē Sumaṅgala was recognized by the British as head of the Peak temple in 1867, but was already the fourteenth monk to hold that position since its creation by Kīrti Śrī, and the sixth under British rule.[116] It is fantastic to imagine this erudite scholar-monk taking on folkloristic qualities in Aryapala's version, screaming at and hitting the *āňḍi* until they fled, driving one to his death. There was no solemnity to this demise, only a comedic comeuppance for unwelcome interlopers.

It is instructive that speaking about the *āňḍi* triggered Aryapala to link Muslims into his train of thought. This suggests that the term still carries catch-all connotations for foreign, unlikable others.[117] Yet Aryapala stopped short of heaping vituperations upon Muslims. He began to head that way, summoning old demons of misinformation about Muhammadan worship, but seemed to mentally reevaluate his point as he dragged out his sentences with languorous enunciation, reverting to a common refrain about pluralism at the Peak, where all are free to worship. That this came only as a conciliatory coda to a divisive story shows how portrayals of pluralism often ring hollow, a problem discussed further in chapter 5.

Aryapala and I reached the foot of the mountain in time for breakfast, and we were in Ratnapura by noon. We immediately headed for the roundabout in the center of town. Aryapala's friend sold betel chews from a small stand there. He introduced himself: "My name is Anil, but if you say that to people around here, nobody will know who you're talking about. If you ask for Kalu Malli [black little brother] who sells betel by the clock tower, everyone will know." Kalu Malli had been up the mountain many times, more than he bothered to count, but had not ascended in several years. Loquacious, with an enormous grin, Kalu Malli knew almost every passerby in Ratnapura and had a constantly rotating audience for his endless stream of stories. Amused by our arrival, he began spinning tale after tale about the Peak. Before long, he landed on Āňḍiyamalatänna. According to Kalu Malli's rollicking version, the *āňḍi* who died was killed by a young monk, furious that Buddha statues in trailside shrines had been replaced by icons of Siva and Parvati. Kalu Malli mimed how this monk grabbed the *āňḍi* by his robes and tossed him from the mountain with a "judo throw." The special additions to Kalu Malli's story likely stemmed from the fact that he was also the local martial arts instructor, with a Bruce Lee poster hanging over his bed at home.

Aryapala started to interject, as only hours before he had delivered a different version of the Āṇ̌diyamalatänna story. But the name "Hikkaduwe Sumangala" had only begun to form on his lips when the bustle of the marketplace interrupted him and the moment was lost. Aryapala was more reserved in Ratnapura, cultivating a mystique appropriate for a head *kapurāla* to Saman, the most important god in town. As he yielded to Kalu Malli, the Āňḍiyamalatänna mytholith expanded, facets added to suit the personal interests of its narrator. Still, the stories could ultimately coexist because the basic function of the mythic tool was the same. The *āňḍi* were invasive and unwelcome, and violence directed against them, even by monks, was thereby authorized. In this way, the *āňḍi* became the antithesis of Buddhists at the Peak.

Thus, although Sinhala and Tamil authors traded in similar mytholithic structures throughout this chapter, especially with tales linking Siva, mountain, and watershed, the edges of their stories were hewn differently. Whereas Siva is all powerful in Tamil texts, he is at best a benign metaphor and at worst an unwelcome interloper in Sinhala compositions. The pluralism of the Peak once again appears far from harmonious, though its landscape retains potential for generating comparable outlooks.

PART III

Being Like a Mountain

5

Pilgrimage Ethics from Pluralism

ඉතා බොසො පවු පරදාර කල උනී෴
කතා බොසෝ අරගල නැතුව අසමිනී෴
සිතා ගතොත් මෙම සසරට සවුසතුනී෴
පතා ගනිමුව වඳුන් ශම සිතිනී෴

Very great demerit was defeated
Hearing many stories without disputes
If all beings in this world are considered
Let us all aspire to worship mindfully.[1]

The above verse is inscribed in a large palm-leaf compilation of Sinhala poetry meant for singing on pilgrimage. Most such songs are no longer used by those who rush up and down the Peak, with little time for poems. In slower eras, however, the laborious practice of copying manuscript books itself spurred poetic creativity. Unlike most verses in this 1857 compilation, this quatrain is seemingly an original composition of the scribe, one Senbakuṭṭi Kulasēkara Appu, who added it as a coda to the customary songs. Its sentiments are noble, suggesting ideal behavior in a pluralistic space, where many stories (*katā*) can be heard without disputes (*aragala*) when all beings bound in the worldly cycle of births are mindfully taken into consideration.

As the previous chapters have shown, however, the many multireligious stories of the Peak have not coexisted without conflict. Muslim and Hindu myths have been dismantled or dismissed by those Buddhists who wish for sole ownership of the Peak. So does pluralism actually exist there? The answer depends on how it is defined. What I call "presumed pluralism" is a stock definition that assumes harmony prevails at the Peak, with little or no reflection on how different religious groups actually coexist. It holds that the place wields a power over pilgrims that effaces all divisions or disputes. This discourse is touted in tourist literature, newspapers, academic articles, and government offices.[2] Arguing that this presumed pluralism does not really exist, I offer the alternative of planetary pluralism. This does not assume harmony, but instead considers all the agents in this mountain's story, human and nonhuman, living and nonliving, as a dynamic plurality that structures pilgrimage. This planetary perspective recognizes that all environments, pilgrimages included, fluctuate, with both divisive and cooperative encounters among beings. Maintaining the positive parts of pluralism is therefore not automatic, but an objective that must be pursued. Pilgrimage in this sense is not apolitical, and portraying it as such can mask injustices, just as treating nature as apolitical is of little use in negotiating accords to execute environmental conservation. In order to defeat demerit and hear the many stories of the Peak without disputes, the differences among them are precisely what must be considered, to work through political contentions by mindfully recognizing them.

Reflecting the content of these stories, this chapter reads the religious and ecological pluralism of the Peak together over three main parts. The first section recounts the local histories of pilgrimage ethics that are tied to environmental history. How people behave partly depends on what sort of landscape they must traverse—the harder the climb, the better the behavior. With less forest at present, pilgrims purportedly have worse manners and more diluted piety, while the powers of guardian gods diminish with a loss of woods and the disappearance of major animal actors. Controlling behavior, especially how pilgrims treat the environment, is therefore a key concern at the Peak. The second section examines attempts to mitigate human impact on the environment through religious language, considering conservation injunctions common on signage along the trail in 2016 as one discourse where the Peak's presumed pluralism falters, with environmental campaigns revealing Sinhala Buddhist biases. This is part of the broader issue of Buddhist hegemony at the Peak, which excludes non-Buddhists, and even non-elite Buddhists, from certain ritual practices on the summit. This leads to the third section of this chapter, where I present pilgrimage ethics through the Peak's planetary pluralism. In the face of increasing Buddhist hegemony, I counter that Buddhist thought, in its canonical, philosophical, poetic, and ethnographic instantiations, promotes unbounded understandings of interactive ecological and religious pluralities.[3] When pilgrims tell stories of Saman's wilderness powers, or draw connections between the Buddha dharma and natural laws, lessons about the Peak's plural world emerge from the forest. Interpretations of pilgrimage as entangled with wilderness ultimately show how humanity can never fully control the Peak, ecologically or religiously, but is still equipped to cooperate upon it.

But why focus primarily on Buddhism in a book about pluralism? My reasons are partly practical, as synthesizing theories from three different religious traditions alongside political ecology would quickly make this chapter unwieldy. It is also practical in the sense that Buddhists are the ones who currently control the mountain, and so recommendations for better practices of stewardship may be most effectively expressed through Buddhist commitments. Of course, other perspectives on pilgrimage also recur here as a pluralistic measure. For theoretical reasons, I also employ Buddhist concepts for their productive resonances with ecology. This is not the simplistic equation of Buddhism and ecology that characterized early writings on the topic, but a demonstration of their complementary languages.[4] I suggest that Buddhist ideas are an example of what William Connolly calls "process philosophy," which helps us "come to terms more closely with a world composed of interacting force fields set on different scales of chronotime that compose an evolving universe open to an uncertain degree."[5] This chapter presents an array of Buddhist expressions about the interrelatedness and uncertain evolution of things, as well as the suffering that arises from our attachment to what Michel Serres calls the "mastery and possession" of the world.[6] Attempts to dominate and appropriate sever the connectedness of things in the name of ownership, presuming an unrealistic power over the world. These same habits of mastery and possession imperil not only natural habitats, but also the Peak's human habitus of religious pluralism.

Countering the erosion of equitable pilgrimage requires cultivating a religious attention toward maintaining habitable environments for a plurality of beings. As Serres suggests, "the term *religion* expresses exactly this trajectory, this review or prolonging whose opposite is called *negligence*. . . . The notion of negligence makes it possible to understand our time and our climate."[7] Losing attentiveness to the world blinds us to its problems and our faults, making us negligent caretakers of our environments. Building on Serres, Latour argues that *all* collective groups are religious, united in their attention to one thing or another: "But there are collectives that *neglect* many elements that *other collectives* consider extremely important and that they need to care for constantly." Despite their differences, however, religiousness also makes collectives more aware of one another, as they "become attentive to the shock, the scandal, that the *lack of care* on the part of one collective can represent for another. In other words, to be religious is first of all to become attentive to that to which others cling. It is thus, in part, to learn to behave as a diplomat."[8] If sustaining the pluralism of the Peak requires that different parties speak to one another, each collective must develop its own tools of amicable discourse. For Buddhists, identifying how we cling to misguided views that result in a lack of care for others has been a central concern for centuries, as has encouragement toward the attentive correction of these faults. Beyond mere scriptural injunction, this is enacted in various worship practices at the Peak. Vijaya Nagarajan notes how some rituals can be "ways of paying attention to the ground that we walk on daily. They remind us that we are embedded in and dependent on the earth."[9] The rituals conducted around a mountain famous for a footprint are certainly good candidates for remembering our embedded treading.

It may be that we need to heed the pluralistic world in the manner of a pilgrim who carefully attends to the Buddha's foot. Buddha feet are full of details, patterned with 108 auspicious marks (*maṅgala lakuṇa*). Of course, the stone indentation on the summit is unmarked, but cloths are placed atop it as offerings, embroidered with the traditional outline of the footprint and its symbols of fortune, wisdom, and power (fig. 5.1). Some devotees spend weeks crafting such cloths before going on pilgrimage, stitching patterns or drawing the marks with glitter glue and bedazzling them with rhinestones as a meditation on the footprint they will visit at the Peak. So many of these homemade cloth offerings accumulate over the season that they are regularly collected and delivered to the head monk's *vihāra* in Pelmadulla, where they are strung up beneath the eaves of the buildings to display during the closing ceremonies for the worship season.

Covering the stone footprint with illustrated cloth or metal is a practice that dates back centuries. The marks have also been recited in Pali poetry like Vedeha's *Samantakūṭavaṇṇanā* and in Sinhala verse like the *Purāṇa Himagata Varṇanāva* copies sold in Chandra's stall.[10] The latter poem refers to two sacred soles in all its verses about auspicious marks. Likewise, Senbakuṭṭi Kulasēkara Appu includes a verse in his poetry compilation that describes worshiping at a pair of footprints:

> Red and white flowers are heaped up extensively, compressed
> upon the impressed soles
> As when they were placed, the sacred soles have two-hundred-
> sixteen auspicious marks
> Placed like the moon, existing for the whole time of the four eons
> Always worship the soles placed on that earthly plane until
> *moksha* is seen.[11]

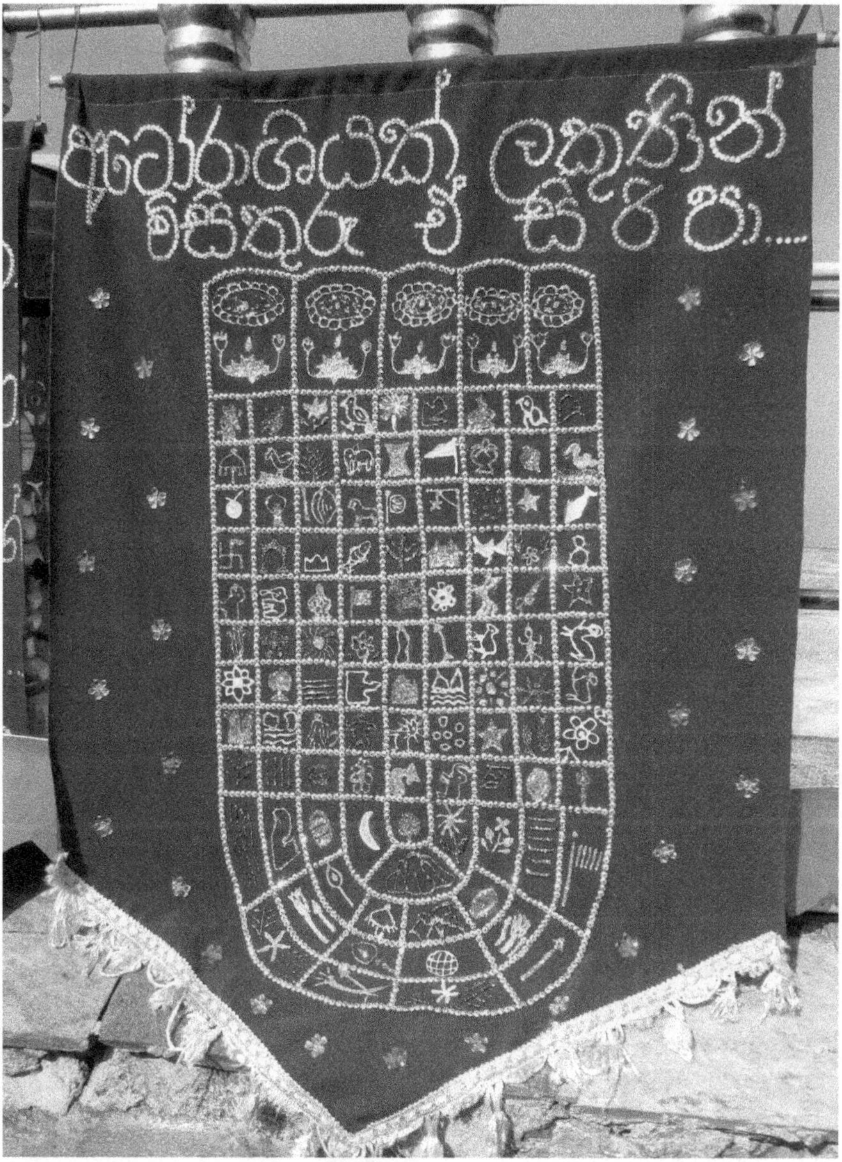

FIGURE 5.1. Homemade footprint cloth tied to summit railing

As the poet suggests, the marks do more than simply decorate. They are part of the deep time phenomenon discussed in chapter 1, connecting the pilgrim to the past across a celestial expanse of time, and encouraging reflection on existence. The Buddha's footprint encompasses heaven and earth, its auspicious marks including animals, plants, gods, stars, lakes, rivers, and many other mountains, with room for Kailash, too. This makes the Buddha's feet "a mirror reflecting the whole world," as the Pali poem *Pajjamadhu* put it.[12]

This expansive cosmos in the Buddha's foot also reflects the equally expansive ethic of kindness he prescribed, one he once articulated in terms of feet:

> For the footless, I have loving-kindness;
> I have loving-kindness for those with two feet;
> for those with four feet, I have loving-kindness;
> I have loving-kindness for those with many feet.
> . . .
> All beings, all living things,
> all creatures, everyone,
> may they see all good fortune,
> and may nothing bad come to anyone.[13]

This was part of the Buddha's reply in the *Ahirāja Sutta* (Discourse on snake kings) to a report that a monk had died from snakebite. He reasoned that it was the monk who needed to display more loving-kindness (*metta*) to the snakes for them to return the favor. Yet the above verses that close the discourse show the Buddha scaling the *metta* ethic up from the specific case at hand. As Buddhaghosa notes in his commentary, *Ahirāja Sutta* up to this point explains "particular loving-kindness" (*odissakametta*) specific to the snake case, but "with this 'all beings' now general loving-kindness (*anodissakametta*) begins to be explained." Buddhaghosa then glosses the entities mentioned: "in this sense, all of these beings, living things, and creatures [*sattā pāṇā bhūtā*] are synonyms for persons [*puggala*]."[14] The term *puggala* most often refers to people, and the human element is certainly important for the Peak, as accords among religious groups are required for flourishing pluralism. Yet Buddhaghosa here likely uses a secondary sense of *puggala* that encompasses all beings, whether animal, ghost, god, or even element, as the semantic range of *bhūtā* is especially expansive.[15] Whether human or nonhuman, *metta* is a helpful ethic, what Maria Heim calls "a much more capacious way of being, one that is not distorted or hemmed in by one's usual prejudices, resentments, hatreds, and aversions."[16] To this end, Buddhaghosa's broad application of the *puggala* category is especially fitting for a modern audience, as personhood is precisely what many ecology scholars and activists attempt to attribute to pieces of the nonhuman world, even if only for legal standing.[17] Of course, no person can stand without support, making Buddhaghosa's gloss of "good fortune" (*bhadra*) quite apt, as he modifies it with the word *ārammaṇa*, meaning "support," "help," or "footing,"[18] thereby tempering the vagaries of luck and omens otherwise associated with fate and fortune. This firmer sort of fortune must be intentionally enacted with loving-kindness, as the "bad" (*pāpa*) one hopes to avoid can arise from human demerits just as easily as events beyond our control. At the Peak, this means all pilgrims must help secure stable footing for one another, human or otherwise, as steady as the perfectly level feet of a Buddha and equally expansive in their measure of what is worthy for inclusion, even collectives sometimes seen as threats. Buddha feet do not fear fangs of snakes, for their soles contain these footless ones, too, including Vāsuki, the same serpent who hangs from Siva's shoulders. If there is space for all these beings in the Buddha's footprint, they should have a place in the world. This requires cultivating an expansive capacity for creaturely kindness, even if it means the forest maintains more dangerous forms, as many more voices in this chapter will recommend.

As Buddhist poetics help build the ethics represented here, the verses of several Sinhala bards grace the pages to come. One poet appears most often as a guide through this forest of pluralism: K. H. Juvānisā. He stands as an example of a devout Buddhist able to accommodate eclectic pluralities at the Peak, both religiously and ecologically, as expressed in his 1923 *Śrī Pāda Gaman Vistaraya* (Description of the Sri Pada journey). This is not a work of high poetry. Its basic vocabulary and repetitive phrasings led one Sinhala scholar to call it "unskilled" or "untrained" (*nupuhuṇu*), although he acknowledged the simple didactic quality may have been so children could participate in singing it.[19] Juvānisā certainly saw himself as a Buddhist teacher, encouraging readers to "take this book and look well into the *dharma* of Gautama the Sage Lord," thereafter showing his own devotion with several verses about the Buddha's enlightenment and visits to Lanka before the actual pilgrimage description.[20] He also notes his deep experience with the pilgrimage: "The amount I've worshiped at Siripāda is now thirty-five journeys, including the one from today."[21] Taking on this teaching role, Juvānisā was unafraid to critique Buddhists he found behaving badly, including those who were too exclusionary. Juvānisā personally revered a diverse pantheon, invoking over a dozen deities alongside the Buddha, and noting in particular that permission to enter the forest was granted to pilgrims by both Saman and Siva:

> Having remembered God Sumana Saman,
> giving merit clusters at appropriate places,
> receiving warrant to go into the forest,
> God Sumana Saman has given us protection.
>
> God Isivara we have remembered.
> Having worshiped our Buddha's foot,

> I give to you, too, this merit that was received.
> We have also received warrant from thou.[22]

Juvānisā therefore differs from his contemporary John de Silva, discussed in chapter 4, not only because Juvānisā allows Siva to legitimately coexist at the Peak, but also because his unpretentious verses are less for erudite appreciation, and more to carry through song his ethical points about pilgrimage into a public sphere of ritual practice. In the process, Juvānisā rejects exclusivity at the Peak with lessons from the Buddha as well as the forest, just as this chapter aims to do.

Paradise Lost?

The kids are not all right. So an elder contingent of mountain workers often told me. Chandra gazed out of her trailside tea stall one evening as a group of young people cackled out peals of laughter between yelling the call and response chant about going to worship. Chandra spoke wistfully of another time: "Before, when people came all wearing white and reciting *Tunsarana*, what a beautiful sight it was to see the crowds coming. Now people wear inappropriate clothes and don't recite *Tunsarana*. They are only shouting and shouting, 'Worship! Worship! Worship!'" Although some shops, Chandra's included, still sold print copies of the poem called *Tunsarana* (Triple refuge), only a small minority of pilgrims sung it while climbing. The number of palm-leaf manuscripts of the poem indicate its recitation was once common enough to inspire substantial investment in this painstaking bookmaking method.[23] While printing made copies of *Tunsarana* more available than ever, the poem appears less used, part of what changed the sounds and sights that mattered to Chandra.

The shopkeeper Ranjit had similar thoughts about pilgrims today who never experienced the old hardships of the Peak. A middle-aged man with a shaved head, but with a large and bushy gray beard, he had an ascetic look about him, appropriately taking propriety very seriously in the confines of pilgrimage. Thinking the Hatton trail had become too easy for authentic devotion, Ranjit criticized the gaggles of kids who came shouting, or were only interested in the "love scene." He took me on an imagined journey into the past to frame how pilgrimage behavior had changed:

> If we look back a hundred years . . . for the group that had come back then, little brother, these roads were difficult. Small roads. Right? Rain! Wind! Fog!

> So there is no light; lights were put in 1950, no? There are no lights. There are not shops with everything to eat. Everything has to be bound up and placed on the head. It is indeed difficult to go. That means one or two days of hardship using lamps with coconut oil and things like that. So because this trip is difficult, people have believed, having come here, that they will not be able to return. They will die. It doesn't happen that way. Lord Buddha doesn't let it happen like that. God Saman doesn't let it happen like that. But people have fear . . . They have written over their lands, homes, and everything to someone . . . have written a deed . . . Because of that, those people became accustomed to a way of speaking out of fear . . . fear is one thing, and the other is devotion. Being compassionate [*karuṇā karanavā*].

Ranjit's scene contained the common tropes of a remembered Peak of the past. People writing their last wills and giving land deeds to their children before pilgrimage was a story I heard several times.[24] A colonial source recorded what could happen if deeds were unspecified: "In old age and extreme weakness [Kapuwatte Kumarihami] undertook a pilgrimage to Adam's Peak, and died in February 1884, when she was being carried down the mountain on the back of one of her vassals. There was a contest for her estate by many remote relations."[25] Death itself was a fearsome component to pilgrimage, which Ranjit saw as connected to the compassion with which one needed to travel.[26] By "a way of speaking out of fear," Ranjit referred to a special language once used in forests at the Peak and elsewhere, often describing negative things as positive. Heavy loads are called light, and the verb for "to go" becomes "to be compassionate" (*karuṇā karanavā*). Of this old jungle tongue (*kälē bhāṣā*), that is the only phrase still regularly used at the Peak.[27]

If we go back a century in Sinhala poetry, we see that many journeys were still taken entirely on foot, and mountain trails snaked through full forests, with descriptions that corroborate Ranjit's depiction. Journeys lasted for weeks, rather than the weekend daytrips pilgrims now enjoy. Hardships became especially pronounced after pilgrims entered "Himagata," a name for the Peak that also includes its circumference of forested hills and valleys for miles around the summit. During his ascent of the Peak in 1844, Prince Waldemar of Prussia depicted this territory by focusing his artistic gaze on the great distance between the last constructed shelter on the pilgrimage path and the summit (fig. 5.2). Poems by veteran pilgrimage gurus like Lavarenti warn of this dangerous terrain:

> Except for the house-or-door-lacking Himagata, friend,
> without a village, from this place on it's only mountains.

FIGURE 5.2. "Last Rest-house on the Way to Adam's Peak" by Prince Waldemar of Prussia

Due to various wild animals, let us go in a row.
I speak of it much too clumsily; you should go and see.[28]

As with the forest panoply from *Saman Sirita* that leapt through chapter 1, the hills were still filled with dangerous creatures, requiring attentive sight to truly understand it and thereby survive within it.

Juvānisā likewise had much advice to offer about keeping the pilgrim group united, healthy, and sane when in dark labyrinths of foreboding forests. He refers to these difficulties of the jungle repeatedly throughout his poem, and emphasizes his firsthand experience when stating his authorial intentions at the end:

Gone from place to place in the forest and being hidden
Having entered the forest and become afraid
The Himagata god becomes the assistance
Therefore tying tributes for the Lord God
...
When going in the forest like this, friend
Counting everyone in the group

Adding the number all together
The guru does it like this
. . .
For two or three days being in the forest
Entering the forest and becoming sorrowful
Walking in the forest without an end
Now the god's command is beheld

I thought to speak poetry about this
As the details there in the forest appeared to me
Going mad and staying put was apparent
Nonsensical speaking and crying was apparent.[29]

Jungle animals, scary weather, scanty supplies, sore bodies, or sagging morale could all sink pilgrims into deep wooded sorrows, or even madness. This forced their guru to track them carefully, and perform proper practices for safe passage, as practical as taking headcounts and as tenuous as calling out for compassion (*karuṇāva*) or tying tribute (*paňḍuru*) coins as offerings for the god of Himagata. Juvānisā intriguingly leaves this god unnamed throughout the poem; he is likely referring to Saman, but possibly implying Siva, too, considering his earlier verse and the Himalayan homophony of the name Himagata. Juvānisā seems to leave his invocations open to any god of the forest who might help.[30]

Poetry itself was also recommended for staving off jungle madness. One author endorsed recitation of *Tunsarana* for this purpose.[31] Likewise, many verses in manuscripts of *Samanala Hälla* poems allowed pilgrims to sing about the difficulty of their journey:

Unable to descend on the path and go happily due to mountain
  streams and falls
One's woozy body shivering and shaking, the cold, too, striking
  in the forest
The cold and inability to see the surroundings cause fear in the
  high water
Having become aware and taken the precepts, worship the
  sacred foot on Samanala.[32]

As this verse suggests, the perils of the landscape are part of what drives people to make ethical commitments like observing the Buddhist precepts.

Ranjit told me how, without natural threats instilling a fear of the forest on modern trails, some youth no longer come with proper comportment, nor bother to recite the customary poetry:

> Now, the older group, the group with devotion, coming to worship while saying "*sadhu sadhu*," reciting *Tunsarana—tun sarana* means Buddha, Dharma, Sangha—in that way they spoke . . . That bunch with great devotion and strength came to worship here. Now, out of a hundred there are maybe ten or fifteen like that . . . Girls are here, boys are here, and they are not going compassionately [*karuṇāvayi nähä*], not reciting *Tunsarana*. Some, not all . . . So, girls and boys are here going together for the love scene in that way. There are inappropriate clothes, harsh words in the mouth, sometimes saying things people don't like, laughing . . . So, little brother, those we cannot call correct. There are 365 days per year. There's only one day here . . . On that day, they're not here twenty-four hours, no? Six or five or seven hours. So, for these five hours we can go correctly, no? Beautifully speaking without a harsh word in the mouth. Without the love scene. In that way we can go, no? Three hours silently up and three hours silently down we can go.

Ranjit's imagination of the poetic past, when singing *Tunsarana* was a standard pilgrimage ritual, has disillusioned him toward the younger generation's informal rush up the mountain. Yet mouthy kids have seemingly been a perennial problem, scolded in past poems just as some still are today. A poet in 1890 endorsed "constructive speech" (*väḍa äti bas*) like his own ethical advice, and condemned "unconstructive words for laughs" (*väḍa näti vada sināvaṭa*).[33] Lavarenti likewise notes that when "Himagata is on both sides . . . trained youths will not blather rough words in their mouths."[34] Being trained (*purudäti*) to go on pilgrimage like this was partly due to safety, as, according to Juvānisā, juvenile talk was another trigger for jungle madness:

> Going to Samanala while playing
> Don't go while harassing, friend
> If you harass, it will happen like this
> You will run into the forest unable to be caught
>
> Now hear about the ones like this
> They walk now losing consciousness

Why do they lose consciousness?
Because people go cracking various jokes.[35]

The fact that so many poets felt such injunctions necessary suggests the etiquette of pilgrimage speech was often broken.

Ranjit's passing mention of "harsh words" also alludes to a real problem of harassment on the trail, where some men inflict violence, including sexual harassment of local and foreign women, or insults and threats against non-Buddhists. Yet Ranjit seemed particularly peeved by the flirtatious canoodlers. Ironically, his stall offered the exact items that catered to the youth fashion of "the love scene." He did a steady business selling key chains, bracelets, necklaces, barrettes, headbands, sunglasses, rings, and even combs and mirrors (fig. 5.3). Ranjit was polite. He preferred we chat when customers were absent, but he said he was only pointing out problems that would also upset Saman.

FIGURE 5.3. Items for sale in Ranjit's shop

Yet Ranjit's concerns about this love scene were not new either. A 1974 novel by T. B. Ilangaratne implied that multiple generations of youth had been using pilgrimage to elude parental oversight and snuggle with sweethearts:

> "Going on pilgrimage in two separate buses with a lot of others won't do any harm."
>
> "No. Certainly not in the bus. When they start climbing in the night in the cold, the young will know how to warm themselves. These pilgrimages particularly to Adam's Peak are arranged for that purpose. Have you forgotten our young days?"[36]

People old enough to be Ranjit's grandparents were thus once guilty of the same amorous transgressions he attributed to today's youth. Still older poems voiced similar concerns about romantic socializing. In a work from the temperance movement of the 1930s, entitled *The Lament of Mother Lanka, or the Great Divine Wrath*, the party scene at the Peak was excoriated, skewering dishonorable pilgrimage gurus in its critique of intoxicated revelers who were more interested in dancing, matchmaking, and singing inappropriate songs than in sincere worship:

> Some louts of low vile groups
> Like savage beasts doing various mockeries
> Climb to the charming mountain summit and dance and sport
> Drinking dreadful gin brandy and ganja, becoming intoxicated
> inhumans
>
> Bringing toddy to be drunk, women sing wild *baila*
> They stop with girls, having caught onto the playful songs well
> The groups of toddy-drunken mindless gurus are like pigs
> Bringing immaturity like this, the vile group goes on pilgrimage
>
> Having aimed well for beautiful precious ones
> Untamed, going only to be wedded couples
> Lewd boundless people go to Samanala
> In the group those guru idiots also encourage that
>
> The thief-called-guru's stomach lump filling for himself
> To drink liquor, thus they take the funds for supplies
> Dear forgiving King Sakra, this is really not a lie
> Courageous conquered Sri Lanka thus went to ruin.[37]

This lament of Mother Lanka was almost identical to one I heard from Chandra, as she decried trip leaders who collected money just to "make a party" out of the pilgrimage.[38] Contrary to her and Ranjit's vision of a virtuous pilgrimage prevailing before the trail was paved or lit, enough infrastructure evidently existed by the turn of the twentieth century for people to turn the trip into a festival of merrymaking up and down the mountain.

The main material agents of this ethical change were the roads and rails described in chapter 2. Without the challenge of a weeklong hike, revelry easily ensued. Illustrations of trains and cars speeding to and from the Peak were featured on the cover of M. G. K. Jōn Perēra's *Sri Pada Pilgrimage, or Former Customs and Current Customs* in 1924. Although transportation went unmentioned in his poem, his main topic was pilgrim behavior, showing Buddhists of this period struggling with what they, too, saw as a decline in piety practices. Almost a century before Chandra and Ranjit's complaint, Perēra claimed reciting "proper poems" like *Tunsarana* was a thing of the past, that people were now only shouting slogans like *karuṇāva* rather than actually enacting their meaning: "Wanting to offer across the eardrums, that is the *karuṇāva* those ones do indeed."[39] This same verse also prefigured Ranjit's complaints of harassment: "Shamelessly having gone to a row of shops, creeping around girls." Another verse criticized the vain love scene in general:

> Face powder applied, whiskers twisted, some people tie two hair combs,
> while pouring out festive rosewater to forever spread the fragrance.
> Although gone from home to perform merit, along the road that's not remembered.
> Behaving flirtatiously while on the road, some people sit and laugh happily.[40]

Perērapreferred the older manner of pilgrimage, which he envisioned as one of humble appearances, sharing of food, and attention to purity and religious rites:

> Grinding and bundling five culinary spices and chilies to make food,
> having also bundled white clothing like this to wear for the journey,
> heads washed and bathed, clothes put on, they go to the nearby *vihara*,
> taking the five precepts and eight precepts like *sastras*, and listening to the Dharma.[41]

Although this portrays the past as ideally normative, the "old ways" are always seductive. Despite Perēra's complaints about changes in his own time, a Sinhala scholar of the 1970s reminisced of Perēra's era as idyllic, with more bullock carts than cars.[42] In turn, the 1970s were a time about which people in 2016 reminisced to me. Each former age allegedly provides the purer pilgrimage, as the actually fluid past is repeatedly idealized into a constant standard.

Nevertheless, new challenges in controlling pilgrim behavior have certainly arisen, with problems that temperance poets would not have anticipated. As pilgrim numbers have grown exponentially over the past century, so has their environmental footprint on the Peak. Ranjit noticed this, too, taking me behind his shop to show me the layers of plastic bags embedded in the soil; some he guessed were decades old. So while signage along the trail in 2016 did contain injunctions or poetic quatrains to discourage drinking or smoking on pilgrimage, warnings against harming the wilderness reserve have become even more common, usually packaged with a Buddhist message.

Buddhist Hegemony in Conservation and Ritual

Religious language in environmental messages at the Peak is not subtle, even on signs erected by government organizations like the Central Environmental Authority (Madhyama Parisara Adhikāriya). One Hatton-trail sign, for example, used specific ethical vocabulary that made its message particular to Buddhists: "The most necessary time for your loving-kindness [*mettāva*], compassion [*karuṇāva*], sympathetic joy [*muditāva*], and equanimity [*upēkṣāva*] is at this sacred ground. By even your breath, may the environment cool [*parisariya nivēvā*]!" These terms are significant for a Buddhist who knows them as "the four immeasurables," virtues cultivated to attain nirvana. The trail sign then likened humans to bodhisattvas, whose traits liberate the environment, as the breath's cooling effect was *nivēvā*, also meaning "to extinguish," a verbal form of nirvana. It was a new way of encouraging environmental conservation by using the cooling bodhisattva motifs of older texts, as in how Juvānisā described Saman:

> God Sumana Saman proceeds
> Wielding a whisk fan of three leagues
> Stirring the winds for the Sage like this
> Worshiping the Sage Lord's foot.[43]

With human breath cooling the environment like divine winds cooled the Buddha, the Central Environmental Authority left a layered metaphor to direct Buddhists toward deeper consideration of conservation. Other local offices, like the Ambagamuwa Divisional Council (Ambgamuva Prādēśiya Sabhāva) posted signs with direct appeals to pilgrimage leaders: "Noble group-entrusted guru, inform everyone in the groups who arrived with you so as to not discard waste anywhere in this most sacred merit ground that received the touch of Gautama Buddha, where God Sri Sumana Saman resides." In general, government-sponsored signs made ubiquitous use of Buddhist religious language, unlike many signs from private businesses such as banks, which omitted direct religious references in a general call for sustainability, or used vaguer phrasings like "sacred ground," applicable to any religion.

Religious terminology may be appropriate for certain conservation messages at a wilderness reserve that is also a pilgrimage site, but this language can also warp the promotion of pluralism at the Peak, hindering environmental projects in the process. The fact that the vast majority of signage was only in Sinhala is the most obvious example of bias limiting the conservation conversation. Although Sinhala is the majority language of Sri Lanka, it is a relative minority around Nallathanni. The Central Province Agricultural and Environmental Ministry recently took some bilingual initiative by creating new signs in a campaign called "The Environment Is Sacred" (Sinhala: *parisaraya pūjanīyayi*; Tamil: *cuṟṟāṭal puṉitamāṉatu*). They were posted along the road between Maskeliya and Nallathanni, near Tamil settlements. The campaign slogan was printed above, and the messages below varied, but the Sinhala was always on top. On some, there was essentially no difference between the Sinhala and Tamil. Other signs, however, lost something in translation. The most egregious example was in the heart of Nallathanni, just below the trailhead. The Sinhala message read: "Like the mind of you who arrive at this beautiful sacred ground made worshipful by the touch of the Buddha foot, let us purify the environment, too." This linked the Buddhist values of pilgrimage with the ecological ethics of a wilderness reserve. The Tamil message, however, had problems: "Like the minds of those who arrive at the sacred ground made worshipful by the glory of the Lord Buddha, clean the environment, too." The sign did not adapt its religious language to Hindu standards, and the Buddha was presented as the only option for the owner of the footprint. Nor did it extend the pronoun "you" to its Tamil reader. Moreover, the verbs were different. Sinhala sentences always had the *-mu* verbal ending, connoting a communal "let's do it" sentiment. While a similar construction did appear in most Tamil messages with the equivalent *-ōm* verbal ending, the above Tamil message had the verb as a formal imperative (*tūymaiyākkuṇkaḷ*), connoting a command to the Tamils to pick up after the pure-minded Buddhists. Considering most mountain labor is Tamil, the message could be read as intentionally insulting. One local blamed Buddhists in particular for littering, claiming Hindus ate and drank before or after, not during, pilgrimage. Nallathanni residents do not need a reminder that they are the ones collecting trash after every weekend surge of pilgrims who discard garbage uncaringly. Such a board is therefore an ominous sign. Just as with religious pluralism, one cannot assume automatic accords will prevail in environmentalism, nor that Buddhist invocations of nature are always innocent. Wilderness reserves can be used to overtly promote an allegedly pluralistic shared heritage, but covertly play to a Buddhist base by evicting non-Buddhists from the land, as has occurred at other pilgrimage sites like Kataragama.[44] Bad bilingual signs are but one example of creeping Buddhist hegemony that thrives in spaces where control of behavior is paramount.

The summit of the Peak is the most controlled of all. Even its flora has almost been regulated out of existence. Above the cement, only the heartiest of plants forge forth in the last cracks of parent rock (fig. 5.4). Good behavior in the form of soft sounds and modest dress, including removing hats and shoes, is enforced by signs, monks, police, and other stern staff and pilgrims. Prohibition of photography is enforced by the constant footprint guard, and the selfies below are kept in check by reminders that it is untoward to take photos with one's back toward the shrine building. Yet strict control can also prevent ritual pluralism at the Peak by exclusivity, so some seeking the summit may feel as squeezed as the last plants.

As noted previously, the Buddhist domination of the Peak began in earnest after Ven. Morotunduve Dhammānanda became head monk in 1954.[45] Yet no one monk could change a whole culture. Buddhicization of the Peak was surely supported from the ground up, promoting prejudices of a Buddhist base with reservations about Hindus and Muslims at the Peak. To see how such Buddhist hegemony was felt, consider a 1955 Tamil travelogue by S. Jeyarācā, a student of Jaffna Hindu College. He likely climbed via Nallathanni, describing a sign of Hindu representation: "At first everyone properly started to climb the mountain, and at the beginning there was a *gopuram* tower visible." As Jeyarācā climbed, he relayed an interaction with other pilgrims at a rest stop: "there was a rest hall and water amenities were manifested through pumps. To rest the legs, we stayed there for some minutes. In mass, men, women, and children of the Sinhala *jāti* went saying 'Sadu, Sadu.' They saw us and shouted 'Aro Hara' in faulty pronunciation. So we, too, called out 'Sadu Sadu.'" This encounter seems friendly enough, Buddhists and Hindus exchanging each other's exclamations of sacred affirmation. Although mispronunciation might suggest mockery,

FIGURE 5.4. Last plants on the summit

Jeyarācā did not seem bothered by it. He was more perturbed by what happened at the summit deity shrine: "On the front side, glass doors were fastened. Inside, an image of Lord Krishna, made of gold, and some various other images were installed there, with electrical lights brightly shining. We, in accordance with Saiva religion, burned camphor, worshiped, and then turned to the other shrine. A person from the Sinhala *jāti*, who saw us leaving, kicked the burning camphor with his leg and extinguished it. By that, they showed this mountain as belonging to them quite well."[46] Although this is the same shrine space where Saman's statue is, Jeyarācā showed no knowledge of that deity. Perhaps he interpreted Saman as Krishna. Perhaps there actually was a Krishna statue in that shrine, if it once held a more diverse pantheon.[47] Yet the Saiva style of worship Jeyarācā practiced was rejected by a Buddhist pilgrim. Summit rituals are still controlled by allowing only certain offerings, limiting religious others. Jeyarācā's camphor being kicked out is a type of experience recreated by new waves of exclusionary Buddhists. During the civil war, Tamils traveling to the Peak took steps to efface their identities.[48] These pressures did not all abate in the postwar period. In April 2017, a group of forty-five pilgrims from Jaffna, carrying orange flags of Siva's bull Nandi, said they were threatened by Buddhists who told them not to bring banners or shout *ōm nama civvāyā* to praise Siva on the way.[49]

The aura of exclusion that exists at the summit can even be directed by Buddhists toward their own coreligionists. On this point, Juvānisā's critique in *Śri Pāda Gaman Vistaraya* becomes most forceful. In a section titled "Verses to Recite at Mahagiridamba," he admonishes those who "guard" (*mura karannē/räkinnē*) the trail at this spot just below the summit:

To climb Mahagiridamba, friends,
open the space to go to worship.
Are you not allowing worship, friends?
Why are guards there, friends?

In the country, a crowd having come like this,
in their own group to worship like that.
So on that mountain are guards like that,
for their own people to worship like that.

Oh why does the guard stay there?
Oh why is this pain caused?
From this guarding are quarrelling words.
How are the barred people going to worship?

Do not attack the minds of those going to worship.
Open the Rajamāvata trail to go.
From guarding there is not any merit, friend.
When going to worship, why guard?[50]

These guards stationed near the summit may have barred non-Buddhists, but seemingly kept other Buddhists away, too, as the summit was protected for particular pilgrimage parties to worship privately. Juvānisā accuses these people of "guarding their own wives and children, and not giving any consolation to others."[51] At one point, he suggests this prejudice is caste based, a definite possibility at a time when pilgrimages were customarily "organized with neighbors of common caste":[52]

It was told to our Buddha
that the Sage went for alms like the *roḍī* caste.
As the Enlightened King was walking,
"Do not take those offerings," was said.

By that demerit that remains up to today,
when going to worship, they say "no."
So, meritorious ones, look here.
Now we are going to worship here.[53]

Juvānisā criticizes those who would refuse a devotee's worship with an apparent reference to the *Vasala Sutta* of the Pali canon. Guards at the Peak are likened to the Brahmin of that teaching, who shouted at the Buddha, calling him an outcaste (*vasala*) as the Buddha came on alms rounds while a sacrifice was being readied at the Brahmin's house.[54] Instead of *vasala*, Juvānisā substitutes the term *roḍī*, the outcaste rank of the Sinhala system, to reiterate the message of the *sutta* that teaches the true measure of character comes from action and not birth status. Juvānisā therefore emphasizes the lack of merit that comes from guarding, and presses forward to worship with his group. Meanwhile, his tone toward his opponents remains respectful, addressing them as friends, just as the Buddha humbled the Brahmin by not being angered at his insult. As Juvānisā's verses were sung aloud, they were likely meant to shame anyone who would inhibit earnest pilgrims. Their content certainly differed from traditional songs in circulation. A verse from the *Samanala Hälla* corpus, for example, is more idealistic, claiming that, on pilgrimage, "people in the country born in various castes are equally united in hand."[55] Compared to such sentiments, Juvānisā made a critical intervention against a myth of presumed pluralism operative in his own day, attempting to hold his peers to the Buddhist values of canonical teachings and pilgrimage poems.

There are still moments of elite Buddhists exercising exclusion over other Buddhists on the summit. The Tamil account of Jeyarācā provides an example of this with respect to a particular Buddhist ritual—the worship of the footprint by washing it. Jeyarācā documents a time before it became a V.I.P. event. When he witnessed it in 1955, this washing was seemingly a common form of worship that many pilgrims performed: "Below the canopy a footprint was visible. As before, we worshiped and stood there. By standing like this, we witnessed the Sinhala *jāti*'s worship method there. Since their worship method was novel, it was amazing to us. First, pouring a little water and rubbing turmeric on that, having drained and taken a portion of that water for themselves, the rest was poured on top of the footprint, and afterward they covered the foot with cloth, worshiped, put that cloth aside and left."[56] Rubbing turmeric on the footprint and then pouring water, some of which is collected by pilgrims, still happens at the Peak, but now only twice a week, under strict conditions.

The Guarded Work of Kemmura

Wednesdays and Saturdays are *kemmura* days at the Peak. The term *kemmura* is also applied to other Lankan temples, signifying days when the resident god is most powerful, generally Wednesday and Saturday, when shrines are often ritually cleansed. At the Peak, *kemmura* days necessitated a special afternoon *puja*, with a washing of the footprint and the entire upper compound. It seemed to hearken to stories cited in chapter 1 about rains washing the summit. As the footprint is now enclosed, humans take the place of clouds to bathe it. Those allowed to rub the turmeric or pour the water are only monks, summit staff, and invited personages of import. Institution of this official *kemmura puja* happened in 1984 according to Aryapala, the head *kapurāla* priest for the summit Saman shrine, who described it as both a religious commitment and an election promise: "It was a vow [*bhārayak*]. . . . A head monk before in the past . . . had made a vow in order to request votes. 'If votes are given,' he said, 'we will . . . have the *kemmura puja*'. . . . That means for this *kemmura* here. As far as *kemmura* in general, for around two-thousand years it has been done continuously." Bringing the ancient *kemmura* rites to the Peak was part of the politics that shaped so much pilgrimage infrastructure. The *puja* began as a conduit for consolidating monastic power, which is a function it retains decades later.

When I witnessed the *kemmura puja*, the general public was removed from the area and asked to wait below while the resident monks, *kapurāla* priests, police officers, and other summit staff worked. Any non-monks wore all white, with handkerchief covering their heads. I was given permission to attend and observe for my research by Ven. Gnanasumana, a resident monk of the summit, on the suggestion of Aryapala, always supportive of my studies. This happily coincided with a day when dozens of monks from Kurunegala arrived, with an equally large group of lay devotees, complete with their own sound system, to perform a massive flower *puja*, with an entire flower throne, flower parasol, and flower fans to be offered. After this, the monks were invited to participate in the *kemmura puja*.

It began with a preliminary sweeping by police officers and summit staff, and then a lot of cleaning all at once. The Saman *kapurālas* tended to their shrine, and the monks performed the ritual washing of the footprint. This began by removing all offerings and decorations, including its normal covering of a silk pillow embroidered with a *śrīpāda* illustration. The footprint rock was then rubbed with a turmeric paste made with milk and lime juice. The monks crowded around, taking turns, staining their hands orange. A resident monk of the summit directed the group, next filling silver jugs with water, and a dash of sacred ash, to pour over the footprint. As he poured, other monks chanted in

Pali. Rosewater was then sprinkled on the footprint and around the summit. The water that ran from the footprint flowed out of small drains, where some was collected in another silver jug for distribution to devotees, who drink it as a panacea. The shrine's décor was then reassembled, while the cleaning action returned outside, and the whole compound was soaked with a hose. Normally the police officers do the bulk of this work, but that day, the large group of visiting monks filled the summit with a sea of sweeping saffron robes (fig. 5.5). Once everything was washed, the resident monks worshiped privately. The public was then let back into the upper compound for the usual afternoon *puja*, with processed offerings, chanted Pali, Sinhala blessings, and dedications of accrued merit to Saman.

That first day I was an observer, but the next Saturday, I returned for the *kemmura puja* and became a participant, as I did for many *kemmura* days thereafter. Since large groups of visiting monks were rare, my general sweeping labor was appreciated. A broom was put into my hand straightaway on the second day. This regular engagement allowed me to befriend many summit police officers, in whose quarters I changed into my white clothes and had tea before our work. The police of the summit lived in a four-room cement building, each room with two or three bunk beds. There was a corner for boiling tea beside a

FIGURE 5.5. Scrubbing the summit during the *kemmura puja*

tap-and-bucket bathroom. The tight quarters lacked privacy, but were kept at a cozy temperature with space heaters counteracting the chilling wind outside. Men slept with sheets over their heads at intervals, preparing for overnight shifts. The summit police were chosen by the head monk, Ven. Dhammadinna, and all came from the Ratnapura district. I asked if working on the summit was a merit-making activity. An older officer agreed wholeheartedly: "Often when we are working in our service, we don't get a chance to go home, to go to the temple, or offer alms [*dāna*] for monks. So working here is a good opportunity to make merit." The work of this ritual, however, does not preclude levity. While there is a hushed solemnity among those performing the rubbing and bathing of the footprint itself, when the work turns to outside scrubbing, with the hose vigorously spraying, levity arises with artful dodges of the powerful water stream. There is also casual chatting between officers and monks, and some smiling at the sight of pilgrims waiting on the level below, scattering when water begins pouring down the steps.

The *kemmura puja* is beautiful and fun, but it is also marked by its exclusivity. One must be clergy or a handpicked layperson to be present. Those waiting below sometimes crept to the gate to glimpse the action. Some asked why they had to leave. "How can we wash the compound if you all are here?" was how the workers generally replied. There is a practical aspect to limiting the number of people on the summit and thus making space to scrub everything. Workers were often soaked by the end. Exclusivity, however, also signals the privilege of witnessing a special event, separating elites from others. For one, it is a solely male ritual. While women have adopted more prominent roles in some pilgrimage group leadership,[57] they remain barred from participating in the summit *kemmura*. Overall, the fact that only particular laypeople—such as police officers, politicians, wealthy donors, or anthropologists—are allowed to witness and participate in the ritual at the discretion of the resident monks reinforces clerical power. In turn, Buddhist ritual hegemony is ensured.

The concept of *kemmura* itself sanctions exclusivity, signifying ritually important time marking off space. It has mytholithic edges, a tool for making mountain stories. I was told that *kemmura* days often bring beams of light streaking across the sky, interpreted as gods coming to worship. Some trailside shopkeepers read rains as nature cleansing itself in preparation for divine worship on *kemmura*. The concept also appears in folktales, *kemmura* being when one might encounter Saman or another spirit walking in the woods as a man in white.[58] The word *kemmura* thereby stands for Buddhist power on the mountain, the most ritually potent days demanding the most ritually elite participants for merit making.

Yet, even faced with ritual exclusion, the Peak itself still reminds us of what is shared across religious actors in the common stakes of sacred landscapes. When Jeyarācā descended the mountain and listened to the jungle awaken at dawn, enveloped in a panoply of sound, he finally heard the right Tamil elocution of the praise phrase that the Sinhala pilgrims had mispronounced: "Because it was the time of the sunrise, on both sides of the path the jungle beasts and birds were resounding. This sound to our ears was drawn like 'Aro Hara.' In a short time, we passed half the distance."[59] Jeyarācā thus joined the Sinhala poets who were also enchanted by forest songs, but heard these in his own tongue. If different groups that have difficulty talking with one another are seen as already communicating with a third party—the mountain itself—new avenues of collaborative ritual action may open.

A Natural Pilgrimage Ethic: Cooperation Over Control

The nature of religious and ecological pluralism is often obscured through categorical language that divides the world into separate boxes. This includes the word "nature" itself, as the European Enlightenment and its colonial arms generally held "civilization" apart from "nature," the latter alternately shown as more real, dangerous, beautiful, researchable, exploitable, or conquerable than civilization. A separable, scalable, and useable nature, one grown in reserves, encouraged an idea of escape into nature, instead of always already living in it.[60] While the Sinhala word most commonly translated as "nature"—*sobādahama*, from the Sanskrit *svabhāva-dharma*—likely absorbed certain senses from the English term, Buddhist thought has its own long history of classing the world into civilization or wilderness, and reserving specific tracts for preservation. Precolonial "forbidden forests" in Lanka, for example, functioned as groves reserved for royalty, or acted as security buffers for villages. The subsequent colonial state then re-created the royal model, instituting national reserves in the late nineteenth century as game refuges for hunting.[61] For the Peak in particular, its watershed made it important to protect, as Ratnapura Government Agent H. Wace wrote in 1887 to inspire more funding: "Two of the largest rivers in the Island take their rise in the villages under the Peak, and the conservation of forests at their source and along their source should be a matter of interest to the Forest Department. I trust that next year will witness a more generous policy."[62] Today, the Wildlife Conservation Department at the Peak continues this mission, with ever-elusive funding now supplemented by local and multinational banks in step with neoliberal reincarnations of colonial nature, exerting control through the borders and boundaries that come with conservation.

But when pilgrims at the Peak speak of *sobādahama*, they do not always mean the sort of nature biologists catalog and environmentalists conserve. The term is expansive, as Padmasiri de Silva noted how "*svabhāva dharma* captures the lawful nature of the universe within which humans and nature live."[63] So *sobādahama* is nature writ large, from human nature to animal instinct, from forest groves to physical laws. This closely connects *sobādahama* to the idea of dependent origination (*paṭiccasamuppāda*), which "sees the world as a network of many-sided, reciprocal causal patterns which interact . . . very broadly used to refer to all phenomena, so that tables and chairs, rivers, mountains and animals, as well as humans, are phenomena which dependently originate."[64] This is not a simplistic universalism where all is equal and in perfect balance. Interruptions of impermanence pervade Buddhist nature. The first Pali text to take up the question of *svabhāva*—meaning an inherent essence, substance, or nature—was *Paṭisambhidāmagga*, an analytic synthesis of Abhidhamma philosophy, which sorts the world into its most fundamental constituent forms, conditions, and causalities. Fittingly, this text only mentions *svabhāva* in its section on emptiness—the Buddhist teaching that nothing has any intrinsic quintessence—explaining that "the born material form is empty of inherent nature [*jātaṃ rūpaṃ sabhāvena suññaṃ*]."[65] There are no truly autonomous essences, as all living beings and material forms are made of impermanent aggregates subject to conditional arising. So *svabhāva-dharma* as nature is really natureless in its ever-changing interdependencies. According to Nāgārjuna, the foremost philosopher of emptiness, "those things which are dependently arisen are not endowed with *svabhāva*, because there is no *svabhāva*. Why? Because of the dependence on causes and conditions."[66] I suggest that cultivating a pluralistic pilgrimage ethic requires accepting this natural state of no-nature, seeing humans as transient in a world of always variable conditional assemblages.

Such nature is neither perfect nor permanent. Behaving well in it requires compassionate action predicated on cooperation rather than forcible control. This is the type of ethic Juvānisā prescribed to counter those who reserved the summit for their own private groups. He suggested a more meritorious way to guard:

> Look here, it is good if you guard like this:
> Giving space on the path to come and go,
> so comforts are provided to this crowd,
> so boons are received from the Lord God.[67]

The real way to win divine favor is by facilitating pilgrimage for others, not blocking their way, but protecting their comings and goings. Such actions are rewarded by gods like Saman because they spread the same spirit of support that characterizes his own bodhisattva status. Such comradery is especially necessary due to the difficulties of the journey, and Juvānisā suggests that by feeding and consoling companions, shepherding them and "driving the group ahead, without being afraid when entering the forest," a pilgrimage leader earns the moral authority to ask the Himagata god for assistance in overcoming jungle perils.[68] As the resident guardian of the Peak's footprint and forest, Saman's powers to support or punish people are often said to operate through natural elements, humbling humans to seek permission to move within the forest. Of course, the forest must exist in the first place for this power to be operative.

Sustaining Endangered Forest Hāskam

Sri Lankans do not often use fancy Pali terms like *paṭiccasamuppāda* to talk about *sobādahama*. When I started asking for stories at the Peak, it was far more common for people to articulate their thoughts through Saman using the colloquial term *hāskam* to describe his miraculous agency linked to the mountain forest. This term is employed to describe powers of other Lankan deities or saints and their shrines. It is often translated as "miracle," but is perhaps better captured with "marvel," as *hāskam* can extend beyond single events to describe a sustained source of wonderment.[69] At the Peak, *hāskam* extends even further, existing not only inside shrine walls or singular rituals, but also in the power of the entire rainforest and mountain range of which Saman is part. Here *hāskam*'s wondrous potentialities encapsulate related agencies of forest animals, elements, and deities in a web of coexistence on the mountain. Yet *hāskam* and *paṭiccasamuppāda* are not equivalent. *Hāskam*, measuring power, may increase or decrease, but its marvels always work through the consistently interdependent world. Anthropologist Rohan Bastin characterizes *hāskam* as "religious potentiality."[70] This certainly fits with Saman's potential to bestow boons, but I also encountered uses of the term *hāskam* that exceed the religious. When people speak of the forest, the potentiality deepens from divine marvels to the natural wonders of ecology. Forest *hāskam* includes the destructive energy of water and the strength of stone. It is the forest continually recalibrating itself, as in seasonal rains that cleanse impurities and keep away pilgrims for a period of regeneration, giving animals an opportunity to worship. An example of what Nagarajan calls "embedded ecologies," those "implicit and embodied ways of seeing and relating to the natural world,"[71] *hāskam* is cited as the reason why certain plants only grow in the Peak's particular climate and elevation. It is why some animals live there and nowhere else, especially rare or dangerous beasts like leopards and elephants, including Saman's elusive white tusker.[72] In a way, the verses from *Saman Sirita* in chapter 1 can be read as a forest *hāskam* elegy, with interrelated agencies of plants, animals, and stone. In this sense, *hāskam* becomes more than simply miracles *in* a forest. It is the miracle *of* the forest.

One stall on the Hatton trail where I regularly stopped for a chat was owned by H. M. Surasena, a veteran shopkeeper who helped build the Sri Pada Japanese Peace temple in the 1970s. His son, about my age, was nicknamed "Japan," and occasionally came to help on busy weekend nights. However drowsy, he enjoyed giving me lessons in Buddhist philosophy when we met the following morning. Like many who lived near the mountain, he brought up *hāskam* unprompted when describing the landscape. For Japan, it extended down to geological bedrock of the hills: "So this jungle has a lot of *hāskam*. That's difficult for many people to understand. Though these mountains seem like earth, they're not earthen hills. They're a creation of stone. Granite. . . . The whole entire mountain is pure granite. Right on top there is earth of only ten or fifteen feet. The vegetation actually grew in that. There's a *hāskam* like that." Japan also attributed *hāskam* to the gemstones within the rock, which he said came down in the form of rain, back when God Saman ruled these lands as a king. It is generally difficult to separate Saman from the mountain and its forest. His miraculous powers operate through the landscape itself.

When people speak of Saman's *hāskam*, they often refer to how the god compassionately aids the ascent of pilgrims. Two friends in their early twenties, on their fifth trip to the Peak, answered my question about *hāskam* by explaining how hard it is to climb a mountain, yet when people are climbing here, there is not much difficulty. Indeed, the boys became a manifestation of marvelous assistance for another pilgrim, Rosa, who has worked on the Peak for thirty-seven years and been to the summit over two hundred times. As she told me in her characteristic deadpan fashion, "I would climb seven times a season if I had seven legs." Hers was the stall just a few steps down the trail from Chandra's, dug out from the hillside, one of the few without electricity. She burned an oil lamp at night and sold colas in glass bottles. We climbed on a windy, rainy day, and the boys took turns carrying Rosa's fruit offerings. She answered my question on Saman's *hāskam* by detailing his boons: a house for her, a job for her younger brother. "Look see, everything was given. For that reason I am living happily. Everything was given. If you ask God Saman, having not eaten meat or fish, if you worship correctly, that will really be true." Rosa gave another anecdote: "When an animal of mine died, I was not eating and was crying. I said to Lord God Saman, 'I have come to your Makara Torana shrine.' Saying that, I did a *puja*. But I was sad, no? Then when I returned home, there they were—two animals. He had brought them from somewhere and given them. Cats! I was very happy having seen them." Rosa's experience saw Saman's compassion in boons for her family, and associated the god with power over animals. Most importantly, Rosa noted how miracles were contingent upon devotee behavior. If one asks favors of Saman, especially when living and working in his forest, certain right actions must be practiced. Vegetarianism, abstinence, and regular worship are all prerequisites.

What happens when one displeases Saman? Is there an edge to his *hāskam*? Asking people whether Saman punishes (*daňḍuvam karanne*) yielded a range of responses. Some were sure that Saman, as a bodhisattva, would never harm. The shopkeeper Ranjit was adamant: "No! God Saman does not punish. However, Lord Buddha said, if you do good things the result will be good. If you do bad things, the result will be bad.... Karma works in that way... but God Saman doesn't punish." I asked Ramagiri, who has worked as a *kapurāla* priest for the summit Saman shrine for thirty-nine years, whether the god punishes ne'er-do-wells. He said, "Yes, he will punish. Various troubles will be caused. That is, if you come badly." He didn't elaborate just then, but I brought it up again later, asking whether the god actually punished by his own hand. "No, no, no, it's not like that. It's as if done through power [*balayen*]," he said, citing an example of someone suffering temporary jungle madness as "only the appearance of giving punishment." According to Ramagiri, Saman gave just a taste of rebuke, a warning to correct behavior by showing humans not to trifle with divine power. Some credit lesser deities as Saman's enforcers, like the sorcerous god Suniyan.[73] Others cite unnamed forest spirits, tree gods, and will-o'-the-wisps—"the innumerable ruling *devas* and *devatās* of the forest."[74] As Ramagiri noted, these minor deities act autonomously, for to order violence is as bad as doing it: "God Saman doesn't send them. If he sent them it would be a demerit. If I say, do this, kill this person, it's a demerit for me.... As I said before, he'll show a bit of trouble, but after that, having given difficulties, he'll remove them. He doesn't like causing demerit, no? He has attained *sōvān*." *Sōvān* (Pali: *sotāpatti*) represents a status of "stream enterer," upon which there are no more negative rebirths, a first step for bodhisattvas on the path to enlightenment.[75] Ramagiri, like many others, cited Saman's achievement of *sōvān* as the reason the god must act compassionately. To prevent any demerit for Saman, the wilderness acts on his behalf.

As nature executes its own powers to protect itself, the animals, plants, water, and stone of the whole mountain region stand guard. A recent Sinhala book about the Peak includes a section called "*Hāskam* of the Sri Pada Range" (*siripā aḍaviyē hāskam*), which argues that difficulties of ascent recorded by Europeans were due to their impurity.[76] Animals allegedly punished the foreigners for dining on bacon and brandy in the woods, and W. Knighton wrote that "with the noise of elephants, cheetahs, jungle cats, jungle fouls and crows, it was utterly impossible to doze."[77] Later British observers were more aware of these traditions, as a Ratnapura government agent noted the special forest language used while walking the Kuruwita trail: "The pilgrim dares not murmur on this route for fear of the Saman Deviyo. His burden (bara) he calls 'light' (Sehelluwa): the stones against which he hits his feet are mercies (Karunawa) and even the leeches are blessings in disguise."[78] So terms of compassion like *karuṇāva*, the most uttered word on pilgrimage, are said partly from fear, as earning divine compassion also means forgoing complaints. Nothing in Saman's forest should be insulted, down to stones and leeches.

Worms are another agent of forest *hāskam*, as I was told by the *kapurāla* of the Saman shrine at the Sitagangula stream on the Hatton trail. He twice tried to bring a fish dinner across the river to the shrine, but within minutes, his food was infested. The same thing happens to fruit people remove. You can eat it in the forest, but worms will prevent you from carrying it out.[79] Similar stories of retributive wilderness *hāskam* abound, from monkey armies or other animals.[80] The head *kapurāla* Aryapala told me one afternoon: "Saman has attained *sōvān*, right? But, despite that, if people do bad, that punishment will surely be received. Yesterday or the day before, a person speaking inappropriately went down and was stung by hornets." While stories of forest *hāskam* express Saman's power, it is ultimately natural laws that set things right, whether through the appetites of leeches and worms, or the anger of primates and insects. It need not even be a living thing that takes retribution. Chandra enjoyed telling me tales about the Peak's wondrous waters:

> Having worked here for forty years, we've seen a lot of things. I can rightly say that God Saman's power here is real. One time, a man died suddenly, leaving his wife and two children. His son came to the Sri Pada forest to see if he could hunt some deer . . . to see if he could bring some food to cook. He was in the jungle for a few days. Then there was a lot of rain, every day just raining raining raining. One day we heard . . . someone screaming in the forest. The police and everyone were afraid to go into the jungle and look, even as the screaming continued. But we found a set of boys who work in the sweets shops to go into the forest and find the person screaming. There they found the boy. He had been swept over a waterfall, fallen and broken. The boys carried him out of the forest and brought him to the hospital. That's the reality of the god. If you do bad, the god will strike.

However, instead of Saman literally striking, a crush of water did the work, washing out the threat. The mountain and forest thereby defray responsibility for retribution, allowing Saman to guard without causing suffering or even needing to command it himself. These mountain myths thereby represent a type of Buddhist "moral naturalism" that Heim also identifies in canonical texts: "Moral naturalism means that the external world is inscribed with a moral order. This is expected in a world structured according to karma because making merit is a natural process, in the sense that it bears fruit independently of human or divine arrangements."[81] This is the same logic animating the Buddha's response to a snakebite in the *Ahirāja Sutta*. Following his verse about having loving-kindness for creatures with any number of feet, he recites a mirroring verse that requests "no harm come to me" from the footless, two-footed, four-footed, and many footed.[82] The expectation is that virtuous action is reflected back by the environment.

It is therefore fitting that natural retribution at the Peak is often delivered against those who would take too much from the land. In this sense, Saman's forest delivers a lesson similar to the *Vasala Sutta* that inspired Juvānisā, where, as the Buddha teaches the Brahmin what sorts of people are really outcastes, he includes "one who takes what has not been given, whether in the village or the forest, stealing the belongings of others." Buddhaghosa's commentary elaborates on the division of the world into the civilized and the wild, as "village here includes a village, a town, a city, together with their vicinities; apart from this, the rest is forest." Yet this is only to make clear that the rule applies equally to both, as "belongings of others" includes "the unrelinquished possessions of other beings, whether a living being or inanimate object."[83] With his use of the most general Pali terms for all things animate (*satto*) and inanimate (*saṅkhāro*), Buddhaghosa ethically charges the whole world. If one considers Saman to be one of the "other beings" (*parasattā*) in the case of the Peak, its entire environment is rightly protected under his ownership.

The extent to which Saman is interwoven with the total mountain, from bedrock to woods to watershed, means many do not distinguish between the *hāskam* of the god and that of his forested range (*aḍaviya*). Ven. Kassapa, however, who runs a small rest house for pilgrim monks on the Hatton trail, did draw a firm line to preserve Saman's innocence: "There can be a great difference. The god's *hāskam* only causes good things. For example, on the Ratnapura side, when people come, some say they see a man in white up ahead of them. He is always just ahead as they climb. But when they reach the summit, he's not there. They did not pass him along the way, yet he's no longer there. That type of *hāskam* is the god's *hāskam*. But when bad things happen to people with bad behavior, that's the *hāskam* of the forest." Yet Ramagiri did not see a need to separate *hāskam*: "There's not a difference. This is the Saparagamuwa district . . . Saman governs this Saparagamuwa and looks after it well. No troubles are given. Some little tiny things come. But big things don't come." Likewise, Dayananda Kapumahatya of the *devale* by the Maussakelle dam outside Nallathanni agreed: "Both are the same, meaning God Saman's seat of influence, his jurisdiction. . . . this Samanala Range and the whole region generally are linked to him." These two *kapurālas* interpreted *hāskam* of forest and god as equivalent because the forest was Saman's territory, the land imbued with divine power. Ranjit saw it similarly: "That forest being separate and God Saman's *hāskam* being separate? It's not that way. If you look at the forest, it's our ground, the trees, the medicinal gardens, the climate. So those are one. Now these flowering trees you can't grow elsewhere; they only grow here. If you cut a branch and take it elsewhere, it does not grow; it's not like that. Therefore, both are one." For Ranjit, finding where exactly forest ended and god began was impossible. Divinity was in the forest, responsible for its unique climate, flora, and fauna, a natural *hāskam*.

When I told Ranjit I wanted to study the whole environment of the Peak, he said: "The whole environment [*parisaraya*] of Sri Pada. That means there are the trees and vines, the animals, the river, but also we, too, are here. You have us, the shops, the steps, the electricity, the lights, the water board. There is all that, too." Ranjit realized a panoply of beings and buildings made up the nature of the modern Peak. He also knew that shifting too many of these surroundings from living to concrete forms would enfeeble the miraculous powers of this forest, decreasing its *hāskam*. Ranjit and many others told me the *hāskam* of the forest was in decline. As Ven. Kassapa put it, "When bad things happen to people with bad behavior, that is the *hāskam* of the forest. These days, however, because the path is so developed, the power [*balavēga*] and difficulty of the forest have been reduced." As woods were cut to facilitate greater numbers of pilgrims, the buffer of difficulty decreased, and fewer natural agents are now available to channel Saman's guardian powers. The threatening beasts described in early twentieth-century poems were quite varied:

> Elephants, panthers, sambar—leopards, tigers, bears—
>   dangerous animals—
> cruel vipers—horrible pythons—are in this forest—in fearless
> mentality—God Saman really—will provide aid to us.[84]

> Panthers—elephants—wild buffalo with ferocity
> Filled with snakes—herons—poisonous serpents
> Noise-giving parrots—starlings always calling
> The ruler of Samankula is indeed thou, Sumana.[85]

Such animals are now rare enough to avoid rather than frighten humans. Encroachment harms *hāskam*, as it makes the forest too heavily human. Without jungle challenges to check people, some feared the situation would only deteriorate.

The former forest *hāskam* that made pilgrimage harder may also have encouraged a pluralistic ethic. As a poet put it in 1891, "the forest especially removes all prejudice [*agatiya*]," causing pilgrims to "always guard against the ten demerits [*dasa akusal*]," so that "there are good people who give refuge without limit."[86] People in 2016 still spoke about pilgrims cooperating to overcome obstacles. Sharing food, clothes, walking sticks, or encouraging words can ease the challenges of chilly slopes, as shared discomfort decreases callous behavior. In other contexts, Leela Prasad has likewise noted a potential of bodily struggle to foster cooperative ethics, as "physical discomfort . . . engenders a metaphysical awareness that transforms an enigmatic other into a deeply familiar presence."[87] While the Peak has lost some wilderness tests, the sheer feat of ascending its elevation is always daunting. As noted in chapter 2, the challenge of the climb is part of its meritorious nature. Juvānisā went so far as to argue that putting able bodies to this physical test, interrupting our comfortable lives but ultimately benefitting our future, is the only way to take full advantage of our time as humans:

> Equipped with eyes, ears, and mouth,
> hands and feet not broken, but comfortably placed,
> the time of being born in this world is passing.
> If you don't go to Samanala, for what are you living?[88]

Discomfort remains a requirement to generate mountaineering merit. And although other pilgrimage difficulties have decreased in modern times, Juvānisā's advice to push ourselves can also effectively apply to the challenges of a crowded plural space, where hegemonic control needs interruption for all beings to pursue their shared struggle.

While many at the Peak think human infrastructure reduces forest *hāskam*, at least one shopkeeper argued the opposite. As the trail was more developed and easier, he said, the *hāskam* of the forest increased. After all, he explained, it had been Saman's wish to facilitate pilgrimage to this footprint relic. The fact that so many people are now able to go is proof of the god's power, and, as people come to worship him, his *hāskam* will only grow. His logic matches the examples in chapter 2, where environmental alterations, especially clearing forests to facilitate worship, had long been deemed meritorious. Yet *hāskam* might be further recharged if human interventions into the forest are centered on its regrowth rather than removal. The marvelous potentiality of a wilderness plurality may be reinvigorated to facilitate masses of pilgrims and maintain living accords among mountain beings, with an ethos of cooperation reinforced by Buddhist thought.

Where Nature Dharma and Buddha Dharma Meet

As the words for "nature" (*sobādahama*) and "Buddhism" (*bududahama*) share a suffix of *dahama* or *dharma*, it was easy to phrase intriguing interview questions about whether they were connected. People at the Peak had much to say about their interaction, some even calling them equivalent.[89] Ajith had been working as the manager of the Siddhalepa Ayurvedic rest stop on the Hatton trail for the past twenty-two years. He described the natural changes he witnessed: "Before, animals on this side came close to the road, but now people are going here and there shouting '*hu! hu!*,' no? Now, before, when this was like a forest, there were more animals than there are now." When I asked him about *sobādahama* being tied to *bududahama*, he explained:

> *Bududahama* originally was created of *sobādahama*. The Lord Buddha we believe in, he fulfilled his aim . . . becoming aware beneath a tree. Even in the time before he fulfilled that aim, that was a revered tree. Therefore, the importance of *sobādahama* has to be confirmed, that even before *bududahama* it was correct. Without it, we couldn't live, no? That Lord Buddha explained to us, no? He said *sobādahama* is important, to love *sobādahama*, according to his Buddhist view. In Buddhist philosophy [*darśana*], that which has a chief place is *sobādahama*.

Ajith was one of several people to answer my question about *bududahama* and *sobādahama* with the story of the enlightenment under a bodhi tree (*Ficus religiosa*), a natural object already revered before the Buddha's arrival.[90] Yet the Buddha's use of the tree imprinted it with his power, making it a sacred relic like his footprint atop the Peak.

The fact that memories of the Buddha are visible in nature is one reason to protect it, an injunction repeated to me by many at the Peak, including Ven. Gnanasumana, the senior monk who lived most of the year on the summit and annually witnessed the rainforest reclaim the trail in the offseason before being cut back again. His response to my question about a *bududahama* and *sobādahama* connection was characteristically brief and gruff, but informative: "Yes. Lord Buddha loves the trees and leaves of *sobādahama*. Lord Buddha said to preserve [*itiri karanna*] leaves and trees of *sobādahama*, to do such to *sobādahama*. Those two go as one." He then paused before adding: "But people are destroying *sobādahama*. The environment [*parisaraya*] is completely being destroyed. Bottles are brought. Plastic is brought. All are discarded. And how many trees are cut? Mm. Now *sobādahama* does not have a significance. People don't respect it. As much as it will be destroyed, they will destroy it." By attributing teachings on nature preservation to the Buddha, Ven. Gnanasumana positioned *bududahama* as a guardian of *sobādahama*, although the monk seemed pessimistic about the future prospects of environmental health.

Others said *bududahama* lent one the ability to recognize *sobādahama*, protecting nature and one's karmic trajectory in it. Kalu Malli, the Ratnapura betel salesman introduced in chapter 4, linked *sobādahama* and *bududahama* without my asking when describing the power of a forest near the Peak where he said a fearsome *rakshasa* guardian lived, who was Saman's secretary and Aryapala Kapumahatya's bodyguard. I asked Kalu Malli to elaborate, and he said, "There's *sobādahama* and *bududahama*. Both are joined. *Bududahama* introduces us to *sobādahama*. *Bududahama* gives us an awareness of *sobādahama*. Otherwise, the way we live now, we are separated from *sobādahama*. We don't know it. We have these vehicles, this cement everywhere, but *bududahama* reminds us of *sobādahama*. Actually *bududahama* is a method for being well in *sobādahama*. That way, we're able eventually to no longer exist, to exit from samsara and receive nirvana." Kalu Malli emphasized how *bududahama* meant living well in *sobādahama*, something he executed in his own life through physical fitness, walking for transport, turning off the village streetlamps in the morning, and feeding local children and urban wildlife around the Ratnapura clock tower. Kalu Malli highlighted the soteriological significance of a successful existence in *sobādahama*, a lifestyle that eventually led to nirvana.

Still, the concept of *bududahama* taming *sobādahama* also pervades Buddhist thought, a trope that can be counterproductive for pluralism and conservation if used to evoke a conquest over nature and submission of all beings. The insights of those who live near the Peak, however, offer paths around this, keeping with a philosophy of dependent origination where humans can wield influence, but *sobādahama* ultimately follows its own flows. Such thoughts were articulated by monks of the small Nāgadīpa temple and rest house in Nallathanni, where the first signboard marking Saman's boundary stands, and where some give offerings and take the five precepts before proceeding. Ven. Silavamsa emphasized the importance of the mountain as a watershed, essential to the health and wealth of populations below: "For the life given by rivers, this is a chief place. The rivers go and fill the reservoirs, and the people then farm paddy." The other monk, Ven. Narada, in his sixteenth season of service, explained the protective power of *bududahama*, believing it enhanced *hāskam* in the area, allowing nature to regulate itself: "Up to now, from thirty to forty years ago, this place has changed a lot. Here *bududahama* and *sobādahama* are greatly elevated. That means there is a huge *hāskam*. After the groups increase, after this place is dirtied, it rains through *sobādahama*. It rains and it all becomes purified here . . . Recently, there was a forest fire near one of the tea plantations here. During the fire, a great rain came and extinguished the flames. This is the link between *bududahama* and *sobādahama*." Both monks' comments represent a give-and-take between humans and *sobādahama*. For Ven. Silavamsa, *sobādahama* was life-giving, flush with fresh waters for cultivation. In this sense, *sobādahama* inspires its own taming, encouraging people to collect the waters of the mountain to canalize, irrigate, and farm. This is a reminder not only that humans are architects within *sobādahama*, manipulating its parameters to generate new forms, but also that nature itself gives rise to the conditions that allow this. Ven. Narada then offered a reminder of how human intrusions in *sobādahama* can overstep. In his examples—whether discarding too much garbage or starting forest fires—*sobādahama* adjusted to human error by its aqueous agency. In this sense, it was nature that tamed the human, most effectively at the Peak because of *bududahama*, as the sacred footprint's consecration gives the mountain environment extra *hāskam*. So the woods do find ways to renew as human influence mingles with jungle. One long-time shopkeeper described the relationship between *sobādahama* and *bududahama*: "*bududahama* has influence [*balapäm*]. In that influence, it is always speaking to everything, wind, rain, sunlight, by that indeed. Compared to other places in Sri Lanka, that is greater at Sri Pada." I asked what the influence did. "Control, control. Indeed control. If something of humanity's is too great to take, it has balanced it." The word I translate as "control" is *pālanaya*. It carries many connotations, including governance, guardianship, management, mastery, power, rule, sway, etc. The way this shopkeeper put it, *bududahama* influenced *sobādahama* to protect nature from humanity's too overzealous exploitation. This was not a control in terms of mastery, but a guardianship that refreshed ecologies.

Control came in rains, or through animals. Food waste is consumed by jungle beasts like wild boar, who grow to huge girth off this high-caloric trash, skittishly crashing through underbrush. Dogs also help to pick over garbage piles. Dogs are a good representation of the tenuous human control over nature, showing that a species created through taming can still leave the leash entirely. Evolved and bred as allies, dogs settle with humans. But most dogs in Sri Lanka are not pampered pets. The dog world exists in outdoor packs, at the edges of human life, feeding off scraps. And when humans move to the forest, dogs migrate with them. In part, they rely on humans, but dogs may realize the woods are full of sustenance, too, and disappear into its groves, sometimes permanently. If one hikes the Ratnapura trail at night, forest packs can be heard howling. I found this human-canine-forest interplay summated wonderfully on a cardboard sign hanging from a shop on the Hatton trail, which read: "Throw trash into the forest for dogs only." In other words, don't toss anything that a dog could not eat, an acknowledgment of the reality of forest dogs who lives off both the woods and refuse. The injunction was accompanied by a fitting illustration—a dog-headed man in stick-figure form, a dog of human nature.

Dogs are like us and we are like dogs, an idea articulated in myth for millennia as "we humans have grown up with dogs at our sides."[91] More than mere monsters, dogmen represent natural codependence. As Eduardo Kohn wrote of a different forest: "In their mutual attempts to live together and to make sense of one another, dogs and people . . . increasingly come to partake in a sort of shared trans-species habitus."[92] As forest dogs stray off human edges to execute their own ecological effects, they are still trained on their old masters' excess. Having followed people to the forest, the dogs who join the mountain ecology in turn keep a check on humanity.

Stray dogs are occasionally driven off with rocks, but someone else usually throws them a bone. According to karmic logic, dogs are not only like us, they once *were* us, or might yet be. Lowly births show them settling bad karma. This was explained to me by Ven. Gunasiri, the resident monk at the Makara Torana shrine, who often dispensed ethical sermons to pilgrims about to pass through that portal, marking entry into a more concentrated circle of God Saman's power. Ven. Gunasiri was a frequent conversation partner whenever I passed the spot, and when I asked about the link between *sobādahama* and *bududahama*, he explained the workings of rebirth: "Now, according to *bududahama*, if you do sin or make merit, those have consequences. There will be birth in the god world, or there will again be a birth in the human world, that is if you make merit. So if you do sin, there is hell for beings. Following that, you need to look for where dogs are living, there the soul is born. And it's according to *bududahama* that there are these things." *Bududahama* again connoted awareness and intent within the forces of *sobādahama*. Those who want to avoid the dog life must get to merit making. Dogs, meanwhile, can only live in *sobādahama*, ignorant of *bududahama* and the karmic mechanisms of their inferiority. Still, some dogs may be settling karma on the mountain. People jokingly referred to them as guides, leading people up and down the Peak, likely hoping for scraps. Some even sang the passing singsong blessing to them, usually reserved for human pilgrims: "May God Sumana Saman bless the dogs going to worship!" To disregard dogs is to discard their lessons, their warnings via both *bududahama* and *sobādahama*. The implication of the dog-person continuum should encourage awareness of an important fact: we are all beings bound in similar fates.

There was no cuter example of this at the Peak than the case of a kitten. While animals like dogs may become less human when introduced to the forest, some jungle animals become more human, and adopt pets. So Chandra's husband, Mathu, told me in their shop one afternoon. There was a small kitten there, wandered in from who knows where. It snuggled in my lap for warmth and soon fell asleep. Mathu told me the kitten did not care whose body it found; it just wanted to snuggle. The day before, he said, something amazing happened. The kitten was lying in the sun just outside the shop with a larger cat that stayed with Chandra and Mathu. A troupe of macaques swung down from the trees. The older cat, afraid of monkeys, fled to hide inside. The tiny kitten just stood and mewed, complaining of lost heat. So one of the macaques came and gently picked it up, cradling it for a bit and stroking its fur. Mathu said he just stared at the scene, amazed. Eventually the macaque moved on with its clan, setting the kitten down and returning to the trees, but for a few moments, it had done what humans do when a kitten mews—cradled it, cuddled it, comforted it. The interspecies habitus of the Peak presents its own ethics of interdependency. As the poets have long done, we must listen to the forest.

Of course, we cannot simply meow in response. Animal imitation was an inappropriate ascetic ethic that the Buddha said only resulted in rebirth as an animal, as "the dog-duty ascetic . . . reappears in the company of dogs."[93] A better goal is to live well with *sobādahama*, by bringing *bududahama* into forest groves. The number of monks actually meditating in the Peak forest is minor, giving them a mythical status among workers and pilgrims.[94] But the Buddhist ethic to be well in *sobādahama* goes beyond dwelling in groves. Padmasiri de Silva argues that environmental degradation is all part of a larger *dukkha*, or suffering, which *bududahama* strives to alleviate. He translates *dukkha* as "basic disharmony," relating it to an early use of the word for cartwheels with broken pegs.[95] If this metaphor is applied to the Peak, I suggest that the spokes of healthy forest engagement have loosened, while those of ritual control have been overtightened, threatening to pitch pilgrimage off a sustainable path. Keeping it all spinning, even if not harmoniously singing, requires pieces be forged together from plural ethics that encompass ecological and religious concerns.

Pitfalls of Presumed Pluralism

Presumed pluralism assumes that pilgrimage provides a neutral context where religious spaces are freely and harmoniously shared. An idealistic "peace" is frequently associated with this sort of pluralism, especially by outsiders who contrast their perception of perpetual violence elsewhere on the island with the quiescence of the Peak. A magazine article from 1961, for example, casts this dichotomy in perpetuity: "All through Ceylon's long history of invasion and internal strife, with their legacy of resentment and jealousy of the smaller communities, the Peak remained a place of peace. And though resentment culminated in bloody racial riots as recently as 1958, it is still a place of peace today."[96] A magazine article from 2007 repeats this refrain, as its author, an academic but not a scholar of Sri Lanka, mentions the country's civil war repeatedly, though never in context. Instead, the war is simply meaningless violence, "madness erupted," the "historical musculature" that mars his desired first impression of the island as "an unspoiled, unpeopled place, an Eden where problems are swept away on a cinnamon breeze."[97] Primed to see harmony at the Peak, the author juxtaposes it to war at every turn, so a line of pilgrims climbing in the dark becomes a comment on their ethnicities fading "in the dimness . . . Perhaps for at least these few hours they could forget."[98] It suggests that only religious observance, magically removed from the rest of real life, keeps Sri Lankans from each other's throats. This presumed pluralism, by making communal relations into a caricature, only masks a reality of misunderstandings, disagreements, negotiations, and compromise at the Peak. The mountain's more complex past indicates that Buddhists, Muslims, Saivas, and Christians have shared spaces with cooperative curiosity, but also sectarian conflicts. Such a narrative is less tidy, but more accurately depicts the challenge of plural religious interests flourishing at the Peak.

There are moments, however, when stock stories of presumed pluralism do seem to carry important weight, as when religious minorities invoke it to justify their presence at the Peak, or even in the country.[99] When the national flag was being designed in 1948, some Tamils, attempting to prevent the Sinhala lion from dominating, as it now does, suggested the Peak be the symbol for the nation.[100] The Peak had already been imprinted on a 1947 stamp to commemorate the new constitution of an independent Ceylon (fig. 5.6). Presumed pluralism is also supported by the inclusive Hindu theology among many highland Tamils I met at the Peak. Jegathasa, for example, was a Hatton native finishing his first decade as a shop owner. He guessed he had been to the summit 150–200 times in his life. I asked why, thinking he was once a courier, but his answer was devotion: "I go! The god is there, no? I believe." He explained how he made a name for himself as an ice cream seller, with a small cooler set up beneath a trademark red umbrella, recognized as the "ice-selling uncle." This led to a stall that now sported a full soft-serve machine, making his benches a popular stop for tired pilgrims. "It is because of the god's help that this situation has

FIGURE 5.6. The Peak on the horizon of new governance in a 1947 stamp commemorating a new constitution

come about. So if I want to work the shop for another two years, or build a house, or buy a vehicle, for that, maybe God Saman, God Siva, Adam Bawa [Father Adam], *someone* is helping me. It is due to that honor that I go and do a *puja*." I asked if any *puja*s were for specific gods. Jegathasa responded inclusively: "We will offer to everyone. God Siva, God Saman, Adam Bawa, Jesus Christ, to all of them we go and give. They're all gods, no? Each one is a god. So we go and give a *puja*. By their great protection we're in the forest here, alone without anything, no? We're here six months, no? Because of that in that way we will do a *puja* and come . . . So each season we make pilgrimage two times, when the shop is going to begin and when it is finished." Jegathasa tried to get me to deliver a verdict on which claim to the footprint seemed most plausible, but I said there was no way to know. He understood my hesitance to judge. "That means whatever god it is, this place is the important thing," he said. "It could be God Siva's, or it could be Lord Buddha's, or it could be Jesus Christ's, or Adam's Peak, Adam Bawa, it could be like that. Whoever it is, although it's that god, the *place* is most important. Without this sort of belief, hundreds of thousands of people wouldn't be coming, no? Not making pilgrimage, no? Or they're coming otherwise for fun, for play. Whatever the purpose, there is an honor [*nambuvak*]. Because of that indeed people come." So Jegathasa offered his *puja* to any and all deities, saints, or prophets present. He was not one to determine who exactly was assisting him, only that some higher power must be. He even saw fit to extend possible footprint ownership to Jesus, a first as far as I had encountered. This pluralistic harmony could exist in one spot for Jegathasa because the physical place was what he found truly important about the Peak. It was only natural for different religions to map their gods onto such an impressive environment.

Although I would not begrudge Jegathasa his perspective, such stories of the Peak may also allow the Sri Lankan state and other sponsors to ignore the needs of non-Buddhists, relying on a presumed pluralistic power to unify people. This discourse of neatly bounded religions magically becoming harmonious in special contexts thrives in state channels, like the government's proposal for UNESCO to recognize the Peak as a World Heritage Site.[101] The entire central highlands currently have world-heritage status for biodiversity, but the Peak is not recognized by itself. A proposal was submitted in 2010 to include it in a stretch of heritage sites, "Seruwila to Sri Pada." The list featured several disparate places, all supposedly in a pilgrimage circuit along the Mahaweli River. The proposal continually stressed the multireligious nature of the project, but its argument was scattershot, and its mytholith of the Peak was misshapen, recycling the old European invention that some Christians held the footprint as that of St. Thomas. This proposal presumed a pluralism that avoided the heavy lifting of critical historical investigation and concealed problems behind labels of four separate-but-equal "world religions" living in harmony. The language of the proposal thereby mimicked the rhetoric of the United Nations and its promotion of religious freedom as a universal human right. This idea of religious identity presumes a free market of intentionally chosen faiths, which are pinned as demographic badges, and used in negotiations. This has long been true of Sri Lanka, where public displays of religious identity are common, and the universalized categories of Buddhist, Christian, Hindu, and Muslim are used as signs to measure rights and representation.[102]

Recent scholarship, however, has questioned the efficacy of framing rights with religious categories, which can further inflame prejudice, marginalize minorities, and obscure the real roots of injustice. Most fundamentally, as Elizabeth Hurd puts it, "religion is too unstable a category to be treated as an isolable identity, whether the objective is to attempt to separate religion from law and politics or design a political response to 'it.'"[103] Although secular governments are ideally meant to secure "freedom of religion" for citizens, while states ostensibly remain free *from* religion, putting this into practice still involves a heavy amount of religious regulation by the state. In the process, minorities are often fetishized into monoliths, frameable as threatening to majorities and their own rights.[104] Majorities may feel obligated to accommodate minorities in lip service to secularism, but often make reservations as delimited or isolating as possible. As Saba Mahmood attests, "the regulation of religion under secularism has . . . [made] it more, rather than less important to the identity of the majority and minority populations. This process has resulted in the intensification of interreligious inequality and conflict, the valuation of certain aspects of religious life over others, and the increasingly precarious position of religious minorities in the polity."[105] In Sri Lanka specifically, a secular-style constitution guarantees freedom of religion, but nevertheless gives primacy of place to Buddhism, yielding waves of legislations and litigations that fuel political "economies of expert religion."[106] Divisive results are laid bare everywhere, especially in education, where religious instruction is present in public schools but segregated, with students tracked to study only the religion of their parents, a misconstrual of religious equality that has been eloquently critiqued by Sri Lankan high schoolers themselves.[107] For these reasons, conventional religious labels seem inadequate for representing or managing pluralism at the Peak.

As religion cannot be separated from the rest of life, its static categories can be traded for the ground they stand on, to draw more organic ideas of pluralism from the Peak itself. Starting from the natural world helps circumvent the artifice of human designations. As Lefebvre put it: "A rock on a mountainside, a cloud, a blue sky, a bird on a tree—none of these, of course, can be said to lie. Nature presents itself as it is, now cruel, now generous. It does not seek to deceive; it may reserve many an unpleasant surprise for us, but it never lies. So-called social reality is dual, multiple, plural."[108] While Lefebvre's contrast between the natural and social serves his point, I argue that even honest nature can be multiple and plural, which is precisely why it can model an ethic of dynamic pluralism that transcends inert social labels. The metamorphic events that made the Peak's rock, for example, can be read pluralistically, as Connolly notes how different cooling rates mean "each crystallization of lava into granite exhibits a unique pattern that is neither predictable in advance nor replicable."[109] Similarly, pilgrimage ethics are unpredictably forged moment to moment on the trail, responsive to time, place, and personages encountered. Instead of assuming shared pilgrimage means equal worship spaces or an automatic overlap of religious values, Peak pluralism begins from the mountain up, considering how common ecological entanglements entwine diverse human assemblies. This is a pluralism greater than the sum of respective myths about the footprint. It attends to the footprints pilgrims leave, tracing mass movements and individual encounters among persons, rocks, water, plants, and animals. From this mountainous theory, a connected pilgrimage ethic emerges, based not on carving up the mountain among religions, but on sustaining all beings at the Peak.

Forest Lessons on Living Well

The office of the Wildlife Conservation Department on the Hatton trail is a small concrete building with three rangers. They inspect the region, on the trail and off, document incidents of rare animals like leopards, and manage daily affairs, like issuing permits to shopkeepers, and coordinating the gathering of plastic for recycling. The office holds a collectable, conservable version of "nature," with taxidermied animals, charts of species, and elephant and deer skulls. Brochures from a dusty filing cabinet I was shown listed the wealth of flora and fauna species in the Peak Wilderness Reserve: "419 plant species, along with more than 1095 herbarium species, have been identified at Peak Wilderness. Of the 19 endemic genera found in Sri Lanka, 11 were discovered at Peak Wilderness, with most of it originating from the montane forest." Another brochure was for use on the Ratnapura trail, listing species one could expect to find at different elevations. Its cover announced: "This field guide is designed to facilitate your nature-based experience, a meaningful one. It will help you to learn while enjoying the unparalleled marvels of nature that we have inherited . . . Traveling responsibly can reduce adverse impacts and help to conserve the natural heritage of Peak Wilderness." Both brochures conveyed a conservation message with the idea that nature is something to be experienced, enjoyed, and inherited, but also kept within a remote reserve.

Upali Gunasekara was a ranger at the wildlife office in 2016. He was one of the more philosophically inclined people I met on the mountain, not only in the canonical sense of being well-read in Aristotle, Hegel, Marx, Weber, etc., but also in his constant consideration of difficult problems, especially regarding human relationships with the environment. Upali knew that sustainable futures were not achieved by people simply dipping their toes into a wilderness weekend, on a nature trail paved with cement. A more wholesale scale of thinking needed reevaluation. He was eager for me to read a Sinhala article he had published, titled "Violation of Nature's Constitution." It gave a history of how Protestant capitalism was to blame for commodifying nature and promoting distant views of God and the afterlife that justified worldly gain. This made us all cultural slaves to trade (*väḷaňda siṭina api saňskrutika vahalun vemu*) and promoted megaconsumerism (*ati paribhōjanavādaya*). Foreign influence in Sri Lanka encouraged this new annihilationist religious thought (*ucchēdavādī nava āgamika cintanaya*), especially after the opening of the Sri Lankan economy in 1977. The language of Upali's article was dense and technical, and he admitted many would have difficulty reading it, but his alternative to the religion of megaconsumerism was one a villager would know. This "Sinhala Conservation Policy" (*saňrakṣaṇa pratipadāva*) was articulated with a quatrain of folk poetry, a traditional children's song that taught a sustainable ethic:

> On this tree greatly—there are sweet oranges
> Ripe and ready—bowed to the ground—branches become heavy
> For little sister and for me—there are two fruits
> To pluck more is wrong, child—we do not do such things.[110]

Upali believed such generational wisdom needed new promotion, as it remains relevant to future survival.

Similar sustainable ethics for the Peak forest have recurred for generations. A 1929 poem, for example, promoted conservative consumption on the way to the summit:

> Guava, pomegranate, and mandarin in the Himagata
> Strong *himbuṭu* vines being heavy with fruit

Rich oranges and more various fruits are there
You must eat cleverly without plucking them

Remember God Sumana Saman
Do not break those fruit vines there
Existing elephants seen, be not afraid
Seeking nirvana, dress for the journey.[111]

These lines mention fruits and the medicinal *himbutu* plant, its vines also used as binding materials. Yet the pilgrims were told to not to break the vines, and only eat fruit that was ripe enough to fall without plucking. These injunctions recall Saman's guarding presence in the woods, which is also evident in verses on forest gardens and the privileged knowledge of their cultivators:

Breadfruit, jack, plantain bunches, and great pineapple
Talipot, coconut, areca nut, and betel joined together
Among the cliffs there are multitudes of various fruits
. . .
When going in the Himagata there are various signs. [*lakunē*]
In the forest place to place are also home gardens in the grove.
. . .
The god is without appearance only.
How can it be if farmers saw him in the forest?[112]

Saman is normally invisible, but those familiar with the forest, who know how to read its signs and coax it to bear so many fruits, are graced with divine perspective. Of course, to ascribe some pristine environmental ethic to this poem would be foolhardy. It also promotes some deforestation for better pilgrimage infrastructure:

While there, some people cut bamboo trees
They clear, bundle, and carry them away happily
Along the path, clearing the trees is good
Giving merit to the god, let us go to Sri Pada happily.[113]

Some might also question the ability of old songs to adequately address present problems. Being careful about how much fruit to pluck is a reasonable ethic to promote in a village of a dozen families, but can it feed a city of millions like Colombo? Still, poetic forest ethics retain relevance in another way. The most famous element in our present eco-crises is carbon, and humans have realized that forests keep it cycling into the ground and not altering the atmosphere. Retaining the remaining forest land is thus a crucial component of sustainable futures, and management of reserves is achieved with local knowledge of signs that indicate woodland health.

Making records of forest wisdom, including the theology of its ecology, has been a component of previous conservation studies. In the largest survey of the Peak Wilderness to date, Anoja Wickramasinghe stressed: "The commitment of the fringe dwellers and the pilgrims to protecting the wilderness is closely related to their beliefs about and affinity with the forest. They have strong ethics which stop them exploiting the forest. . . . An 84 year-old man . . . said: 'The Samanala-adawiya is our soul, its water, greens, soils, flora and fauna have nourished thousands of people; my ancestors and my children.' "[114] More recent scientific studies of Sri Lankan wilderness management framed by climate change support the effectiveness of forest-fringe villages and "home-garden" agroforestry in providing a buffer for denser reserves of woods and storing more carbon. Home gardeners find profit in the jungle without clearing its trees, using the produce that poets praised. Increased canopy cover also creates more wildlife habitats, guarded by humans who monitor its health to sustainably reap its wealth.[115] Groves are sometimes reserved in religious terms, via unnamed forest gods living in the densest forbidden regions. Likewise, Wickramasinghe recorded opinions that proclaimed a unity of gods and other beings in the jungle, so each plant was a microcosm for the full forest, imbued with its life-sustaining properties: "It is full of life and invisible powers that extends generosity toward us in the outskirts. Every life form, the trees, shrubs, herbs, bamboo, rhizomes, moss, pandanas and weeds of the 'Samanala Adaviya,' carries its wholistic features. We believe that nature itself has made us live outside to retain the purity of 'Samanala Adaviya,' to retain the gods of the forest and deities who are in a better position to safeguard the forest."[116] The plans of nature dictate that humans should live on its fringes, as beings with special stakes in protecting its health. Through human guardianship of the environment, divine power is also maintained. In this way, humanity sustaining the forest in turn sustains *hāskam*, which then helps to guard the forest even further than humans ever could. Such scientific surveys of forest-fringe dwellers are only the latest in a long-standing fascination with the mythic wild men of Sri Lanka, as those who intimately know the jungle are made a part of it by outside observers.[117] For example, in an 1891 pilgrimage poem, forest-fringe villagers are described as a species of fauna:

> Charcoal-like black-colored row of teeth, the body decrepit
> Brown-colored cloth having donned, girded to the knees
> Villagers appearing like groups of monkeys lovingly.[118]

Likewise, a 1966 book called *Piṭisara Minissu* (Wild people) depicts forest-fringe dwellers in a single interdependent habitus, so "trees, vines, and animals exist abundantly through the lives of one another. This conjoined influence is to the point that if one species disappeared for any reason, another species will die."[119] Such romanticized ecological awareness is translated into pilgrimage ethics through signs at the Peak that directly encourage interdependent perspectives, like a board that reads, "These trees and vines give us life," posted on a rare stretch of the Hatton trail that was still significantly forested (fig. 5.7).

Through intentional interventions, some problems that Wickramasinghe recorded in 1995 have found workable solutions. The cement trails lessen the erosive impact on the forest by encouraging pilgrims to stick to one path, although even this cannot contain the biggest crowds. Garbage collection has also improved, as has sanitation, and the water-reclamation plant helps considerably in this regard. Other problems, however, have only morphed into new forms. Deforestation demands decreased when propane replaced firewood as fuel for most shops, but nonrenewable natural gas releases more carbon. Further improvements remain but imagined possibilities, like more permanent cement shops, so all need not be rebuilt anew every year. Such buildings would

FIGURE 5.7. "These trees and vines give us life"

require less annual clearing of the surrounding forest. This would allow trees near the shops to regenerate into larger forms with attentive pruning, and shopkeepers could then cultivate home gardens at the Peak, the produce of which would make a valuable market among pilgrims who value its forest of origin. This would also be another avenue for political display, fulfilling government initiatives promising millions more home gardens.[120]

The idea that some cement in the right places can help more green to grow may seem counterintuitive, but it is a realistic ethic, a workable compromise with the intractable scale of humanity on the plant. It is an example of what Anna Tsing calls "disturbance-based ecologies in which many species live together without either harmony or conquest."[121] The idea of achieving pure harmony in nature is just as much of a fantasy as the pure harmony of religious pluralism at the Peak, but in both cases accords can be forged. It is therefore appropriate that a cement intervention with environmental benefit—the Peak's water-reclamation plant—also represents one of the better instantiations of pluralism on the mountain (fig. 5.8). State funded and constructed by engineering firms, the plant required an alliance between the expertise of Colombo elites, mostly Sinhala, and the physical labor and continued residence of the highland Tamil population, who built it and now reside as maintenance workers in the adjacent dormitory. When the final signboard for the plant was placed after it began operations in 2016, its names were significant: the Sripadasthanaya Sewerage Scheme in Sinhala and English, and the Sivanolipada Sewerage Scheme in Tamil. This was the closest to the summit that any official designation of Siva had been in some time. In this case, cooperation led to more consciously plural representation, albeit still downstream of the toilets. As an essential service, however, the Peak's water-reclamation plant indicates one way that human and ecological equity can be forged from discord in dire times, inviting higher aspirations for the future.

Elevating pilgrimage ethics means taking seriously the "supererogatory" side of Buddhist ethics and exceeding conventional expectations of selflessness.[122] If one follows the Buddhist teaching that nature lacks any intrinsic nature—*svabhāvadharma* with an empty *svabhāva*—it leads to all categories being only provisional, including conventional identities like religion and ethnicity. This emptiness of things means the Peak can have no absolute owner, only interdependent pieces that are continually reordered. This suggests the most control humans can claim is a form of stewardship, taking responsibility for aiding the mountain's many pilgrims, human and otherwise. For Buddhists, this requires enacting what Alan Sponberg has called a "hierarchy of compassion." Unlike conventional hierarchies of domination, "the vertical dimension here is . . . the range of progressively greater degrees of awareness and ethical sensibility

FIGURE 5.8. Cooperation in a disturbed ecology at the Peak's water-reclamation plant

available to all life-forms."[123] Enlightened ones and humans with hopes for enlightenment are best positioned to spread compassion the widest. This is why Buddhas and bodhisattvas who tame nature do so to convey compassion, as when Saman extends nirvana potential to many beings as the guardian of the mountain:

> God Sumana Saman, to become the future Buddha
> Causing humans to worship like strings of pearls
> Mind having aspired, making the intention fulfilled
> Causing your tusker, like you, to become a Buddha
> . . .
> Having entered amid the forest and kept Buddha virtue
> Having aspired to nirvana, made to recall Sage virtues
> Lord God Saman greatly offered to the foot
> So now may we receive nirvana comfort.[124]

By facilitating so many strands of people to come on pilgrimage and by making his original offerings to the Buddha foot, Saman put all beings on the path to enlightenment, all the way through to the elephant world of Saman's tusker vehicle.[125] The Peak's pilgrimage is an excellent space in which to cultivate such an ethic, considering that the word for compassion (*karuṇā*) is called out so frequently by pilgrims during their ascents. Genuinely enacting a compassionate hierarchy best serves this plural mountain of diverse beings who are constitutive of and responsible for each other.

This intertwining of existence is a sort of a dance, a description Sinhala poets applied to forests. K. D. G. Perērā's 1926 pilgrimage poem vividly described such scenes:

> Elephants, oxen, and bears in the great forest
> Love for listening to their resounding noises
> Becoming Buddha-virtued, let us all go alike
> Behold, friends, in the incense affectionately
> . . .
> Lizards, snakes and such, elephants, oxen, bears
> Dancing animals, monkeys, and forest people
> With united minds, sinners receiving merit
> This dance is visible, easily being faultless.[126]

The idea of an entire pilgrimage group uniting their minds and becoming filled with Buddha virtue (*buduguṇa*) is common to such poetry, but Perērā's inclusion of animals extends this conjoined being into the environment. The merit-making dance of pilgrimage spreads in the forest, animating all the sentience on mountain slopes to stretch toward perfection. The "sinners" are those making demerit (*pavkarasun*), presumably through the regular predations of forest life. Perērā has such faults karmically ameliorated by the overall concord of the forest dance. The movements cause all beings to receive the merit made in the larger hierarchy of compassion, as the dancing animals appropriately appear amid other verses about prior Buddhas and their enlightenments. In turn, the metaphor of dance can convey not only how forest beings interact, but also how we should conduct ourselves to remain open to the forest. As Tsing writes of mushroom foragers, "being in the forest this way might be considered dance: lines of life are pursued through senses, movements, and orientations. The dance is a form of forest knowledge."[127] As human and nonhuman signs intertwine, the knowledge whirled up in the process displays what Timothy Morton calls "ecognosis," which is "like knowing, but more like letting be known. It is something like coexisting. . . . Knowing in a loop."[128] For Buddhists, cultivating such knowledge of the world comes with moral obligations. A sort of ecognosis thus appears in Nāgārjuna's ethics for aspiring bodhisattvas, as natural elements teach us how to "always be an object of enjoyment for all sentient beings . . . as are the earth, water, fire, wind, herbs, and wild forests."[129] As circles of beings let one another be known in grooves of forest soundscapes, humans who are situated to best practice compassion and loving-kindness can actively foster a flourishing coexistence through intentional mutualism.

Like forest ecologies, the religious pluralism at the Peak may also work best by letting itself be known, not dictated. In the same vein as Latour's point that humans can better cooperate with nature through "the art of governing without mastery,"[130] the head monk and other Buddhist leaders could position themselves more like stewards than sentries of Sri Pada. As Juvānisā noted a century ago, no merit comes from inhibiting the worship of other pilgrims. With less stricture, shrines and rituals might blossom more freely on the trails and summit, on mountain slopes broad enough to shoulder divinities as plural as their stone and life. There is still no perfect harmony, as Tsing notes: "Every instance of collaboration makes room for some and leaves out others. . . . The best we can do is aim for 'good-enough' worlds, where 'good-enough' is always imperfect and under revision."[131] Religious meetings must therefore be negotiated by revisable pilgrimage ethics rather than by mandated rules of worship. Embracing disagreements and discomforts of shared ritual space, "out of reciprocal appreciation for the element of contestability in these domains,"[132] can be productive in itself, another difficulty to add to the physical travails that pilgrims say generate merit. In turn, a healthy multireligious public may emerge. As Leela Prasad puts it, "co-being is not a state of utopian togetherness . . . [It] becomes possible only when individuals and private collectives endure physical discomfort, risk, and uncertainty."[133] Tensions generate perpetually renegotiable agreements about what is shared, accords crafted to maintain multiple trajectories of flourishing, while also profitably cooperating on issues of mutual import. As Connolly contends, such an "ethos of engagement can support a more multifarious pluralism . . . a *pluralism* in which multiple possibilities of connection open up across several lines of difference."[134] This entails forming consensuses while acknowledging there is no sole consensus. It means thinking like a forest, and not losing it for the trees by keeping the broad view of a mountain.

Nevertheless, the pursuit of "macropolitical" agendas like promoting the plural heritage of the Peak, or preserving the ecology of the Peak, requires everyday "micropolitical" actions with an "ethos of engagement" that builds working coalitions around compromise.[135] Buddhist philosophy supports such an ethos, evident in canonical and vernacular texts as well as in the opinions of those who work on the Peak today. The impermanence of all things fills the world with dynamic potentiality through perpetual change, necessitating continual adaptations and accommodations. For this philosophy to guide those

Buddhists in control of the Peak, they must remain open to allying themselves with varied religions and rituals in their midst. Although Sri Lanka's political system has created expectations for overt government support of a broadly construed Buddhist *sāsana*, the continued pursuit of plural coexistence remains possible in part through long-standing Lankan Buddhist standards of toleration, including the "imperial toleration" of compassionate rulers or the "cosmological toleration" of fluid pantheons that assimilate other gods and spirits.[136] Consider a poetic verse that neatly encapsulates cosmological toleration at the Peak, spanning so many of the mythic personages and places that populate the pages of this book:

> With the refuge of the gods, brahmas, Siva, Uma, and the Sun
> and Moon gods
> With the gems of Uma's Lord [Siva], God Ganesh, and God
> Kadirakumara
> In the shade beneath the sacred feet imprinted on the stones of
> Mecca and Samanala
> Although there are errors in all the verses, free them from faults
> by those powers.[137]

The poet interweaves Buddha footprints with Saiva deities and Islamic influences to commence his ritual song and cleanse his verses of literary mistakes. In the process, he does not simply appropriate Siva, Mecca, etc., for Buddhists, but lends key Buddhist terminology to laud Siva, as one can take refuge (*saraṇa*) from him and other gods just as one can take the refuge of the Buddha, Dharma, and Sangha. Likewise, Siva and his divine family are described as gems (*ruvan*), another common designation for the Buddha, Dharma, and Sangha. The poet thereby elevates a diversity of religious elements with respectful language, causing this verse to incidentally express the ethic of the *Metta Sutta*—one of the most recited passages from the Pali canon:

> One should develop loving-kindness for the whole world,
> a state of mind without boundaries—
> above, below, and across,
> unconfined, without enmity or adversaries.[138]

Despite this well-known injunction to recognize an unbounded cosmos, some Buddhists would prefer to prohibit pluralistic parity. As Latour notes, "if pluralism is so rare, appearances notwithstanding, it is because there is always a deity waiting in ambush that demands to be made commensurable with no other."[139] There are indeed many who claim the summit as a solely Buddhist space. The current head monk has done well to permit some alternative ritual programming at the Peak, but it is telling that this has mainly been to accommodate foreign Buddhists or local Tamil laborers who revere Vishnu, a god more fully absorbed and subordinated within the Buddhist pantheon than Siva.[140] A complete *metta* ethic remains to be enacted at the Peak through the dissolution of ritual boundaries in all directions.

To pursue pluralism with adequate alacrity, one cannot wait for imperial toleration to be benevolently dispensed from above. It is therefore heartening to see other local forms of tolerant micropolitics already underway in certain places on the Peak. Such activities are varied, including grassroots environmental cleanup days advertised to both Tamil and Sinhala pilgrims, the presence of local Tamils on the summit staff with special roles in Buddhist rituals like the *kemmura* cleansing, and the general adoption of the bodhisattva Saman as a guardian god shared by local Hindus.[141] What these examples have in common is attention to the specific space of the Peak and respect for its land. As Lefebvre notes, oftentimes "a space-related issue spurs collaboration . . . between very different kinds of people."[142] Such nuanced pluralities must be continually cultivated to resist the broad strokes of nationalists seeking a purified space, so their homogenous shouts do not drown out the interactive song and dance of the Peak.

Consider one final example of successfully plural micropolitics on another signboard promoting environmentally sustainable behavior. This one was erected at the roundabout near the Maussakelle dam on the Hatton side of the mountain, at the turn for the final seven-kilometer trip to Nallathanni. The road snakes around the bright blue-green reservoir, beside tea terraces and groves of foreign pines for failed reforestation projects, their tannins too acidic for local undergrowth. The signboard was from the "Environment Is Sacred" campaign, which also made the problematic bilingual board discussed above. This sign, however, was more easily translatable among multiple religious idioms. Alongside an image of Saman, the Sinhala read: "God Sumana Saman's blessing for you who help to protect the environment of the Sri Pada sacred ground!" The Tamil was vaguer, but productive in that way: "Our Lord [*perumāṉ*] bless those who help protect the environment of the Sri Pada mountain pilgrimage site." *Perumāṉ* is a fairly open-ended title, often applied to Siva, but generic enough for almost any god, Saman included. It is even a term that Tamil Muslims have applied to the Prophet Muhammad.[143] The sign therefore allows for a plurality of beliefs. Although it lacks the Tamil name "Sivanolipadamalai" for the Peak, instead using Śrī Pātamalai, this might be a basic case of Sanskrit vocabulary in Tamil, not necessarily a Sinhala imposition. Many highland

Tamils do call the Peak Sri Pada for short, and its meaning of "sacred foot" does not contradict the beliefs of Hindus, Muslims, or Christians, perhaps projecting the same pluralistic intent as *perumāṉ*. Likewise, one highland Tamil author has argued that the title "Sri Pada" is considerate of "regional unity" (*tēciya oṟṟumai*) since it is the name of hotels, restaurants, and tea estates owned and operated by Tamils.[144]

Even seemingly small word choices can make space for new religious assemblages instead of ritual hegemony. This would ultimately fulfill the aspirations of so many Buddhist poets like Juvānisā, who hoped that "when going in the Lord God's forest . . . all sufferings are removed, providing comforts for all people," with generated merit "to be received by all people."[145] Truly taking all pilgrims into account means crafting a space that works for all. In turn, by acknowledging that the Peak has many users, the above conservation sign suits the deeper stakes of the pact it promotes. With some basis of religious cooperation, attention can then be codirected onto the ecology, which requires its own negotiated agreements in a multispecies pluralism. To show what myths the Peak may offer for the deepest sort of ecological stakes we face, this book's conclusion turns to the final frontiers of co-being in the expansive troubles of the Anthropocene.

Conclusion

Deep Stakes

ballan biruvāṭa kanda kaḍā väṭennē nähä.
The mountain does not collapse for dogs barking.

—Sinhala proverb[1]

If the Peak is a mountain at a center of the world, the meaning of "world" might be read in two ways: as "the global—a singularly human story—and the planetary, a perspective to which humans are incidental."[2] I have shown these worlds of the Peak in overlap, with the Peak as its own actor across a human history of oceanic trade, royal courts, colonialism, and modern religious conflict. In doing so, I have worked toward the type of history Dipesh Chakrabarty prescribes for the Anthropocene, "to bring together intellectual formations that are somewhat in tension with each other: the planetary and the global; deep and recorded histories; species thinking and critiques of capital."[3] Yet the Anthropocene, a term coined in the year 2000, is still being defined.[4] It stands for the epoch when human agency in planetary processes assumed a geologic scale, with major alteration of carbon, phosphorous, and nitrogen cycles, and massive displacement of soil and water, contributing to a multispecies extinction event. These are the sorts of changes that previously only occurred from forces like tectonic plates and planetary orbit. Now humanity pushes hard on the planet, too, and the planet is pushing back.

The Mythic Lithic in the Anthropocene

Geologists have yet to officially adopt "Anthropocene" as an epochal successor to the current Holocene, and its meaning, especially its dating, continues to be debated. Some suggest long timelines, whether beginning from the start of human agriculture, the age of colonial exterminations, or the Industrial Revolution. The deeper timeframes lend an important perspective about human behavior, as "human cultures have for centuries, even millennia, caused greenhouse gas emissions or eradicated potential carbon sinks and thus *participated* in climate dynamics . . . *Participation* is the key word here. Human and natural actors have formed a common historical process in which they cannot be neatly differentiated."[5] As Latour succinctly says, "we *are* the atmosphere."[6] Geologists, however, need a more definitive "golden spike" for epochs, readable in rock.[7] The year 1945 is one choice, as a radioactive stratigraphy was layered with the nuclear age, a definitively new chapter in the record of the earth.[8] Other scholars, like Donna Haraway, reject the term "Anthropocene" for wrongly blaming all humans for these capitalist crises and further promoting anthropocentrism.[9] As Haraway has long been attuned to mythology, however, always reminding us that "the stories we tell matter," she surely recognizes that the idea of the Anthropocene has grown beyond any one critical intervention. The Anthropocene has become its own mytholith, rapidly expanded with a staggering range of scholarly reflection in the span of two decades and used for multifarious ends, including to encourage more or less human intervention in ecology. Even those who reject the Anthropocene by name still pick it up and shape it.

The Anthropocene edge I find useful here agrees with William Connolly: "It is first and foremost a geological term set in relation to the trends and periodic volatilities of other geological periods."[10] For this reason, the Anthropocene encourages thought on especially deep scales, the sort that can spark profound humility in humanity. Even the classic Indic invocation meant to glorify kings for "as long as the sun and the moon exist," also carries an implication that, if time is read in its full cosmic deepness, someday these will not exist. Beyond any present climate challenge, nothing can stop the sun from dying, which truly makes every human question on the planet one "of how we wish to live whatever time is left for the human species."[11] Before the Anthropocene accelerated the spread of deep time in various discourses, those who had such a deep temporal scope were mostly geologists. John McPhee recorded their ensuing existential reflections: "Geologists, dealing always with deep time, find that it seeps into their beings and affects them in various ways." The stunning suddenness of humanity can lead to indifference or pessimism: " 'You care less about civilization.' . . . 'Mammalian species last, typically, two million years. We've about used up ours.' " Yet McPhee quoted others who held almost salvational visions: "If you free yourself from the conventional reaction to a quantity like a million years, you free yourself a bit from the boundaries of human time. And then in a way you do not live at all, but in another way you live forever."[12] Geohistory provides a mythic picture with immense perspective, allowing humans to intellectually transcend the temporal limits of their mortality.

When wielding the Anthropocene mytholith, many scholars have consciously used theories of myth to animate geology, telling stories of stones "to discern in the most mundane of substances a liveliness."[13] Such forays into geological animation include Connolly's rereading of the Book of Job to find its "volcano God . . . closer to a lava flow bubbling along implacably with intense heat and energy."[14] Others have used "the mythological . . . for exploring the idea of geological life," finding "identity, or even empathy, between man and stone."[15] Still others have tried to revise a "geontological" divide, which overly separates living from nonliving, by using different mythic pictures to reweave these categories, be they the "dreamings" of Australian aboriginal communities,[16] or those Western continental philosophers who envisioned a "mineralogy of being" that stones possess.[17] In this world of animate rocks, the Peak can also contribute, helping humans think on multiple scales by seeing what it means to be a mountain.

Being Like a Mountain

The phrase "thinking like a mountain" was introduced into the mid-twentieth-century ecological movement by Aldo Leopold, who regretted his younger years hunting wolves for no reason, which led to too many deer, who denuded their mountain and then starved to death, leading Leopold to realize: "Only the mountain has lived long enough to listen objectively to the howl of a wolf."[18] Thinking like a mountain was then used as a slogan by other environmentalists highlighting interdependent ecologies.[19] Centuries earlier, however, the need to see reality from a mountain's point of view had already been preached by the Japanese Sōtō Zen master Dōgen. In 1240, Dōgen delivered his *Sansuikyō*, or *Mountains and Waters Sutra*, which builds upon a koan that states, "the blue mountains are constantly walking." Dōgen begins by explaining how "the mountains lack none of their proper virtues; hence, they are constantly at rest and constantly walking. We must devote ourselves to a detailed study of this virtue of walking . . . [as] one ought not doubt that the mountains walk simply because they may not appear to stride like humans."[20] In an era before plate-tectonics theories, walking mountains would seem particularly paradoxical, but if walking is a metaphor for impermanence here, then of course both mountains and humans are constantly walking, even if mountains may appear more permanent than us (i.e., constantly at rest) on a human time scale. Dōgen explains how the world contains a multiplicity of different perspectives, as "the way of seeing mountains and waters differs according to the type of being,"[21] a point he illustrates wonderfully with a flowing stream. While we see the stream as flowing, "fish see water as a palace . . . they do not view it as flowing. And, if some onlooker were to explain to them that their palace was flowing water, they would surely be just as amazed as we are now to hear it said that mountains flow."[22] From the vantage point of a fish, the mountain may be what flows. Shohaku Okumura explains in his modern commentary why such multiperspectivity is an important trait to cultivate: "If I think there is only one center of the world and it's me, that's a problem. If we think that there are numberless centers, this means that everyone of us is the center of the world. We can respect everyone."[23] Natural formations like mountains and waters can model this virtue of boundless accommodation of others. Echoing his description of virtuous mountains, Dōgen writes that "water is nothing but water's 'real form just as it is.' Water is the virtue of water."[24] Okumura elaborates: "Mountains and waters have no defilement. Mountains are simply being mountains and accepting all beings within them. Oceans do not reject water from any river."[25] Dōgen's call to understand how mountains walk in order to know ourselves is more than just a philosophical riddle. It is an ethical injunction.

Can the Peak help its pilgrims practice the same sort of knowing and being? Can we learn how the mountain experiences the Anthropocene, and so come to better know ourselves? To start, we must learn how to look for the signs of the epoch written on the Peak. From the very beginning of a climb, whether on the Hatton or Ratnapura side, one must notice a lack of forest, the ensuing extra sunlight making daytime ascents more difficult. The Peak's lower garments were sheared as part of "a worldwide supplanting of local biota in favor of an imported portmanteau of profitable species,"[26] yielding rolling ridges of tea bushes in this case. Meanwhile, if one climbs on opening day, or during a busy weekend, the Peak trail is a microcosm of Anthropocene overpopulation, with traffic jams of international bodies stuck for hours, pilgrim queues squeezed by the summit bottleneck (fig. Con.1).

The mountain surely notices the nonsacred environmental footprint that all the pilgrim feet leave, as piles of half-burnt trash struggle to decompose on the clear-cut edges of paved trails. In some spots, including at the summit itself, trash has become embedded into layer upon layer of soil, marking decades of discarding (fig. Con.2). This is the stratigraphy of the Anthropocene, the "anthropogenic deposits" that are building a "novel strata . . . both lithostratigraphal and biostratigraphal, for it comprises the built environment

FIGURE CON.1. The crowd on opening day near the summit

(a kind of trace fossil system in the making) that humans have created."[27] As the mountain's geological materials were carved out for summit construction space, its rubble was remixed with plastics, metal alloys, and glass, to form a new Peak body. Lady Lanka's diadem is now forged in part from artificial materials. Such unsightly effects are rallying cries for some to table their singularly human problems for a bigger picture. Responding to anti-Muslim memes about Sri Pada that circulate on Facebook, one page posted pictures of embedded trash on the trail, with the caption: "Sri Pada needs to be rescued not from the Muslims, but from our Buddhists."[28]

Thinking like a mountain entails concern about such natural alterations, but also an acknowledgment that this concern is really for our human selves. However much we trash it, the mountain will outlive us. Even if all agree to become dog-persons, learning to see our being as coeval with the nonhuman, all our barking at or about the mountain will never make it crumble. In this way, meditating on the mountain's relative permanence allows deep visions of both past and future, a fitting perspective for an Anthropocene that is "asking us to extend to the future the faculty of understanding that historians routinely extend to humans of the recorded past."[29] There are signs at the Peak that encourage pilgrims to think this way. Consider two examples, one from

FIGURE CON.2. Anthropocene strata on the summit

each side of the mountain. A banner on the Hatton trail was hung near the Makara Torana during the midseason by the Damsak Padanama, or Dharma Wheel Foundation, of Avissawella. It encouraged pilgrims to responsibly remove trash because of how long it takes to degrade. The rest of the sign was a long list of times—the decay rates of various garbage. It began with small scales, listing easily biodegradable items: 3–4 weeks for a banana leaf, 1 month for a paper leaf, 2 months for an apple core or cardboard. The middle of the list grew to a scale that could consume most of a human life: 25–40 years for leather sandals, and 50–80 for rubber sandals or small plastics. The lower level of the list was anchored by a more mountainous scale of temporality over many human generations: 200–500 years for aluminum cans, 450 years for plastic bottles, and 200–1,000 years for plastic bags. Last was glass, spending the most future time with the Peak at 1–2 million years. About a million pilgrims walked past this poster in 2016. How many actually read its temporal stratigraphy of trash is unknown, but it shows one possible strategy for mountain thinking. Using the deep time that attaches naturally to the Peak, it encourages a more responsible ecological consciousness by reminding people how long the mountain will remain with their things, and that more human-made materials are less likely to recycle well into planetary systems.

Another sign, on the Ratnapura trail, took a different approach to time. Hung outside the Ceylon Electricity Board camp, it asked passing pilgrims to "stop a bit," and look around. This sign tried to slow time down for a moment, asking people to be fully on the mountain, not huffing ahead, but absorbing it all:

> Take a breath,
> and a bit of the purity on earth from the wind . . .
> Be silent,
> trees and leaves will speak to you . . .
> Love,
> trees and leaves will love you . . .
> Experience
> the environmental beauty pleasantly . . .
> Lift your foot,
> so as to not be a weight for the great earth.
> Take away
> all the things you brought without footprints.
> Promise
> to be without any error
> . . . so as to protect this for future generations.

By stopping to simply *be* on the Peak, to breathe in the mountain, to listen to it, to love it, one can mold the proper mindset to tread lightly. Being part of the mountain encourages action as faultless as Dōgen believed mountains were, so that the Peak environment can continue to tell its stories to generations of pilgrims.

Still, more is surely needed. Perhaps it is time for the Peak to have its own political representative, someone to take the time to relay the needs of trees and leaves back to human debates. Stories of animated nature and vital materials are only decorative without a political follow through. As Latour put it, "the fiction resides not in giving water a voice, but in believing that one *could get along without* representing it *by a human voice* capable of making itself understood by other humans."[30] If the Peak had a seat in parliament, it would certainly upset the usual notions of modern state territory, but also thereby acknowledge that the planetary supersedes political borders. As seen in chapter 1, premodern authors of Lankan boundary books had the Peak touch each of the three main divisions of the island. Instead of being an inert object under human control, the Peak was an independent landmark around which fluid human politics continually reorganized. It may need to watch over still more political reshuffling, in a world where climatic changes mean that "what a territory signifies has been totally disrupted: it is no longer the old pastoral landscape of well-marked fields . . . it is rather the violent *reappropriation* of all human claims *by the Earth itself*."[31] As the planet is already redrawing our territories, appointing political representation for natural formations like the Peak seems eminently sensible.

Deleuze and Guattari, introducing their idea of "geophilosophy," describe how "the earth constantly carries out a movement of deterritorialization on the spot, by which it goes beyond any territory. . . . It merges with the movement of those who leave their territory en masse, with crayfish that set off walking in file at the bottom of the water, with pilgrims or knights who rise in a celestial line of flight. The earth . . . brings together all the elements in a single embrace while using one or another of them to deterritorialize territory."[32] The history of a mountain at a center of the world traffics across many territories. The preceding chapters have shown the Peak drawing pilgrims from near and far, crossing open seas and political gulfs to ascend its slopes. The Peak was an Islamic land on medieval maps made over oceans half a world away. It was a southern extension of Himalayan heights, to match other realms of Saiva space. It anchored temporality, connecting many former Buddhas across ages. Still, the Peak also transcended all these mythically malleable realms, retaining an ultimate sovereignty in a geohistory that walks at its own pace.

One of the strangest reflections ever composed about the Peak concerns these geological forces and their indifference to human suffering and religious supplication:

> Nature's impassiveness and irresponsiveness are terrible. One feels that—if helpless to aid the groaning millions who through the long, long centuries

> have climbed her rocky flanks and scaled her wind-swept summit to reach a little nearer to the God who dwells in the aching blue above them—the mountain, in sheer sorrow for their useless toil and grief . . . should long ago have crumbled into dust and fragments. One can hardly help feeling a foolish exaltation that in the end, no matter how far off it be, the very mountain itself must be thrown down and levelled with the plain. But there is a terror in this, too.
>
> . . .
>
> Plains rise and mountain ranges fall . . . soft and impalpable touches of cloud hands and the gentle wearing of the summer rain are the agents of destruction; but the impassivity of granite crags themselves must give way before their soft invincibility. Therein lies the terror of it.[33]

This anonymous introspective from 1886 may represent a proud colonial hero staring down his ultimate defeat. The Peak would outlive any empire. Yet his barking about superstition could not make the mountain collapse, so he only dreamt of a day he would never see, when the Peak would also disappear. Addicted to control, he trembled facing the fact that "nature" was truly uncontrollable. This remains an Anthropocene anxiety, as humans are now as powerful as geological forces, but still lack any real control. Yet a geophilosophical frame might also be used to dispel terror, to inspire and instruct. As the Buddha once exclaimed to compliment his disciple's forbearance in meditation:

> As a mountain of rock is unwavering, well settled,
> so a monk whose delusion is ended
> doesn't quiver—
> just like a mountain.[34]

Skillfully maintaining attentive mindfulness is being like a mountain, a state without fearful trembling or being shaken by distraction, because reality is made plain without delusions.

This reality comes with discomforts, but they are what make it instructive, as when those walking mountains begin to rush in on us. In the *Pabbatūpama Sutta*, or *Mountain Simile Discourse*, the Buddha poses questions to a king who is "intoxicated with the intoxication of sovereignty . . . having conquered a great sphere of territory on earth." The Buddha asks him to imagine a scenario in which "someone trustworthy and reliable" from each direction reports "a great mountain high as the clouds coming this way, crushing all living beings . . . If, great king, such a great peril should arise, such a terrible destruction of human life, the human state being so difficult to obtain, what should be done?"[35] The king rightly responds that the only thing to be done in that case is live by the dharma and perform righteous and meritorious deeds. The Buddha elaborates that aging and death are likewise rolling in on the king, also reasons to live by the dharma. The king concurs that there are no ways of fighting this coming foe, as all methods of warfare—whether elephants, cavalry, chariot, infantry, political subterfuge, or wealth—will prove useless. Aging and death, as earthly forces unto themselves that make life fleeting, are more powerful, showing the importance of doing good as a human who is aware enough to make merit in the face of this terrible destruction.

This simile adapts well to the Anthropocene if the mountains are also made to stand for the planetary agencies that now threaten the fundamental possibility of the human state, "so difficult to obtain." Buddhaghosa's commentary on this *sutta* is also instructive, relaying the afterlife of the sermon when the king retells it to an army of thieves who have captured him. Buddhaghosa explains how the thieves and king became trapped together in a dark forest, unable to advance at night due to the danger of being "impaled by stakes affixed for planting." So, as they are stuck together, the leader of the thieves, knowing of the king's visits to the Buddha, asks for a sermon, realizing that "this king, being troubled, unable to restrain himself, will expound the Dhamma through instruction, and I will understand."[36] This image of unlikely allies forged in darkness, pressed in by unexpected manmade threats and the fundamental agencies of nature, learning to converse in order to live virtuously, is one answer to the Buddha's question, more relevant than ever: "[With] death rolling in . . . what should be done?" Considering that mountainous change is already impersonally and indifferently rolling in on us, it certainly seems time for pilgrims to band together in the dark. I therefore turn to one last group of beings who cross territories en masse, more members of the nonhuman collective of Peak pilgrims whom we might follow, "to think of ethics in terms of movement."[37]

Following the Butterflies

It is perhaps a strange way to end, to only now reveal the meaning of the Peak's most common poetic name—Samanala. But this may save the best for last. Most say the name Samanala comes from the word for butterfly, *samanalayā*, a theory bolstered by their annual presence at the Peak.[38] The myth of butterflies on pilgrimage was recorded by British colonial authors, as "travellers find themselves haunted by clouds of innumerable butterflies of large size and many colours. Their assembling at this season (when their life is nearly finished) is preparatory, saith native tradition, to their taking flight for Adam's Peak in the interior, whereon they will worship the footprint of Buddha, and therefore die content."[39] By all accounts, the butterfly population in Lanka was once much greater, especially in the southwestern coastal strip, which has lost much leaf cover to concrete. During migratory seasons for both humans and insects, colonial visitors to Colombo described scenes that are impossible to fathom today.

In his article on one of the first butterfly breeding experiments in the colony, Major Neville Manders recalls: "By a coincidence a migratory flight of butterflies was in full swing on the day I landed in Ceylon, October 25, 1895, and I certainly thought that I had stepped into a land of butterflies. The harbour, streets, and large promenade, the Galle Face by the sea-shore, was alive with butterflies, and . . . looked for all the world like a snow-storm."[40] Storms of butterflies in the city have dried to drizzles of late, and without this coastal larval ground, the subsequent highland migrations have also declined. Older employees at the Peak said the butterflies had undoubtedly diminished in recent decades. Clouds of them once stretched over the sky like a jet stream, winding toward the summit. The annual wave is now less immense, but many insects still come to pay their respects, sticking to the summit at the end of their lives. Butterflies are present on all inhabited continents, across which many species migrate, sometimes for thousands of miles and even overseas. They are therefore a natural sort of pilgrim, those beings on the move, though their motivation for migration remains fairly mysterious in its complexity. Is it innate? Does it depend on food supply? Rainfall? Spawning grounds? In the heyday of colonial science, positivists were positive there was a definitive answer more specific than the mythic, though they could not quite conjure it with their limited data.

Entomologist C. B. Williams classed the pilgrimage theory as a passing curiosity. Starting his section on "Sources of Information," he wrote: "Unidirectional flights of butterflies . . . have been for long a source of wonder to the inhabitants of Ceylon, and the natives have even evolved a superstition as to their goal and have thought the insects to be on a pilgrimage to Adam's Peak or elsewhere."[41] Williams, however, was more interested in empirical observations, recording times, directions, species, and weather. Compiling all mentions of migration he could find, Williams concluded that at least 69 species, out of 234 total recorded, took part in migrations, and he isolated the main seasons of October–December and February–April, the latter overlapping with Peak pilgrim migrations. Yet Williams deduced no further: "There are many exceptional flights which do not fit into the general scheme. . . . Further information is needed on every point before reliable conclusions can be drawn."[42] More than seventy observations could say little about *why* butterflies were moving about or were drawn to the Peak region in particular. Williams implied that a veritable army of observers, coordinated across regions over years, would be needed to find a final answer, to understand how the butterfly defied territories.

In the end, Major Manders's map from three decades earlier still summarized the situation well. He could identify the spawning grounds with circles on the coast, but most arrows of migration ended in question marks, especially near the Peak region, where they branched into a triplicate of confusion. Following butterflies is difficult. Question marks persist, and it seems unlikely that funding will ever manifest for a study comprehensive enough to exhaustively explain the multispecies butterfly/moth highland migration. In which case, what would it mean to provisionally accept the idea that the butterflies are on pilgrimage? Might this still be our best explanation for the phenomenon, in the sense of being the most useful?

Although Samanala is the most common name for the Peak in Sinhala poetry, butterflies have appeared in surprisingly few verses over the years. When they do flutter through, however, they carry potent imagery that effaces the divide between human and nonhuman, even as the verses acknowledge key differences between insects as us. Consider three examples from consecutive generations of Sinhala poets. In the modern resurgence of *sandeśa* poems, an 1895 composition used the butterfly as its messenger, with opening verses expressing an insect elegy. The butterfly is described as a lovely lady and compared to the Peak for this reason, for "what other girls in the world are there to speak of, friend?" The poem also institutes a trope about the silence of butterflies, repeated in later Sinhala verse: "Risen into the belly of the sky, will the lady not speak when coming?" Nevertheless, she still has important duties to perform, such as "making known truly beautiful floral wealth" by "keeping the job of desiring lianas and vines." She has something to teach humans, too: "having lived without practicing deception" with "nobility able to match polished high-born people, for the assembly of the world there is no other except you."[43] The term used for this assembly (*sabāva*) connotes something decidedly political, suggesting that humans should be as honest as butterflies in their governments, and seeming to presage the twenty-first-century pundits who recommend legal representation for natural actors.

In 1932, another messenger poem sent a butterfly on a proxy pilgrimage to the Peak, to make and share merit on behalf of the author and deliver a missive to God Saman lamenting the modern degradation of pilgrim manners. This

Samanala Hasuna also devotes its opening verses to elegizing the *samanala* courier:

> Hail, in healthy comfort—Received mindfully in the belly of
> the sky
> Butterfly, my friend—Shining beautifully like golden flowers
>
> Like the journey of the drawn and released arrow, the trip is
> necessary.
> Though without hard sounds, for you there is passionate wisdom.
> Continually pleasing, you have a soft face like sewn garlands,
> like the bloomed moon-white waterlily when my mind has seen.
>
> Like a disaster destroying the beings below,
> they must spend up to a month there to go to the vault of the sky.
> As desired, your journey is possible without fatigue or feebleness.
> Except for you, is there another one equal in this world?[44]

The poet lauds the butterfly's Peak pilgrimage as a required force, driven like the kinetic energy of a loosed arrow. He also praises the butterfly's effortless flying ascent, making the monthlong toils of humans to reach the summit on foot look disastrous by comparison, and thereby giving poetic expression to the fact that "there are achievements in other species that put to shame their corollaries or substitutes in us."[45] Nevertheless, the poet notes that even the butterfly may be grounded by "unfortunate winds" near the summit, forced onto the steps like its human counterparts subject to the same planetary forces.[46] Overall, however, the butterfly seems the more proficient pilgrim in this poem, holding its own silent insight—its passionate wisdom without hard sounds. The merit-making insect climbs at a faster clip, able to ascend without motivating noise, not needing to shout or sing like the other beings in the forest below.

Likewise, the 1972 poem "A Butterfly Story" describes the insect's "muteness entangling in a dharma eternally." The wisdom of butterflies is its own dharma, but this truth is elusive, a silent rest within the wilderness symphony. We must thus watch butterflies closely to follow them. The author of "A Butterfly Story" longed to transform into one: "Filled with happy freedom and nonviolent virtue, why can't a person be a butterfly?"[47] As noted in chapter 5, however, ethics are not achieved simply by humans becoming other animals. Our simultaneous attraction to and essential differences from butterflies are well represented in the words for the insect that almost seem to try to *sound* the way a butterfly *looks*. Tongues flap or flutter like wings in the English butterfly, the German *Schmetterling*, the Sinhala *samanala*, or the Hindi *titili*. The silent wisdom of the butterfly may enchant, but tongues must still translate it into human vocalizations.

The best we may do is to follow the butterflies, in the sense of embracing a state of co-being, where facilitating their own Peak pilgrimage is just as worthy of political representation as the construction of infrastructure. The old poets hint at such cooperation, as *Samanala Hasuna* depicts its butterfly messenger resting from strenuous travel on human structures, "setting down wings at this time in a well-guarded place, the relieved wings releasing cramps atop the rampart."[48] I saw similar flashes of such co-being practiced on the summit—the migration terminus where butterflies and moths cling to every surface (fig. Con.3). Before the ritual *kemmura puja* washing of the footprint, each insect was carefully removed by hand, or lightly swept away so as to not be harmed by the waters, even though their life cycles were ending. Ideally, this co-being would expand to facilitate butterfly pilgrimage at every stage, from larval grounds to fluttering end.

To start, this would require restoring local greenery, as some around Colombo have begun to do.[49] The Sri Lankan scientists who now follow butterflies have noted that their populations flourish in spots regenerating back to

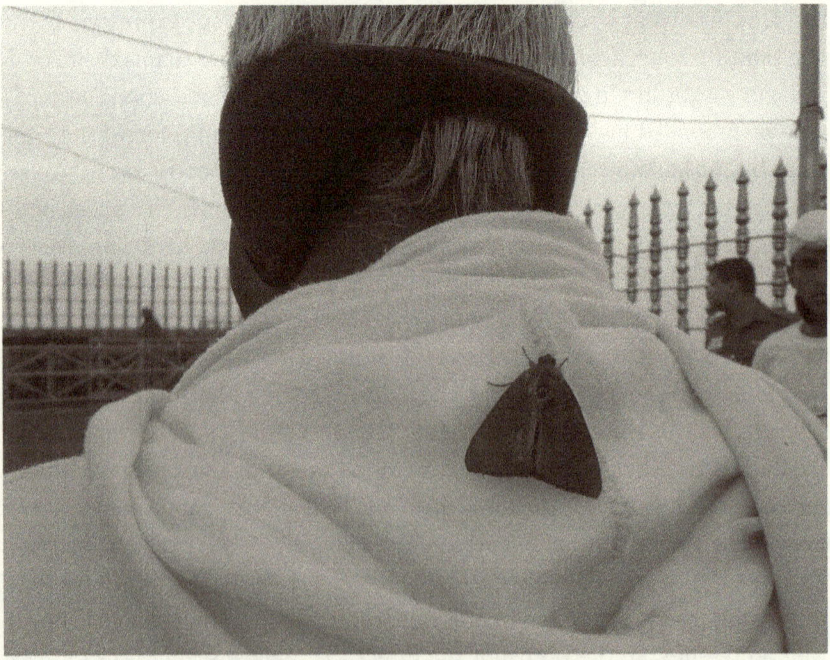

FIGURE CON.3. Co-being on the summit

forests. When humans stop clearing, abundant shrubs spring up in the sunlight, growing a wealth of food. Afterward, as primary forests succeed into shading secondary-growth trees, butterfly density may decline, but the overall species diversity can increase.[50] Butterflies thereby demonstrate an ability to adapt in disturbed ecologies, acting as an enchanting indicator that humans are on a proper path, their colorful fluttering beauty able to be appreciated by a plurality of pilgrims.[51]

Yet the planetary scales of the Anthropocene mean that habitat management is no longer only a local matter. The cascading consequences of changing climates could negatively impact butterfly populations at every stage of their life. When Major Manders conducted his butterfly breeding through temperature experiments, he unwittingly generated data that might foretell the heated future of a carbon-overloaded atmosphere. At unusually cold temperatures, a small number of his larva survived until maturation, but it did not work at all in the other direction: "The attempt to keep pupæ in abnormally hot dry atmosphere failed—the pupæ all dried up. . . . It shows that the constitution of the larvæ is somewhat delicate."[52] So we are left with a choice of two ways to follow the butterflies: by joining them as earthbound pilgrims, or by ignoring them and other planetary systems at our peril, until it all dries up. The mountain may help make our myths, but only we can use them. The Peak will be there regardless of how we choose to do so. Humanity can only aspire to its deep future.

Notes

Abbreviations

CNML	Colombo National Museum Library
SLNA	Sri Lanka National Archives
UPL	University of Peradeniya Library

Introduction

1. Most interviews were audio-recorded and later translated from Sinhala to English by me. When I was unable to record, I took notes by hand and reconstructed conversations afterward. I translate the ideas of interviewees as literally as possible. Ellipses indicate places where I have omitted phrases for brevity.
2. Bruno Latour, *We Have Never Been Modern*, trans. Catherine Porter (Cambridge, MA: Harvard University Press, 1993).
3. Qadri Ismail, *Abiding by Sri Lanka: On Peace, Place, and Postcoloniality* (Minneapolis: University of Minnesota Press, 2005), xxx.
4. For this reason, although I draw inspiration from postcolonial theorists of Sri Lanka like Qadri Ismail, Ananda Abeysekara, and David Scott, endorsing their theories of "post-empiricism" and calls to "de-authorize history," especially in the way I present my own book as a mythic construction, I cannot fully follow them in abandoning empirical arguments altogether. Sri Lankans still take history seriously, and it would be impossible to abide by Sri Lanka and intervene in its most contentious discourses without it. The evidentiary ethos of empiricism may still have an important role to play, even when discourses are deconstructed and critiqued, at times giving critique itself firmer ground on which to stand, especially as the dangers of a "post-fact" world are increasingly apparent.

5. Leela Prasad, *The Audacious Raconteur: Sovereignty and Storytelling in Colonial India* (Ithaca, NY: Cornell University Press, 2020), 106.
6. Henri Lefebvre, *The Production of Space*, trans. Donald Nicholson-Smith (Oxford: Blackwell, 1991), 330–32.
7. By the "Pali canon," I refer to the set of texts known as the *Tipitaka*, or "Three Baskets," developed over centuries and then codified in Sri Lanka during the early first millennium and closed by the time of the canonical commentaries attributed to Buddhaghosa in the fifth century. See Steven Collins, "On the Very Idea of the Pali Canon," *Journal of the Pali Text Society* 15 (1990): 89–126. My citations refer to English translations. When modified by me, I have consulted the Pali *Tipitika* edition compiled by the Sixth Buddhist Council in 1958, available at www.tipitika.org.
8. Much has been penned on Sinhala nationalism and its links to the Sri Lankan civil war, fought between government forces and the Liberation Tigers of Tamil Eelam (LTTE) from 1983 to 2009. The war, its ethno-linguistic-religio-nationalist preconditions, and its post-war continuations are key reasons for the imperiled state of pluralism in Sri Lanka. For a summary of the full arc of this political history, see Neil DeVotta, "The Liberation Tigers of Tamil Eelam and the Lost Quest for Separatism in Sri Lanka," *Asian Survey* 49, no. 6 (2009): 1021–51. For an analysis of how Sinhala-Buddhist nationalism developed over the twentieth century, see Harshana Rambukwella, *The Politics and Poetics of Authenticity: A Cultural Genealogy of Sinhala Nationalism* (London: UCL Press, 2018).
9. Lefebvre, *The Production of Space*, 332, 287; emphasis in the original.
10. Nihal Perera, *People's Spaces: Coping, Familiarizing, Creating* (New York: Routledge, 2016), 16.
11. *Dhammapada*, 2.8. See John Ross Carter and Mahinda Palihawadana, eds., *The Dhammapada* (New York: Oxford University Press, 1987), 116. This verse also appears in the voice of Brahmā Sahampati in Bhikkhu Bodhi, *The Connected Discourses of the Buddha: A Translation of the Saṃyutta Nikāya* (Boston: Wisdom, 2000), 232.
12. James Emerson Tennent, *Ceylon: An Account of the Island, Physical, Historical, and Topographical, with Notices of Its Natural History, Antiquities, and Productions* (London: Longman, Green, Longman, and Roberts, 1859), 2:132.
13. E. F. C. Ludowyk, *The Footprint of the Buddha* (London: George Allen and Unwin, 1958), 20.
14. G. van der Leeuw, *Religion in Essence and Manifestation*, trans. J. E. Turner, 2 vols. (New York: Cloister Library, Harper and Row, 1963), 54–55.
15. Mircea Eliade, *Patterns in Comparative Religion*, trans. Rosemary Sheed (New York: Meridian Books, 1958), 99–100.
16. Ludowyk, *The Footprint of the Buddha*, 20.
17. CNML 104/Z2: W. A. G. Juvānis, *Śrīpādavandanāva Hevat Giripada Lakara* (Moraketiya: Vijēpāla Yantrālaya, 1929), v. 83: "galak unat unveyi mēgamanē."
18. In anthropology, for example, see Donna J. Haraway, *When Species Meet* (Minneapolis: University of Minnesota Press, 2008); *Staying with the Trouble: Making Kin in the Chthulucene* (Durham, NC: Duke University Press, 2016); Annu Jalais, *Forest of Tigers: People, Politics and Environment in the Sundarbans* (New Delhi: Routledge, 2010); Eduardo Kohn, *How Forests Think: Toward an Anthropology Beyond the Human* (Berkeley: University of California Press, 2013); Anna Lowenhaupt Tsing, *The Mushroom at the End of the World: On the Possibility of Life in Capitalist Ruins* (Princeton, NJ: Princeton University Press, 2015).
19. Jane Bennett, *Vibrant Matter: A Political Ecology of Things* (Durham, NC: Duke University Press, 2010), viii.

20. E.g., Sonia Hazard, "The Material Turn in the Study of Religion," *Religion and Society: Advances in Research* 4 (2013): 58–78; Donovan O. Schaefer, *Religious Affects: Animality, Evolution, and Power* (Durham, NC: Duke University Press, 2015); Manuel A. Vásquez, *More than Belief: A Materialist Theory of Religion* (New York: Oxford University Press, 2011).
21. David Haberman, *Loving Stones: Making the Impossible Possible in the Worship of Mount Govardhan* (New York: Oxford University Press, 2020); Luke Whitmore, *Mountain, Water, Rock, God: Understanding Kedarnath in the Twenty-First Century* (Oakland: University of California Press, 2018).
22. Russell T. McCutcheon, *Critics Not Caretakers: Redescribing the Public Study of Religion* (Albany: State University of New York Press, 2001), 66.
23. Eliade, *Patterns in Comparative Religion*, 216.
24. Gananath Obeyesekere, *The Cult of the Goddess Pattini* (Chicago: University of Chicago Press, 1984), 283. This reflects the "compilational tendencies in literate traditions . . . the steadily increasing accretion of myths." E. J. Michael Witzel, *The Origins of the World's Mythologies* (New York: Oxford University Press, 2012), 98–99.
25. Benoit B. Mandelbrot, *The Fractal Geometry of Nature* (New York: W. H. Freeman, 1983), 1.
26. William Skeen, *Adam's Peak: Legendary Traditional, and Historic Notices of the Samanala and Srí-Páda with a Descriptive Account of the Pilgrims' Route from Colombo to the Sacred Foot-Print* (Colombo: W. L. H. Skeen, 1870), 9, 53.
27. Andrew Shryock, Daniel Lord Smail, and Timothy K. Earle, eds., *Deep History: The Architecture of Past and Present* (Berkeley: University of California Press, 2011), 30–31; emphasis in the original.
28. Similar attempts have been made to read history like a pearl, that is, "nacreous in its approach: akin to the formation of a pearl, it accretes layers in concentric, interlocking form." Tamara Fernando, "Seeing Like the Sea: A Multispecies History of the Ceylon Pearl Fishery 1800–1925," *Past and Present*, no. 254 (February 2022): 133.
29. Mircea Eliade, *The Quest: History and Meaning in Religion* (Chicago: University of Chicago Press, 1969), 76.
30. Leszek Kołakowski, *The Presence of Myth*, trans. Adam Czerniawski (Chicago: University of Chicago Press, 1989), 25, 29.
31. Michel Serres, *Religion: Rereading What Is Bound Together*, trans. Malcolm DeBevoise (Stanford, CA: Stanford University Press, 2022), 30.
32. Claude Lévi-Strauss, *The Raw and the Cooked: Introduction to a Science of Mythology*, vol. 1, trans. John Weightman and Doreen Weightman (New York: Harper and Row, 1970), 3, 5.
33. A similar point, albeit avoiding the term "myth," is made by Marisol de la Cadena, *Earth Beings: Ecologies of Practice Across Andean Worlds* (Durham, NC: Duke University Press, 2015), 27.
34. As Eliade noted, "we are not always able to show everything 'that happened' in a chronological perspective . . . in order to claim that we are writing the history of religions." Mircea Eliade, *Shamanism: Archaic Techniques of Ecstasy*, trans. Willard R. Trask (Princeton, NJ: Princeton University Press, 1964), xvi.
35. Serres, *Religion*, 53.
36. Latour, *We Have Never Been Modern*, 75.
37. P. E. P. Deraniyagala, "The Stone Age and Cave Men of Ceylon," *Journal of the Ceylon Branch of the Royal Asiatic Society* 34, no. 92 (1939): 359–60.
38. Claude Lévi-Strauss, "The Structural Study of Myth," *Journal of American Folklore* 68, no. 270 (1955): 443.

39. Deraniyagala, "The Stone Age and Cave Men of Ceylon," 360.
40. John Davy, "A Description of Adam's Peak. In a Letter Addressed to Sir Humphry Davy, F.R.S. Ll.D," *Journal of Science and the Arts* 5, no. 9 (1818): 25.
41. Tomoko Masuzawa, *The Invention of World Religions, or, How European Universalism Was Preserved in the Language of Pluralism* (Chicago: University of Chicago Press, 2005); Jonathan Z. Smith, *Relating Religion: Essays in the Study of Religion* (Chicago: University of Chicago Press, 2004), 179–96. Although the concept of discrete religions was universalized in the modern period, there are many premodern examples of boundaries around different ritual traditions in shared spaces being policed by orthodox interests, as shown throughout this book and elsewhere, e.g., Dionigi Albera, " 'Why Are You Mixing What Cannot Be Mixed?': Shared Devotions in the Monotheisms," *History and Anthropology* 19 (2008): 37–59.
42. William E. Connolly, *Pluralism* (Durham, NC: Duke University Press, 2005), 63; emphasis added. For an example of a shared site in South Asia where pluralism is intentionally pursued and carefully cultivated, see Anna Bigelow, *Sharing the Sacred: Practicing Pluralism in Muslim North India* (New York: Oxford University Press, 2010).
43. Jeremy F. Walton and Neena Mahadev, "Religious Plurality, Interreligious Pluralism, and Spatialities of Religious Difference," *Religion and Society: Advances in Research* 10 (2019): 82. See also Martin E. Marty, "Pluralisms," *Annals of the American Academy of Political and Social Science* 612 (2007): 16.
44. Pamela E. Klassen and Courtney Bender, "Habits of Pluralism," in *After Pluralism: Reimagining Religious Engagement*, ed. Pamela E. Klassen and Courtney Bender (New York: Columbia University Press, 2010), 8.
45. Lefebvre, *The Production of Space*, 382.
46. Walton and Mahadev, "Religious Plurality," 82. Likewise, Veena Das argues "religious pluralism is the normal condition in which religious subjectivities are formed." Veena Das, "Cohabitating an Interreligious Milieu: Reflections on Religious Diversity," in *A Companion to the Anthropology of Religion*, ed. Janice Boddy and Michael Lambek (West Sussex: Wiley Blackwell, 2013), 82. Thus Jonathan Walters wonders: "Are there any religions, at any period/s of history, whose adherents were not participants in multireligious situations?" Jonathan S. Walters, "Multireligion on the Bus: Beyond 'Influence' and 'Syncretism' in the Study of Religious Meetings," in *Unmaking the Nation: The Politics of Identity and History in Modern Sri Lanka*, ed. Pradeep Jeganathan and Qadri Ismail (Colombo: Social Scientists' Association, 2009), 48–49.
47. Klassen and Bender, "Habits of Pluralism," 6.
48. Elaine Fisher, *Hindu Pluralism: Religion and the Public Sphere in Early Modern South India* (Oakland: University of California Press, 2017), 193.
49. Benjamin Schonthal, "The Tolerations of Theravada Buddhism," in *Toleration in Comparative Perspective*, ed. Vicki A. Spencer (Lanham, MD: Lexington Books, 2018), 181.
50. Schonthal, "The Tolerations of Theravada Buddhism," 185–86. This type of toleration fits the model of "antagonistic tolerance" developed by Robert Hayden. In this model, the Peak is a good example of a site where majoritarian religious actors are tempted to exert dominance, due to its "centrality" and high level of "perceptibility." See Robert M. Hayden et al., *Antagonistic Tolerance: Competitive Sharing of Religious Sites and Spaces* (New York: Routledge, 2016), 15.
51. Schonthal, "The Tolerations of Theravada Buddhism," 184–85.
52. Bennett, *Vibrant Matter*, 21.

53. Lefebvre, *The Production of Space*, 137.
54. The paradigmatic denominational approach is seen in the volumes published by Harvard's Center for the Study of World Religions, which essentially inaugurated the subfield of religion and ecology. Examples of works on ironic harms of religion, or shortcomings of religious environmentalism, include Cheryl Colopy, *Dirty, Sacred Rivers: Confronting South Asia's Water Crisis* (New York: Oxford University Press, 2012); Eliza E. Kent, *Sacred Groves and Local Gods: Religion and Environmentalism in South India* (Oxford: Oxford University Press, 2013); K. Sivaramakrishnan, "Ethics of Nature in Indian Environmental History," *Modern Asian Studies* 49, no. 4 (2015): 1261–310; Emma Tomalin, *Biodivinity and Biodiversity: The Limits to Religious Environmentalism* (Burlington: Ashgate, 2009).
55. E.g., Georgina Drew, *River Dialogues: Hindu Faith and the Political Ecology of Dams on the Sacred Ganga* (Tucson: University of Arizona Press, 2017); David Haberman, *People Trees: Worship of Trees in Northern India* (New York: Oxford University Press, 2013); Haberman, *Loving Stones*; Jalais, *Forest of Tigers*; Vijaya Nagarajan, *Feeding a Thousand Souls: Women, Ritual, and Ecology in India—an Exploration of the Kōlam* (New York: Oxford University Press, 2018); Anand Vivek Taneja, *Jinnealogy: Time, Islam, and Ecological Thought in the Medieval Ruins of Delhi* (Stanford, CA: Stanford University Press, 2018); Whitmore, *Mountain, Water, Rock, God*.
56. Ananda Abeysekara, "The Un-Translatability of Religion, the Un-Translatability of Life: Thinking Talal Asad's Thought Unthought in the Study of Religion," *Method and Theory in the Study of Religion* 23 (2011): 258; emphasis in the original. See also Vikash Singh, *Uprising of the Fools: Pilgrimage as Moral Protest in Contemporary India* (Stanford, CA: Stanford University Press, 2017), 28–31.
57. *Purāṇa Himagata Varṇanāva*, v. 113. Like most poems sold on the trail, the edition in Chandra's stall contained no date or publication information. For an academic edition of this text, see Dayāpāla Jayanetti, ed., *Vaňdanā Kavi Sāhityaya* (Colombo: Samayavardhana, 2005), 35–56.

1. Rock, Water, and Montane Agency

1. *Saman Sirita*, v. 64.
2. A. R. Crawford and R. L. Oliver, "The Precambrian Geochronology of Ceylon," *Special Publication—Geological Society of Australia* 2 (1969): 283–306.
3. P. G. Cooray, "The Precambrian of Sri Lanka: A Historical Review," *Precambrian Research* 66 (1994): 3–18; A. Kröner, K. V. W. Kehelpannala, and E. Hegner, "Ca. 750–1100 Ma Magmatic Events and Grenville-Age Deformation in Sri Lanka: Relevance for Rodinia Supercontinent Formation and Dispersal, and Gondwana Amalgamation," *Journal of Asian Earth Sciences* 22 (2003): 279–300.
4. M. B. Katz and N. S. W. Kensington, "The Precambrian Metamorphic Rocks of Ceylon," *Geologische Rundschau* 60 (1971): 1523–49.
5. M. B. Katz, "Sri Lanka-Indian Eastern Ghats-East Antarctica and the Australian Albany Fraser Mobile Belt: Cross Geometry, Age Relationships, and Tectonics in Precambrian Gondwanaland," *Journal of Geology* 97, no. 5 (1989): 646–48; A. Kröner, "African Linkage of Precambrian Sri Lanka," *Geologische Rundschau* 80, no. 2 (1991): 429–40; C. B. Dissanayake and Rohana Chandrajith, "Sri Lanka-Madagascar Gondwana Linkage: Evidence for a Pan-African Mineral Belt," *Journal of Geology* 107 (1999): 223–35.

6. C. B. Dissanayake, Rohana Chandrajith, and H. J. Tobschall, "The Geology, Mineralology and Rare Element Geochemistry of the Gem Deposits of Sri Lanka," *Geological Society of Finland* 72 (2000): 5–20; M. Sandiford et al., "Thermal and Baric Evolution of Garnet Granulites from Sri Lanka," *Journal of Metamorphic Geology* 6 (1988): 351–64.
7. Kröner, "African Linkage of Precambrian Sri Lanka."
8. S. U. Deraniyagala, *The Prehistory of Sri Lanka: An Ecological Perspective* (Colombo: Department of Archaeological Survey, Government of Sri Lanka, 1992), 2:488.
9. P. W. Vitanage, "The Geology, Structure and Tectonics of Sri Lanka and South India," in *Recent Advances in the Geology of Sri Lanka: Proceedings of the Symposium on the Geology of Sri Lanka, Peradeniya, 1983* (Paris: CIFEG, 1985), 14.
10. M. J. Fernando and A. N. S. Kulasinghe, "Seismicity of Sri Lanka," *Physics of the Earth and Planetary Interiors* 44 (1986): 99–106.
11. D. N. Wadia, "The Ring of Waterfalls in Central Ceylon and Its Bearing on the Geological Structure and Earth Movements," *Spolia Zeylanica* 23, no. 1 (1941): 20.
12. E.g., Yasuhito Osanai et al., "Metamorphic Evolution of High-Pressure and Ultrahigh-Temperature Granulites from the Highland Complex, Sri Lanka," *Journal of Asian Earth Sciences* 28 (2006): 20–37.
13. Tissa Munasinghe and C. B. Dissanayake, "A Plate Tectonic Model for the Geologic Evolution of Sri Lanka," *Journal of the Geological Society of India* 23 (August 1982): 369–80.
14. John McPhee, *Basin and Range* (New York: Farrar, Straus, Giroux, 1981), 20, 127.
15. McPhee, *Basin and Range*, 79.
16. Ludwig Wittgenstein, *On Certainty*, ed. G. E. M. Anscombe and G. H. von Wright, trans. Denis Paul and G. E. M. Anscombe (Oxford: Blackwell, 1969), §§94–95; emphases added.
17. Wittgenstein, *On Certainty*, §143.
18. Wittgenstein, *On Certainty*, §§97, 99.
19. Thomas S. Kuhn, *The Structure of Scientific Revolutions*, 4th ed. (Chicago: University of Chicago Press, 2012), 3.
20. Martin J. S. Rudwick, *Bursting the Limits of Time: The Reconstruction of Geohistory in the Age of Revolution* (Chicago: University of Chicago Press, 2005); Stephen Jay Gould, *Time's Arrow, Time's Cycle: Myth and Metaphor in the Discovery of Geological Time* (Cambridge, MA: Harvard University Press, 1987); Martina Kölbl-Ebert, ed., *Geology and Religion: A History of Harmony and Hostility* (London: Geological Society, 2009).
21. Rudwick, *Bursting the Limits of Time*, 94.
22. Pratik Chakrabarti and Joydeep Sen, " 'The World Rests on the Back of a Tortoise': Science and Mythology in Indian History," *Modern Asian Studies* 50, no. 3 (2016): 808–40.
23. Rudwick, *Bursting the Limits of Time*, 148–49.
24. Cooray, "The Precambrian of Sri Lanka."
25. Karl Scherzer, *Narrative of the Circumnavigation of the Globe by the Austrian Frigate Novara, in the Years 1857, 1858, & 1859*, vol. 1 (London: Saunders, Otley, 1861), 416.
26. Georg Frauenfeld, "Ausflung Nach Dem Adamspik Auf Ceylon," *Sitzungberichte der Kaiserlichen Akademie der Wissenschaften* 37 (1859): 796. "Dort der Schauplatz einer Handlung, hier der Ausgangspunkt einer Mythe."
27. G. N. Wright, *A Guide to the Lakes of Killarney* (London: Baldwin, Cradock, and Joy, 1822), 47.
28. James Emerson Tennent, *Ceylon: An Account of the Island, Physical, Historical, and Topographical, with Notices of Its Natural History, Antiquities, and Productions* (London: Longman, Green, Longman, and Roberts, 1859), 1:14–15.

29. Steven Collins, "The Discourse on What Is Primary (Aggañña-Sutta): An Annotated Translation," *Journal of Indian Philosophy* 21 (1993): 301–93.
30. E.g., Stanley J. Tambiah, *World Conqueror and World Renouncer: A Study of Buddhism and Polity in Thailand Against a Historical Background* (Cambridge: Cambridge University Press, 1976).
31. Collins, "The Discourse on What Is Primary," 341.
32. *Ṛg Veda*, X, 129. Richard F. Gombrich, "The Buddha's Book of Genesis?," *Indo-Iranian Journal* 35 (1992): 159–78. Cycling worlds can also be read as a rejection of a stagnant hierarchical cosmogony of castes advanced by Brahmins: Nalin Swaris, *The Buddha's Way to Human Liberation: A Socio-Historical Approach* (Nugegoda: Sarasavi Publishers, 2008), 225.
33. This also occurs in *Saṃyutta Nikāya* (hereafter referred to as SN) of the Pali canon, where the Buddha uses several similes to describe *saṃsāra* as "without discoverable beginnings" (*anamatagga*), comparing the time it would take for "a great stone mountain" to wear away from the brush of a silk cloth every hundred years to the length of just one of the many hundreds of thousands of eons that have existed (SN 15.5).
34. Collins, "The Discourse on What Is Primary," 357.
35. This story of world creation became a regular trope in Lankan texts, from religious works like Buddhaghosa's *Visuddimagga* and Buddhaputra's *Pūjāvaliya* to chronicles like *Rājavaliya* and many local histories.
36. James Hutton, "Theory of the Earth; or an Investigation of the Laws Observable in the Composition, Dissolution, and Restoration of Land Upon the Globe," *Transactions of the Royal Society of Edinburgh* 1, no. 2 (1788): 304.
37. *The Minor Anthologies of the Pāli Canon*, vol. 3: *Chronicle of Buddhas (Buddhavaṃsa) and Basket of Conduct (Cariyāpiṭaka)*, trans. I. B. Horner (Bristol: Pali Text Society, 1975), 96–97. See also Jonathan S. Walters, "Buddhist History: The Sri Lankan Pāli Vaṃsas and Their Commentary," in *Querying the Medieval: Texts and the History of Practices in South Asia* (New York: Oxford University Press, 2000), 103.
38. Don Martino de Zilva Wickremasinghe, H. W. Codrington, and S. Paranavitana, eds., *Epigraphia Zeylanica: Being Lithic and Other Inscriptions of Ceylon* (London: Published for the Government of Ceylon by H. Frowde, 1928), 2:217.
39. Prior Buddhas were mentioned in earlier pilgrimage poems like *Samanala Vistaraya* (CNML AL/14, ff. 15, 32; CNML AJ/14, f. 16) as well as *Samanala Hälla* (UPL 277809, f. 1b; UPL 278540, f. 4a). The manuscript dates are c. 1850, but these poetic traditions likely began in the seventeenth and eighteenth centuries. For a printed example, see CNML 104/T14: Ugat Kāvyakkārayek, *Śrīpādapatmaya Vandanāgātha Saha Abhinava Himagatavarṇanāva* (Granthalokayantrālaya: K. Dāvit Perērā, 1902), vv. 10, 58–60.
40. *Purāṇa Samanala Vandanā Kāvyaya*, v. 30. Reprinted in Dayāpāla Jayanetti, ed., *Vaňdanā Kavi Sāhityaya* (2005), 81–93. It was a fad to title Sinhala works *purāṇa* in the nineteenth and early twentieth centuries, but this does not indicate actual ancientness. This poem likely dates to the late nineteenth century. Nor does the Sinhala *purāṇa* prefix indicate much similarity with Hindu *purāṇa* texts, although they do share a cosmically large temporal scope.
41. CNML 104/B20: Hēnepola G. K. Ratnasēkara, *Sūvisi Vivaraṇa Śrī Pāda Vandanāva* (Maradana: Śrī Laṃkōdaya Yantrālaya, 1923).
42. CNML 104/C8: *Śrī Pādavarṇanā Kāvyaya Hevat Śrīpāda Alaṅkāraya* (D. P. D. Raṇatuṅga Appuhāmi, 1910), vv. 17–27; CNML 104/C8: Dehigama Paṇḍita Samarasiṅha Puṅcibaṇḍāra, *Buduguṇa Kavi Nohot Śrī Pāda Vandanāva* (Henarathgoda: Siriyālōka Mudraṇālaya, 1922), vv. 6–35. See also

CNML 104/B6: Varallē M. G. C. Abhayasiṅha, *Siripā Väňduma* (Matale: D. E. A. Guṇavardana, 1917), vv. 21–44.

43. CNML 104/Z2: W. Ātar Ähäliyagoḍa Baṇḍāra, *Buduguṇa Mālāva* (Colombo: Viliyam Kōnāra Basnāyaka Raṇasiṃha Baṇḍāra, 1928), v. 100.
44. CNML 104/Z2: Attuḍāvē Hārmanis Jayasēkara, *Sirilaka Siripada Lakara Saha Abhinava Vandanā Kāvyaya* (Panadura: D. C. Raṇavaka, 1932), v. 3.
45. CNML 104/K4: K. D. G. Perērā, *Śrī Pāda Vandanā Gamana* (Sevyaśrī Yantrālaya: J. A. Guṇsēna, 1926), v. 7.
46. E.g., Charles Hallisey, "The Care of the Past: The Place of Pastness in Transgenerational Projects," in *On Religion and Memory*, ed. Babette Hellemans, Willemein Otten, and Burcht Pranger (New York: Fordham University Press, 2013).
47. Puṅcibaṇḍāra, *Buduguṇa Kav Nohot Śrīpāda Vandanāva.*
48. Richard F. Gombrich, *Buddhist Precept and Practice: Traditional Buddhism in the Rural Highlands of Ceylon*, 2nd ed. (London: Clarendon Press, 1995), 150.
49. N. B. M. Seneviratna, ed., *Siṃhala Kāvya Saṃgrahaya: Mātara Yugaya* (Colombo: Laṃkā Jātika Kautukāgāra Prakāśana, 1964), 218. *Samanala Hälla* songs are further explained in chapter 4.
50. "Niti vaňdin nitarama häma kalē"; "niti cirākal"; "niti dun."
51. Rudwick, *Bursting the Limits of Time*, 96.
52. Mrs. Col. Walker, "Journal of an Ascent to the Summit of Adam's Peak," in *Companion to the Botanical Magazine*, ed. W. J. Hooker (London: Samuel Curtis, 1835), 12.
53. John Capper, "The Tourist in Ceylon," in *All the World Over*, ed. Edwin Hodder (London: Thomas Cook and Son, 1875), 35.
54. William Howard Russell, *My Diary in India, in the Year 1858-9* (London: Routledge, Warne, and Routledge, 1860), 85.
55. CNML 104/Z11: H. K. B. D. Amarasinghe, *Tarunangana Sandesaya* (Hingulwala: T. B. Kulatunga and M. B. Kulatunga, 1934), v. 48.
56. For examples of an invocation (*yatikāva*) to Saman, see Premakumara De Silva, "God of Compassion and the Divine Protector of Sri Pada: Trends in Popular Buddhism in Sri Lanka," *Sri Lanka Journal of the Humanities* 34 (2008): 93–107.
57. Dhammadinnācārya Vimalakīrti, *Saddharmaratnākaraya*, ed. V. D. S. Guṇavardhana (Colombo: Samayavardhana Pothala Samāgama, 2001), 304.
58. Archibald Campbell Lawrie, *Gazetteer of the Central Province* (Colombo: Government Press: 1896), 1:vii.
59. Benjamin Bailey, *Poetical Sketches of the Interior of the Island of Ceylon: Benjamin Bailey's Original Manuscript, 1841*, ed. Rajpal K. de Silva (London: Serendib Publications, 2011), 125.
60. *Samantakūṭavaṇṇanā*, v. 725. I am guided by Vedeha Thera, *In Praise of Mount Samanta* [Samantakūṭavaṇṇanā], trans. Ann Appleby Hazlewood (London: Pali Text Society, 1986); I render my own translations from Deniyāyē Paññālōka, ed., *Prācīta Madhyama Vibhāgayaṭa Niyamita Samantakūṭavaṇṇanā* (Colombo: Samayavardhana Pothala Samāgama, 2001).
61. H. U. Pragnaloka, ed., *Purāṇa Sivpada Saṃgrahava* (Colombo: Government Publications, 1952), 198.
62. H. A. P. Abeyawardana, *Boundary Divisions of Mediaeval Sri Lanka* (Polgasovita: Academy of Sri Lankan Culture, 1999), 205. This sentence appears almost identically in the *Lakvidiya* (p. 208). Different wording of the same concept also appeared in the *Tri Siṃhalē Kaḍaim* manuscript used for the first printed edition: A. J. W. Mārambē, ed., *Tri Siṃhalē Kaḍaim Saha Vitti*

(Mahanuvara: Laṃkāpradīpa Yantrālaya, 1926). Still another version of this sentence is found at the start of Or.6607(2): *Kaḍayuru saha Bōdhivaṃsa Lēkhanaya*. Unless otherwise noted, all manuscripts with British Library call numbers cited in this book have been consulted through their transliterated portions available in K. D. Somadasa, ed., *Catalogue of the Hugh Nevill Collection of Sinhalese Manuscripts in the British Library*, 7 vols. (London: British Library, 1987–1995). It is worth noting that the very first word in the Sinhala sentences is *Samanṭakūta*.

63. In Abeyawardana, *Boundary Divisions*, 202. See also Mārambē, *Tri Siṃhalē Kaḍaim Saha Vitti*, 41; *Uḍahē Vāhäṭē Kaḍayim Kavi*, in Pragnaloka, *Purāṇa Sivpada Saṃgrahava*, 6.
64. *Tahandi kavi*, in W. Ātar Da Silva and Guṇapāla Malalasēkara, eds., *Siṅhala Janasammata Kāvya* (Colombo: S. Goḍagē saha Sahōdarayō, 1935; reprint, 2013), p. 163, vv. 1234–35. See also "the Samanala direction" mentioned in Or.6615(366): *Mäṇikpāla Sāntiya*.
65. See *Laṅkādvīpayē Kadaim*, in Abeyawardana, *Boundary Divisions*, 199.
66. Pragnaloka, *Purāṇa Sivpada Saṃgrahava*, 208–9. An even longer version of this poem appears in Bandula Liyanagē, ed., *Ruvan Kavi* (Kuruviṭa: Isuru Mudraṇa, 1995), 61–62.
67. Steven P. Hopkins, "Love, Messengers, and Beloved Landscapes: *Sandesakavya* in Comparative Perspective," *International Journal of Hindu Studies* 8, no. 1–3 (2004): 29–55.
68. Charles Hallisey, "Works and Persons in Sinhala Literary Culture," in *Literary Cultures in History: Reconstructions from South Asia*, ed. Sheldon Pollock (Berkeley: University of California Press, 2003), 699.
69. Maha Thero Sri Rahula, *Selalihini Sandesa*, ed. K. W. De A. Wijesinghe (Colombo: Godage International Publishers, 2006), v. 25.
70. McPhee, *Basin and Range*, 81.
71. Maturin M. Ballou, *The Pearl of India*, 2nd ed. (Boston: Houghton, Mifflin, 1895), 12, 14.
72. John F. Hurst, *Indika: The Country and the People of India and Ceylon* (New York: Harper and Brothers, 1891), 244.
73. Allister MacMillan, *Seaports of India and Ceylon: Historical Descriptive Commercial Industrial Facts, Figures, and Resources* (London: W. H. and L. Collingridge, 1928), 397.
74. Sumathi Ramaswamy, *The Lost Land of Lemuria: Fabulous Geographies, Catastrophic Histories* (Berkeley: University of California Press, 2004).
75. W. S. W. Ruschenberger, *Narrative of a Voyage Round the World, During the Years 1835, 36, and 37; Including a Narrative of an Embassy to the Sultan of Muscat and the King of Siam* (London: Richard Bentley, 1838), 1:268.
76. See "A New Mapp of the Island of Zeloan," in John Thornton, *The English Pilot. The Third Book. Describing the Sea-Coasts, Capes, Headlands, Straits, Soundings, Sands, Shoals, Rocks, and Dangers. The Islands, Bays, Roads, Harbors and Ports in Oriental Navigation* (London: John How, 1703).
77. *Samantakūṭavaṇṇanā*, v. 724.
78. K. C. Naṭarācā, ed., *Tirikoṇācala Purāṇam* (Colombo: Intucamaya Kalācāra Aluvalkar Tiṇaikkaḷam, 1997), 7:10. Samanai is the traditional name for the Peak in Lankan Tamil literature, as explained in chapter 4.
79. Raimy Ché-Ross, "Munshi Abdullah's Voyage to Mecca: A Preliminary Introduction and Translation," *Indonesia and the Malay World* 28, no. 81 (2000): 186–87.
80. George Thambyahpillay, "Tropical Cyclones and the Climate of Ceylon," *University of Ceylon Review* 17, nos. 3–4 (1959): 137–80.
81. Ché-Ross, "Munshi Abdullah's Voyage to Mecca," 187.

82. From Albrecht Herport, *A Short Description of a Nine-Year East-Indian Journey* (1669), reprinted in Behr et al., *Germans in Dutch Ceylon*, trans. R. Raven-Hart (Colombo: Colombo National Museum, 1953), 26.
83. J. Drew Gay, *The Prince of Wales in India, or from Pall Mall to the Punjab* (New York: R. Worthington, 1877), 114.
84. Christopher Schweitzer, *Journal and Diary of His Six Years' East-Indian Journey* (1682), reprinted in Behr et al., *Germans in Dutch Ceylon*, 41, 65–66.
85. Florence Caddy, *To Siam and Malaya in the Duke of Sutherland's Yacht "Sans Peur"* (London: Hurst and Blackett, 1889), 67.
86. *Rājāvaliya*, trans. A. J. Suraweera (Ratmalana: Sarvodaya Vishva Lekha, 2000), 15.
87. Gananath Obeyesekere, *The Cult of the Goddess Pattini* (Chicago: University of Chicago Press, 1984). In India, Pattini was Kannaki, tragic heroine of the Tamil *Cilappatikāram*. She became a bodhisattva in the Buddhist context.
88. *Devol Deviyannē Kathāva*, v. 128, in P. E. P. Deraniyagala, ed., *Deva Varṇanā Kāvya* (Colombo: Ceylon National Museum, 1960), 15. See also Or.6615(378): *Vāhala Devol Vīdiya Kavi*.
89. S. J. Sumanasēkara Baṇḍā, *Guru Haṭana Hevat Sokari Nāṭakaya* (Colombo: Goḍagē saha Sahōdarayō, 2005), p. 43, v. 75.
90. William Skeen, *Adam's Peak: Legendary Traditional, and Historic Notices of the Samanala and Srí-Páda with a Descriptive Account of the Pilgrims' Route from Colombo to the Sacred Foot-Print* (Colombo: W. L. H. Skeen, 1870), 5.
91. McPhee, *Basin and Range*, 47.
92. Vitanage, "The Geology, Structure and Tectonics of Sri Lanka and South India," 14. See also P. G. Cooray, *An Introduction to the Geology of Ceylon* (Colombo: National Museums of Ceylon, 1967), 255–58.
93. *A Conversation Between a Christian and a Pilgrim—Śrī Pādaya Gäṇaya* (Colombo: Wesleyan Mission Press for Ceylon Religious Tract Society, 1871), 7.
94. *Samantakūṭavaṇṇanā*, v. 789.
95. Ḥamd-allāh Mustawfī, *The Geographical Part of the Nuzhat-Al-Qulūb*, trans. G. Le Strange (Leyden: E. J. Brill, 1919), 186–87.
96. Quoted in Carl Ernst, "India as a Sacred Islamic Land," in *Religions of India in Practice*, ed. Donald S. Lopez (Princeton, NJ: Princeton University Press, 1995), 559–60.
97. Robert DeCaroli, *Haunting the Buddha: Indian Popular Religions and the Formation of Buddhism* (New York: Oxford University Press, 2004).
98. *Käṭakirilli Sandeśaya*, v. 12, in *Kataragama Deviňduṇṭa Sandeśa Kavi 1700–1900* (Dehiwala: Tisara Prakāśakayō, 1970). My reading is informed by P. B. G. Hēvāvasam, *Mātara Yugayē Sāhityadharayan Hā Sāhitya Nibandhana* (Saṃskrutika Kaṭayutu Piḷibaňda Depārtimentuva, 1966), 339.
99. Amy L. Allocco, "Fear, Reverence and Ambivalence: Divine Snakes in Contemporary South India," *Religions of South Asia* 7 (2013): 230–48.
100. There are two extant versions of this poem printed from manuscripts. I have translated and analyzed them, positing Kaviraja as a cross-generational collective name, in Alexander McKinley, "Farming Songs from the Poet King: Translation and Explication of a Sinhala *Janakavi* Work," *Sri Lanka Journal of the Humanities* 41, no. 1–2 (2017): 64–117.
101. *Laṅkā Vistaraya*, in V. D. Da Länarōl, *Goyam Kav Saha Neḷum Kav* (Colombo: M. D. Guṇasēna saha Samāgama, 1946), p. 121, vv. 948–49. A similar description of the Mahaweli Ganga as a *nāga* as emerging from its home in Samangira is found in Or.6607(24): *Mahaväli Gaňga Vänīma*.

102. Antecedents of this mountain/*nāga*/river imagery occur in the Pali canon. *Nāga* habitats running the full length of a watershed appear twice as similes in *Saṃyutta Nikāya* (SN 45.151; 46.1). Buddhaghosa then explains in his commentary that female *nāgas* "ascend the rivers to the Himalayas to give birth there. They then train their young in the mountain ponds until they have mastered the art of swimming." See Bhikkhu Bodhi, *The Connected Discourses of the Buddha: A Translation of the Saṃyutta Nikāya* (Boston: Wisdom, 2000), 1554, 1567, 1897n39.
103. *Laṅkā Vistaraya*, in Da Länarōl, *Goyam Kav saha Neḷum Kav*, p. 122, v. 957.
104. Da Silva and Malalasēkara, *Siṅhala Janasammata Kāvya*, v. 1707.
105. Gananath Obeyesekere, *The Creation of the Hunter: The Vädda Presence in the Kandyan Kingdom: A Re-Examination* (Colombo: Sailfish, 2022), 134, 153. See also H. Parker, *Ancient Ceylon* (London: Luzac, 1909), 139.
106. Or.6615(412) and Or.6615(488): *Gaṅgē Baṇḍāra Kavi*; UPL 277817: *Gaṅgē Baṇḍāra Kavi*; CNML AJ/14: *Gaṅgā Vistaraya*. These manuscripts date to the nineteenth century, but are likely copies of songs that originated a century or two earlier.
107. *Gaṅgē Baṇḍāra Kavi*, in Tissa Kāriyavasam, ed., *Siri Laka Devivaru: Hiyū Nevil Kāvyāvali Āśrayeni* (Colombo: S. Goḍagē saha Sahōdarayō, 1991), 81. A similar verse appears in Or.6611(16): *Gaṅga Vistaraya*, f. 9.
108. Kaḍarodagama Sudhīra, *Saparagamu Paḷātē Diya Äli Puda Sirit Vimarśanaya (Ratnapura Distrikkaya Āśrayeni)* (Colombo: S. Godagē saha Sahōdarayō, 2005). See also Or.6615(127): *Sīma Bändīma*.
109. E.g., Or.6607(23): *Mahaväli Gaṅga Vistaraya*, Or.6611(16): *Gaṅga Vistarya*, and Or.6611(17): *Gaṅga Vistarya Kavi*. Or.6611(16) and Or.6611(17) were read via copies at CNML 82/X5 and CNML 82/V19. See also *Mahaväli Gaṅgā Vistaraya*, in Pragnaloka, *Purāṇa Sivpada Saṃgrahava*, 9.
110. Or.6607(24): *Mahaväli Gaṅga Vänīma*, consulted via a copy at CNML 82/W15.
111. *Nava Baṇḍāra Kavi*, in Kāriyavasam, *Siri Laka Devivaru*, 143. In one version, the Hulu or Suḷu Gaṅga is appointed as Gaṅgē Baṇḍāra's queen: Gedara Pinhāmi, *Dolahadeviyangē Kavipota Saha Dalumura Upata* (Mahanuvara: T. M. Migel Appu, 1900), v. 128. See also CNML AJ/14: *Gaṅga Vistaraya*, v. 2.
112. *Tirikoṇācala Purāṇam*, 7:22.
113. *Tirikoṇācala Purāṇam*, 7:23–24.
114. C. Nākaliṅkapiḷḷai, ed., *Takṣiṇa Kailāca Purāṇam* (Jaffna: N. Kumāracuvāmi, 1928), 44–45. This was originally a Sanskrit text translated into Tamil with the modern "Sivanolipadamalai" moniker for the mountain. It likely postdates *Tirikoṇācala Purāṇam*. See chapter 4 for more on these sources.
115. "A Short Account of the Mission of Ceylon," in V. Perniola, *The Catholic Church in Sri Lanka: The Dutch Period*, vol. 2, *1712–1746: Original Documents Translated Into English* (Dehiwala: Tisara Prakasakayo, 1983), 124–25.
116. J. Carver, *The New Universal Traveller. Containing a Full and Distinct Account of All the Empires, Kingdoms, and States in the Known World* (London: G. Robinson, 1779), 44.
117. W. Heine, "From Berlin to Japan: A Trip to Adam's Peak," *Illustrirte Zeitung*, October 13, 1860, reprinted in R. K. de Silva, ed., *19th Century Newspaper Engravings of Ceylon—Sri Lanka: Accompanied by Original Texts with Notes and Comments* (London: Serendib Publications, 1998), 381–82.
118. *Purāṇa Samanala Vandanā Kāvyaya*, vv. 28, 33–35, reprinted in Jayanetti, *Vaṅdanā Kavi Sāhityaya*.

119. Al-Bīrūnī, *The Book Most Comprehensive in Knowledge on Precious Stones: Al-Beruni's Book on Mineralogy* [Kitāb al-Jamāhir fī Ma'rifat al-Jawāhir], trans. Hakim Mohammed Said (Islamabad: Pakistan Hijra Council, 1989), 39.
120. Aḥmad ibn Yūsuf al-Tīfāshī, *Arab Roots of Gemology: Ahmad Ibn Yusuf Al Tifaschi's Best Thoughts on the Best of Stones*, trans. Samar Najm Abul Huda (London: Scarecrow Press, 1998), 94.
121. W. W. Rockhill, "Notes of the Relations and Trade of China with the Eastern Archipelago and the Coast of the Indian Ocean During the Fourteenth Century," *T'oung Pao* 16, no. 3 (1915): 380.
122. Ana Gunatilaka, "Role of Basin-Wide Landslides in the Formation of Extensive Alluvial Gemstone Deposits in Sri Lanka," *Earth Surface Processes and Landforms* 32 (2007): 1863, 1872.
123. *Laṅkā Vistaraya*, in *Goyam Kav saha Neḷum Kav*, vv. 953, 955.
124. P. E. P. Deraniyagala, "Some Fossil Animals from Ceylon," *Journal of the Ceylon Branch of the Royal Asiatic Society* 33, no. 88 (1935): 165–68; P. E. P. Deraniyagala, "Some Fossil Animals from Ceylon. Part 2," *Journal of the Ceylon Branch of the Royal Asiatic Society* 34, no. 91 (1938): 231–39; P. E. P. Deraniyagala, "The Stone Age and Cave Men of Ceylon," *Journal of the Ceylon Branch of the Royal Asiatic Society* 34, no. 92 (1939): 351–73; P. E. P. Deraniyagala "The Hippopotamus as an Index to Early Man in India and Ceylon," *Science and Culture* 7, no. 2 (1941): 66–68; P. E. P. Deraniyagala, "Some Aspects of the Prehistory of Ceylon, Part I," *Spolia Zeylanica* 23, no. 2 (1943): 93–115; P. E. P. Deraniyagala, *The Pleistocene of Ceylon*, Ceylon National Museums Natural History Series (Ceylon: Government Press, 1958); P. E. P. Deraniyagala, "Prehistoric Archaeology in Ceylon," *Asian Perspectives* 7 (1963); 189–95; S. U. Deraniyagala, *The Prehistory of Sri Lanka*; S. U. Deraniyagala, *The Prehistory and Protohistory of Sri Lanka* (Colombo: Central Cultural Fund, 2007); Kenneth A. R. Kennedy, *God-Apes and Fossil Men: Paleoanthropology of South Asia* (Ann Arbor: University of Michigan Press, 2000); Nikos Kourampas et al., "Rockshelter Sedimentation in a Dynamic Tropical Landscape: Late Pleistocene-Early Holocene Archaeological Deposits in Kitugala Beli-Lena, Southwestern Sri Lanka," *Geoarcheology: An International Journal* 24, no. 6 (2009): 677–714; Nimal Perera et al., "People of the Ancient Rainforest: Late Pleistocene Foragers at the Batadomba-Lena Rockshelter, Sri Lanka," *Journal of Human Evolution* 61 (2011): 254–69.
125. McPhee, *Basin and Range*, 24–25. This was equally true of one of Deraniyagala's predecessors in Lankan geology: Rasoul Sorkhabi, "Ananda K. Coomaraswamy: From Geology to *Philosophia Perennis*," *Current Science* 94, no. 3 (2008): 394–401.
126. Perera et al., "People of the Ancient Rainforest," 256.
127. John Still, *The Jungle Tide*, 3rd ed. (Edinburgh: W. Blackwood and Sons, 1930), 32–33.
128. K. R. Perera, *Samanaḷagamana Saha Śripādavandanāva* (Colombo: K. D. Siyadōris Appuhāmi, 1890), v. 60: "helikeruvē māvata ätraja visin."
129. Still, *The Jungle Tide*, 32. Elephant ascents of the Peak are also mentioned in Alfred Russel Wallace, *The Geographical Distribution of Animals: With a Study of the Relations of Living and Extinct Faunas as Elucidating the Past Changes of the Earth's Surface* (New York: Harper and Brothers, 1876), 11; Adolphus E. L. Rost, "Adam's Peak (Ceylon) in 1902," *Journal of the Royal Asiatic Society of Great Britain and Ireland* (1903): 657.
130. Caddy, *To Siam and Malaya in the Duke of Sutherland's Yacht*, 311.
131. CNML 82/V19: *Gaṅga Vistarya Kavi*, f. 2a; the original is Or.6611(17).
132. *Samantakūṭavaṇṇanā*, v. 726.
133. W. A. F. Dharmavardhana, ed., *Parevi Sandeśa Kāvya Varṇanāva* (Colombo: Guṇasēna, 1967), v. 61.

134. Vedeha Thera, *In Praise of Mount Samanta*, vv. 729–31, 733–37.
135. Vimalakīrti, *Saddharmaratnākaraya*, 302–3.
136. Still, *The Jungle Tide*, 30.
137. Seneviratna, *Siṃhala Kāvya Saṃgrahaya*, 218.
138. Deriyanagala's father, Paulus Pieris, wrote that "the text of Saman Sirita is in a very confused state," but concluded that the final king mentioned was Bhuvanekabāhu VII (r. 1521–1551); see P. E. Pieris, *Ceylon: The Portuguese Era, Being a History of the Island for the Period 1505–1658* (Colombo: Colombo Apothecaries, 1913), 1:570. Deriyanagala concurred with this in his article on *Saman Sirita*, but, in his printed edition, the last king seems to be Vīra Parakramabāhu (r. 1477–1489), or Dharma Parakramabāhu (r. 1489–1513). Either a leaf went missing while the manuscript was being copied and edited, or the poem may be several decades earlier than Pieris and Deriyanagala thought.
139. P. E. P. Deraniyagala, "The Saman Sirita, a Hymn to the Presiding Deity of Mount Saman," *Spolia Zeylanica* 29, no. 2 (1961): 301–3.
140. Animals and their arrangements, for example, bore similarities with forest elegies in poems like *Girā Sandeśa* (vv. 169–94). Thanks to Bandara Herath for pointing out this comparison.
141. *Saman Sirita*, v. 65, reprinted in Deraniyagala, *Deva Varṇanā Kāvya*, pp. 51–77. The manuscript from which Deraniyagala worked may now be lost, but a nearly identical manuscript labeled *Samandevi Varuṇa* exists at CNML 7/I1.
142. *Saman Sirita*, v. 52.
143. *Saman Sirita*, v. 51.
144. *Saman Sirita*, v. 61.
145. *Saman Sirita*, v. 60.
146. *Saman Sirita*, v. 37.
147. *Saman Sirita*, v. 32.
148. *Saman Sirita*, v. 30.
149. Amal Uḍavatta, *Śrī Pāda Aḍaviya: Saṃskrutika Vividhatvaya Saha Jaiva Vividhatvaya* (Dankotuwa: Vāsana Pot Prakāśakayō, 2014); Guṇasēkara Guṇasōma, *Samandevi Aḍaviya Janakatā* (Colombo: Fāsṭ Pabliṣin, 2013); Raṃjanī Dedduvakumāra Mahinda Amugoḍa, *Siripā Vanayē Yōgī Bhikṣuvak Samaṅga* (Maharagama: Katru Prakāśanayak, 2008); Tilak Sēnāsiṃha, *Saman Deviyangē Aḍaviya (Śrīpāda Aḍaviyē Cārikā Saṭahan Peḷak)* (Kudabollana: Udaya Prinṭars Änḍ Pabliṣars, 1997).

2. The Workaday Mountain

1. Miki Namba, "Becoming a City: Infrastructural Fetishism and Scattered Urbanization in Vientiane, Laos," in *Infrastructures and Social Complexity: A Companion*, ed. Penny Harvey, Casper Brunn Jensen, and Atsuro Morita (New York: Routledge, 2017), 76–86.
2. Victor Turner, "The Center Out There: Pilgrim's Goal," *History of Religions* 12, no. 3 (1973), 229.
3. Henri Lefebvre, *Writings on Cities*, trans. Eleonore Kofman and Elizabeth Lebas (Cambridge: Blackwell, 1996), 109. Kaviraja, for example, calls Samanala a city several times, using the terms *pura* and *nuvara*. See *Laṅkā Vistaraya*, vv. 71, 73–74, in Alexander McKinley, "Farming Songs from the Poet King: Translation and Explication of a Sinhala *Janakavi* Work," *Sri*

Lanka Journal of the Humanities 41, no. 1–2 (2017): 64–117. See also CNML 85/D18: *Samanaḷa Väňdīma*, f. 1b.

4. Lefebvre, *Writings on Cities*, 195.
5. Henri Lefebvre, *The Urban Revolution*, trans. Robert Bononno (Minneapolis: University of Minnesota Press, 2003), 118.
6. Brian Larkin, "The Politics and Poetics of Infrastructure," *Annual Review of Anthropology* 42 (2013): 328.
7. Ismail Fajrie Alatas, "The Poetics of Pilgrimage: Assembling Contemporary Indonesian Pilgrimage to Ḥaḍramawt, Yemen," *Comparative Studies in Society and History* 58, no. 3 (2016): 608.
8. Andrew Barry, "Infrastructure and the Earth," in *Infrastructures and Social Complexity: A Companion*, ed. Penny Harvey, Casper Brunn Jensen, and Atsuro Morita (New York: Routledge, 2017), 187.
9. Premakumara De Silva, "Kings, Monks and Pre-Colonial States: Patrons of the Temple of the Sacred Footprint," in *Asian Art and Culture: A Research Volume in Honor of Ananda Coomaraswamy*, ed. Anura Manatunga et al. (Department of Information: Government of Sri Lanka, 2012), 41–53.
10. Don Martino de Zilva Wickremasinghe, H. W. Codrington, and S. Paranavitana, *Epigraphia Zeylanica: Being Lithic and Other Inscriptions of Ceylon* (London: Published for the Government of Ceylon by H. Frowde, 1904–1934), 2:217. This record of Vijayabāhu's endowments is corroborated by the first extension of the *Mahāvaṃsa*, in the thirteenth century: *Cūḷavaṃsa, Being the More Recent Part of the Mahāvaṃsa*, trans. Wilhelm Geiger and C. Mabel Rickmers (Delhi: Motilal Banarsidass Pvt., 1996), 60:64–67. Translations from this edition are modified by me throughout using Wilhelm Geiger, ed., *Cūlavaṃsa: Being the More Recent Part of the Mahāvaṃsa* (London: Pali Text Society, 1980).
11. *Cūḷavaṃsa*, 80:24.
12. Wickremasinghe, Codrington, and Paranavitana, *Epigraphia Zeylanica*, 3:31. See also S. Paranavitana and C. E. Godakumbara, eds., *Epigraphia Zeylanica: Being Lithic and Other Inscriptions of Ceylon*, vol. 5, part 3 (Ceylon: Government Press, 1965), 446.
13. Mayurapāda Buddhaputra, *Pūjāvaliya* (Colombo: M. D. Guṇsēna saha Samāgama, 2015), 784.
14. There have been movements at various times to identify this cave as Bhagavalena, also known as Divāguhāwa; see SLNA 45/341: Ratnapura government agent diary, February 28, 1929; Kiriällē Ñāṇavimala, *Saparagamu Darśana* (Ratnapura: Śāstrādaya Yantrālaya, 1967), 64–74. Since the late 1990s, however, a cave named Baṭatoṭa-lena near Eratne has generally been accepted as Divāguhāva; see Kevin Trainor, "The Buddha's 'Cave of the Midday Rest' and Buddhist Relic Practices in Sri Lanka," *Material Religion* 9, no. 4 (2013): 516–21.
15. John Still, *The Jungle Tide*, 3rd ed. (Edinburgh: W. Blackwood and Sons, 1930), 26.
16. The legible remains of these lines are recorded in Kiriällē Ñāṇavimala, *Sabaragamuvē Päraṇi Liyavili* (Nugegoda: Mānavahitavādi Lēkhaka Parṣadaya, 2001), 30–32.
17. Guṇasēkara Guṇasōma, *Samandevi Aḍaviya Janakatā* (Colombo: Fāsṭ Pabliṣin, 2013), 155, 173, 183, 187.
18. A version in thirteen verses is found in Or.6615(503)II: *Samanaḷa Uppättiya*; excerpts are included in the *Samanala Vistaraya* tradition: CNML AL/14, f. 10; CNML AJ/14, f. 8. Several verses were also incorporated into *Purāṇa Himagata Varṇanāva*, vv. 27–32.
19. CNML 104/C8: S. Lakpatiraṇa, *Situm Sahita Śrī Pāda Vandanāva Hā Bhātiya Raja Kālayē Śrī Pādaya Soyā Dun Koṭāgē Kathāva* (W. Viliyam Perērā saha D. M. Kannangara, 1920).

20. CNML 104/C8: Attuḍāvē Hārmanis Jayasēkara, *Siripadahälla* (Aluthgama: Saddharmaprakāśa Yantrālaya, 1924), vv. 11–12.
21. *Culavamsa*, 85:118–21.
22. *Culavamsa*, 86:9–12.
23. *Culavamsa*, 86:21–28.
24. *Samantakūṭavaṇṇanā*, v. 754.
25. Buddhaputra, *Pūjāvaliya*, 795.
26. C. E. Godakumbura, *Panavitiya Ambalama Carvings* (Colombo: Archaeological Department, 1981), 20–21.
27. John M. Senaveratna, *Dictionary of Proverbs of the Sinhalese: Including Also Their Adages, Aphorisms, Apologues, Apothegms, Bywords, Dictums, Maxims, Mottoes, Precepts, Saws, and Sayings: Together with the Connected Myths, Legends, and Folk-Tales* (Colombo: Times of Ceylon, 1936), 82.
28. Penny Harvey and Hannah Knox, "The Enchantments of Infrastructure," *Mobilities* 7, no. 4 (2012): 521.
29. *Culavamsa*, 86:3–8.
30. *Culavamsa*, 88:48; Buddhaputra, *Pūjāvaliya*, 801.
31. *Saman Sirita*, vv. 193–207.
32. Jonathan S. Walters, "Lovely Lady Lanka: A Tenth-Century Description," *Sri Lanka Journal of the Humanities* 19, no. 1–2 (1993): 45–47. Walters's translation slightly modified by me.
33. Alan Strathern, "Towards the Source-Criticism of Sitavaka-Period Heroic Literature, Part Two: The *Sitavaka Hatana*: Notes on a Grounded Text," *Sri Lanka Journal of the Humanities* 34, nos. 1–2 (2008): 70.
34. Rōhiṇi Paraṇavitāna, ed., *Sītāvaka Haṭana* (Śrī Laṅkā Rajayē Mudraṇa Depārtamēnttuva: Madhyama Saṅskrutika Aramudala, 1999), v. 166.
35. *Sītāvaka Haṭana*, vv. 173–76. The final verse reads: "naraniňdu sada la pā | jayatilaka bū pā | lakdivaṭa siri pā | nuvara pävatī upā."
36. The only other source I have found mentioning Mayadunne's pilgrimage is *Suḷu Rājavaliya*, completed in 1820, in which this king makes a large oil *puja* to the summit lamp, and then has 780 stone steps carved at Heramitipana on his way down in order to accumulate merit. *Suḷu Rājavaliya* (Colombo: Ratna Pot Prakāśakayō, 2005), 32.
37. *Sītāvaka Haṭana*, vv. 458–60, 702.
38. *Sītāvaka Haṭana*, vv. 696, 698–99.
39. Stephen C. Berkwitz, "Strong Men and Sensual Women in Sinhala Buddhist Poetry," in *Religious Boundaries for Sex, Gender, and Corporeality*, ed. Alexandra Cuffel, Ana Echevarria, and Georgios T. Halkias (New York: Routledge, 2019), 63–77.
40. McKinley, "Farming Songs from the Poet King."
41. Abaya Aryasinghe, *The Deities and Demons of Sinhala Origin* (Nugegoda: Deepanee, 2000), 58–59.
42. CNML 104/Z2: W. A. G. Juvānis, *Śrīpādavandanāva Hevat Giripada Lakara* (Moraketiya: Vijēpāla Yantrālaya, 1929), vv. 208–10; K. R. Perera, *Samanaḷagamana Saha Śripādavandanāva* (Colombo: K. D. Siyadōris Appuhāmi, 1890), vv. 41–42; CNML 104/Z2: M. S. Pranāndu, *Samanala Hasuna* (Pānadura: M. Jēsan Pranāndu, 1932), v. 13; Don Kornēlis Ponsēkā, *Sumaṇa Śaila Mārgā Laṅkāraya Hevat Sumanaselmagalakara* (Sarasavisaňdaräsa Mudrāyantra Śālāvē, 1891), v. 57.
43. Ñāṇavimala, *Sabaragamuvē Päraṇi Liyavili*, 35–36; John Still, "Notes on Adam's Peak and Some of the Paths in the Range," *Spolia Zeylanica* 5 (1908): 85.
44. Still, "Notes on Adam's Peak," 83.

45. "Exploring of Adam's Peak: A Lofty and Sacred Mountain in the Island of Ceylon," *La belle assemblée: or Court and fashionable magazine*, December 1816, 268–69.
46. H. C. P. Bell, *Report on the Kuṭṭāpiṭiya Sannasa* (Kandy: Miller, 1925), 14. For sample correspondence on this issue from 1826, see William Skeen, *Adam's Peak: Legendary Traditional, and Historic Notices of the Samanala and Srí-Páda with a Descriptive Account of the Pilgrims' Route from Colombo to the Sacred Foot-Print* (Colombo: W. L. H. Skeen, 1870), 356–57.
47. SLNA 45/345: Ratnapura government agent diary, January 5, 1933.
48. SLNA 45/345: Ratnapura government agent diary, July 22, 1933.
49. For a history of the 1867 election of Hikkaduvē Sumaṅgala, see Anne M. Blackburn, *Locations of Buddhism: Colonialism and Modernity in Sri Lanka* (Chicago: University of Chicago Press, 2010). There are three thick twentieth-century casefiles about election controversies of the high priest position: SLNA 45/2964, 45/2965, 45/2966.
50. *Administration Reports* 1906: I4. A nearly complete set of these reports from the mid-nineteenth century to the present are shelved in the public reading room of the SLNA. I cite them here by year and page number.
51. Amna Khalid, "'Subordinate' Negotiations: Indigenous Staff, the Colonial State and Public Health," in *The Social History of Health and Medicine in Colonial India*, ed. Biswamoy Pati and Mark Harrison (New York: Routledge, 2009), 45–73.
52. E.R.P., "Adam's Peak: Ceylon," *Literary Gazette: A Weekly Journal of Literature, Science, and the Fine Arts* 1084 (October 28, 1837): 689.
53. *Administration Reports* 1906: H8; 1907: H6–H7.
54. *Administration Reports* 1914: I4.
55. *Administration Reports* 1914: I4.
56. *A Conversation Between a Christian and a Pilgrim—Śrī Pādaya Gäṇaya* (Colombo: Wesleyan Mission Press for Ceylon Religious Tract Society, 1871), 4–5.
57. E.g., Juvānis, *Śrīpādavandanāva*, v. 58.
58. *Käṭakirilli Sandeśaya*, v. 53.
59. CNML 104/T14: Ugat Kāvyakkārayek, *Śrīpādapatmaya Vandanāgātha Saha Abhinava Himagatavarṇanāva* (Granthalokayantrālaya: K. Dāvit Perērā, 1902), vv. 97–98.
60. CNML AL/14; f. 50. See chapter 5 for more on this text and its scribe. The usual irregularities of manuscript spelling are found: "anbalamak kerevvottin sit nokāmäli sit pähädī | pembaranäsiya samagin gos ē surapura upadī | anbara pili sah̆da vilasin dilihena ran viman ladī | tanbaramin śarasunu sursen pirivaramin ävidī."
61. CNML 104/S8: D.D.L., *Siri Pāda Gaman Vistaraya* (Colombo: Lakdiv, 1891), v. 24.
62. D.D.L., *Siri Pāda Gaman Vistaraya*, vv. 76, 78. The word I translate as "nation" here is *heḷa*, which could refer to the island of Lanka, or the Sinhala language or people.
63. *Administration Reports* 1935: I6. "A temporary hospital with two wards—one for males and the other for females—of six beds each was opened and equipped at Heramitipana owing to the malaria epidemic."
64. *Administration Reports* 1907: I4.
65. SLNA 45/335: Ratnapura government agent diary, March 4, 1914.
66. Nihal Perera, *People's Spaces: Coping, Familiarizing, Creating* (New York: Routledge, 2016), 194–95, 214.
67. Susan Leigh Star, "The Ethnography of Infrastructure," *American Behavioral Scientist* 43, no. 3 (1999): 380.
68. Lefebvre, *The Urban Revolution*, 25–26.

69. Jōn Da Silvā, *Śrīpāda Śatakaya* (Colombo, 1912), v. 84. UPL call number: RES 294.3 NAR. Here "water machine" is *jala yatura*. This poet and poem are further discussed in chapters 3 and 4.
70. Juvānis, *Śrīpādavandanāva*, v. 132.
71. Juvānis, *Śrīpādavandanāva*, v. 116.
72. *Gīta vatura pompē hanḍa denavā*. CNML 104 C/8: T. H. Udāris, *Śrīpāda Vandanāva Saha Gālu Kōralē Siṭa Yana Vandanākārayingē Gaman Vistaraya* (Ambalangoḍa: Vijaya Yantrālaya, 1923), v. 47. Full translation in Alexander McKinley, "The Spacing of Pilgrimage: Two Journeys to Sri Pada in Sinhala Verse," *SAGAR: A South Asia Research Journal* 25 (2017): 96–130.
73. Juvānis, *Śrīpādavandanāva*, vv. 135–36.
74. *Administration Reports* 1936: I5.
75. SLNA 45/348: Ratnapura government agent diary, March 18, 1936. Subscriptions (*sammādam*) were also given for the water pumps at Lihinihela, or Nilihela, according to Da Silvā, *Śrīpāda Śatakaya*, v. 87.
76. Lisa Björkman, *Pipe Politics, Contested Waters: Embedded Infrastructures of Millennial Mumbai* (Durham, NC: Duke University Press, 2015), 232.
77. SLNA 45/349: Ratnapura government agent diary, April 1, 1937.
78. See SLNA 45/2955: Buddhist Temporalities correspondence, and John D. Rogers, "Religious Belief, Economic Interest and Social Policy: Temple Endowments in Sri Lanka During the Governorship of William Gregory, 1872–77," *Modern Asian Studies* 21, no. 2 (1987): 349–69.
79. SLNA 45/2955: Buddhist Temporalities correspondence; SLNA 45/3313: temple and *devale* land register.
80. SLNA 45/2955: Buddhist Temporalities correspondence.
81. Mädauyangoḍa Vimalakīrti, *Vimalakīrtigē Siṃhala Āṇḍuva* (Colombo: S. Goḍagē saha Sahōdarayō, 2001), 224–31.
82. SLNA 45/2955: Buddhist Temporalities correspondence.
83. SLNA 45/2956: Buddhist Temporalities correspondence.
84. SLNA 45/2956: Buddhist Temporalities correspondence.
85. SLNA 45/2956: Buddhist Temporalities correspondence.
86. SLNA 45/2956: Buddhist Temporalities correspondence.
87. Premakumara De Silva, "'Colonial Governmentality': Legal and Administrative Technologies of the Governance of Sri Pada Temple in Sri Lanka," in *Theravada Buddhism in Colonial Contexts*, ed. Thomas Borchert (New York: Routledge, 2018), 121–37.
88. SLNA 45/334: Ratnapura government agent diary, February 20, 1913.
89. SLNA 45/336: Ratnapura government agent diary, February 27, 1915.
90. SLNA 45/2963: Buddhist Temporalities correspondence. Another example of the Peak trustee clashing with private donors occurred during early efforts to electrically illuminate the Peak in the 1930s, when the trustee was upset the illumination society collected donations from pilgrims. See K. M. Vitarana, *Sri Pada: Adam's Peak, the Holy Mountain of Religious Amity and Miracles* (Nugegoda: Sarasavi Publishers, 2011), 62–75.
91. SLNA 45/335: Ratnapura government agent diary, March 5, 1914.
92. SLNA 45/2963: Buddhist Temporalities correspondence.
93. SLNA 45/2963: Buddhist Temporalities correspondence.
94. *Administration Reports* 1922: I2.
95. SLNA 45/338: Ratnapura government agent diary, January 26, 1922.
96. *Administration Reports* 1907: I4.

97. Simon Sawers and Henry Marshall, *Recollections of a Journey from Kandy to Caltura, by Way of Adam's Peak, Made in the Year 1819* (Edinburgh: Royal College of Physicians of Edinburgh, 1823), 9.
98. James L. A. Webb, *Tropical Pioneers: Human Agency and Ecological Change in the Highlands of Sri Lanka, 1800–1900* (Athens: Ohio University Press, 2002).
99. SLNA 53/5: Arthur Morice to Sir H. Robinson, November 18, 1865.
100. SLNA 45/341: Ratnapura government agent diary, February 26, 1929.
101. *Administration Reports* 1912–1913: I20.
102. SLNA 45/338: Ratnapura government agent diary, August 21, 1924.
103. SLNA 45/341: Ratnapura government agent diary, September 6, 1928. Less than five years later, this road was again in need of major repairs, suggesting its heavy use. See SLNA 45/345: Ratnapura government agent diary, February 9, 1933.
104. Kumari Jayawardena and Rachel Kurian, *Class, Patriarchy and Ethnicity on Sri Lankan Plantations: Two Centuries of Power and Protest* (New Delhi: Orient BlackSwan, 2015), 26.
105. *Administration Reports* 1911–1912: I7.
106. SLNA 45/336: Ratnapura government agent diary, February 27, 1915.
107. SLNA 45/348: Ratnapura government agent diary, March 8, 1936.
108. SLNA 45/349: Ratnapura government agent diary, March 29, 1937.
109. Letter reprinted in Vitarana, *Sri Pada*, 121.
110. *Administration Reports* 1914: I4, B3.
111. Archibald Campbell Lawrie, *A Gazetteer of the Central Province of Ceylon* (Colombo: Government Press, 1896), 1:334.
112. E. B. Denham, *The Census of Ceylon, 1911. Town and Village Statistics* (Colombo: H. C. Cottle, 1912), 68.
113. *Administration Reports* 1908: B7.
114. Lawrie, *A Gazetteer of the Central Province of Ceylon*, 2:540.
115. David Ker, "Climbing Up Adam's Peak: A Night of It on Top Amid Queer Surroundings," *New York Times*, May 20, 1888, 13.
116. A notable exception describing the Hatton route and arrival via train is CNML 104/C8: G. M. Salā, *Samanala Gamanā Laṅkāraya* (Kegalle: Vidyākalpa Yantrālaya, 1924). This is translated in McKinley, "The Spacing of Pilgrimage."
117. *Administration Reports* 1906: I4; 1908: I5; 1909: I6; 1913: I5; 1919: I3; 1920: I3; 1921: I2.
118. *Administration Reports* 1906: B5; 1907: B8; 1908: B7; 1913: B4. For some other vastly different accounts of pilgrim numbers, see Blackburn, *Locations of Buddhism*, 22–23n45.
119. Denham, *The Census of Ceylon, 1911*, 2.
120. CNML 104/BB2: Välitara Dharma Śrī S. Hētumuni, "Samanoḷa Girimudunēdī," *Sarasavi Mäduru* 1, no. 10 (August/September 1933): 189–90; Munidāsa Subhāvikrama, "Samanoḷa Mudunēdī," *Sarasavi Haňḍa* 1, no. 1 (March 1934): 6; T. B. Vikramasiṅha, "Mahakaňdugala Matadī," *Siṅhala Kav Kiruḷa* 12, no. 3 (1934): 43. Concentration of population is also why pilgrimage sites remained important to postcolonial politics; see, e.g., Elizabeth Nissan, "Polity and Pilgrimage Centres in Sri Lanka," *Man* 23, no. 2 (1988): 253–74.
121. Premakumara De Silva, "Anthropological Studies on South Asian Pilgrimage: Case of Buddhist Pilgrimage in Sri Lanka," *International Journal of Religious Tourism and Pilgrimage* 4, no. 1 (2016): 21n3. Estimates for 1992 were 1.5 million via the Hatton trail and 0.5 million via Ratnapura and Kuruwita: Anoja Wickramasinghe, *People and the Forest:*

Management of the Adam's Peak Wilderness (Battaramulla: Sri Lanka Forest Department, 1995), 60.

122. This information comes from the 2006 Project Design Document submitted to the UNFCCC Clean Development Mechanism program, available at https://cdm.unfccc.int/Projects/DB/SGS-UKL1182345245.07/view.
123. The word that Rukmal used translated as "miraculous power" is *hāskam*, discussed further in chapter 5.
124. There is another Makara Torana on the Ratnapura trail, discussed in chapter 5.
125. N. Serena Tennekoon, "Rituals of Development: The Accelerated Mahaväli Development Program of Sri Lanka," *American Ethnologist* 15, no. 2 (1988): 294–310; Bandura Dileepa Witharana, *Negotiating Power and Constructing the Nation: Engineering in Sri Lanka* (Colombo: Tambapanni Academic Publishers, 2022).
126. See the 1942 directives to the society from the civil defense commissioner reprinted in Vitarana, *Sri Pada*, 146.
127. Letter from electrical engineer, government installations, to the public trustee, Colombo, April 25, 1949, in Vitarana, *Sri Pada*, 163.
128. Letter from C. V. Wickramasinghe, president of the Brotherhood, to the Peak trustee, July 13, 1949, in Vitarana, *Sri Pada*, 164–65.
129. Printed in Amal Uḍavatta, *Śrī Pāda Aḍaviya: Saṃskrutika Vividhatvaya Saha Jaiva Vividhatvaya* (Dankotuwa: Vāsana Pot Prakāśakayō, 2014), 131–32.
130. Maria Heim, *Words for the Heart: A Treasury of Emotions from Classical India* (Princeton, NJ: Princeton University Press, 2022), 55–56.
131. Uḍavatta, *Śrī Pāda Aḍaviya*, 186–87.
132. Reprinted in Maḍalagama Vajirabuddhi Himi, *Dēva Purāṇaya: Saman Deviňdu Hā Saman Devola*, ed. Saviman Urugoḍawatta (Balangoda: Sunil Śānta Vīrasēkara, 2007), 407–20.
133. Garrett Field, *Modernizing Composition: Sinhala Song, Poetry, and Politics in Twentieth-Century Sri Lanka* (Oakland: University of California Press, 2017), 28–30.
134. *Samandeviňduni!*, vv. 1, 6–7. Included in a compilation volume under SOAS University of London Library: XII.Sinh.JP.10/108205.
135. Letter from the Peak trustee to the public trustee, Colombo, January 9, 1950, reprinted in Vitarana, *Sri Pada*, 166.
136. Letter from Peak trustee to W. G. Sarnolis, secretary of S.S.V. P.A.S.S., reprinted in Vitarana, *Sri Pada*, 177.
137. See Mrs. Col. Walker, "Journal of an Ascent to the Summit of Adam's Peak," in *Companion to the Botanical Magazine*, ed. W. J. Hooker (London: Samuel Curtis, 1835), 2–14.
138. James Hingston, *The Australian Abroad. Branches from the Main Routes Around the World. Series 2. Ceylon, India, and Egypt* (London: Sampson Low, Marston, Searle, and Rivington, 1880), 42.
139. "Śrī Pādasthānayē Vihāra Maluva," *Savadeśa Mitrayā* Vesak Atirekaya (BE 2473), 58. Thanks to Kitsiri Jayasekara, whom I met on the mountain, for showing me his copy of this publication.
140. Still, "Notes on Adam's Peak," 82.
141. See also Daniel Bass, *Everyday Ethnicity in Sri Lanka: Up-Country Tamil Identity Politics* (Colombo: Social Scientists' Association, 2015); Christopher Neubert, "Power, Everyday Control, and Emerging Resistance in Sri Lanka's Plantations," *Contemporary South Asia* (2015): 1–14; Mythri Jegathesan, *Tea and Solidarity: Tamil Women and Work in Postwar Sri Lanka* (Seattle: University of

Washington Press, 2019). Unique boons of local pilgrimage economies are also found in comparable contexts elsewhere, e.g., Luke Whitmore, *Mountain, Water, Rock, God: Understanding Kedarnath in the Twenty-First Century* (Oakland: University of California Press, 2018), 37–38.

142. Mahathera Abhayaraja Pirivena Valgampaya, *Rājaratnākaraya (the Gem Mine of Kings)*, trans. Kusuma Karunaratne (Colombo: Central Cultural Fund, 2008), 81.
143. Thomas Skinner, *Fifty Years in Ceylon* (London: W. H. Allen, 1891), 178–79.
144. SLNA 45/333: Ratnapura government agent diary, January 6, 1912.
145. SLNA 45/333: Ratnapura government agent diary, January 7, 1912.
146. James S. Duncan, *In the Shadows of the Tropics: Climate, Race and Biopower in Nineteenth Century Ceylon* (Burlington: Ashgate, 2007).
147. Walker, "Journal of an Ascent to the Summit of Adam's Peak," 7.
148. Ker, "Climbing Up Adam's Peak," 13.
149. Talal Asad, *Genealogies of Religion: Discipline and Reasons of Power in Christianity and Islam* (Baltimore: Johns Hopkins University Press, 1993), 76.
150. Marcel Mauss, "Techniques of the Body," in *Incorporations*, ed. Jonathan Crary and Sanford Kwinter (New York: Zone, 1992), 470.
151. Skeen, *Adam's Peak*, 230.
152. *Cūḷavaṃsa*, 97:16.
153. E. Valentine Daniel, *Charred Lullabies: Chapters in an Anthropography of Violence* (Princeton, NJ: Princeton University Press, 1996), 60.
154. Premakumara De Silva, "Reordering of Postcolonial Sri Pāda Temple in Sri Lanka: Buddhism, State, and Nationalism," *History and Sociology of South Asia* 7, no. 155 (2013): 155–76.
155. Gāmiṇi Baṇḍāra Ilaṅgattilaka, "Janapati Guvanē Siṭa Picca Mal Isiddī Śrī Pāda Maḷuva Sādu Nadin Giňgum Deyi," *Divayina*, February 8, 2014.
156. Ruvira Abēmānna, "Siripāda Kaňda Mudunaṭa Doḷos Mahē Pahanayi Ghaṇṭārayayi Genā Mahā Helikopṭar Meheyuma," *Mavbim*, January 11, 2014, 8; Ranmalī Sōmasiri, "Kaḷugalen Kaḷa Doḷosmahēpahana Siripā Maḷuvaṭa Guvanin Genagiya Trāsajanaka Meheyuma," *Lakbima*, January 12, 2014, 16.
157. Kelum Bandara and Yohan Perera, "Election to Select Chief Incumbent of Sri Pada Vihare, Rigged: UNP," *Daily Mirror*, December 2, 2011; Kelum Bandara and Yohan Perera, "Sri Pada: UNP Accuses Government of Disgraceful Conduct," *Daily Mirror*, December 3, 2011; Saman Indrajith, "Election Rigged, Alleges UNP: Election of Chief Incumbent of Sri Pada Vihara," *The Island*, December 2, 2011; L. B. Senaratne, "Siri Pada Election: Kandy Lawyers to Lodge Protest," *Sunday Times*, December 4, 2011.
158. Sumanā Vīratuṅga, *Kavi Situvili* (Colombo: Mavbima Kartru Maṇḍalaya, 2014), 15–17.
159. R. Aśōka A. Dharmasēna, *Uttama Muṇi Siripā* (n.d.), i.
160. Although highland Tamils had no tangible association with the LTTE separatists of the civil war, this did not stop local Sinhala officials from treating them with suspicion. See Daniel Bass, "Paper Tigers on the Prowl: Rumors, Violence and Agency in the Up-Country of Sri Lanka," *Anthropological Quarterly* 81, no. 1 (2008): 269–95.
161. Sri Lankan advertising firms have long been sensitive to religious contexts. See Steven Kemper, *Buying and Believing: Sri Lankan Advertising and Consumers in a Transnational World* (Chicago: University of Chicago Press, 2001).
162. Henri Lefebvre, *The Production of Space*, trans. Donald Nicholson-Smith (Oxford: Blackwell, 1991), 48.
163. Lefebvre, *Writings on Cities*, 169.

3. Adam's Peak and Buddhist Visions of Mecca

1. Johan Elverskog, *Buddhism and Islam on the Silk Road* (Philadelphia: University of Pennsylvania Press, 2010).
2. Llewelyn Morgan, *The Buddhas of Bamiyan* (Cambridge, MA: Harvard University Press, 2012).
3. Yi-Fu Tuan, *Space and Place: The Perspective of Experience* (Minneapolis: University of Minnesota Press, 1977), 6.
4. E.g., Peter Bishop, *The Myth of Shangri-La: Tibet, Travel Writing, and the Western Creation of Sacred Landscape* (Berkeley: University of California Press, 1989).
5. Paul Carter, *The Road to Botany Bay: An Exploration of Landscape and History* (New York: Knopf, 1988), xxiv.
6. Rohaṇa is also the moniker for the Peak in some Sanskrit texts, being the local name for the southern kingdom of Lanka.
7. Al-Bīrūnī, *Kitāb Al-Jamāhir Fī Ma'rifat Al-Jawāhir*, trans. Hakim Mohammed Said (Karachi: Pakistan Historical Society, 2001), 52.
8. Abū 'Ubayd al-Bakrī (d. 1094) in his *Mu'jam mā ista'jam*, quoting someone named al-Mamdāni, cited in Markus Aksland, *The Sacred Footprint: A Cultural History of Adam's Peak* (Bangkok: Orchid Press, 2001), 119.
9. Donald S. Lopez and Peggy McCracken, *In Search of the Christian Buddha: How an Asian Sage Became a Medieval Saint* (New York: Norton, 2014).
10. S. M. Stern, Sophie Walzer, and Muḥammad ibn 'Alī Ibn Bābawayh al-Qummī, *Three Unknown Buddhist Stories in an Arabic Version* (Columbia: University of South Carolina Press, 1971).
11. Daniel Gimaret, *Le livre de Bilawhar et Būdāsf selon la version arabe ismaélienne* (Geneva: Droz, 1971), 83.
12. *The Balavariani (Barlaam and Josaphat), a Tale from the Christian East Translated from the Old Georgian*, trans. David Marshall Lang (Berkeley: University of California Press, 1966), 71.
13. *The Balavariani*, 71n1.
14. George Ratcliffe Woodward and Harold Mattingly, *St. John Damascene: Barlaam and Ioasaph* (New York: Macmillan, 1914), 63.
15. Gui de Cambri, *Barlaam and Josaphat: A Christian Tale of the Buddha*, trans. Peggy McCracken (New York: Penguin, 2014), 17.
16. Manuel de Faria e Sousa, *The Portugues Asia*, trans. John Stevens (London: Printed for C. Brome, 1695), 2:510.
17. Solomon Caesar Malan, *The Book of Adam and Eve* (London: Williams and Norgate, 1882); Michael Stone, "The Death of Adam: An Armenian Adam Book," *Harvard Theological Review* 59, no. 3 (July 1966): 283–91; Michael Waldstein and Frederik Wisse, eds., *The Apocryphon of John: A Synopsis of Nag Hammadi Codices Ii,1, Iii,1, and Iv,1 with Bg 8502,2*, vol. 33 (Leiden: E. J. Brill, 1995).
18. Hugh Kennedy, *The Court of the Caliphs: The Rise and Fall of Islam's Greatest Dynasty* (London: Weidenfeld and Nicolson, 2004); Travis E. Zadeh, *Mapping Frontiers Across Medieval Islam: Geography, Translation, and the 'Abbāsid Empire* (London: I. B. Tauris, 2011).
19. David Allen Scott, "The Iranian Face of Buddhism," *East and West* 40, no. 1/4 (1990): 43–77; Jamsheed K. Choksy, "Sailors, Soldiers, Priests, and Merchants: Reappraising Iran's Early Connections to Ceylon," *Iranica Antiqua* 48 (2013): 363–91.
20. *The History of Al-Ṭabarī* [Ta'rīkh al-rusul wa'l-mulūk], trans. Franz Rosenthal (Albany: State University of New York Press, 1989), 1:184–86.

21. *The History of Al-Ṭabarī*, 290–92.
22. Ibn Abbas would have been only an infant when Abu Talib died. Considering his age, some interpret all hadith that go back to Ibn Abbas as a conglomeration of folktales.
23. *The History of Al-Ṭabarī*, 292.
24. Ranabir Chakravarti, "Reaching Out to Distant Shores: Indo-Judaic Trade Contacts (up to C.E. 1300)," in *Indo-Judaic Studies in the Twenty-First Century: A View from the Margin*, ed. Nathan Katz (New York: Palgrave Macmillan, 2007), 19–43.
25. *The History of Al-Ṭabarī*, 292.
26. *The History of Al-Ṭabarī*, 296–97.
27. Ibn al-Kalbī, *The Book of Idols, Being a Translation from the Arabic of the Kitāb Al-Asnām*, trans. Nabih Amin Faris (Princeton, NJ: Princeton University Press, 1952), 43–44.
28. Engseng Ho, *The Graves of Tarim: Genealogy and Mobility Across the Indian Ocean* (Berkeley: University of California Press, 2006).
29. Tarif Khalidi, *Islamic Historiography: The Histories of Mas'ūdī* (Albany: State University of New York Press, 1975), 23–27.
30. *'Aḫbār Aṣ-Ṣīn Wa L-Hind: Relation de la Chine et de l'Inde*, trans. Jean Sauvaget (Paris: Société d'édition Les Belles Lettres, 1948), 4. I have translated from Sauvaget's French.
31. Perween Hasan, "The Footprint of the Prophet," *Muqarnas* 10 (1993): 335–43.
32. Ashraf Jamal, "Telling and Selling on the Indian Ocean Rim," in *Indian Ocean Studies: Cultural, Social, and Political Perspectives*, ed. Shanti Moorthy and Ashraf Jamal (New York: Routledge, 2010), 403–4.
33. Suhanna Shafiq, *Seafarers of the Seven Seas: The Maritime Culture in the Kitāb 'ajā'ib Al-Hind (the Book of the Marvels of India) by Buzurg Ibn Shahriyār (D. 399/1009)*, Islamkundliche Untersuchungen (Berlin: Klaus Schwarz Verlag, 2013).
34. Buzurg ibn Shahriyār, *The Book of the Wonders of India: Mainland, Sea, and Islands* [Kitāb 'Ajā'ib al-Hind], trans. G. S. P. Freeman-Grenville (London: East-West Publications, 1981), 106.
35. James E. Montgomery, "Serendipity, Resistance, and Multivalency: Ibn Khurradādhbih and His *Kitāb Al-Masālik Wa-L-Mamālik*," in *On Fiction and Adab in Medieval Arabic Literature*, ed. Philip F. Kennedy (Wiesbaden: Harrassowitz Verlag, 2005), 198–201.
36. Zadeh, *Mapping Frontiers Across Medieval Islam*, 16–17.
37. Montgomery, "Serendipity, Resistance, and Multivalency," 214; Zadeh, *Mapping Frontiers Across Medieval Islam*, 44–48.
38. C. Barbier de Meynard, "Le livre des routes et des provinces, par Ibn Khordadbeh," *Journal Asiatique* (January–February 1865): 285–86. I have translated from the French.
39. Gerald R. Tibbets, "The Beginnings of a Cartographic Tradition," in *The History of Cartography*, vol. 2, book 1, *Cartography in the Traditional Islamic and South Asian Societies*, ed. J. B. Harley and David Woodward (Chicago: University of Chicago Press, 1992), 92–93.
40. Zadeh, *Mapping Frontiers Across Medieval Islam*, 18.
41. *El-Mas'ūdī's Historical Encyclopaedia, Entitled "Meadows of Gold and Mines of Gems,"* trans. Aloys Sprenger (London: Oriental Translation Fund, 1841), 1:352.
42. *El-Mas'ūdī's Historical Encyclopaedia*, 59.
43. Al-Muqaddasī, *The Best Divisions for Knowledge of the Regions, Aḥsan Al-Taqāsīm Fī Ma'rifat Al-Aqālīm*, trans. Basil Collins (Reading: Garnet Publishing, 2001), 12–13.
44. Montgomery, "Serendipity, Resistance, and Multivalency," 193–94.
45. Al-Bīrūnī, *Kitāb Al-Jamāhir Fī Ma'rifat Al-Jawāhir*, 52.
46. Al-Bīrūnī, *Kitāb Al-Jamāhir Fī Ma'rifat Al-Jawāhir*, 51.

47. *Arab Navigation in the Indian Ocean Before the Coming of the Portuguese, Being a Translation of Kitāb Al-Fawā'id Fī Uṣūl Al-Baḥr Wa'l-Qawā'id of Aḥmad B. Mājid Al-Najdī*, trans. G. R. Tibbetts (London: Royal Asiatic Society of Great Britain and Ireland, 1971), 184–85.
48. *Arab Navigation in the Indian Ocean*, 219, 221.
49. *Arab Navigation in the Indian Ocean*, 221n14.
50. Konrad Miller, *Mappae Arabicae*, ed. Heinz Gaube, Beihefte zum Tübinger Atlas des Vonderen Orients (Wiesbaden: Dr. Ludwig Reichert Verlag, 1986), 2:30–32.
51. Andreas Kaplony, "Comparing Al-Kāshgharī's Map to His Text: On the Visual Language, Purpose, and Transmission of Arabic-Islamic Maps," in *The Journey of Maps and Images of the Silk Road*, ed. Philippe Forêt and Andreas Kaplony (Leiden: Brill, 2008), 145.
52. See translated map at http://commons.wikimedia.org/wiki/File:Kashgari_map.jpg.
53. Johan Elverskog, *Uygur Buddhist Literature*, Silk Road Studies (Turnhout: Brepols, 1997).
54. Semih Tezcan, *Das Uigurische Insadi-Sūtra* (Berlin: Akademie-Verlag, 1974), 71. I have translated from the German.
55. Maḥmūd al-Kāšġarī, *Compendium of the Turkic Dialects (Dīwān Luġāt at-Turk)*, trans. Robert Dankoff and James Kelly (Duxbury, MA: Harvard University Printing Office, 1982), 1:270.
56. Emel Esin, "An Aspect of Turkish Mediacy in the Westward Transmission of Eastern Culture, in the Case of Mysticism," in *Proceedings of the Thirty-First International Congress of Human Sciences in Asia and North Africa, Tokyo-Kyoto, 31st August–7th September 1983* (1983), 379. See also Emel Esin, "On the Relationship Between the Iconography in Musim Uyġur Manuscripts and Buddhist Uyġur Eschatology," in *Altaistic Studies: Papers at the 25th Meeting of the Permanent International Altaistic Conference at Uppsala June 7–11 1982*, ed. Gunnar Jarring and Staffan Rosén (Stockholm: Almqvist and Wiksell International, 1985).
57. S. Magbul Ahmad, "Cartography of Al-Sharīf Al-Idrīsī," in *The History of Cartography*, vol. 2, book 1, *Cartography in the Traditional Islamic and South Asian Societies*, ed. J. B. Harley and David Woodward (Chicago: University of Chicago Press, 1992), 156–72.
58. *India and the Neighbouring Territories in the Kitāb Nuzhat Al-Mushtāq Fi'khtirāq Al-'āfāq of Al-Sharīf Al-Idrīsī*, trans. S. Magbul Ahmad (Leiden: E. J. Brill, 1960), 27.
59. Ahmad, "Cartography of al-Sharīf al-Idrīsī," 158.
60. *The Travels of Ibn Baṭṭūṭa A.D. 1325–1354*, trans. H. A. R. Gibb and C. F. Beckingham (London: Hakluyt Society, 1994), 4:835–36.
61. Donovan O. Schaefer, *Religious Affects: Animality, Evolution, and Power* (Durham, NC: Duke University Press, 2015), 17.
62. *The Travels of Ibn Baṭṭūṭa*, 4:838.
63. *The Travels of Ibn Baṭṭūṭa*, 4:847.
64. Chandra Richard De Silva, *Sri Lanka: A History* (New Delhi: Vikas Publishing House, 1987), 93–94.
65. *The Travels of Ibn Baṭṭūṭa*, 4:848–49.
66. *The Travels of Ibn Baṭṭūṭa*, 4:850.
67. *The Travels of Ibn Baṭṭūṭa*, 4:850.
68. "In the city there are 300 wells, 500 houses of valiant and powerful ministers, 500 houses of dancing women, 500 houses of Brahmins, 800 houses of dhobis, 800 houses of potters, 700 carpenters' sheds, 4 stables for horses, 3 stables for elephants, 2 herds of hunting buffalos, an aviary, a kennel, and 700 powerful skilled and trained warriors." F. Modder, "Kurunegala Vistaraya; with Notes on Kurunegala, Ancient and Modern," *Journal of the Ceylon Branch of the Royal Asiatic Society* 13, no. 44 (1893): 38.

69. *The Travels of Ibn Battūta A.D. 1325–1354*, trans. H. A. R. Gibb (Cambridge: Hakluyt Society, 1962), 2:314. Ibn Battuta had earlier visited this sheikh's tomb in Persia.
70. *The Travels of Ibn Baṭṭūṭa*, 4:849–50.
71. Geert Jan van Gelder, "To Eat or Not to Eat Elephant: A Travelling Story in Arabic and Persian Literature," *Bulletin of SOAS* 66, no. 3 (2003): 419–30.
72. *The Travels of Ibn Baṭṭūṭa*, 4:852.
73. *The Travels of Ibn Baṭṭūṭa*, 4:853.
74. *The Reḥla of Ibn Baṭṭūṭa (India, Maldive Islands and Ceylon)*, trans. Mahdi Husain (Baroda: Oriental Institute, 1953), 223n6.
75. *The Travels of Ibn Baṭṭūṭa*, 4:853.
76. *The Travels of Ibn Baṭṭūṭa*, 4:853–55.
77. *The Travels of Ibn Baṭṭūṭa*, 4:851.
78. A. G. Sūrasēna, *Paurāṇika Janapravāda Hā Janaśrāti* (Talavatugoḍa: Ḍī Sī Guṇasēkara, 2000), 30.
79. Lorna Dewaraja, *The Muslims of Sri Lanka: One Thousand Years of Ethnic Harmony, 900–1915* (Colombo: Lanka Islamic Foundation, 1994).
80. Ameer Ali, "Muslims in Harmony and Conflict in Plural Sri Lanka: A Historical Summary from a Religio-Economic and Political Perspective," *Journal of Muslim Minority Affairs* 34, no. 3 (2014): 227–42.
81. See also Alexander McKinley, "Merchants, Maidens, and Mohammedans: A History of Muslim Stereotypes in Sinhala Literature of Sri Lanka," *Journal of Asian Studies* 81 (2022): 523–40.
82. Rebecca R. Darley, "'Implicit Cosmopolitanism' and the Commercial Role of Ancient Lanka," in *Sri Lanka at the Crossroads of History*, ed. Zoltán Biedermann and Alan Strathern (London: UCL Press, 2017), 44–65.
83. Alexander Johnston, "A Letter to the Secretary Relating to the Preceding Inscription," *Transactions of the Royal Asiatic Society of Great Britain and Ireland* 1, no. 2 (1826): 537–48; J. C. van Sanden, *Sonahar: A Brief History of the Moors of Ceylon* (Colombo: Daily Mail Press, 1925), 117–18.
84. *Saman Sirita*, v. 142.
85. John F. Dickson, "Service Tenures Commission. Report of the Service Tenures Commissioner, for 1870," in *Ceylon: Indische Volksbelangen*, ed. A. W. P. Verkerk Pistorius (The Hague: Martinus Nijhoff, 1874), 206; Lorna Dewaraja, "The Muslims in the Kandyan Kingdom (c. 1600–1815): A Study of Ethnic Integration," in *Muslims of Sri Lanka: Avenues to Antiquity*, ed. M. A. M. Shukri (Beruwala: Jamiah Naleemia Institute, 1986), 219–20, 232n48.
86. E.g., Archibald Campbell Lawrie, *A Gazetteer of the Central Province of Ceylon* (Colombo: Government Press, 1896), 1:7.
87. Lawrie, *A Gazetteer of the Central Province*, 1:139, 1:217, 1:220–21, 1:223; Archibald Campbell Lawrie, *A Gazetteer of the Central Province of Ceylon* (Colombo: Government Press, 1898), 2:807.
88. Mecca appears in *Samanala Vistaraya* and the *Samanaḷa Hālla* tradition, which are difficult to date. Puñcibaṇḍāra Sannasgala places the latter in the "Kandyan period" (*mahavuvara kālayē*), rejecting the 1902 printed edition's claim that Vidāgama Maitreya wrote it in the fifteenth century. See Puñcibaṇḍāra Sannasgala, *Siṃhala Sāhitya Vaṃśaya* (Colombo: Lēkhavus Mudraṇālaya, 1964), 583; CNML 104/T14: Vīdāgama Mahānētra Prasādamūla Maitreya, *Purāṇa Samanala Hälla* (Colombo: Granthālokayantrālaya, 1902). No extant manuscripts of *Samanaḷa Hālla* predate the nineteenth century, but their large number, with varying lengths and verses, some shared, some unique, suggests our historical snapshot represents

a widespread cross-generational tradition, making a century or two prior a reasonable origin range. The earliest mention anywhere of the Buddha's visit to "Mecca" (*makkama*) may be *Śrī Laṃkādvīpayē Kaḍaim*, a boundary book for Gampola circa the fourteenth century. Of course, its extant manuscripts are also later copies with possible interpolations. H. A. P. Abeyawardana, *Boundary Divisions of Mediaeval Sri Lanka* (Polgasovita: Academy of Sri Lankan Culture, 1999), 37–42, 192.

89. CNML 85/D18: *Samanaḷa Väňdīma*, f. 9a. This manuscript composition, which, contrary to the catalogue title cited here, is named *Samangira Vändīma Kavi* on its wooden cover, is similar in style to *Samanaḷa Hālla* verse, but repeats the name Samangira instead of Samanala to anchor the final line that enjoins pilgrims to worship the sacred foot on the Peak.
90. *Samaṇaḷa Vistaraya* in V. D. Da Länarōl, *Goyam Kav Saha Neḷum Kav* (Colombo: M. D. Guṇasēna saha Samāgama, 1946), v. 1005. It matches v. 68 in CNML AL/14: *Samanala Vistaraya*, and v. 42 in CNML AJ/14: *Samanala Vistaraya*. These manuscript copies are also c. 1850s, but a seventeenth- or eighteenth-century origin for this work is likely.
91. *Purāṇa Himagata Varṇanāva*, v. 25.
92. Jason Neelis, *Early Buddhist Transmission and Trade Networks: Mobility and Exchange Within and Beyond the Northwestern Borderlands of South Asia* (Leiden: Brill, 2011), 106–8.
93. B. E. Perērā, *Śrī Pāda Lāñchana: Samantakūṭa Parvataya Hā Divā Guhāva* (Nugēgoḍa: Prasanta Mudraṇa, 1979), 55, 59.
94. CNML 104/C8: T. H. Udāris, *Śrīpāda Vandanāva Saha Gālu Kōralē Siṭa Yana Vandanākārayingē Gaman Vistaraya* (Ambalangoḍa: Vijaya Yantrālaya, 1923), v. 39. Cf. *Kälaṇi Hālla* [c. 18th century], v. 32, which reverses the right and left; in Dayāpāla Jayanetti, ed., *Vaňdanā Kavi Sāhityaya* (Colombo: Samayavardhana, 2005), 102.
95. *Abhinava Himagata Varṇanāva*, v. 122. The edition I used from UPL lacked a cover. The 1902 edition, with slight variations, is CNML 104/T14. See also Karuṇādāsa Rūpasiṃha, *Śrī Pāda Vandanā Sāhitya* (Colombo: Äs Goḍagē saha Sahōdarayō, 2013), 126.
96. E.g., Sūrasēna, *Paurāṇika Janapravāda Hā Janaśrāti*, 29.
97. *Purāṇa Himagata Varṇanāva*, v. 7; *Abhinava Himgata Varṇanāva*, v. 20.
98. Or.6615(378): *Vāhala Devol Vīdiya Kavi*, f. 7a, v. 2. Similar verses describing Devol's sighting of the Peak and subsequent Samanala settlement are also found in Or.6615(172): *Devel Devi Kavi* and Or.6615(399): *Maha Devel Vīdiya*. The Devol manuscripts and other deity palm leaves from the Hugh Nevill collection date to the nineteenth century. Like the Samanala songs discussed above, these copies likely reproduced a tradition dating at least a century earlier. Somadasa suggests the multidecked ships with glass windows in Devol poetry mean it originated in the late seventeenth or eighteenth century. See K. D. Somadasa, ed., *Catalogue of the Hugh Nevill Collection of Sinhalese Manuscripts in the British Library* (London: British Library, 1993), 6:340.
99. Gananath Obeyesekere, *The Cult of the Goddess Pattini* (Chicago: University of Chicago Press, 1984), 307.
100. Or.6615(236) and Or.6615(237).
101. See Nevill's full note for Or.6615(236) in P. E. P. Deraniyagala, ed., *Sinhala Verse (Kavi), Collected by the Late Hugh Nevill* (Colombo: Ceylon National Museums, 1954), 1:7. The Or.6615(237) manuscript also had Devol land at Bēruvala, a predominantly Muslim town on the southwest coast.
102. Or.6615(170): *Devel Kavi*, f. 8a, v. 1.
103. Or.6615(171): *Devel Kavi: Vāsala Devel Bāge Yāgaya*, f. 4a, v. 2.

104. Obeyesekere, *The Cult of the Goddess Pattini*, 307–8.
105. *Aravali Mantaraye Kavi*, in N. B. M. Seneviratna, ed., *Siṃhala Kāvya Saṃgrahaya: Mātara Yugaya* (Colombo: Laṃkā Jātika Kautukāgāra Prakāśana, 1964), 263.
106. Or.6615(299): *Huniyan Yak Yādinna*, Or.6615(340): *Kaḍavara Puvata*, Or.6615(360): *Vaḍiga Paṭuna.*
107. Or.6615(34): *Hata Aḍiya*, Or.6615(36): *Dos Harane*, Or.6615(390): *Kaḍavara Puvata*, Or.6615(458)II: *Dan Udiyāgē Kathāva*, Or.6615(475): *Kini Kaṇḍa Upata*, Or.6615(492): *Rīri Yak Kavi.* It is interesting to note that the author of *Rīri Yak Kavi*, Dingiri Baṇḍā, was from a prominent family of Aluthgama, a village beside Beruwala with a significant Muslim population.
108. CNML 22/C1: *Rīri Yak Kavi*, f. 2b. Also appears in CNML 22/I2, f. 2b. See also Nōman Siripāla, *Sabaragamu Janakaviyē Samāja Muhuṇuvara* (Nugēgoḍa: Piyasiri Prinṭin Sisṭams, 1999), 30.
109. Or.6615(83): *Ilandāri Deviyangē Kavi*, f. 12a, v. 1.
110. Or.6615(322): *Abuta Deviyange Kavi*; reprinted in Tissa Kāriyavasam, ed., *Siri Laka Devivaru: Hiyū Nevil Kāvyāvali Āśrayeni* (Colombo: S. Goḍagē saha Sahōdarayō, 1991), 1.
111. Or.6611(265): *Upulvan Asna.*
112. *Vannam saha Savudam Kavi*, in W. Ātar Da Silva and Guṇapāla Malalasēkara, eds., *Siṅhala Janasammata Kāvya* (Colombo: S. Goḍagē saha Sahōdarayō, 1935), v. 525.
113. Or.6615(340) and Or.6615(434); reprinted in Kāriyavasam, *Siri Laka Devivaru*, 30, 44.
114. *Bali Sanniya*, in Seneviratna, *Siṃhala Kāvya Saṃgrahaya: Mātara Yugaya*, 266.
115. Some *sanni* ceremonies Obeyesekere observed also insulted Muslims: Gananath Obeyesekere, "The Ritual Drama of the Sanni Demons: Collective Representations of Disease in Ceylon," *Comparative Studies in Society and History* 11, no. 2 (1969): 190.
116. Sūrasēna, *Paurāṇika Janapravāda Hā Janaśrāti*, 26–30. See also Śrīyāṇi Rājapakṣa, *Sabaragamu Kumāra Samayama* (Colombo: S. Goḍagē saha Sahōdarayō, 2000), 63.
117. Jonathan Spencer et al., *Checkpoint, Temple, Church and Mosque: A Collaborative Ethnography of War and Peace* (London: Pluto Press, 2015), 161.
118. Obeyesekere, *The Cult of the Goddess Pattini*, 146.
119. Dennis B. McGilvray, *Crucible of Conflict: Tamil and Muslim Society on the East Coast of Sri Lanka* (Durham, NC: Duke University Press, 2008), 75–77.
120. *Pāru Māle*, in Seneviratna, *Siṃhala Kāvya Saṃgrahaya: Mātara Yugaya*, 202.
121. *Demaḷa Vayinaḍaya*, in Da Länarōl, *Goyam Kav Saha Neḷum Kav*, p. 22, v. 155. See also *Siṃhala Demaḷa Valinaḍaya*, in P. B. G. Hēvāvasam, ed., *Pantis Kōlmura Kavi* (Colombo: Pradīpa Prakāśakayō, 1974), p. 341, v. 4. Obeysekere found the *Valinaḍaya* performance to be mostly moribund in the ritual tradition he studied: Obeyesekere, *The Cult of the Goddess Pattini*, 244.
122. Obeyesekere, *The Cult of the Goddess Pattini*, 337. Obeyesekere dates the origins of the *pataha* poetic tradition to the seventeenth century. The verse cited here from Da Länarōl is likely from a nineteenth-century manuscript.
123. *Pataha*, in Da Länarōl, *Goyam Kav Saha Neḷum Kav*, p. 46, v. 342. Also in Hēvāvasam, *Pantis Kōlmura Kavi*, p. 111, v. 113.
124. Lawrie, *A Gazetteer of the Central Province*, 1:332.
125. M. B. Mohamed Ghouse, "Folk Songs of the Moors," in *The First Twenty One Years: Moors' Islamic Cultural Home, 1944–1965* (Colombo: Moors' Islamic Cultural Home, 1965), 42. I have retranslated the verse.
126. H. C. P. Bell, "Sinhalese Customs and Ceremonies Connected with Paddy Cultivation in the Low-Country," *Journal of the Ceylon Branch of the Royal Asiatic Society* 8, no. 26 (1883): 50.
127. Bell, "Sinhalese Customs and Ceremonies Connected with Paddy," 52.

128. J. P. Lewis, "The Language of the Threshing-Floor," *Journal of the Ceylon Branch of the Royal Asiatic Society* 8, no. 29 (1884): 268.
129. Likewise, see Torsten Tschacher, "Can 'Om' Be an Islamic Term? Translations, Encounters, and Islamic Discourse in Vernacular South Asia," *South Asian History and Culture* 5, no. 2 (2014): 195–211.
130. T. S. Dharmabandhu, ed., *Jana Kav Dahasa: Patē, Potē, Hā Gamē—Goḍa Pavatnā Jana Kav* (Colombo: M. D. Guṇasēna saha Samāgama, 1956), v. 520.
131. *Rājāvaliya*, 2–4.
132. Or.6611(104): *Patasa.*
133. Dickson, "Service Tenures Commission," 185.
134. Lawrie, *A Gazetteer of the Central Province*, 1:223.
135. Qadri Ismail, "Unmooring Identity: The Antinomies of Elite Muslim Representation in Modern Sri Lanka," in *Unmaking the Nation: The Politics of Identity and History in Modern Sri Lanka*, ed. Pradeep Jeganathan (New York: SSA Sri Lanka, 2009), 62–107.
136. SLNA 45/336: Ratnapura government agent diary, July 8–9, 1915.
137. Ameer Ali, "The 1915 Racial Riots in Ceylon (Sri Lanka): A Reappraisal of Its Causes," *South Asia* 4, no. 2 (1981): 1–20; George Rowell, "Ceylon's Kristallnacht: A Reassessment of the Pogrom of 1915," *Modern Asian Studies* 43, no. 3 (2009): 619–48; McKinley, "Merchants, Maidens, and Mohammedans."
138. Ronit Ricci, *Banishment and Belonging: Exile and Diaspora in Sarandib, Lanka and Ceylon* (Cambridge: Cambridge University Press, 2019).
139. Tayka Shu'ayb 'Ālim, *Arabic, Arwi and Persian in Sarandib and Tamil Nadu* (Chennai: Imāmul 'Arūs Trust, 1993), 8–9, 643.
140. Aptuṟ Ṟahīm, *Muslim Tamiḻp Pulavarkaḷ* (Chennai: Yuṉivarsal Paplişars aṇṭ Puk Cellars, 1980), 9.
141. Sumathi Ramaswamy, *The Lost Land of Lemuria: Fabulous Geographies, Catastrophic Histories* (Berkeley: University of California Press, 2004).
142. Torsten Tschacher, "Drowning in the Ocean of Tamil: Islamic Texts and the Historiography of Tamil Literature," in *Literature and Nationalist Ideology: Writing Histories of Modern Indian Languages*, ed. Hans Harder (New Delhi: Social Science Press, 2011), 59–60. As Ḥāfiẓ M. K. Sayyid Ahmad claims, "Adam spoke Tamil." 'Ālim, *Arabic, Arwi and Persian in Sarandib and Tamil Nadu*, 775.
143. Arthur C. Dep, *The Egyptian Exiles in Ceylon (Sri Lanka)* (Colombo: Praveena Press, 2011).
144. John Chinaman, "Colombo, Ceylon: The Pearl Drop on the Brow of India—Land of Beauty and Spicy Fragrance," *Baltimore Sun*, March 16, 1887, 5.
145. Moncure Daniel Conway, *My Pilgrimage to the Wise Men of the East* (Boston: Houghton, Mifflin, 1906), 162–66.
146. CNML 104/FF14: *Arābihaṭana Hevat Siṅhala Kaviyen Racanā Karaṇalada Misaradeśika Yuddhaya* (Lakmiṇipagaṇ Yantrālaya, 1883), vv. 59–61.
147. I. L. M. Abdul Azeez, *A Criticism of Mr. Ramanathan's "Ethnology of the 'Moors' of Ceylon"* (Colombo: Moors' Islamic Cultural Home, 1957), 11.
148. M. M. Thawfeeq, *Muslim Mosaics* (Colombo: Moors' Islamic Cultural Home, 1972), 110. A newspaper version of this story is laminated and hangs in the main foyer at the Dewatagaha *masjid*. It was also repeated to me by an elderly mosque trustee in 2016.
149. For other famous Muslims who visited the Peak in the nineteenth century, see M. M. Thawfeeq, "Muslim Saints and Shrines in Sri Lanka," in *The First Twenty One Years: Moors' Islamic*

Cultural Home, 1944–1965 (Colombo: Moors' Islamic Cultural Home, 1965), 40; Thawfeeq, *Muslim Mosaics*, 125.

150. R. Vasundhara Mohan, *Identity Crisis of Sri Lankan Muslims* (Delhi: Mittal Publications, 1987), 72–75; Dennis B. McGilvray, "Sri Lankan Muslims: Between Ethno-Nationalism and the Global *Ummah*," *Nations and Nationalism* 17, no. 1 (2011): 45–64; Zarin Ahmad, "Contours of Muslim Nationalism in Sri Lanka," *South Asian History and Culture* 3, no. 2 (2012): 269–87.
151. Satarupa Bhattachariya, Chris Kamalendran, and Asif Fuard, "The Divided Brotherhood: Jihad in Lanka: Sectarianism Takes Root as Muslim Groups Battle It Out in Beruwala," *Sunday Times*, August 2, 2009. See also Ameer Ali, "Kattankudy in Eastern Sri Lanka: A Mullah-Merchant Urban Complex Caught Between Islamist Factionalism and Ethno-Nationalisms," *Journal of Minority Muslim Affairs* 29, no. 2 (2009): 184–94; Spencer et al., *Checkpoint, Temple, Church and Mosque*.
152. Farzana Haniffa, "Piety as Politics Amongst Muslim Women in Contemporary Sri Lanka," *Modern Asian Studies* 42, no. 2/3 (2008): 347–75.
153. Ameer Ali, "Political Buddhism, Islamic Orthodoxy and Open Economy: The Toxic Triad in Sinhalese-Muslim Relations in Sri Lanka," *Journal of Asian and African Studies* 49, no. 3 (2014): 298–314.
154. E.g., John Still, *The Jungle Tide*, 3rd ed. (Edinburgh: W. Blackwood and Sons, 1930), 23.
155. Imtiyaz Yusuf, "Muslim-Buddhist Relations Caught Between Nalanda and Pattani," in *Ethnic Conflict in Buddhist Societies in South and Southeast Asia*, ed. K. M. de Silva (Colombo: International Centre for Ethnic Studies, 2015), 157–93; Kalinga Tudor Silva, "Gossip, Rumor, and Propaganda in Anti-Muslim Campaigns of the Bodu Bala Sena," in *Buddhist Extremists and Muslim Minorities: Religious Conflict in Contemporary Sri Lanka*, ed. John Clifford Holt (New York: Oxford University Press, 2016), 119–39.
156. R. Spence Hardy, *A Manual of Budhism, in Its Modern Development; Translated from Singhalese Mss* (London: Partridge and Oakey, 1853), 212. Jonathan Forbes observed in 1827 that at "a clear space of ground at the base of the [Peak] cone. . . . we saw the grave of a Mohammedan saint who probably considered himself fortunate in closing his pilgrimage, and resting in peace, so near the place at which the father of mankind . . . had been obliged to stand." Jonathan Forbes, *Eleven Years in Ceylon. Comprising Sketches of the Field Sports and Natural History of That Colony, and an Account of Its History and Antiquities* (London: R. Bentley, 1840), 1:174. No graves remain to be seen.
157. Maṇippulavar Marutūr Ē. Majīt, *Mattiya Kiḻakkil Iruntu Maṭṭakkaḷappu Varai* (Kalmunai: Marutūr Veḷiyīṭṭup Paṇimaṉai, 1995), 29.
158. Premakumara De Silva, "Reordering of Postcolonial Sri Pāda Temple in Sri Lanka: Buddhism, State, and Nationalism," *History and Sociology of South Asia* 7, no. 155 (2013): 155–76.
159. Victor C. de Munck, "Sufi and Reformist Designs: Muslim Identity in Sri Lanka," in *Buddhist Fundamentalism and Minority Identities in Sri Lanka*, ed. Tessa J. Bartholomeusz and Chandra Richard De Silva (Albany: State University of New York Press, 1998), 121.
160. Guṇasēkara Guṇasōma, *Samandevi Aḍaviya Janakatā* (Colombo: Fāsṭ Pabliṣin, 2013), 28–30.
161. McKinley, "Merchants, Maidens, and Mohammedans."
162. Mupisāl Apūpakkar, "Āyuḷil Oru Muṟaiyāvatu Ātam Malaikku Celvōm," *Asian News*, March 15, 2021.
163. Majīt, *Mattiya Kiḻakkil Iruntu Maṭṭakkaḷappu Varai*, 28–34; M. M. M. Nūṟulhak, *Ciṟupāṉmaiyiṉar Cila Avatāṉaṅkaḷ* (Sainthamaruthu: Marutam Kalai Ilakkiya Vaṭṭam, 2002), 46–48.
164. Ivaṉ Cañcāri, "Marakatattīvīl Ulakiṉ Mutaṟcuvaṭu," *Cilōṉ Muslim*, February 5, 2016, 6.

165. Although this piece of ephemera is undated, I would estimate a range around 1960–1970. It must predate 1983, when it entered the collection of the Nationaal Museum van Wereldculturen. The bottom of the poster reads "Maskeliya (Ceylon)," which suggests it also precedes the country's name change to Sri Lanka in 1972.
166. Thanks to Hunter Bandy for explaining the Arabic to me.
167. E.g., Ulrich Marzolph, "From Mecca to Mashhad: The Narrative of an Illustrated Shi'i Pilgrimage Scroll from the Qajar Period," *Muqarnas* 31 (2014): 207–42.
168. The Nationaal Museum van Wereldculturen holds one such example; see inventory number RV-5224-0-7: https://hdl.handle.net/20.500.11840/840174.
169. Latheef Farook, *Nobody's People: The Forgotten Plight of Sri Lanka's Muslims* (Colombo: South Asia News Agency, 2009), 340, 370–80; Luke Alexander Heslop, "On Sacred Ground: The Political Performance of Religious Responsibility," *Contemporary South Asia* 22, no. 1 (2014): 21–36; Philip Friedrich, "Adjudicating Antiquity: The Politics of Historical Confrontation at Devanagala, Sri Lanka," in *Buddhist Extremists and Muslim Minorities: Religious Conflict in Contemporary Sri Lanka*, ed. John Clifford Holt (New York: Oxford University Press, 2016), 140–63; Alexander McKinley and Merin Shobhana Xavier, "The Deconstruction of Dafther Jailani: Muslim and Buddhist Contests of Original History in Sri Lanka," *History of Religions* 62, no. 3 (2023): 254–83.
170. Glenn Bowman, "Grounds for Sharing—Occasions for Conflict: An Inquiry Into the Social Foundations of Cohabitation and Antagonism," in *Post-Ottoman Coexistence: Sharing Space in the Shadow of Conflict*, ed. Rebecca Bryant (Oxford: Berghahn, 2016), 258.
171. Aksland, *The Sacred Footprint*, 107–8. Much of this is circulated through Facebook. One Muslim site archived a television appearance by a monk claiming the Arabs stole Mecca: https://www.facebook.com/video.php?v=551834401526034&fref=nf. Meanwhile, Sinhala nationalist Facebook pages like "Siṃha Haňḍa" (The Lion's Roar) have posted propaganda images of Abraham's Meccan footprints with text claiming they belong to Buddha. News blogs from far-right Sinhala nationalists claim the same; see Shripal Nishshanka Fernando, "Qabbah and Buddhas Foot Print," posted on *Lankaweb*, February 13, 2012, http://www.lankaweb.com/news/items/2012/02/13/qabbah-buddhas-foot-print/.
172. Justin W. Henry, *Ravana's Kingdom: The Ramayana and Sri Lankan History from Below* (New York: Oxford University Press, 2022).
173. Jōn Da Silvā, *Śrīpāda Śatakaya* (Colombo, 1912), v. 44.
174. J. Da Silvā, *Śrīpāda Śatakaya*, vv. 14–15. See chapter 4 for more on this poem. Da Silva may have posited Noah's sons as Ravana's progeny to endorse the idea that a large portion of Ravana's Lankan kingdom was lost in a flood. Henry, *Ravana's Kingdom*, 38–39. In an opposite mythic maneuver, the Malay text *Hikayat Seri Rama* uses the character of Ravana to reaffirm the presence of Adam in Lanka and his footprint atop the Peak. Ricci, *Banishment and Belonging*, 160–63.
175. As quoted in Jayaratna Patiraāracci, "Ṭolamiṭa Anuva Makkama Kalā Oya Muhudu Sīmāvayi!," *Budusaraṇa*, July 10, 2008. See also Mänävē Vimalaratna, "Rāvaṇā Parapurē Säňgavuṇa Toraturu," *Divayina*, July 22, 2009. In this article, Vimalaratna also interprets *yonaka* as the Jaffna peninsula.
176. W. F. Gunavarḍana, ed., *Kokila Sandeśaya* (Colombo: Peramuna, 1945), v. 202.
177. Sucarita Gamlat and A. Adikāri, eds., *Mūlika Piriven Pot: Siṃhala Hōḍiya, Nampota, Maňgul Lakuṇa, Gaṇadevi Hälla, Vadan Kavi Pota, Buddhagadyaya, Sakaskaḍa* (Colombo: Äs Godagē saha Sahōrdarayō, 1988), 31.

178. Jayaratna Patiraāracci, *Dakuṇu Budu Siripatula Pihiṭi Makkama Saha Rāvaṇa Rajugē Sellipi* (Boralesgamuwa: Udaya Grāfiks, 2005), 14: "mema pradēśayē jivat vana kisiweku mema pradēśayē makkamak gäna asā näta. e kisiweku itihāsaya hadārā nomäti bävini."
179. Gananath Obeyesekere, "Religious Symbolism and Political Change in Ceylon," in *The Two Wheels of Dhamma: Essays on the Theravada Tradition in India and Ceylon*, ed. Gananath Obeyesekere, Frank Reynolds, and Bardwell L. Smith (Chambersburg, PA: American Academy of Religion, 1972), 65; emphasis in original.
180. Patiraāracci, "Ṭolamiṭa Anuva Makkama Kalā Oya Muhudu Sīmāvayi!"
181. Seneviratna, *Siṃhala Kāvya Saṃgrahaya: Mātara Yugaya*, 193.
182. J. A. Sumanapāla Samarasēkara, *Tovil: Devol Maḍuva Hā Aṭasanniya Piḷibaňda Samāja Vidyātmaka Vigrahayak* (Colombo: Guṇasēna, 1995), 80–81.
183. Henry, *Ravana's Kingdom*, 152.
184. E.g., Jayaratna Patiraāracci, "Jana Kaviyā Duṭu Vam Siripādaya Saha Dakuṇu Siripādaya," *Budusaraṇa*, January 22, 2008.
185. Recorded and posted on Facebook on October 29, 2013: https://www.facebook.com/video.php?v=599697530093928&set=vb.125347604146957&type=3&permPage=1.
186. A wealth of videos from these events can be found on the SLTJ Facebook page: https://www.facebook.com/sltjsinhala.
187. Patiraāracci, *Dakuṇu Budu Siripatula Pihiṭi Makkama*, 40, 45n31. Ravana historiography has already helped dismantle buildings at Dafther Jailani: McKinley and Xavier, "The Deconstruction of Dafther Jailani"; Henry, *Ravana's Kingdom*, 131–34. See also Samanth Subramanian, *This Divided Island: Stories from the Sri Lankan War* (Haryana: Penguin India, 2014), 222–31.
188. David Scott, "Dehistoricizing History," in *Unmaking the Nation: The Politics of Identity and History in Modern Sri Lanka*, ed. Pradeep Jeganathan and Qadri Ismail (New York: SSA Sri Lanka, 2009), 20–33.
189. Schaefer, *Religious Affects*.
190. In Mullapiṭiyē K. H. Da Silva and Abhayasiṃha Vijayaśrīvardhana, *Siṃhala Sähäli*, ed. Vibhavi Vijayasrīvardhana, 2nd ed. (Colombo: Äs Goḍagē saha Sahōdarayō, 2009), 170.
191. E.g., Bhikkhu Bodhi, *The Suttanipāta: An Ancient Collection of the Buddha's Discourses Together with Its Commentaries* (Somerville, MA: Wisdom, 2017), 289.

4. Admitting and Forbidding Siva at the Peak

1. C. S. Navaratnam, *A Short History of Hinduism in Ceylon and Three Essays on the Tamils* (Jaffna: Sri Sanmuganatha Press, 1964), 64.
2. CNML 104/Z2: M. S. Pranāndu, *Samanala Hasuna* (Panadura: M. Jēsan Pranāndu, 1932), v. 34.
3. On a return visit to the Peak in July 2023, however, I observed a much larger *kōvil* built right at the trailhead and dedicated in August 2022, at a spot that had previously only contained a small statue of Ganesh. It had since been expanded into a full Ganesh shrine, including stone images of Ganesh, a Siva lingam, and Siva's bull Nandi, as well as wall paintings of Siva and Parvati. It was constructed with money from the Tamil Hindus living in Nallathanni, indicating how income generated by the pilgrimage industry may increase the potential for Hindu representation, at least on the lower stretches of the trail.

4. As reported in the book by the CSD lieutenant met in chapter 2: R. Aśōka A. Dharmasēna, *Uttama Muṇi Siripā* (n.d.), 24.
5. Most details Buddhists mentioned were not actually in the *Mahāvaṃsa*, but later texts like *Pūjāvaliya*. Another version of the Saiva story was recorded from a Hindu priest in Colombo in 2002, but it, too, was only a few sentences: Premakumara De Silva, "Reordering of Postcolonial Sri Pāda Temple in Sri Lanka: Buddhism, State, and Nationalism," *History and Sociology of South Asia* 7, no. 155 (2013): 159.
6. E. Valentine Daniel, *Charred Lullabies: Chapters in an Anthropography of Violence* (Princeton, NJ: Princeton University Press, 1996).
7. Anand Vivek Taneja, *Jinnealogy: Time, Islam, and Ecological Thought in the Medieval Ruins of Delhi* (Stanford, CA: Stanford University Press, 2018), 63.
8. This is comparable to the relative everyday importance of Bhairav versus Shiva in the Kedarnath region of the Himalayas, although Kedarnath still has many stories of Shiva. It is also notable that Shiva's presence there is expressed most directly through the mountain rather than any shrine or image. See Luke Whitmore, *Mountain, Water, Rock, God: Understanding Kedarnath in the Twenty-First Century* (Oakland: University of California Press, 2018), chap. 2.
9. Sasikumar Balasundaram, "An Indentured Tamil Goddess: Mariyamman's Migration to Ceylon's Plantations as a Worker," in *Inventing and Reinventing the Goddess: Contemporary Iterations of Hindu Deities on the Move*, ed. Sree Padma (London: Lexington Books, 2014), 103–19; Sasikumar Balasundaram, "Temples and Deities on Plantations," in *Multi-Religiosity in Contemporary Sri Lanka: Innovation, Shared Spaces, Contestation*, ed. Mark P. Whitaker, Darini Rajasingham-Senanayake, and Pathmanesan Sanmugeswaran (New York: Routledge, 2022), 179–91; Daniel Bass, "The Goddess of the Tea Estates: Hindu Traditions and Community Boundaries in the Up-Country of Sri Lanka," *South Asianist* 6 (2018): 23–45.
10. Premakumara De Silva, "Competitive Sharing: Sri Lankan Hindus and Up-Country Tamil Religiosity at the Sri Pada Temple," *South Asianist* 6 (2018): 76–97.
11. Bruce Lincoln, *Theorizing Myth: Narrative, Ideology, and Scholarship* (Chicago: University of Chicago Press, 1999), 208.
12. Lévi-Strauss realized this, openly acknowledging "this book on myth is itself a kind of myth . . . the myth of mythology." Claude Lévi-Strauss, *The Raw and the Cooked: Introduction to a Science of Mythology*, vol. 1, trans. John Weightman and Doreen Weightman (New York: Harper and Row, 1970), 6, 12.
13. Premakumara De Silva, "Religion, History and Colonial Powers: Colonial Knowledge Production on a Popular Sacred Site in Sri Lanka," *Journal of History and Social Sciences* 5, no. 1 (2014): 21–34.
14. William Skeen, *Adam's Peak: Legendary Traditional, and Historic Notices of the Samanala and Srí-Páda with a Descriptive Account of the Pilgrims' Route from Colombo to the Sacred Foot-Print* (Colombo: W. L. H. Skeen, 1870), 35–37.
15. Skeen, *Adam's Peak*, 295.
16. Senarat Paranavitana, *The God of Adam's Peak* (Ascona: Artibus Asiae Publishers, 1958), 21.
17. L. D. Barnett and G. U. Pope, eds., *A Catalogue of Tamil Books in the Library of the British Museum* (London: British Museum, 1909), 261; L. D. Barnett, ed., *A Supplementary Catalogue of the Tamil Books in the Library of the British Museum* (London: British Museum, 1931), 289–90.
18. Paranavitana, *The God of Adam's Peak*, 21.
19. K. N. Sivaraja Pillai, *Agastya in the Tamil Land* (Mylapore: University of Madras, 1930), 2.

20. *Maṇimēkalai, patikam*, lines 11–14. I translate from Cīttalaiccāttaṉār, *Maṇimēkalai*, ed. K. Kalyanasundaram and M. Sivakumar (Project Madurai, 2002).
21. Paranavitana, *The God of Adam's Peak*, 19. The other drama with a similar passage cited by Paranavitana is Rājaśekhara's *Bālarāmāyaṇa*.
22. Paranavitana, *The God of Adam's Peak*, 71.
23. J. R. Sinnatamby, *Ceylon in Ptolemy's Geography* (Colombo: Times of Ceylon, 1968), 70–71.
24. Connecting Tamil to the Greek classics was also a common maneuver in linguistic politics of Tamil Nadu; see Sumathi Ramaswamy, *Passions of the Tongue: Language Devotion in Tamil India, 1891–1970* (Berkeley: University of California Press, 1997).
25. Sinnatamby was not the first to invoke Ptolemy as a proof of "the ancientness of the Tamil language and literature"; see Sumathi Ramaswamy, *The Lost Land of Lemuria: Fabulous Geographies, Catastrophic Histories* (Berkeley: University of California Press, 2004), 118–19.
26. Paranavitana, *The God of Adam's Peak*, 21. His main thesis is that Saman evolved out of the god Yama. It is a highly speculative argument, but it shows Paranavitana's general willingness to admit any other god to the Peak except Siva.
27. Anne E. Monius, *Imagining a Place for Buddhism: Literary Culture and Religious Community in Tamil-Speaking South India*, South Asian ed. (New Delhi: Navayana, 2009), 100–15.
28. *Maṇimēkalai*, canto 11, lines 21–28.
29. Paula Richman, *Women, Branch Stories, and Religious Rhetoric in a Tamil Buddhist Text* (Syracuse, NY: Maxwell School of Citizenship and Public Affairs, Syracuse University, 1988), 200n10.
30. *Maṇimēkalai*, canto 28, lines 107–12, 119–20.
31. E.g., R. A. L. H. Gunawardana, *Robe and Plough: Monasticism and Economic Interest in Early Medieval Sri Lanka* (Tucson: University of Arizona Press, 1979), 233.
32. Max Walleser and Herman Kopp, eds., *Manorathapūraṇī: Buddhaghosa's Commentary on the Aṅguttara-Nikāya*, vol. 2, 2nd ed. (London: Pali Text Society, 1967), III.IV.6, p. 230. Further evidence for the Peak as a first-millennium pilgrimage site comes from the early eighth-century visit of the South Indian monk Vajrabodhi as recorded in his Chinese biography: Jeffrey Sundberg and Rolf Giebel, "The Life of the Tang Court Monk Vajrabodhi as Chronicled by Lü Xiang: South Indian and Śrī Laṅkān Antecedents to the Arrival of the Buddhist Vajrayāna in Eight-Century Java and China," *Pacific World* Third Series, no. 13 (Fall 2011): 129–222.
33. Indira Viswanathan Peterson, *Poems to Śiva: The Hymns of the Tamil Saints* (Princeton, NJ: Princeton University Press, 1989), 205–6. See pp. 222–23 for footprint-poem examples. In general, feet are the focus of worship for almost all Hindu and Buddhist deities.
34. For an example of a poem using all three terms, see Appar, *Tēvāram* 4:96, vv. 3, 9, in *Tēvāram: 2. Appar Et Cuntarar*, ed. T. V. Gopal Iyer (Pondicherry: Institut Français d'Indologie, 1985).
35. Kalāpūcaṇam Cāralnāṭaṉ, *Cintaiyaḷḷum Civaṉoḷipātamalai* (Kotagala: Cāral Veḷiyīṭṭakam, 2009), 12, 47. Hindu pilgrims from other quarters of India may have been more common, too. In 1792, Jonathan Duncan interviewed "two *Fakeers*" in Benares, one of whom had traveled to Lanka to visit Kataragama and "went on to visit the *Sreepud*, or, 'The Divine Foot' situated upon a mountain of extraordinary height." See Jonathan Duncan, "An Account of Two Fakeers, with Their Portraits," *Asiatic Researches* 5 (1799): 39. Likewise, in 1816, the Colombo Magistrate interviewed a "Brahmin Beggar" from Benares who spoke neither Tamil nor Sinhala, but came to Lanka to visit Kataragama and the Peak. See Sujit Sivasundaram, *Islanded: Britain, Sri Lanka, and the Bounds of an Indian Ocean Colony* (Chicago: University of Chicago Press, 2013), 52.

36. V. C. Kantaiyā, ed., *Kaṇṇaki Vaḻakkurai* (Batticaloa: Kāraitīvu Intucamaya Virutti Caṅkam, 1968), 2:164.
37. Vittuvāṉ F. X. C. Naṭarācā, *Īḻattut Tamiḻ Nūl Vāl̲āṟu* (Colombo: Aracu Veḷiyīṭu, 1970), 91–100; Justin W. Henry, "Distant Shores of Dharma: Historical Imagination in Sri Lanka from the Late Medieval Period" (PhD diss., University of Chicago, 2017), 90–95.
38. Makā Vittuvāṉ Ciṅkai Cekarācacēkaraṉ, *Takṣiṇakailāca Purāṇam*, ed. K. C. Naṭarācā (Colombo: Intucamaya Kalāccāra Aluvarkaḷ Tiṇaikkaḷam, 1995), 6:161–62. See also Alexander McKinley, "Making Lanka the Tamil Way: A Temple History at the Crossroads of Landscapes and Watersheds," *South Asian History and Culture* 11, no. 3 (2020): 254–76.
39. Cekarācacēkaraṉ, *Takṣiṇakailāca Purāṇam*, 2:79.
40. Henry, "Distant Shores of Dharma," §3.4.
41. A. Vellupillai, "Historical Evaluation of Kōnēcar Kalveṭṭu," in *Perspectives in Archaeology: Leelananda Prematilleke Festschrift*, ed. Sudharshan Seneviratne (Peradeniya: University of Peradeniya, Department of Archaeology, 1990), 96. S. Pathmanathan, "The Portuguese in Northeast Sri Lanka (1543–1658): An Assessment of Impressions Recorded in Tamil Chronicles and Poems," in *Re-Exploring the Links: History and Constructed Histories Between Portugal and Sri Lanka*, ed. Jorge Flores (Wiesbaden: Harrassowitz Verlag, 2007), 43.
42. Agastya's southern exile is also a common tale in Indian *tala purāṇam*: David Shulman, *Tamil Temple Myths: Sacrifice and Divine Marriage in the South Indian Saiva Tradition* (Princeton, NJ: Princeton University Press, 1980), 142–43.
43. Kavirājāvarōtayaṉ, *Kōṇēcar Kalveṭṭu*, ed. I. Vaṭivēl (Colombo: Intucamaya, Kalācāra Aluvalkaḷ Tiṇaikkaḷam, 1993), 122–23.
44. Sanmugam Arumugam, *Hundred Hindu Temples of Sri Lanka: Ancient, Medieval and Modern*, ed. Thirumugam Arumugam (London: Ohm Books, 2014), 87–88.
45. A. Kumāracuvāmi, ed., *Tirukkaraicaippurāṇam* (Trincomalee: A. Alakakūn, 1952), "Kaṅkai carukkam," v. 31.
46. Kumāracuvāmi, *Tirukkaraicaippurāṇam*, "Kaṅkai carukkam," v. 36.
47. Kumāracuvāmi, *Tirukkaraicaippurāṇam*, "Kaṅkai carukkam," v. 37.
48. Kumāracuvāmi, *Tirukkaraicaippurāṇam*, "Kaṅkai carukkam," v. 38.
49. Kumāracuvāmi, *Tirukkaraicaippurāṇam*, "Kaṅkai carukkam," v. 39. Another work about this temple, labeled "Tirukkaracai antāti," has been digitized through the British Library's Endangered Archives Program (EAP 1260/31/7). Although deterioration of the palm leaves prevents a full reconstruction of the text, the Peak appears as "Mount Samanai" (Camaṉai Kiri) in a section about the Mahaweli River. See image 18: https://eap.bl.uk/archive-file/EAP1260-31-7.
50. K. C. Naṭarācā, ed., *Tirikoṇācala Purāṇam* (Colombo: Intucamaya Kalācāra Aluvalkar Tiṇaikkaḷam, 1997), 1:4.
51. Naṭarācā, *Tirikoṇācala Purāṇam*, 1:5.
52. Naṭarācā, *Tirikoṇācala Purāṇam*, 1:6.
53. Naṭarācā, *Tirikoṇācala Purāṇam*, 7:15.
54. Naṭarācā, *Tirikoṇācala Purāṇam*, 7:13, 7:19.
55. Naṭarācā, *Tirikoṇācala Purāṇam*, 7:11.
56. Kumāracuvāmi, *Tirukkaraicaippurāṇam*, 27.
57. Vē Akilēcapiḷḷai, *Tirukkōṇācala Vaipavam* (Colombo: Tattuva Ñāṉat Tavaccālaip Piracuram, 2000), 9–14. Akilēcapiḷḷai also referred to the Peak as Civajōtipātam in the first sentence of his book, which included it in a list of important Śaiva sites around Lanka.

58. C. Nākaliṅkapiḷḷai, ed., *Takṣiṇa Kailāca Purāṇam* (Jaffna: N. Kumāracuvāmi, 1928), 3. As Nākaliṅkapiḷḷai's title demonstrates, *Taṭcaṇakayilāca Māṉmiyam* is sometimes conflated with *Takṣiṇakailāca Purāṇam*, but they are in fact different texts. Nākaliṅkapiḷḷai obtained the first of his manuscripts in 1906, from a Brahma Sri N. Kumāracuvāmi Guru in Colombo, and the second from a Kirimalai Srimat K. Capāpatin Guru in Jaffna. Considering its content and manuscript history, I would estimate *Taṭcaṇakayilāca Māṉmiyam* was written at some point between 1750 and 1850.
59. Ludo Rocher, *The Purāṇas* (Wiesbaden: Otto Harrassowitz, 1986), 228–29.
60. *The Skanda Purāṇa*, 20 vols. (Delhi: Motilal Banarsidass, 1950–2003), 11:202, v. 159.
61. Nākaliṅkapiḷḷai, *Takṣiṇa Kailāca Purāṇam*, 30–31.
62. Nākaliṅkapiḷḷai, *Takṣiṇa Kailāca Purāṇam*, 97–98.
63. K. Cōmacuntarappulavar, "Īḻakēcari Āṇṭumaṭal Pāṭṭu: Vāyuṟavāḻtti Matiyuraittatu," *Īḻakēcari* 1935, 1.
64. Nākaliṅkapiḷḷai, *Takṣiṇa Kailāca Purāṇam*, 32.
65. Cāralnāṭaṉ, *Cintaiyaḷḷum Civaṉoḷipātamalai*. In his list of the many names of the Peak on p. 62, Camaṉai is absent.
66. CNML 104/C8: Attuḍāvē Hārmanis Jayasēkara, *Siripadahälla* (Alutgama: Saddharmaprakāśa Yantrālaya, 1924), v. 8.
67. *Samantakūṭavaṇṇanā*, v. 741. Hindu mythology is also present elsewhere in Vedeha's poem, as when he describes the connection between the Buddha's mother and father as "like the Himalayas to Siva," or more literally like "the royal mountain" (*girirājā*) to the "the skull-bearer" (*kapālito*). The Himalayas likely represent Parvati, born of the mountains. The phrase "like Sītā to Rāmarāja" is also used to express this deep love (vv. 25–26).
68. D. G. Abhayaguṇaratna, ed., *Pärakumbā Sirita* (Colombo: Ratna Pot Prakāśakayō, 2004), v. 116.
69. R. A. Liyanaāracci, ed., *Alagiyavanna Mukaveṭi Tumāgē Sävul Saṅdēśaya: Sarala Siṅhala Artha Vigrahayen Saha Anvayen Yutu Nava Saṅskaraṇaya* (Colombo: Samayavardhana Pothala Samāgama, 2009), v. 12.
70. Stephen C. Berkwitz, "Sinhala *Sandēśa* Poetry in a Cosmopolitan Context," in *Sri Lanka at the Crossroads of History*, ed. Zoltán Biedermann and Alan Strathern (London: UCL Press, 2017), 105.
71. Liyanaāracci, *Sävul Saṅdēśaya*, vv. 46, 51, 54, 57.
72. Liyanaāracci, *Sävul Saṅdēśaya*, vv. 152–53.
73. CNML 82/V19: *Gaṅga Vistarya Kavi*, ff. 1a, 2a. The original manuscript is Or.6611(17).
74. From *Dolaha Deviyangē Kavi*, in N. B. M. Seneviratna, ed., *Siṃhala Kāvya Saṃgrahaya: Mātara Yugaya* (Colombo: Laṃkā Jātika Kautukāgāra Prakāśana, 1964), 228. See also Gedara Pinhāmi, *Dolahadeviyangē Kavipota Saha Dalumura Upata* (Mahanuvara: T. M. Migel Appu, 1900), vv. 127, 129.
75. H. U. Pragnaloka, ed., *Purāṇa Sivpada Saṃgrahava* (Colombo: Government Publications, 1952), 73.
76. Or.6615(378): *Vāhala Devol Vīdiya Kavi*, f. 12b, v. 4.
77. Eliza E. Kent, *Sacred Groves and Local Gods: Religion and Environmentalism in South India* (Oxford: Oxford University Press, 2013), 34–37.
78. Or.6615(235): *Vīramuṇḍa Alaṅkāraya*, reprinted in Tissa Kāriyavasam, ed., *Siri Laka Devivaru: Hiyū Nevil Kāvyāvali Āśrayeni* (Colombo: S. Goḍagē saha Sahōdarayō, 1991), 195.
79. Benjamin Schonthal, "The Tolerations of Theravada Buddhism," in *Toleration in Comparative Perspective*, ed. Vicki A. Spencer (Lanham, MD: Lexington Books, 2018), 189.

80. *Saman Sirita*, v. 98.
81. Seneviratna, *Siṃhala Kāvya Saṃgrahaya: Mātara Yugaya*, 207.
82. Garrett Field, *Modernizing Composition: Sinhala Song, Poetry, and Politics in Twentieth-Century Sri Lanka* (Oakland: University of California Press, 2017), 23–25.
83. Jōn Da Silvā, *Śrīpāda Śatakaya* (Colombo, 1912), v. 3.
84. J. Da Silvā, *Śrīpāda Śatakaya*, v. 12.
85. J. Da Silvā, *Śrīpāda Śatakaya*, v. 16.
86. J. Da Silvā, *Śrīpāda Śatakaya*, v. 22.
87. J. Da Silvā, *Śrīpāda Śatakaya*, v. 24. It is not clear to me what Da Silvā is referencing, but there is a Telugu work named *Sri Parvata*.
88. Āriyaratna Sunil, ed., *Jōn Da Silvā Nurti Nāṭya Ekatuva* (Colombo: S. Goḍagē saha Sahōdarayō, 2008), 3:117.
89. H. C. P. Bell, *Report on the Kuṭṭāpiṭiya Sannasa* (Kandy: Miller, 1925), 11. Bell's translation slightly modified by me throughout. This *sannasa* was earlier translated by C. Alwis, appearing in Skeen, *Adam's Peak*, 297–300. Bell's translation is more technically precise.
90. The Maḍagammana *sannasa* was reprinted in Kiriällē Ñāṇavimala, *Sabaragamuvē Päraṇi Liyavili* (Nugēgoḍa: Mānavahitavādi Lēkhaka Parṣadaya, 2001), 23–24.
91. *Cūḷavaṃsa, Being the More Recent Part of the Mahāvaṃsa*, trans. Wilhelm Geiger and C. Mabel Rickmers (Delhi: Motilal Banarsidass Pvt., 1996), 93:9–13. Translations are modified by me throughout.
92. S. Pathmanathan, "The Munnesvaram Tamil Inscription of Parākramabāhu VI," *Journal of the Sri Lanka Branch of the Royal Asiatic Society* 18 (1974): 54–69.
93. *Cūḷavaṃsa*, 92:17–19; 97:16–18, 97:31.
94. *Cūḷavaṃsa*, 100:220–27.
95. John Clifford Holt, *The Religious World of Kīrti Śrī: Buddhism, Art, and Politics in Late Medieval Sri Lanka* (New York: Oxford University Press, 1996), 28–39.
96. Gananath Obeyesekere, *The Doomed King: A Requiem for Śri Vikrama Rājasinha* (Colombo: Sailfish, 2017).
97. Gananath Obeyesekere, "Between the Portuguese and the Nāyakas: The Many Faces of the Kandyan Kingdom, 1591–1765," in *Sri Lanka at the Crossroads of History*, ed. Zoltán Biedermann and Alan Strathern (London: UCL Press, 2017), 167.
98. Anne M. Blackburn, *Buddhist Learning and Textual Practice in Eighteenth-Century Lankan Monastic Culture* (Princeton, NJ: Princeton University Press, 2001), 63, 104.
99. Achala Gunasekara-Rockwell, "Hūniyam: Demon to Deity" (PhD diss., University of Wisconsin–Madison, 2011), 196–97.
100. Or.6615(272): *Ăňḍi Kaḍavara Tovil*, f. 1a, v. 1.
101. A. V. Suraweera, *The Rājāvaliya: A Comprehensive Account of the Rulers of Sri Lanka, and the First Ever Translation of the Alakeśvara Yuddhaya* (Colombo: Vijitha Yapa Publications, 2014), part 2, 92. The earlier *Alakeśvara Yuddhaya*, however, identified a Manamperuma Mukaveṭṭi with Veṇḍumāl Iṭṭan, a scribe from South India. See part 1, 25. Manamperuma appeared as his usual *ăňḍi* self in another local *Rājāvaliya*: Gaṇanāth Obēsēkara, ed., *Vanni Rājāvaliya* (Colombo: S. Goḍagē saha Sahōdarayō, 2005), 128, 130, 132.
102. Suraweera, *The Rājāvaliya and Alakeśvara Yuddhaya*, part 2, 52–53, 93–95. Suraveera's English translation replaced *ăňḍiyā* with "fakir," while *jogues* (yogis) was used in Ferñao de Queyroz, *The Temporal and Spiritual Conquest of Ceylon*, trans. S. G. Perera (Colombo: A. C. Richards, 1930), 2:485. The *ăňḍi* were also portrayed in Sinhala folktales as dishonest tricksters with

one another, only pretending to contribute to their communal rice pot. CNML 104/CC4: *Athetha Wakya Deepanya or a Collection of Sinhalese Proverbs, Maxims, Fables &C. Compiled and Translated Into English* (1881), 6.

103. Puñcibaṇḍāra Sannasgala, *Siṃhala Sāhitya Vaṃśaya* (Colombo: Lēkhavus Mudraṇālaya, 1964), 581–83.

104. CNML 82/K1: *Samanaḷa Väňdīma*, f. 1b.

105. UPL 278540: *Samanaḷa Hälla*, f. 6a.

106. This was also implied by the 1788 *Käṭakirili Sandēśaya*'s portrayal of Tamil, Sanskrit, and Pali as ritual languages on the Peak (v. 26). Mentioning these, however, could have simply been a trope of erudition, matching earlier *sandeśa* poems.

107. Rianne Siebenga, "Colonial India's 'Fanatical Fakirs' and Their Popular Representations," *History and Anthropology* 23, no. 4 (2012): 445–66.

108. *A Conversation Between a Christian and a Pilgrim—Śrī Pādaya Gäṇaya* (Colombo: Wesleyan Mission Press for Ceylon Religious Tract Society, 1871), p. 10, vv. 52–53. Verse numbers added by me.

109. Talgaskandē Sujāta, *Śrī Pāda Vandanā Atpota* (Ratnapura: Prinṭ Havus, n.d.), 28. Despite Äňḍiyamalatänna's many appearances in Sinhala Samanala poetry, this is the only verse I have seen that explains its etymology.

110. It was called "Andea Malla Hella" there: "Journey to Adam's Peak, in the Island of Ceylon," *Atheneum; or, Spirit of the English Magazines* 1, no. 7 (July 1, 1817): 477.

111. SLNA 45/341: Ratnapura government agent diary, February 27, 1929.

112. CNML 104/S8: D.D.L., *Siri Pāda Gaman Vistaraya* (Colombo: Lakdiv, 1891), v. 79.

113. CNML 104/Z2: W. A. G. Juvānis, *Śrīpādavandanāva Hevat Giripada Lakara* (Moraketiya: Vijēpāla Yantrālaya, 1929), v. 142.

114. Pranāndu, *Samanala Hasuna*, v. 47.

115. The Hatton-trail Makara Torana was discussed in chapter 2.

116. Bell, *Report on the Kuṭṭāpiṭiya Sannasa*, 14. Aryapala was not the first to make a leap in Peak history from Kīrti Śrī to Hikkaduvē Sumaṅgala. See CNML 104/C8: *Śrī Pādavarṇanā Kāvyaya Hevat Śrīpāda Alaṅkāraya* (D. P. D. Raṇatuṅga Appuhāmi, 1910), vv. 74–75.

117. Coincidentally, a British author also linked Äňḍiyamalatänna to a Muslim. Although he otherwise reproduced the 1827 (pub. 1840) observations of Jonathan Forbes, down to exact phrasings, Charles Pridham's 1849 account also elaborated from unknown sources. So while Forbes recorded a Muslim grave on the trail (cited in chapter 3), Pridham said that at "Aandiyamalletenne, here is the grave of an Aandia or mendicant priest, now a Mohammedan saint. . . . After his body had lain for three months on this spot, resisting the most inveterate causes of decomposition, it was discovered by a hermit from the wilds below . . . who . . . performed the last offices of humanity over the sainted dead." Whether this was a nineteenth-century myth or Pridham's own imagination is uncertain. Charles Pridham, *An Historical, Political, and Statistical Account of Ceylon and Its Dependencies* (London: T. and W. Boone, 1849), 2:614.

5. Pilgrimage Ethics from Pluralism

1. CNML AL/14: *Samanala Vistaraya*, f. 51.

2. E.g., S. S. M. Nanayakkara, "Sri Pada: Sanctuary for All Faiths," *Sunday Observer*, August 27, 2000; Rajika Jayatilake, "Sri Pada: Symbol of Inter-Faith Harmony," *South Asian Life and*

Times, January 2003; John B. Wright, "Sri Pada: Sacred Pilgrimage Mountain of Sri Lanka," *Focus on Geography* 50, no. 2 (2007): 1–6.

3. My use of the term "unbounded" is inspired by Roshni Patel, "Releasing Boundaries, Relieving Suffering, Becoming Pained: An Engagement with Indian Buddhism and Martin Heidegger," *Philosophy East and West* 69, no. 4 (2019): 1053–75.
4. J. Baird Callicott, "The New New (Buddhist?) Ecology," *Journal for the Study of Religion, Nature and Culture* 2, no. 2 (2008): 166–82.
5. William E. Connolly, "Process Philosophy and Planetary Politics," in *Common Goods: Economy, Ecology, and Political Theology*, ed. Melanie Johnson-DeBaufre, Catherine Keller, and Elias Ortega-Aponte (New York: Fordham University Press, 2015), 25.
6. Michel Serres, *The Natural Contract*, trans. Elizabeth MacArthur and William Paulson (Ann Arbor: University of Michigan Press, 1995), 32.
7. Serres, *The Natural Contract*, 47–48.
8. Bruno Latour, *Facing Gaia: Eight Lectures on the New Climatic Regime*, trans. Catherine Porter (Cambridge: Polity Press, 2017), 152.
9. Vijaya Nagarajan, *Feeding a Thousand Souls: Women, Ritual, and Ecology in India—an Exploration of the Kōlam* (New York: Oxford University Press, 2018), 208.
10. *Samantakūṭavaṇṇanā*, vv. 765–70; *Purāṇa Himagata Varṇanāva*, vv. 35–57. See also T. B. Karunaratne, "The Significance of the Signs and Symbols on the Footprints of the Buddha," *Journal of the Sri Lanka Branch of the Royal Asiatic Society* 20 (1976): 47–60.
11. CNML AL/14: *Samanala Vistaraya*, f. 28.
12. *Sabbalokapaṭibimbitadappaṇābhaṃ*. Claudio Cicuzza, *A Mirror Reflecting the Entire World: The Pāli Buddhapādamaṅgala or "Auspicious Signs on the Buddha's Feet"* (Bangkok: Fragile Palm Leaves Foundation, 2011), xvii.
13. Bhikkhu Bodhi, *The Numerical Discourses of the Buddha: A Translation of the Aṅguttara Nikāya* (Somerville, MA: Wisdom, 2012), 456. Translation modified by me.
14. Herman Kopp, ed., *Manorathapūraṇī: Buddhaghosa's Commentary on the Aṅguttara-Nikāya*, vol. 3 (London: Pali Text Society, 1966), IV.VIII.7, p. 103.
15. In another commentary, Buddhaghosa collects meanings of *bhūtā* found throughout the Tipitaka, including "existing . . . the five aggregates . . . the four primary elements . . . an arahant . . . all beings . . . plant life . . . a general term for spirits . . . and the totality of beings." Bhikkhu Bodhi, *The Suttanipāta: An Ancient Collection of the Buddha's Discourses Together with Its Commentaries* (Somerville, MA: Wisdom, 2017), 679.
16. Maria Heim, *Words for the Heart: A Treasury of Emotions from Classical India* (Princeton, NJ: Princeton University Press, 2022), 199–200.
17. Christopher D. Stone, *Should Trees Have Standing? Law, Morality, and the Environment*, 3rd ed. (New York: Oxford University Press, 2010).
18. T. W. Rhys Davids and William Stede, eds., *The Pali Text Society's Pali-English Dictionary* (London: Pali Text Society, 1921–1925), 107.
19. Karuṇādāsa Rūpasiṃha, *Śrī Pāda Vandanā Sāhitya* (Colombo: Äs Goḍagē saha Sahōdarayō, 2013), 149.
20. CNML 104/B20: K. H. Juvānisā, *Śrī Pāda Gaman Vistaraya* (Kegalle: Vidyākalpa Yantrālaya, 1923), vv. 8, 18–33.
21. Juvānisā, *Śrī Pāda Gaman Vistaraya*, v. 116.
22. Juvānisā, *Śrī Pāda Gaman Vistaraya*, vv. 35–36. See also vv. 13–17, 37–44. An earlier Sri Pada poem contains a similarly diverse invocation of gods, including Siva, and many verses meant

to share merit with them: Yon Merañña Siman Hēvāgē Sālis Silvā, *Sirisaraṇabhivādanaya* (Grantha Prakāśayantrālayē, 1892), vv. 10, 56–86.

23. The University of Peradeniya holds thirteen copies: 277347(2), 277406, 277424, 277475, 277529, 277530, 277542, 277957, 278086, 278264(2), 278423, 278540(2), 278974(2). The British Library holds seven copies: Or.6603(50)V, Or.6604(133)I, Or.6604(145)I, Or.6604(179), Or.6604(180), Or.6604(182), Or.6604(198)II. The Wellcome Institute holds five copies: 94 IV, 142, 146, 301 I, and 314 in K. D. Somadasa, *Catalogue of the Sinhalese Manuscripts in the Library of the Wellcome Institute for the History of Medicine* (London: Wellcome Trust, 1996). The Colombo National Museum Library holds at least ten copies, including AL/14, and numbers 1549, 1551, and 1553–1559 in W. A. de Silva, ed., *Catalogue of Palm Leaf Manuscripts in the Library of the Colombo Museum*, vol. 1 (Colombo: Ceylon Government Press, 1938).
24. The common invocation of this history was demonstrated again at the start of the coronavirus pandemic, in March 2020, when the head monk, Ven. Dhammadinna, initially resisted shutting down the pilgrimage, citing the previous danger of the journey on which pilgrims used to perish: Ranjith Rajapaksa and Lasantha Niroshan Perera, "Sri Pada Pilgrimage Will Continue: Prelate," *Daily Mirror*, March 17, 2020. Two days later, however, for the first time in history, the pilgrimage was officially canceled and all traffic to the Peak was blocked off.
25. Archibald Campbell Lawrie, *A Gazetteer of the Central Province of Ceylon* (Colombo: Government Press, 1896), 1:419.
26. Ranjit's mention of "fear and devotion" matches the Indian *bayam-bhakti* discourses about sacred groves, and their own modern decline; see Eliza E. Kent, *Sacred Groves and Local Gods: Religion and Environmentalism in South India* (Oxford: Oxford University Press, 2013), 77.
27. For *kälē bhāṣa* terms, see H. Parker, *Ancient Ceylon* (London: Luzac, 1909), 123–32.
28. CNML 104/S8: D.D.L., *Siri Pāda Gaman Vistaraya* (Colombo: Lakdiv, 1891), v. 68.
29. Juvānisā, *Śrī Pāda Gaman Vistaraya*, vv. 48, 60, 121–22.
30. Juvānisā, *Śrī Pāda Gaman Vistaraya*, vv. 68, 81–82.
31. CNML 104/C8: G. M. Salā, *Samanala Gamanā Laṅkāraya* (Kegalle: Vidyākalpa Yantrālaya, 1924), v. 37.
32. UPL 277607: *Samanaḷa Hälla*, f. 4a.
33. K. R. Perera, *Samanaḷagamana Saha Śripādavandanāva* (Colombo: K. D. Siyadōris Appuhāmi, 1890), v. 50.
34. D.D.L., *Siri Pāda Gaman Vistaraya*, v. 66.
35. Juvānisā, *Śrī Pāda Gaman Vistaraya*, vv. 47, 53.
36. T. B. Ilangaratne, *The Matchmaker* (Colombo: Lake House, 1974), 56.
37. CNML 104/Y8: *Laṅkāmātāvagē Śokaprakāśaya Hevat Mahadeva Kōpaya* (Kosgaslanga: A. K. Romiyel Prērā, 1934), vv. 28–31.
38. For similar critiques, see Bryan Pfaffenberger, "Serious Pilgrims and Frivolous Tourists: The Chimera of Tourism in the Pilgrimage of Sri Lanka," *Annals of Tourism Research* 10 (1983): 57–74; Premakumara De Silva, "'To Worship Our "Boss" (the Buddha)': Youth Religiosity in a Popular Pilgrimage Site in Sri Lanka," in *Ritual Journeys in South Asia: Constellations and Contestations of Mobility and Space*, ed. Christopher Bergmann and Jürgen Schaflechner (New York: Routledge, 2020), 139–56.
39. CNML 104/C8: M. G. K. Jōn Perēra, *Śrī Pādavandanāgamana Nohot Perasirit Saha Dänsirit* (Alutgama: I. D. Jōn Siññō, 1924), vv. 32, 45. Likewise, see CNML 104/Z2: M. S. Pranāndu, *Samanala Hasuna* (Panadura: M. Jēsan Pranāndu, 1932), vv. 104–10.

40. M. G. K. J. Perēra, *Śrī Pādavandanāgamana*, v. 38. Likewise: Pranāndu, *Samanala Hasuna*, vv. 101–3.
41. M. G. K. J. Perēra, *Śrī Pādavandanāgamana*, v. 28.
42. B. E. Perērā, *Śrī Pāda Lāñchana: Samantakūṭa Parvataya Hā Divā Guhāva* (Nugegoda: Prasanta Mudraṇa, 1979), 14–19.
43. Juvānisā, *Śrī Pāda Gaman Vistaraya*, v. 28.
44. Tariq Jazeel, *Sacred Modernity: Nature, Environment, and the Postcolonial Geographies of Sri Lankan Nationhood* (Liverpool: Liverpool University Press, 2013). For an Indian analogue, see Mukul Sharma, *Green and Saffron: Hindu Nationalism and Indian Environmental Politics* (Ranikhet: Permanent Black, 2012).
45. Premakumara De Silva, "Reordering of Postcolonial Sri Pāda Temple in Sri Lanka: Buddhism, State, and Nationalism," *History and Sociology of South Asia* 7, no. 155 (2013): 155–76.
46. S. Jeyarācā, "Eṅkḷ Civaṉoḷipāta Malaip Pirayāṇam," *Intu Iḷaiñaṉ* 15 (1955): 22–24.
47. The smaller summit shrine may have had several earlier forms. Fifty years before Jeyarācā, there was only "a small marble figure of Buddha seated," per Adolphus E. L. Rost, "Adam's Peak (Ceylon) in 1902," *Journal of the Royal Asiatic Society of Great Britain and Ireland* (1903): 656.
48. Sasikumar Balasundaram, "Temples and Deities on Plantations," in *Multi-Religiosity in Contemporary Sri Lanka: Innovation, Shared Spaces, Contestation*, ed. Mark P. Whitaker, Darini Rajasingham-Senanayake, and Pathmanesan Sanmugeswaran (New York: Routledge, 2022), 188.
49. "Civaṉoḷipāta Malaiyil Civakōcam Eḻuppiyavarkaḷukku Accuṟuttal!," *Karudan News—Karuṭaṉiṉ Pārvaiyil*, April 23, 2017.
50. Juvānisā, *Śrī Pāda Gaman Vistaraya*, vv. 91–94.
51. Juvānisā, *Śrī Pāda Gaman Vistaraya*, v. 95.
52. Bryce Ryan, *Caste in Modern Ceylon: The Sinhalese System in Transition* (New Brunswick: Rutgers University Press, 1953), 160.
53. Juvānisā, *Śrī Pāda Gaman Vistaraya*, vv. 98–99.
54. Bodhi, *The Suttanipāta*, 1:7.
55. UPL 278540: *Samanala Hälla*, f. 6a. This seems to have been a relatively free-floating line, incorporated with minor variations into an otherwise entirely different quatrain in UPL 277607: *Samanala Hälla*, f. 5b.
56. Jeyarācā, "Eṅkḷ Civaṉoḷipāta Malaip Pirayāṇam," 24.
57. De Silva, "Anthropological Studies on South Asian Pilgrimage," 26–29.
58. K. M. Vitarana, *Sri Pada: Adam's Peak, the Holy Mountain of Religious Amity and Miracles* (Nugegoda: Sarasavi Publishers, 2011), 81, 84; Guṇasēkara Guṇasōma, *Samandevi Aḍaviya Janakatā* (Colombo: Fāsṭ Pabliṣin, 2013), 182.
59. Jeyarācā, "Eṅkḷ Civaṉoḷipāta Malaip Pirayāṇam," 24.
60. Timothy Morton, *Ecology Without Nature: Rethinking Environmental Aesthetics* (Cambridge, MA: Harvard University Press, 2007). Despite valid critiques of the word by Morton and many others, I continue to use the term "nature" here, as it best translates the interplay of ecological habitat and human habit expressed in the Sinhala *sobādahama*, which is closer to Bruno Latour's concept of a "nature/culture" than to a bounded separate "nature." The term *sobādahama* also avoids the pitfalls of "Western nature" by being empty and impermanent in the Buddhist sense explained below.
61. Nihal Karunaratna, *Udavattekälē: The Forbidden Forest of the Kings of Kandy* (Colombo: Department of National Archives, 1986).

62. *Administration Reports* 1887, p. 34A.
63. Padmasiri de Silva, *Environmental Philosophy and Ethics in Buddhism* (London: Macmillan Press, 1998), 32.
64. Padmasiri de Silva, *Environmental Philosophy and Ethics in Buddhism*, 40.
65. Bhikkhu Ñāṇamoli, *The Path of Discrimination (Paṭisambhidhāmagga)* (Oxford: Pali Text Society, 2014), XX:5. See also Y. Karunadasa, *The Theravāda Abhidhamma: Inquiry Into the Nature of Conditioned Reality* (Somerville, MA: Wisdom, 2019), 40–45.
66. Jan Westerhoff, *The Dispeller of Disputes: Nāgārjuna's Vigrahavyāvartanī* (New York: Oxford University Press, 2010), v. 22. See also John Clark, "On Being None with Nature: Nagarjuna and the Ecology of Emptiness," *Capitalism Nature Socialism* 19, no. 4 (December 2008): 6–29.
67. Juvānisā, *Śrī Pāda Gaman Vistaraya*, v. 97.
68. Juvānisā, *Śrī Pāda Gaman Vistaraya*, vv. 56–66.
69. Rohan Bastin, *The Domain of Constant Excess: Plural Worship at the Munnesvaram Temples in Sri Lanka* (New York: Berghahn, 2002), 5–6.
70. Rohan Bastin, "Saints, Sites, and Religious Accommodation in Sri Lanka," in *Sharing the Sacra: The Politics and Pragmatics of Intercommunal Relations Around Holy Places*, ed. Glenn Bowman (New York: Berghahn, 2012), 107.
71. Nagarajan, *Feeding a Thousand Souls*, 208.
72. Amal Uḍavatta, *Śrī Pāda Aḍaviya: Saṃskrutika Vividhatvaya Saha Jaiva Vividhatvaya* (Dankotuwa: Vāsana Pot Prakāśakayō, 2014), 143–46.
73. Guṇasōma, *Samandevi Aḍaviya Janakatā*, 138; Uḍavatta, *Śrī Pāda Aḍaviya*, 145; Vitarana, *Sri Pada*, 85; Alexander McKinley, "The Apotheosis of Emptiness: God Suniyan and the Soteriological Necessity of Negativity in Sinhala Buddhism," in *The Meaning and Power of Negativity*, ed. Ingolf U. Dalferth and Trevor W. Kimball (Tübingen: Mohr Siebeck, 2021), 352–56. Compare with this proverb: "You may escape from the god Saman Deviyo but you cannot escape his servant Amangalla." Arthur A. Perera, *Sinhalese Folklore Notes* (Bombay: British India Press, 1917), 54.
74. M. G. K. J. Perēra, *Śrī Pādavandanāgamana*, v. 51.
75. In Lankan Pali and Sinhala texts, Saman attains *sōvān* after hearing the Buddha preach, fitting the meaning of *sotāpanna* in the Pali canon as one who heard the *buddha-dhamma*. Peter Masefield, *Divine Revelation in Pali Buddhism* (London: George Allen and Unwin, 1986), 130–36.
76. Navanäliye Vijētuṅga, *Śrī Pādasthānaya* (Navanagara: Dänuma Väḍuma Prakaśayō, 2014), 58.
77. William Skeen, *Adam's Peak: Legendary Traditional, and Historic Notices of the Samanala and Srí-Páda with a Descriptive Account of the Pilgrims' Route from Colombo to the Sacred Foot-Print* (Colombo: W. L. H. Skeen), 1870, 169.
78. SLNA 45/333: Ratnapura government agent diary, February 7, 1912.
79. Likewise: "On the way to Adam's Peak there are to be found sacred orchards where a person may enter and eat any quantity of fruit but will not be able to find his way out if he tries to bring any with him." A. A. Perera, *Sinhalese Folklore Notes*, 6. See also Juvānis, *Śrīpādavandanāva*, v. 113.
80. Guṇasōma, *Samandevi Aḍaviya Janakatā*, 53.
81. Maria Heim, "The Aesthetics of Excess," *Journal of the American Academy of Religion* 71, no. 3 (2003): 541.
82. Bodhi, *The Numerical Discourses of the Buddha*, 456. According to Bhikkhu Bodhi, the final lines of this *sutta* are recited daily by forest monks as a protection against snakebites (1692n760).

83. *The Suttanipāta*, 549. Translation modified by me.
84. M. G. K. J. Perēra, *Śrī Pādavandanāgamana*, 8.
85. D. P. Vettasiṅha, *Śrīpādasthānayaṭa Hā Samandēvālavalaṭa Adhigruhita Siri Sumana Saman Deviyō* (Anula Yantralaya: H. D. D. Guṇasēkara, n.d.), v. 88. Likely c. 1950, based on detailed red-ink cover art featuring Saman with bow and arrow.
86. Don Kornēlis Ponsēkā, *Sumaṇa Śaila Mārgā Laṅkāraya Hevat Sumanaselmagalakara* (Sarasavisaňdaräsa Mudrāyantra Śālāvē, 1891), v. 21.
87. Leela Prasad, "Co-Being, a Praxis of the Public: Lessons from Hindu Devotional (Bhakti) Narrative, Arendt, and Gandhi," *Journal of the American Academy of Religion* 85, no. 1 (2017): 206.
88. Juvānisā, *Śrī Pāda Gaman Vistaraya*, v. 86.
89. Connections between Buddhism and nature are also popular topics for Sinhala publishers: Pūjya Bōmiriyē Dhammapāla, *Bududahama Hā Parisaraya* (Wellampitiya: Śrī Pāli Prakāśakayō, 2000); Pūjya Kanattegoḍa Saddhāratna, *Bududahama Hā Parisara Pavitratāva* (Divulapitiya: Sarasvatī Prakāśana, 2011); Guṇasiri Baṇḍā Vīrasūriya, *Jalaya Parisaraya Minisā Saha Budu Dahama* (Colombo: Āriya Prakāśakayō, 2013).
90. David Haberman, *People Trees: Worship of Trees in Northern India* (New York: Oxford University Press, 2013).
91. David Gordon White, *Myths of the Dog-Man* (Chicago: University of Chicago Press, 1991), 13.
92. Eduardo Kohn, *How Forests Think: Toward an Anthropology Beyond the Human* (Berkeley: University of California Press, 2013), 132.
93. Bhikkhu Ñāṇamoli and Bhikkhu Bodhi, *The Middle Length Discourses of the Buddha: A Translation of the Majjhima Nikāya*, 4th ed. (Somerville, MA: Wisdom, 2015), 493–94.
94. E.g., Raṃjanī Dedduvakumāra Mahinda Amugoḍa, *Siripā Vanayē Yōgī Bhikṣuvak Samaňga* (Maharagama: Katru Prakāśanayak, 2008).
95. Padmasiri de Silva, *Environmental Philosophy and Ethics in Buddhism*, 33.
96. Christina Campbell, "To Be a Pilgrim," *Blackwell's Magazine* (1961). I consulted the reprint in the *Ceylon Observer*. Thanks to the CNML staff for directing me to this piece.
97. Wright, "Sri Pada," 2.
98. Wright, "Sri Pada," 4.
99. Similarly, in the case of the North Indian pilgrimage site studied by Anna Bigelow, its reputation for pluralism "is so integral to the town's identity" that residents work diligently at "constructing and substantiating that identity of peaceful pluralism." Anna Bigelow, *Sharing the Sacred: Practicing Pluralism in Muslim North India* (New York: Oxford University Press, 2010), 154.
100. Satchi Ponnambalam, *Sri Lanka: National Conflict and the Tamil Liberation Struggle* (London: Zed Books, 1983), 72.
101. "Seruwila to Sri Pada (Sacred Foot Print Shrine), Ancient Pilgrim Route Along the Mahaweli River in Sri Lanka," UNESCO, http://whc.unesco.org/en/tentativelists/5531/.
102. For an example of this neatly categorical approach to pluralism, see *Human Rights and Religions in Sri Lanka: A Commentary on the Universal Declaration of Human Rights* (Colombo: Sri Lanka Foundation, 1988).
103. Elizabeth Shakman Hurd, *Beyond Religious Freedom: The New Global Politics of Religion* (Princeton, NJ: Princeton University Press, 2015), 6.
104. Arjun Appadurai, *Fear of Small Numbers: An Essay on the Geography of Anger* (Durham, NC: Duke University Press, 2006).

105. Saba Mahmood, *Religious Difference in a Secular Age: A Minority Report* (Princeton, NJ: Princeton University Press, 2016), 15.
106. Benjamin Schonthal, "Economies of Expert Religion in Sri Lanka," *Journal of Religious and Political Practice* 4, no. 1 (2018): 27–45.
107. Serika Siriwardene, "Rethinking Religious Education," *Daily Mirror*, August 7, 2020.
108. Henri Lefebvre, *The Production of Space*, trans. Donald Nicholson-Smith (Oxford: Blackwell, 1991), 81.
109. William E. Connolly, *Pluralism* (Durham, NC: Duke University Press, 2005), 89.
110. Upāli Guṇasēkara, "Sobādahamē Vyavasthāva Ullaṅghanaya Kirīma," *Vanajīvi/Vaṉavilaṅku/Wildlife* 8, no. 1 (2012): 26.
111. Juvānis, *Śrīpādavandanāva*, vv. 33, 35.
112. Juvānis, *Śrīpādavandanāva*, vv. 87, 91, 155.
113. Juvānis, *Śrīpādavandanāva*, v. 99.
114. Anoja Wickramasinghe, *People and the Forest: Management of the Adam's Peak Wilderness* (Battaramulla: Sri Lanka Forest Department, 1995), 82–83.
115. Mangala De Zoysa and Makoto Inoue, "Climate Change Impacts, Agroforestry Adaptation and Policy Environment in Sri Lanka," *Open Journal of Forestry* 4 (2014): 439–56; Eskil Mattsson et al., "Homegardens as a Multi-Functional Land-Use Strategy in Sri Lanka with Focus on Carbon Sequestration," *AMBIO* 42 (2013): 892–902; Eskil Mattsson et al., "Quantification of Carbon Stock and Tree Diversity of Homegardens in a Dry Zone Area of Moneragala Distrcit, Sri Lanka," *Agroforest Systems* 89 (2015): 435–45; Rekha Nianthi, "Climate Change Adaptation and Agroforestry in Sri Lanka," in *Climate Change Adaptation and Disaster Risk Reduction: An Asian Perspective*, ed. Rajiv Shaw, Juan M. Pulhin, and Joy Jacqueline Pereira (Bingley: Emerald, 2010), 285–305; A. J. Uisso, "Agroforestry Practices as an Option for Climate Change Adaptation: A Review," *Octa Journal of Environmental Research* 3, no. 3 (2015): 219–25.
116. Anoja Wickramasinghe, "Conservation Innovations of Peripheral Communities: Case Study of Adam's Peak Wilderness," *Journal of the National Science Foundation of Sri Lanka* 31, nos. 1–2 (2003): 119.
117. Gananath Obeyesekere, *The Creation of the Hunter: The Vädda Presence in the Kandyan Kingdom: A Re-Examination* (Colombo: Sailfish, 2022). This general myth has distorted earlier work on sacred groves, as explained by Kent, *Sacred Groves and Local Gods*, 6.
118. Ponsēkā, *Sumaṇa Śaila Mārgā Laṅkāraya Hevat Sumanaselmagalakara*, v. 48.
119. Māyāraṅjan, *Piṭisara Minissu* (Colombo: Sūriya Prakāśakayō, 2015), 16.
120. M. A. S. Kumari, K. Kansutisukmongkol, and Y. W. Brockelman, "Plant Diversity in Home Gardens and Its Contribution to Household Economy in Suburban Areas of Sri Lanka," *Environment and Natural Resources Journal* 7 (2009): 12–30.
121. Anna Lowenhaupt Tsing, *The Mushroom at the End of the World: On the Possibility of Life in Capitalist Ruins* (Princeton, NJ: Princeton University Press, 2015), 5.
122. Steven Collins, *Wisdom as a Way of Life: Theravāda Buddhism Reimagined* (New York: Columbia University Press, 2020), 7–9.
123. Alan Sponberg, "Green Buddhism and the Hierarchy of Compassion," in *Buddhism and Ecology: The Interconnection of Dharma and Deeds*, ed. Mary Evelyn Tucker and Duncan Ryūken Williams (Cambridge, MA: Harvard University Press, 1997), 358–59. See also Christopher Ives, "Resources for Buddhist Environmental Ethics," *Journal of Buddhist Ethics* 20 (2013): 557–60.
124. Juvānis, *Śrīpādavandanāva*, vv. 181, 192.

125. The verse about Saman's tusker's enlightenment matches a minority of Buddhist texts claiming animals have some access to the dharma and can improve rebirth trajectories. See Reiko Ohnuma, *Unfortunate Destiny: Animals in the Indian Buddhist Imagination* (New York: Oxford University Press, 2017), 24–28.
126. CNML 104/K4: K. D. G. Perērā, *Śrī Pāda Vandanā Gamana* (Sevyaśrī Yantrālaya: J. A. Guṇsēna, 1926), vv. 24, 51.
127. Tsing, *The Mushroom at the End of the World*, 243.
128. Timothy Morton, *Dark Ecology: For a Logic of Future Coexistence* (New York: Columbia University Press, 2016), 5. Latour also writes of earthly "loops" as multiple, overlapping, and often irregular, not perfect circles or spheres. Bruno Latour, *Facing Gaia: Eight Lectures on the New Climatic Regime*, trans. Catherine Porter (Cambridge: Polity Press, 2017), 139–41.
129. Jeffrey Hopkins, *Nāgārjuna's Precious Garland: Buddhist Advice for Living and Liberation* (Ithaca, NY: Snow Lion, 2007), v. 485.
130. Bruno Latour, *Politics of Nature: How to Bring the Sciences Into Democracy*, trans. Catherine Porter (Cambridge, MA: Harvard University Press, 2004), 235.
131. Tsing, *The Mushroom at the End of the World*, 29, 255.
132. Connolly, *Pluralism*, 123. See also William E. Connolly, *Why I Am Not a Secularist* (Minneapolis: University of Minnesota Press, 1999), 154.
133. Prasad, "Co-Being, a Praxis of the Public," 202.
134. Connolly, *Why I Am Not a Secularist*, 155.
135. Connolly, *Why I Am Not a Secularist*, 148–49.
136. Benjamin Schonthal, "Buddhist Perspectives on Freedom of Religion and Belief," in *Routledge Handbook to Freedom of Religion and Belief*, ed. Silvio Ferrari et al. (New York: Routledge, 2020), 73–87; Benjamin Schonthal, "The Tolerations of Theravada Buddhism," in *Toleration in Comparative Perspective*, ed. Vicki A. Spencer (Lanham, MD: Lexington Books, 2018), 179–96.
137. Or.6615(390): *Kaḍavara Puvata*, f. 1a, v. 1. This verse exemplifies Jim Sykes's point that the practice of offering musical/poetic gifts to deities is a good place to find shared traditions among different religious and ethnic groups: Jim Sykes, *The Musical Gift: Sonic Generosity in Post-War Sri Lanka* (New York: Oxford University Press, 2018).
138. Bodhi, *The Suttanipāta*, 180. Translation modified by me: "Mettañca sabbalokasmi, mānasaṃ bhāvaye aparimāṇaṃ; Uddhaṃ adho ca tiriyañca, asambādhaṃ averamasapattaṃ."
139. Latour, *Facing Gaia*, 156.
140. Premakumara De Silva, "Competitive Sharing: Sri Lankan Hindus and Up-Country Tamil Religiosity at the Sri Pada Temple," *South Asianist* 6, no. 1 (2018): 76–97; John Clifford Holt, *The Buddhist Viṣṇu: Religious Transformation, Politics, and Culture* (New York: Columbia University Press, 2004).
141. Alexander McKinley, "Religious Innovation in the Pilgrimage Industry: Hindu Bodhisattva Worship and Tamil Buddhistness," in *Multi-Religiosity in Contemporary Sri Lanka: Innovation, Shared Spaces, Contestation*, ed. Mark P. Whitaker, Darini Rajasingham-Senanayake, and Pathmanesan Sanmugeswaran (New York: Routledge, 2022), 113–25.
142. Lefebvre, *The Production of Space*, 380.
143. E.g., Maṇippulavar Marutūr Ē. Majīt, *Mattiya Kiḻakkil Iruntu Maṭṭakkaḷappu Varai* (Kalmunai: Marutūr Veḷiyīṭṭup Paṇimaṉai, 1995), 33.
144. Kalāpūcaṇam Cāralnāṭaṉ, *Cintaiyaḷḷum Civaṉoḷipātamalai* (Kotagala: Cāral Veḷiyīṭṭakam, 2009), 12.
145. Juvānisā, *Śrī Pāda Gaman Vistaraya*, vv. 88, 115–16.

Conclusion

1. John M. Senaveratna, *Dictionary of Proverbs of the Sinhalese: Including Also Their Adages, Aphorisms, Apologues, Apothegms, Bywords, Dictums, Maxims, Mottoes, Precepts, Saws, and Sayings: Together with the Connected Myths, Legends, and Folk-Tales* (Colombo: Times of Ceylon, 1936), 38.
2. Dipesh Chakrabarty, "Climate and Capital: On Conjoined Histories," *Critical Inquiry* 41 (2014): 23.
3. Dipesh Chakrabarty, "The Climate of History: Four Theses," *Critical Inquiry* 35, no. 2 (2009): 213.
4. Paul J. Crutzen and Eugene F. Stoermer, "The 'Anthropocene,'" *Global Change Newsletter* 41 (2000): 17–18.
5. Ville Lähde, "Gardens, Climate Changes, and Cultures," in *How Nature Speaks: The Dynamics of the Human Ecological Condition*, ed. Yrjö Haila and Chuck Dyke (Durham, NC: Duke University Press, 2006), 94–95; emphasis in original.
6. Bruno Latour, *Facing Gaia: Eight Lectures on the New Climatic Regime*, trans. Catherine Porter (Cambridge: Polity Press, 2017), 105.
7. Jan Zalasiewicz et al., "Stratigraphy of the Anthropocene," *Philosophical Transactions of the Royal Society* 369 (2011): 1036–55.
8. Jan Zalasiewicz et al., "When Did the Anthropocene Begin? A Mid-Twentieth Century Boundary Is Stratigraphically Optimal," *Quaternary International* 383 (2015): 196–203.
9. Donna J. Haraway, *Staying with the Trouble: Making Kin in the Chthulucene*. Durham, NC: Duke University Press, 2016.
10. William E. Connolly, *Facing the Planetary: Entangled Humanism and the Politics of Swarming* (Durham, NC: Duke University Press, 2017), 32.
11. Claire Colebrook, "Framing the End of the Species," in *Extinction*, ed. Claire Colebrook (Ann Arbor, MI: Open Humanities Press, 2012), n.p.
12. John McPhee, *Basin and Range* (New York: Farrar, Straus, Giroux, 1981), 129.
13. Jeffrey Jerome Cohen, *Stone: An Ecology of the Inhuman* (Minneapolis: University of Minnesota Press, 2015).
14. Connolly, *Facing the Planetary*, 6.
15. Amy Catania Kulper, "Architecture's Lapidarium: On the Lives of Geological Specimens," in *Architecture in the Anthropocene: Encounters Among Design, Deep Time, Science and Philosophy*, ed. Etienne Turpin (Ann Arbor, MI: Open Humanities Press, 2013), 90–92.
16. Elizabeth A. Povinelli, *Geontologies: A Requiem to Late Liberalism* (Durham, NC: Duke University Press, 2016).
17. Eleanor Kaufman, "The Mineralogy of Being," in *Architecture in the Anthropocene: Encounters Among Design, Deep Time, Science and Philosophy*, ed. Etienne Turpin (Ann Arbor, MI: Open Humanities Press, 2013), 153–66.
18. Aldo Leopold, *A Sand County Almanac, and Sketches Here and There* (New York: Oxford University Press, 1949), 129.
19. John Seed et al., *Thinking Like a Mountain: Towards a Council of All Beings* (Philadelphia: New Society Publishers, 1988).
20. *Sansuikyō*, §§2–3. I use Carl Bielefeldt's translation, reprinted in Shohaku Okumura, *The Mountains and Waters Sūtra: A Practitioner's Guide to Dōgen's "Sansuikyō"* (Somerville, MA: Wisdom, 2018), 23–24.
21. *Sansuikyō*, §19. Okumura, *The Mountains and Waters Sūtra*, 28–29.

22. *Sansuikyō*, §32. Okumura, *The Mountains and Waters Sūtra*, 32.
23. Okumura, *The Mountains and Waters Sūtra*, 110.
24. *Sansuikyō*, §45. Okumura, *The Mountains and Waters Sūtra*, 35.
25. Okumura, *The Mountains and Waters Sūtra*, 144.
26. Timothy Clark, *Ecocriticism on the Edge: The Anthropocene as a Threshold Concept* (New York: Bloomsbury, 2015), 101.
27. Zalasiewicz et al., "Stratigraphy of the Anthropocene," 1039–40.
28. Posted on the "Lanka True News" Facebook page, October 31, 2016.
29. Dipesh Chakrabarty, "Postcolonial Studies and the Challenge of Climate Change," *New Literary History* 43, no. 1 (2012): 12. Chakrabarty is commenting on David Archer, *The Long Thaw: How Humans Are Changing the Next 100,000 Years of Earth's Climate* (Princeton, NJ: Princeton University Press, 2009).
30. Latour, *Facing Gaia*, 273; emphasis in original.
31. Latour, *Facing Gaia*, 276; emphasis in original.
32. Gilles Deleuze and Felix Guattari, *What Is Philosophy?*, trans. Hugh Tomlinson and Graham Burchell (New York: Columbia University Press, 1994), 85.
33. "Samanala and Its Shadow," *Cornhill Magazine* 6, no. 31 (January 1886): 44–45.
34. Ṭhānissaro Bhikkhu, *Udāna: Exclamations* (Valley Center, CA: Metta Forest Monastery, 2012), 53.
35. Bhikkhu Bodhi, *The Connected Discourses of the Buddha: A Translation of the Saṃyutta Nikāya* (Boston: Wisdom, 2000), 192.
36. Bhadantācariya Buddhaghosa, *Sāratthappakāsinī Nāma Saṁyuttaṭṭhakathā* (Yangon: Ministry of Religious Affairs, 2008), 153.
37. Whitney A. Bauman, *Religion and Ecology: Developing a Planetary Ethic* (New York: Columbia University Press, 2014), 144.
38. When the word *samanalayō* is used at the Peak, it actually includes both butterflies and moths. While several Sinhala terms for moths exist, *samanala* is a synecdoche for all such insects at the summit, mythically blending with the Peak.
39. Augusta Klein, *Among the Gods, Scenes of India: With Legends by the Way* (London: William Blackwood and Sons, 1895), 10.
40. Neville Manders, "Some Breeding Experiments on *Catopsilia Pyranthe* and Notes of the Migration of Butterflies in Ceylon," *Transactions of the Royal Entomological Society of London* 4 (1904), 703.
41. C. B. Williams, "A Study of Butterfly Migration in South India and Ceylon, Based Largely on Records by Messrs. J. Evershed, E. E. Green, J. C. F. Fryer and W. Ormiston," *Transactions of the Royal Entomological Society of London* 75 (1927): 2.
42. Williams, "A Study of Butterfly Migration," 32.
43. Tiyaḍōr G. Perērā, *Samanaḷa Sandeśaya* (Dharmavardhana Mudra Yantrālayē: Śrīmat Ārtar Älibänk Hävlok, 1895), vv. 2–6.
44. CNML 104/Z2: M. S. Pranāndu, *Samanala Hasuna* (Panadura: M. Jēsan Pranāndu, 1932), vv. 1–3.
45. Connolly, *Facing the Planetary*, 40.
46. Pranāndu, *Samanala Hasuna*, v. 50.
47. First published in the newspaper *Savasa*, July 8, 1972. Reprinted in Piyasēna Mīdeṇiya, *Samanala Katāvak* (Colombo: S. Goḍagē saha Sahōdarayō, 2013), 24–25.
48. Pranāndu, *Samanala Hasuna*, v. 63.

49. Dilrukshi Handunnetti, "An Urban 'Butterfly Experience' in Sri Lanka," *Mongabay*, May 15, 2019.
50. B. M. B. Weerakoon, A. M. R. S. Bandara, and K. B. Ranawana, "Impact of Canopy Cover on Butterfly Abundance and Diversity in Intermediate Zone Forest of Sri Lanka," *Journal of Tropical Forestry and Environment* 5, no. 1 (2015): 41–46.
51. For example, a recent Tamil book about the Peak begins with a chapter on its butterflies: Kalāpūcaṇam Cāralnāṭaṉ, *Cintaiyaḷḷum Civaṉoḷipātamalai* (Kotagala: Cāral Veḷiyīṭṭakam, 2009).
52. Manders, "Some Breeding Experiments," 702–3.

Bibliography

Abēmānna, Ruvira. "Siripāda Kaňda Mudunaṭa Doḷos Mahē Pahanayi Ghaṇṭārayayi Genā Mahā Helikopṭar Meheyuma." *Mavbim*, January 11, 2014, 8.

Abeyawardana, H. A. P. *Boundary Divisions of Mediaeval Sri Lanka*. Polgasovita: Academy of Sri Lankan Culture, 1999.

Abeysekara, Ananda. "The Un-Translatability of Religion, the Un-Translatability of Life: Thinking Talal Asad's Thought Unthought in the Study of Religion." *Method and Theory in the Study of Religion* 23 (2011): 257–82.

Abhayaguṇaratna, D. G., ed. *Pärakumbā Sirita*. Colombo: Ratna Pot Prakāśakayō, 2004.

Abhayasiṅha, Varallē M. G. C. *Siripā Väňduma*. Matale: D. E. A. Guṇavardana, 1917. Colombo National Museum Library 104/B6.

'Aḥbār Aṣ-Ṣīn Wa L-Hind: Relation de la Chine et de l'Inde. Trans. Jean Sauvaget. Paris: Société d'édition Les Belles Lettres, 1948.

Ahmad, S. Magbul. "Cartography of Al-Sharīf Al-Idrīsī." In *The History of Cartography*, vol. 2, book 1, *Cartography in the Traditional Islamic and South Asian Societies*, ed. J. B. Harley and David Woodward, 156–72. Chicago: University of Chicago Press, 1992.

Ahmad, Zarin. "Contours of Muslim Nationalism in Sri Lanka." *South Asian History and Culture* 3, no. 2 (2012): 269–87.

Akilēcapiḷḷai, Vē. *Tirukkōṇācala Vaipavam*. Colombo: Tattuva Ñāṉat Tavaccālaip Piracuram, 2000 (1950).

Aksland, Markus. *The Sacred Footprint: A Cultural History of Adam's Peak*. Bangkok: Orchid Press, 2001.

Alatas, Ismail Fajrie. "The Poetics of Pilgrimage: Assembling Contemporary Indonesian Pilgrimage to Ḥaḍramawt, Yemen." *Comparative Studies in Society and History* 58, no. 3 (2016): 607–35.

Albera, Dionigi. " 'Why Are You Mixing What Cannot Be Mixed?': Shared Devotions in the Monotheisms." *History and Anthropology* 19 (2008): 37–59.

al-Bīrūnī. *The Book Most Comprehensive in Knowledge on Precious Stones: Al-Beruni's Book on Mineralogy* Trans. Hakim Mohammed Said. Islamabad: Pakistan Hijra Council, 1989.

——. *Kitāb Al-Jamāhir Fī Ma'rifat Al-Jawāhir*. Trans. Hakim Mohammed Said. Karachi: Pakistan Historical Society, 2001.

Ali, Ameer. "The 1915 Racial Riots in Ceylon (Sri Lanka): A Reappraisal of Its Causes." *South Asia* 4, no. 2 (1981): 1–20.

——. "Kattankudy in Eastern Sri Lanka: A Mullah-Merchant Urban Complex Caught Between Islamist Factionalism and Ethno-Nationalisms." *Journal of Minority Muslim Affairs* 29, no. 2 (2009): 184–94.

——. "Muslims in Harmony and Conflict in Plural Sri Lanka: A Historical Summary from a Religio-Economic and Political Perspective." *Journal of Muslim Minority Affairs* 34, no. 3 (2014): 227–42.

——. "Political Buddhism, Islamic Orthodoxy and Open Economy: The Toxic Triad in Sinhalese-Muslim Relations in Sri Lanka." *Journal of Asian and African Studies* 49, no. 3 (2014): 298–314.

'Ālim, Tayka Shu'ayb. *Arabic, Arwi and Persian in Sarandib and Tamil Nadu*. Chennai: Imāmul 'Arūs Trust, 1993.

al-Kalbī, Ibn. *The Book of Idols, Being a Translation from the Arabic of the Kitāb Al-Asnām* Trans. Nabih Amin Faris. Princeton, NJ: Princeton University Press, 1952.

al-Kāšġarī, Maḥmūd. *Compendium of the Turkic Dialects (Dīwān Luġāt at-Turk)*. Trans. Robert Dankoff and James Kelly. Vol. 1. Duxbury, MA: Harvard University Printing Office, 1982.

Allocco, Amy L. "Fear, Reverence and Ambivalence: Divine Snakes in Contemporary South India." *Religions of South Asia* 7 (2013): 230–48.

al-Muqaddasī. *The Best Divisions for Knowledge of the Regions, Aḥsan Al-Taqāsīm Fī Ma'rifat Al-Aqālīm* Trans. Basil Collins. Reading: Garnet Publishing, 2001.

al-Tīfāshī, Aḥmad ibn Yūsuf. *Arab Roots of Gemology: Ahmad Ibn Yusuf Al Tifaschi's Best Thoughts on the Best of Stones*. Trans. Samar Najm Abul Huda. London: Scarecrow Press, 1998.

Amarasinghe, H. K. B. D. *Tarunangana Sandesaya*. Hingulwala: T. B. Kulatunga and M. B. Kulatunga, 1934. Colombo National Museum Library 104/Z11.

Appadurai, Arjun. *Fear of Small Numbers: An Essay on the Geography of Anger*. Durham, NC: Duke University Press, 2006.

Apūpakkar, Mupisāl. "Āyuḷil Oru Muṟaiyāvatu Ātam Malaikku Celvōm." *Asian News*, March 15, 2021.

Arab Navigation in the Indian Ocean Before the Coming of the Portuguese, Being a Translation of Kitāb Al-Fawā'id Fī Uṣūl Al-Baḥr Wa'l-Qawā'id of Aḥmad B. Mājid Al-Najdī. Trans. G. R. Tibbetts. London: Royal Asiatic Society of Great Britain and Ireland, 1971.

Arābihaṭana Hevat Siṅhala Kaviyen Racanā Karaṇalada Misaradeśika Yuddhaya. Lakmiṇipagaṇ Yantrālaya, 1883. Colombo National Museum Library 104/FF14.

Archer, David. *The Long Thaw: How Humans Are Changing the Next 100,000 Years of Earth's Climate*. Princeton, NJ: Princeton University Press, 2009.

Arumugam, Sanmugam. *Hundred Hindu Temples of Sri Lanka: Ancient, Medieval and Modern*. Ed. Thirumugam Arumugam. London: Ohm Books, 2014 (1980).

Aryasinghe, Abaya. *The Deities and Demons of Sinhala Origin*. Nugegoda: Deepanee, 2000.

Asad, Talal. *Genealogies of Religion: Discipline and Reasons of Power in Christianity and Islam*. Baltimore: Johns Hopkins University Press, 1993.

Athetha Wakya Deepanya or a Collection of Sinhalese Proverbs, Maxims, Fables &C. Compiled and Translated Into English. 1881. Colombo National Museum Library 104/CC4.

Azeez, I. L. M. Abdul. *A Criticism of Mr. Ramanathan's "Ethnology of the 'Moors' of Ceylon."* Colombo: Moors' Islamic Cultural Home, 1957 (1907).

Bailey, Benjamin. *Poetical Sketches of the Interior of the Island of Ceylon: Benjamin Bailey's Original Manuscript, 1841*. Ed. Rajpal K. de Silva. London: Serendib Publications, 2011.

Balasundaram, Sasikumar. "An Indentured Tamil Goddess: Mariyamman's Migration to Ceylon's Plantations as a Worker." In *Inventing and Reinventing the Goddess: Contemporary Iterations of Hindu Deities on the Move*, ed. Sree Padma, 103–19. London: Lexington Books, 2014.

——. "Temples and Deities on Plantations." In *Multi-Religiosity in Contemporary Sri Lanka: Innovation, Shared Spaces, Contestation*, ed. Mark P. Whitaker, Darini Rajasingham-Senanayake and Pathmanesan Sanmugeswaran, 179–91. New York: Routledge, 2022.

The Balavariani (Barlaam and Josaphat), a Tale from the Christian East Translated from the Old Georgian. Trans. David Marshall Lang. Berkeley: University of California Press, 1966.

Ballou, Maturin M. *The Pearl of India.* 2nd ed. Boston: Houghton, Mifflin, 1895.

Baṇḍā, S. J. Sumanasēkara. *Guru Haṭana Hevat Sokari Nāṭakaya.* Colombo: Goḍagē saha Sahōdarayō, 2005.

Bandara, Kelum, and Yohan Perera. "Election to Select Chief Incumbent of Sri Pada Vihare, Rigged: UNP." *Daily Mirror*, December 2, 2011.

——. "Sri Pada: UNP Accuses Government of Disgraceful Conduct." *Daily Mirror*, December 3, 2011.

Baṇḍāra, W. Ātar Ähäliyagoḍa. *Buduguṇa Mālāva.* Colombo: Viliyam Kōnāra Basnāyaka Raṇasiṃha Baṇḍāra, 1928. Colombo National Museum Library 104/Z2.

Barnett, L. D., ed. *A Supplementary Catalogue of the Tamil Books in the Library of the British Museum.* London: British Museum, 1931.

Barnett, L. D., and G. U. Pope, eds. *A Catalogue of Tamil Books in the Library of the British Museum.* London: British Museum, 1909.

Barry, Andrew. "Infrastructure and the Earth." In *Infrastructures and Social Complexity: A Companion*, ed. Penny Harvey, Casper Brunn Jensen, and Atsuro Morita, 187–97. New York: Routledge, 2017.

Bass, Daniel. *Everyday Ethnicity in Sri Lanka: Up-Country Tamil Identity Politics.* Colombo: Social Scientists' Association, 2015. 2013.

——. "The Goddess of the Tea Estates: Hindu Traditions and Community Boundaries in the Up-Country of Sri Lanka." *South Asianist* 6 (2018): 23–45.

——. "Paper Tigers on the Prowl: Rumors, Violence and Agency in the Up-Country of Sri Lanka." *Anthropological Quarterly* 81, no. 1 (2008): 269–95.

Bastin, Rohan. *The Domain of Constant Excess: Plural Worship at the Munnesvaram Temples in Sri Lanka.* New York: Berghahn, 2002.

——. "Saints, Sites, and Religious Accommodation in Sri Lanka." In *Sharing the Sacra: The Politics and Pragmatics of Intercommunal Relations Around Holy Places*, ed. Glenn Bowman, 107–27. New York: Berghahn, 2012.

Bauman, Whitney A. *Religion and Ecology: Developing a Planetary Ethic.* New York: Columbia University Press, 2014.

Behr, Herport, Schweitzer, and Fryke. *Germans in Dutch Ceylon* Trans. R. Raven-Hart. Colombo: Colombo National Museum, 1953.

Bell, H. C. P. *Report on the Kuṭṭāpiṭiya Sannasa.* Kandy: Miller, 1925.

——. "Sinhalese Customs and Ceremonies Connected with Paddy Cultivation in the Low-Country." *Journal of the Ceylon Branch of the Royal Asiatic Society* 8, no. 26 (1883): 44–93.

Bennett, Jane. *Vibrant Matter: A Political Ecology of Things.* Durham, NC: Duke University Press, 2010.

Berkwitz, Stephen C. "Sinhala *Sandēśa* Poetry in a Cosmopolitan Context." In *Sri Lanka at the Crossroads of History*, ed. Zoltán Biedermann and Alan Strathern, 94–112. London: UCL Press, 2017.

——. "Strong Men and Sensual Women in Sinhala Buddhist Poetry." In *Religious Boundaries for Sex, Gender, and Corporeality*, ed. Alexandra Cuffel, Ana Echevarria, and Georgios T. Halkias, 63–77. New York: Routledge, 2019.

Bhattachariya, Satarupa, Chris Kamalendran, and Asif Fuard. "The Divided Brotherhood: Jihad in Lanka: Sectarianism Takes Root as Muslim Groups Battle It Out in Beruwala." *Sunday Times*, August 2, 2009.

Bhikkhu, Ṭhānissaro. *Udāna: Exclamations*. Valley Center, CA: Metta Forest Monastery, 2012.

Bigelow, Anna. *Sharing the Sacred: Practicing Pluralism in Muslim North India*. New York: Oxford University Press, 2010.

Bishop, Peter. *The Myth of Shangri-La: Tibet, Travel Writing, and the Western Creation of Sacred Landscape*. Berkeley: University of California Press, 1989.

Björkman, Lisa. *Pipe Politics, Contested Waters: Embedded Infrastructures of Millennial Mumbai*. Durham, NC: Duke University Press, 2015.

Blackburn, Anne M. *Buddhist Learning and Textual Practice in Eighteenth-Century Lankan Monastic Culture*. Princeton, NJ: Princeton University Press, 2001.

——. *Locations of Buddhism: Colonialism and Modernity in Sri Lanka*. Chicago: University of Chicago Press, 2010.

Bodhi, Bhikkhu. *The Connected Discourses of the Buddha: A Translation of the Saṃyutta Nikāya*. Boston: Wisdom, 2000.

——. *The Numerical Discourses of the Buddha: A Translation of the Aṅguttara Nikāya*. Somerville, MA: Wisdom, 2012.

——. *The Suttanipāta: An Ancient Collection of the Buddha's Discourses Together with Its Commentaries*. Somerville, MA: Wisdom, 2017.

Bowman, Glenn. "Grounds for Sharing—Occasions for Conflict: An Inquiry Into the Social Foundations of Cohabitation and Antagonism." In *Post-Ottoman Coexistence: Sharing Space in the Shadow of Conflict*, ed. Rebecca Bryant, 258–75. Oxford: Berghahn, 2016.

Buddhaghosa, Bhadantācariya. *Sāratthappakāsinī Nāma Saṁyuttaṭṭhakathā*. Yangon: Ministry of Religious Affairs, 2008.

Buddhaputra, Mayurapāda. *Pūjāvaliya*. Colombo: M. D. Guṇsēna saha Samāgama, 2015.

Caddy, Florence. *To Siam and Malaya in the Duke of Sutherland's Yacht "Sans Peur."* London: Hurst and Blackett, 1889.

Callicott, J. Baird. "The New New (Buddhist?) Ecology." *Journal for the Study of Religion, Nature and Culture* 2, no. 2 (2008): 166–82.

Cambri, Gui de. *Barlaam and Josaphat: A Christian Tale of the Buddha*. Trans. Peggy McCracken. New York: Penguin, 2014.

Campbell, Christina. "To Be a Pilgrim." *Blackwell's Magazine* (1961).

Cañcāri, Ivaṉ. "Marakatattīvīl Ulakiṉ Mutaṟcuvaṭu." *Cilōṉ Muslim*, February 5, 2016, 6.

Capper, John. "The Tourist in Ceylon." In *All the World Over*, ed. Edwin Hodder, 29–40. London: Thomas Cook and Son, 1875.

Cāralnāṭaṉ, Kalāpūcaṇam. *Cintaiyaḷḷum Civaṉoḷipātamalai*. Kotagala: Cāral Veḷiyīṭṭakam, 2009.

Carter, John Ross, and Mahinda Palihawadana, eds. *The Dhammapada*. New York: Oxford University Press, 1987.

Carter, Paul. *The Road to Botany Bay: An Exploration of Landscape and History*. New York: Knopf, 1988.

Carver, J. *The New Universal Traveller. Containing a Full and Distinct Account of All the Empires, Kingdoms, and States in the Known World*. London: G. Robinson, 1779.

Cekarācacēkaraṉ, Makā Vittuvāṉ Ciṅkai. *Takṣiṇakailāca Purāṇam*. Ed. K. C. Naṭarācā. 2 vols. Colombo: Intucamaya Kalāccāra Aluvarkaḷ Tiṇaikkaḷam, 1995.

Chakrabarti, Pratik, and Joydeep Sen. "'The World Rests on the Back of a Tortoise': Science and Mythology in Indian History." *Modern Asian Studies* 50, no. 3 (2016): 808–40.

Chakrabarty, Dipesh. "Climate and Capital: On Conjoined Histories." *Critical Inquiry* 41 (2014): 1–23.

——. "The Climate of History: Four Theses." *Critical Inquiry* 35, no. 2 (2009): 197–222.

——. "Postcolonial Studies and the Challenge of Climate Change." *New Literary History* 43, no. 1 (2012): 1–18.

Chakravarti, Ranabir. "Reaching Out to Distant Shores: Indo-Judaic Trade Contacts (up to C.E. 1300)." In *Indo-Judaic Studies in the Twenty-First Century: A View from the Margin*, ed. Nathan Katz, 19–43. New York: Palgrave Macmillan, 2007.

Ché-Ross, Raimy. "Munshi Abdullah's Voyage to Mecca: A Preliminary Introduction and Translation." *Indonesia and the Malay World* 28, no. 81 (2000): 173–213.

Chinaman, John. "Colombo, Ceylon: The Pearl Drop on the Brow of India—Land of Beauty and Spicy Fragrance." *Baltimore Sun*, March 16, 1887, 5.

Choksy, Jamsheed K. "Sailors, Soldiers, Priests, and Merchants: Reappraising Iran's Early Connections to Ceylon." *Iranica Antiqua* 48 (2013): 363–91.

Cicuzza, Claudio. *A Mirror Reflecting the Entire World: The Pāli Buddhapādamaṅgala or "Auspicious Signs on the Buddha's Feet."* Bangkok: Fragile Palm Leaves Foundation, 2011.

Cīttalaiccāttaṉār. *Maṇimēkalai*. Ed. K. Kalyanasundaram and M. Sivakumar. Project Madurai, 2002. www.projectmadurai.org/pm_etexts/pdf/pm0141.pdf.

"Civaṉoḷipāta Malaiyil Civakōcam Eḻuppiyavarkaḷukku Accuṟuttal!" *Karudan News—Karuṭaṉiṉ Pārvaiyil*, April 23, 2017.

Clark, John. "On Being None with Nature: Nagarjuna and the Ecology of Emptiness." *Capitalism Nature Socialism* 19, no. 4 (December 2008): 6–29.

Clark, Timothy. *Ecocriticism on the Edge: The Anthropocene as a Threshold Concept*. New York: Bloomsbury, 2015.

Cohen, Jeffrey Jerome. *Stone: An Ecology of the Inhuman*. Minneapolis: University of Minnesota Press, 2015.

Colebrook, Claire. "Framing the End of the Species." In *Extinction*, ed. Claire Colebrook. Ann Arbor, MI: Open Humanities Press, 2012.

Collins, Steven. "The Discourse on What Is Primary (Aggañña-Sutta): An Annotated Translation." *Journal of Indian Philosophy* 21 (1993): 301–93.

——. "On the Very Idea of the Pali Canon." *Journal of the Pali Text Society* 15 (1990): 89–126.

——. *Wisdom as a Way of Life: Theravāda Buddhism Reimagined*. New York: Columbia University Press, 2020.

Colopy, Cheryl. *Dirty, Sacred Rivers: Confronting South Asia's Water Crisis*. New York: Oxford University Press, 2012.

Cōmacuntarappulavar, K. "Īḻakēcari Āṇṭumaṭal Pāṭṭu: Vāyuṟavāḻtti Matiyuraittatu." *Īḻakēcari*, 1935, 1–3.

Connolly, William E. *Facing the Planetary: Entangled Humanism and the Politics of Swarming*. Durham, NC: Duke University Press, 2017.

——. *Pluralism*. Durham, NC: Duke University Press, 2005.

——. "Process Philosophy and Planetary Politics." In *Common Goods: Economy, Ecology, and Political Theology*, ed. Melanie Johnson-DeBaufre, Catherine Keller, and Elias Ortega-Aponte, 25–53. New York: Fordham University Press, 2015.

——. *Why I Am Not a Secularist*. Minneapolis: University of Minnesota Press, 1999.

A Conversation Between a Christian and a Pilgrim—Śrī Pādaya Gāṇaya. Colombo: Wesleyan Mission Press for Ceylon Religious Tract Society, 1871.

Conway, Moncure Daniel. *My Pilgrimage to the Wise Men of the East*. Boston: Houghton, Mifflin, 1906.

Cooray, P. G. *An Introduction to the Geology of Ceylon*. Colombo: National Museums of Ceylon, 1967.

——. "The Precambrian of Sri Lanka: A Historical Review." *Precambrian Research* 66 (1994): 3–18.

Crawford, A. R., and R. L. Oliver. "The Precambrian Geochronology of Ceylon." *Special Publication—Geological Society of Australia* 2 (1969): 283–306.

Crutzen, Paul J., and Eugene F. Stoermer. "The 'Anthropocene.'" *Global Change Newsletter* 41 (2000): 17–18.

Cūḷavaṃsa, Being the More Recent Part of the Mahāvaṃsa. Trans. Wilhelm Geiger and C. Mabel Rickmers. Delhi: Motilal Banarsidass Pvt., 1996 (1929).

D.D.L. *Siri Pāda Gaman Vistaraya*. Colombo: Lakdiv, 1891. Colombo National Museum Library 104/S8.

Da Länarōl, V. D. *Goyam Kav Saha Neḷum Kav*. Colombo: M. D. Guṇasēna saha Samāgama, 1946.

Da Silvā, Jōn. *Śrīpāda Śatakaya*. Colombo, 1912.

Da Silva, Mullapiṭiyē K. H., and Abhayasiṃha Vijayaśrīvardhana. *Siṃhala Sähäli*. Ed. Vibhavi Vijayasrīvardhana. 2nd ed. Colombo: Äs Goḍagē saha Sahōdarayō, 2009 (1957).

Da Silva, W. Ātar, and Guṇapāla Malalasēkara, eds. *Siṅhala Janasammata Kāvya*. Colombo: S. Goḍagē saha Sahōdarayō, 1935. Reprint, 2013.

Daniel, E. Valentine. *Charred Lullabies: Chapters in an Anthropography of Violence*. Princeton, NJ: Princeton University Press, 1996.

Darley, Rebecca R. "'Implicit Cosmopolitanism' and the Commercial Role of Ancient Lanka." In *Sri Lanka at the Crossroads of History*, ed. Zoltán Biedermann and Alan Strathern, 44–65. London: UCL Press, 2017.

Das, Veena. "Cohabitating an Interreligious Milieu: Reflections on Religious Diversity." In *A Companion to the Anthropology of Religion*, ed. Janice Boddy and Michael Lambek, 69–84. West Sussex: Wiley Blackwell, 2013.

Davy, John. "A Description of Adam's Peak. In a Letter Addressed to Sir Humphry Davy, F.R.S. Ll.D." *Journal of Science and the Arts* 5, no. 9 (1818): 25.

de la Cadena, Marisol. *Earth Beings: Ecologies of Practice Across Andean Worlds*. Durham, NC: Duke University Press, 2015.

de Munck, Victor C. "Sufi and Reformist Designs: Muslim Identity in Sri Lanka." In *Buddhist Fundamentalism and Minority Identities in Sri Lanka*, ed. Tessa J. Bartholomeusz and Chandra Richard De Silva, 110–32. Albany: State University of New York Press, 1998.

De Silva, Chandra Richard. *Sri Lanka: A History*. New Delhi: Vikas Publishing House, 1987.

de Silva, Padmasiri. *Environmental Philosophy and Ethics in Buddhism*. London: Macmillan Press, 1998.

De Silva, Premakumara. "Anthropological Studies on South Asian Pilgrimage: Case of Buddhist Pilgrimage in Sri Lanka." *International Journal of Religious Tourism and Pilgrimage* 4, no. 1 (2016): 17–33.

——. "'Colonial Governmentality': Legal and Administrative Technologies of the Governance of Sri Pada Temple in Sri Lanka." In *Theravada Buddhism in Colonial Contexts*, ed. Thomas Borchert, 121–37. New York: Routledge, 2018.

——. "Competitive Sharing: Sri Lankan Hindus and Up-Country Tamil Religiosity at the Sri Pada Temple." *South Asianist* 6, no. 1 (2018): 76–97.

——. "God of Compassion and the Divine Protector of Sri Pada: Trends in Popular Buddhism in Sri Lanka." *Sri Lanka Journal of the Humanities* 34 (2008): 93–107.

——. "Kings, Monks and Pre-Colonial States: Patrons of the Temple of the Sacred Footprint." In *Asian Art and Culture: A Research Volume in Honor of Ananda Coomaraswamy*, ed. Anura Manatunga, Sachee Ranaweera, Thilanka Manoj Siriwardana, and Kaushalya Gangadari Gunasena, 41–53. Department of Information: Government of Sri Lanka, 2012.

———. "Religion, History and Colonial Powers: Colonial Knowledge Production on a Popular Sacred Site in Sri Lanka." *Journal of History and Social Sciences* 5, no. 1 (2014): 21–34.

———. "Reordering of Postcolonial Sri Pāda Temple in Sri Lanka: Buddhism, State, and Nationalism." *History and Sociology of South Asia* 7, no. 155 (2013): 155–76.

———. " 'To Worship Our "Boss" (the Buddha)': Youth Religiosity in a Popular Pilgrimage Site in Sri Lanka." In *Ritual Journeys in South Asia: Constellations and Contestations of Mobility and Space*, ed. Christopher Bergmann and Jürgen Schaflechner, 139–56. New York: Routledge, 2020.

de Silva, R. K., ed. *19th Century Newspaper Engravings of Ceylon—Sri Lanka: Accompanied by Original Texts with Notes and Comments.* London: Serendib Publications, 1998.

de Silva, W. A., ed. *Catalogue of Palm Leaf Manuscripts in the Library of the Colombo Museum* Vol. 1. Colombo: Ceylon Government Press, 1938.

De Zoysa, Mangala, and Makoto Inoue. "Climate Change Impacts, Agroforestry Adaptation and Policy Environment in Sri Lanka." *Open Journal of Forestry* 4 (2014): 439–56.

DeCaroli, Robert. *Haunting the Buddha: Indian Popular Religions and the Formation of Buddhism.* New York: Oxford University Press, 2004.

Deleuze, Gilles, and Felix Guattari. *What Is Philosophy?* Trans. Hugh Tomlinson and Graham Burchell. New York: Columbia University Press, 1994 (1991).

Denham, E. B. *The Census of Ceylon, 1911. Town and Village Statistics.* Colombo: H. C. Cottle, 1912.

Dep, Arthur C. *The Egyptian Exiles in Ceylon (Sri Lanka).* Colombo: Praveena Press, 2011. 1983.

Deraniyagala, P. E. P., ed. *Deva Varṇanā Kāvya.* Colombo: Ceylon National Museum, 1960.

———. "The Hippopotamus as an Index to Early Man in India and Ceylon." *Science and Culture* 7, no. 2 (1941): 66–68.

———. *The Pleistocene of Ceylon.* Ceylon National Museums Natural History Series. Ceylon: Government Press, 1958.

———. "Prehistoric Archaeology in Ceylon." *Asian Perspectives* 7 (1963): 189–95.

———. "The Saman Sirita, a Hymn to the Presiding Deity of Mount Saman." *Spolia Zeylanica* 29, no. 2 (1961): 301–3.

———, ed. *Sinhala Verse (Kavi), Collected by the Late Hugh Nevill.* Vol. 1. Colombo: Ceylon National Museums, 1954.

———. "Some Aspects of the Prehistory of Ceylon, Part I." *Spolia Zeylanica* 23, no. 2 (1943): 93–115.

———. "Some Fossil Animals from Ceylon." *Journal of the Ceylon Branch of the Royal Asiatic Society* 33, no. 88 (1935): 165–68.

———. "Some Fossil Animals from Ceylon. Part 2." *Journal of the Ceylon Branch of the Royal Asiatic Society* 34, no. 91 (1938): 231–39.

———. "The Stone Age and Cave Men of Ceylon." *Journal of the Ceylon Branch of the Royal Asiatic Society* 34, no. 92 (1939): 351–73.

Deraniyagala, S. U. *The Prehistory and Protohistory of Sri Lanka.* Colombo: Central Cultural Fund, 2007.

———. *The Prehistory of Sri Lanka: An Ecological Perspective.* 2 vols. Colombo: Department of Archaeological Survey, Government of Sri Lanka, 1992.

DeVotta, Neil. "The Liberation Tigers of Tamil Eelam and the Lost Quest for Separatism in Sri Lanka." *Asian Survey* 49, no. 6 (2009): 1021–51.

Dewaraja, Lorna. "The Muslims in the Kandyan Kingdom (c. 1600–1815): A Study of Ethnic Integration." In *Muslims of Sri Lanka: Avenues to Antiquity*, ed. M. A. M. Shukri, 211–34. Beruwala: Jamiah Naleemia Institute, 1986.

———. *The Muslims of Sri Lanka: One Thousand Years of Ethnic Harmony, 900–1915.* Colombo: Lanka Islamic Foundation, 1994.

Dhammapāla, Pūjya Bōmiriyē. *Bududahama Hā Parisaraya*. Wellampitiya: Śrī Pāli Prakāśakayō, 2000.

Dharmabandhu, T. S., ed. *Jana Kav Dahasa: Patē, Potē, Hā Gamē—Goḍa Pavatnā Jana Kav*. Colombo: M. D. Guṇasēna saha Samāgama, 1956.

Dharmasēna, R. Aśōka A. *Uttama Muṇi Siripā*. n.d.

Dharmavardhana, W. A. F., ed. *Parevi Sandeśa Kāvya Varṇanāva*. Colombo: Guṇasēna, 1967.

Dickson, John F. "Service Tenures Commission. Report of the Service Tenures Commissioner, for 1870." In *Ceylon: Indische Volksbelangen*, ed. A. W. P. Verkerk Pistorius. The Hague: Martinus Nijhoff, 1874.

Dissanayake, C. B., and Rohana Chandrajith. "Sri Lanka-Madagascar Gondwana Linkage: Evidence for a Pan-African Mineral Belt." *Journal of Geology* 107 (1999): 223–35.

Dissanayake, C. B., Rohana Chandrajith, and H. J. Tobschall. "The Geology, Mineralology and Rare Element Geochemistry of the Gem Deposits of Sri Lanka." *Geological Society of Finland* 72 (2000): 5–20.

Drew, Georgina. *River Dialogues: Hindu Faith and the Political Ecology of Dams on the Sacred Ganga*. Tucson: University of Arizona Press, 2017.

Duncan, James S. *In the Shadows of the Tropics: Climate, Race and Biopower in Nineteenth Century Ceylon*. Burlington: Ashgate, 2007.

Duncan, Jonathan. "An Account of Two Fakeers, with Their Portraits." *Asiatic Researches* 5 (1799): 37–52.

E.R.P. "Adam's Peak: Ceylon." *Literary Gazette: A Weekly Journal of Literature, Science, and the Fine Arts* 1084 (October 28, 1837): 689–90.

Eliade, Mircea. *Patterns in Comparative Religion* Trans. Rosemary Sheed. New York: Meridian Books, 1958.

——. *The Quest: History and Meaning in Religion*. Chicago: University of Chicago Press, 1969.

——. *Shamanism: Archaic Techniques of Ecstasy* Trans. Willard R. Trask. Princeton, NJ: Princeton University Press, 1964 (1951).

El-Mas'ūdī's Historical Encyclopaedia, Entitled "Meadows of Gold and Mines of Gems." Trans. Aloys Sprenger. Vol. 1. London: Oriental Translation Fund, 1841.

Elverskog, Johan. *Buddhism and Islam on the Silk Road*. Philadelphia: University of Pennsylvania Press, 2010.

——. *Uygur Buddhist Literature*. Silk Road Studies. Turnhout: Brepols, 1997.

Ernst, Carl. "India as a Sacred Islamic Land." In *Religions of India in Practice*, ed. Donald S. Lopez, 556–63. Princeton, NJ: Princeton University Press, 1995.

Esin, Emel. "An Aspect of Turkish Mediacy in the Westward Transmission of Eastern Culture, in the Case of Mysticism." In *Proceedings of the Thirty-First International Congress of Human Sciences in Asia and North Africa, Tokyo-Kyoto, 31st August–7th September 1983*, 378–79. 1983.

——. "On the Relationship Between the Iconography in Musim Uyġur Manuscripts and Buddhist Uyġur Eschatology." In *Altaistic Studies: Papers at the 25th Meeting of the Permanent International Altaistic Conference at Uppsala June 7–11 1982*, ed. Gunnar Jarring and Staffan Rosén, 37–52. Stockholm: Almqvist and Wiksell International, 1985.

"Exploring of Adam's Peak: A Lofty and Sacred Mountain in the Island of Ceylon." *La belle assemblée: or Court and fashionable magazine*, December 1816, 268–69.

Faria e Sousa, Manuel de. *The Portugues Asia*. Trans. John Stevens. 3 vols. London: Printed for C. Brome, 1695.

Farook, Latheef. *Nobody's People: The Forgotten Plight of Sri Lanka's Muslims*. Colombo: South Asia News Agency, 2009.

Fernando, M. J., and A. N. S. Kulasinghe. "Seismicity of Sri Lanka." *Physics of the Earth and Planetary Interiors* 44 (1986): 99–106.

Fernando, Tamara. "Seeing Like the Sea: A Multispecies History of the Ceylon Pearl Fishery 1800–1925." *Past and Present*, no. 254 (February 2022): 127–60.

Field, Garrett. *Modernizing Composition: Sinhala Song, Poetry, and Politics in Twentieth-Century Sri Lanka*. Oakland: University of California Press, 2017.

Fisher, Elaine. *Hindu Pluralism: Religion and the Public Sphere in Early Modern South India*. Oakland: University of California Press, 2017.

Forbes, Jonathan. *Eleven Years in Ceylon. Comprising Sketches of the Field Sports and Natural History of That Colony, and an Account of Its History and Antiquities*. 2 vols. London: R. Bentley, 1840.

Frauenfeld, Georg. "Ausflung Nach Dem Adamspik Auf Ceylon." *Sitzungberichte der Kaiserlichen Akademie der Wissenschaften* 37 (1859): 789–802.

Friedrich, Philip. "Adjudicating Antiquity: The Politics of Historical Confrontation at Devanagala, Sri Lanka." In *Buddhist Extremists and Muslim Minorities: Religious Conflict in Contemporary Sri Lanka*, ed. John Clifford Holt, 140–63. New York: Oxford University Press, 2016.

Gamlat, Sucarita, and A. Adikāri, eds. *Mūlika Piriven Pot: Siṃhala Hōḍiya, Nampota, Maṅgul Lakuṇa, Gaṇadevi Hälla, Vadan Kavi Pota, Buddhagadyaya, Sakaskaḍa*. Colombo: Äs Godagē saha Sahōrdarayō, 1988.

Gay, J. Drew. *The Prince of Wales in India, or from Pall Mall to the Punjab*. New York: R. Worthington, 1877.

Geiger, Wilhelm, ed. *Cūlavaṃsa: Being the More Recent Part of the Mahāvaṃsa*. London: Pali Text Society, 1980.

Ghouse, M. B. Mohamed. "Folk Songs of the Moors." In *The First Twenty One Years: Moors' Islamic Cultural Home, 1944–1965*, 42–43. Colombo: Moors' Islamic Cultural Home, 1965.

Gimaret, Daniel. *Le livre de Bilawhar et Būdāsf selon la version arabe ismaélienne*. Geneva: Droz, 1971.

Godakumbura, C. E. *Panavitiya Ambalama Carvings*. Colombo: Archaeological Department, 1981.

Gombrich, Richard F. "The Buddha's Book of Genesis?" *Indo-Iranian Journal* 35 (1992): 159–78.

——. *Buddhist Precept and Practice: Traditional Buddhism in the Rural Highlands of Ceylon*. 2nd ed. London: Clarendon Press, 1995. 1971.

Gopal Iyer, T. V., ed. *Tēvāram: 2. Appar Et Cuntarar*. Pondicherry: Institut Français d'Indologie, 1985.

Gould, Stephen Jay. *Time's Arrow, Time's Cycle: Myth and Metaphor in the Discovery of Geological Time*. Cambridge, MA: Harvard University Press, 1987.

Guṇasēkara, Upāli. "Sobādahamē Vyavasthāva Ullaṅghanaya Kirīma." *Vanajīvi/Vaṉavilaṅku/Wildlife* 8, no. 1 (2012): 23–27.

Gunasekara-Rockwell, Achala. "Hūniyam: Demon to Deity." PhD diss., University of Wisconsin–Madison, 2011.

Guṇasōma, Guṇasēkara. *Samandevi Aḍaviya Janakatā*. Colombo: Fāsṭ Pabliṣin, 2013.

Gunatilaka, Ana. "Role of Basin-Wide Landslides in the Formation of Extensive Alluvial Gemstone Deposits in Sri Lanka." *Earth Surface Processes and Landforms* 32 (2007): 1863–73.

Gunavarḍana, W. F., ed. *Kokila Sandeśaya*. Colombo: Peramuna, 1945.

Gunawardana, R. A. L. H. *Robe and Plough: Monasticism and Economic Interest in Early Medieval Sri Lanka*. Tucson: University of Arizona Press, 1979.

Haberman, David. *Loving Stones: Making the Impossible Possible in the Worship of Mount Govardhan*. New York: Oxford University Press, 2020.

——. *People Trees: Worship of Trees in Northern India*. New York: Oxford University Press, 2013.

Hallisey, Charles. "The Care of the Past: The Place of Pastness in Transgenerational Projects." In *On Religion and Memory*, ed. Babette Hellemans, Willemein Otten, and Burcht Pranger, 89–99. New York: Fordham University Press, 2013.

——. "Works and Persons in Sinhala Literary Culture." In *Literary Cultures in History: Reconstructions from South Asia*, ed. Sheldon Pollock, 689–746. Berkeley: University of California Press, 2003.

Handunnetti, Dilrukshi. "An Urban 'Butterfly Experience' in Sri Lanka." *Mongabay*, May 15, 2019.

Haniffa, Farzana. "Piety as Politics Amongst Muslim Women in Contemporary Sri Lanka." *Modern Asian Studies* 42, no. 2/3 (2008): 347–75.

Haraway, Donna J. *Staying with the Trouble: Making Kin in the Chthulucene*. Durham, NC: Duke University Press, 2016.

——. *When Species Meet*. Minneapolis: University of Minnesota Press, 2008.

Hardy, R. Spence. *A Manual of Budhism, in Its Modern Development; Translated from Singhalese Mss.* London: Partridge and Oakey, 1853.

Harvey, Penny, and Hannah Knox. "The Enchantments of Infrastructure." *Mobilities* 7, no. 4 (2012): 521–36.

Hasan, Perween. "The Footprint of the Prophet." *Muqarnas* 10 (1993): 335–43.

Hayden, Robert M., Tuğba Tanyeri-Erdemir, Timothy D. Walker, Aykan Erdemir, Devika Rangachari, Manuel Aguilar-Moreno, Enrique López-Hurtado, and Milica Bakić-Hayden. *Antagonistic Tolerance: Competitive Sharing of Religious Sites and Spaces*. New York: Routledge, 2016.Hazard, Sonia. "The Material Turn in the Study of Religion." *Religion and Society: Advances in Research* 4 (2013): 58–78.

Heim, Maria. "The Aesthetics of Excess." *Journal of the American Academy of Religion* 71, no. 3 (2003): 531–54.

——. *Words for the Heart: A Treasury of Emotions from Classical India*. Princeton, NJ: Princeton University Press, 2022.

Henry, Justin W. "Distant Shores of Dharma: Historical Imagination in Sri Lanka from the Late Medieval Period." PhD diss., University of Chicago, 2017.

——. *Ravana's Kingdom: The Ramayana and Sri Lankan History from Below*. New York: Oxford University Press, 2022.

Heslop, Luke Alexander. "On Sacred Ground: The Political Performance of Religious Responsibility." *Contemporary South Asia* 22, no. 1 (2014): 21–36.

Hētumuni, Välitara Dharma Śrī S. "Samanoḷa Girimudunēdī." *Sarasavi Mäduru* 1, no. 10 (August/September 1933): 189–90.

Hēvāvasam, P. B. G. *Mātara Yugayē Sāhityadharayan Hā Sāhitya Nibandhana*. Saṃskrutika Kaṭayutu Piḷibaňda Depārtimentuva, 1966.

——, ed. *Pantis Kōlmura Kavi*. Colombo: Pradīpa Prakāśakayō, 1974.

Hingston, James. *The Australian Abroad. Branches from the Main Routes Around the World. Series 2. Ceylon, India, and Egypt*. London: Sampson Low, Marston, Searle, and Rivington, 1880.

The History of Al-Ṭabarī. Trans. Franz Rosenthal. Vol. 1. Albany: State University of New York Press, 1989.

Ho, Engseng. *The Graves of Tarim: Genealogy and Mobility Across the Indian Ocean*. Berkeley: University of California Press, 2006.

Holt, John Clifford. *The Buddhist Viṣṇu: Religious Transformation, Politics, and Culture*. New York: Columbia University Press, 2004.

——. *The Religious World of Kīrti Śrī: Buddhism, Art, and Politics in Late Medieval Sri Lanka*. New York: Oxford University Press, 1996.

Hopkins, Jeffrey. *Nāgārjuna's Precious Garland: Buddhist Advice for Living and Liberation.* Ithaca, NY: Snow Lion, 2007.

Hopkins, Steven P. "Love, Messengers, and Beloved Landscapes: *Sandesakavya* in Comparative Perspective." *International Journal of Hindu Studies* 8, no. 1–3 (2004): 29–55.

Human Rights and Religions in Sri Lanka: A Commentary on the Universal Declaration of Human Rights. Colombo Sri Lanka Foundation, 1988.

Hurd, Elizabeth Shakman. *Beyond Religious Freedom: The New Global Politics of Religion.* Princeton, NJ: Princeton University Press, 2015.

Hurst, John F. *Indika: The Country and the People of India and Ceylon.* New York: Harper and Brothers, 1891.

Hutton, James. "Theory of the Earth; or an Investigation of the Laws Observable in the Composition, Dissolution, and Restoration of Land Upon the Globe." *Transactions of the Royal Society of Edinburgh* 1, no. 2 (1788): 209–304.

Ilangaratne, T. B. *The Matchmaker.* Colombo: Lake House, 1974.

Ilaṅgattilaka, Gāmiṇi Baṇḍāra. "Janapati Guvanē Siṭa Picca Mal Isiddī Śrī Pāda Maḷuva Sādu Nadin Giṅgum Deyi." *Divayina*, February 8, 2014.

India and the Neighbouring Territories in the Kitāb Nuzhat Al-Mushtāq Fi'khtirāq Al-'āfāq of Al-Sharīf Al-Idrīsī. Trans. S. Magbul Ahmad. Leiden: E. J. Brill, 1960.

Indrajith, Saman. "Election Rigged, Alleges UNP: Election of Chief Incumbent of Sri Pada Vihara." *The Island*, December 2, 2011.

Ismail, Qadri. *Abiding by Sri Lanka: On Peace, Place, and Postcoloniality.* Minneapolis: University of Minnesota Press, 2005.

——. "Unmooring Identity: The Antinomies of Elite Muslim Representation in Modern Sri Lanka." In *Unmaking the Nation: The Politics of Identity and History in Modern Sri Lanka*, ed. Pradeep Jeganathan and Qadri Ismail, 62–107. New York: SSA Sri Lanka, 2009. (1995).

Ives, Christopher. "Resources for Buddhist Environmental Ethics." *Journal of Buddhist Ethics* 20 (2013): 541–71.

Jalais, Annu. *Forest of Tigers: People, Politics and Environment in the Sundarbans.* New Delhi: Routledge, 2010.

Jamal, Ashraf. "Telling and Selling on the Indian Ocean Rim." In *Indian Ocean Studies: Cultural, Social, and Political Perspectives*, ed. Shanti Moorthy and Ashraf Jamal, 403–17. New York: Routledge, 2010.

Jayanetti, Dayāpāla, ed. *Vaṅdanā Kavi Sāhityaya.* Colombo: Samayavardhana, 2005.

Jayasēkara, Attuḍāvē Hārmanis. *Sirilaka Siripada Lakara Saha Abhinava Vandanā Kāvyaya.* Panadura: D. C. Raṇavaka, 1932. Colombo National Museum Library 104/Z2.

——. *Siripadahälla.* Aluthgama: Saddharmaprakāśa Yantrālaya, 1924. Colombo National Museum Library 104/C8.

Jayatilake, Rajika. "Sri Pada: Symbol of Inter-Faith Harmony." *South Asian Life and Times*, January 2003.

Jayawardena, Kumari, and Rachel Kurian. *Class, Patriarchy and Ethnicity on Sri Lankan Plantations: Two Centuries of Power and Protest.* New Delhi: Orient BlackSwan, 2015.

Jazeel, Tariq. *Sacred Modernity: Nature, Environment, and the Postcolonial Geographies of Sri Lankan Nationhood.* Liverpool: Liverpool University Press, 2013.

Jegathesan, Mythri. *Tea and Solidarity: Tamil Women and Work in Postwar Sri Lanka.* Seattle: University of Washington Press, 2019.

Jeyarācā, S. "Eṅkḷ Civaṉoḷipāta Malaip Pirayāṇam." *Intu Iḷaiñaṉ* 15 (1955): 22–25.

Johnston, Alexander. "A Letter to the Secretary Relating to the Preceding Inscription." *Transactions of the Royal Asiatic Society of Great Britain and Ireland* 1, no. 2 (1826): 537–48.

"Journey to Adam's Peak, in the Island of Ceylon." *Atheneum; or, Spirit of the English Magazines* 1, no. 7 (July 1, 1817): 477.

Juvānis, W. A. G. *Śrīpādavandanāva Hevat Giripada Lakara.* Moraketiya: Vijēpāla Yantrālaya, 1929. Colombo National Museum Library 104/Z2.

Juvānisā, K. H. *Śrī Pāda Gaman Vistaraya.* Kegalle: Vidyākalpa Yantrālaya, 1923. Colombo National Museum Library 104/B20.

Kantaiyā, V. C., ed. *Kaṇṇaki Vaḻakkurai.* Batticaloa: Kāraitīvu Intucamaya Virutti Caṅkam, 1968.

Kaplony, Andreas. "Comparing Al-Kāshgharī's Map to His Text: On the Visual Language, Purpose, and Transmission of Arabic-Islamic Maps." In *The Journey of Maps and Images of the Silk Road,* ed. Philippe Forêt and Andreas Kaplony. Leiden: Brill, 2008.

Kāriyavasam, Tissa, ed. *Siri Laka Devivaru: Hiyū Nevil Kāvyāvali Āśrayeni.* Colombo: S. Goḍagē saha Sahōdarayō, 1991.

Karunadasa, Y. *The Theravāda Abhidhamma: Inquiry Into the Nature of Conditioned Reality.* Somerville, MA: Wisdom, 2019.

Karunaratna, Nihal. *Udavattekälē: The Forbidden Forest of the Kings of Kandy.* Colombo: Department of National Archives, 1986.

Karunaratne, T. B. "The Significance of the Signs and Symbols on the Footprints of the Buddha." *Journal of the Sri Lanka Branch of the Royal Asiatic Society* 20 (1976): 47–60.

Kataragama Deviňduṇṭa Sandeśa Kavi 1700–1900. Dehiwala: Tisara Prakāśakayō, 1970.

Katz, M. B. "Sri Lanka-Indian Eastern Ghats-East Antarctica and the Australian Albany Fraser Mobile Belt: Cross Geometry, Age Relationships, and Tectonics in Precambrian Gondwanaland." *Journal of Geology* 97, no. 5 (1989): 646–48.

Katz, M. B., and N. S. W. Kensington. "The Precambrian Metamorphic Rocks of Ceylon." *Geologische Rundschau* 60 (1971): 1523–49.

Kaufman, Eleanor. "The Mineralogy of Being." In *Architecture in the Anthropocene: Encounters Among Design, Deep Time, Science and Philosophy,* ed. Etienne Turpin, 153–66. Ann Arbor, MI: Open Humanities Press, 2013.

Kavirājāvarōtayaṉ. *Kōṇēcar Kalveṭṭu.* Ed. I. Vaṭivēl. Colombo: Intucamaya, Kalācāra Aluvalkaḷ Tiṇaikkaḷam, 1993.

Kāvyakkārayek, Ugat. *Śrīpādapatmaya Vandanāgātha Saha Abhinava Himagatavarṇanāva.* Granthalokayantrālaya: K. Dāvit Perērā, 1902. Colombo National Museum Library 104/T14.

Kemper, Steven. *Buying and Believing: Sri Lankan Advertising and Consumers in a Transnational World.* Chicago: University of Chicago Press, 2001.

Kennedy, Hugh. *The Court of the Caliphs: The Rise and Fall of Islam's Greatest Dynasty.* London: Weidenfeld and Nicolson, 2004.

Kennedy, Kenneth A. R. *God-Apes and Fossil Men: Paleoanthropology of South Asia.* Ann Arbor: University of Michigan Press, 2000.

Kent, Eliza E. *Sacred Groves and Local Gods: Religion and Environmentalism in South India.* Oxford: Oxford University Press, 2013.

Ker, David. "Climbing Up Adam's Peak: A Night of It on Top Amid Queer Surroundings." *New York Times,* May 20, 1888, 13.

Khalid, Amna. "'Subordinate' Negotiations: Indigenous Staff, the Colonial State and Public Health." In *The Social History of Health and Medicine in Colonial India,* ed. Biswamoy Pati and Mark Harrison, 45–73. New York: Routledge, 2009.

Khalidi, Tarif. *Islamic Historiography: The Histories of Mas'ūdī*. Albany: State University of New York Press, 1975.

Klassen, Pamela E., and Courtney Bender. "Habits of Pluralism." In *After Pluralism: Reimagining Religious Engagement*, ed. Pamela E. Klassen and Courtney Bender, 1–28. New York: Columbia University Press, 2010.

Klein, Augusta. *Among the Gods, Scenes of India: With Legends by the Way*. London: William Blackwood and Sons, 1895.

Kohn, Eduardo. *How Forests Think: Toward an Anthropology Beyond the Human*. Berkeley: University of California Press, 2013.

Kołakowski, Leszek. *The Presence of Myth*. Trans. Adam Czerniawski. Chicago: University of Chicago Press, 1989 (1966).

Kölbl-Ebert, Martina, ed. *Geology and Religion: A History of Harmony and Hostility*. London: Geological Society, 2009.

Kopp, Herman, ed. *Manorathapūraṇī: Buddhaghosa's Commentary on the Aṅguttara-Nikāya* Vol. 3. London: Pali Text Society, 1966.

Kourampas, Nikos, Ian A. Simpson, Nimal Perera, Siran U. Deraniyagala, and W. H. Wijeyapala. "Rockshelter Sedimentation in a Dynamic Tropical Landscape: Late Pleistocene-Early Holocene Archaeological Deposits in Kitugala Beli-Lena, Southwestern Sri Lanka." *Geoarcheology: An International Journal* 24, no. 6 (2009): 677–714.

Kröner, A. "African Linkage of Precambrian Sri Lanka." *Geologische Rundschau* 80, no. 2 (1991): 429–40.

Kröner, A., K. V. W. Kehelpannala, and E. Hegner. "Ca. 750–1100 Ma Magmatic Events and Grenville-Age Deformation in Sri Lanka: Relevance for Rodinia Supercontinent Formation and Dispersal, and Gondwana Amalgamation." *Journal of Asian Earth Sciences* 22 (2003): 279–300.

Kuhn, Thomas S. *The Structure of Scientific Revolutions*. 4th ed. Chicago: University of Chicago Press, 2012 (1962).

Kulper, Amy Catania. "Architecture's Lapidarium: On the Lives of Geological Specimens." In *Architecture in the Anthropocene: Encounters Among Design, Deep Time, Science and Philosophy*, ed. Etienne Turpin, 87–110. Ann Arbor, MI: Open Humanities Press, 2013.

Kumāracuvāmi, A., ed. *Tirukkaraicaippurāṇam*. Trincomalee: A. Alakakūn, 1952.

Kumari, M. A. S., K. Kansutisukmongkol, and Y. W. Brockelman. "Plant Diversity in Home Gardens and Its Contribution to Household Economy in Suburban Areas of Sri Lanka." *Environment and Natural Resources Journal* 7 (2009): 12–30.

Lähde, Ville. "Gardens, Climate Changes, and Cultures." In *How Nature Speaks: The Dynamics of the Human Ecological Condition*, ed. Yrjö Haila and Chuck Dyke, 78–105. Durham, NC: Duke University Press, 2006.

Lakpatiraṇa, S. *Situm Sahita Śrī Pāda Vandanāva Hā Bhātiya Raja Kālayē Śrī Pādaya Soyā Dun Koṭāgē Kathāva*. W. Viliyam Perērā saha D. M. Kannangara, 1920. Colombo National Museum Library 104/C.8.

Laṅkāmātāvagē Śokaprakāśaya Hevat Mahadeva Kōpaya. Kosgaslanga: A. K. Romiyel Prērā, 1934. Colombo National Museum Library 104/Y8.

Larkin, Brian. "The Politics and Poetics of Infrastructure." *Annual Review of Anthropology* 42 (2013): 327–43.

Latour, Bruno. *Facing Gaia: Eight Lectures on the New Climatic Regime*. Trans. Catherine Porter. Cambridge: Polity Press, 2017.

——. *Politics of Nature: How to Bring the Sciences Into Democracy*. Trans. Catherine Porter. Cambridge, MA: Harvard University Press, 2004.

——. *We Have Never Been Modern*. Trans. Catherine Porter. Cambridge, MA: Harvard University Press, 1993.

Lawrie, Archibald Campbell. *A Gazetteer of the Central Province of Ceylon*. 2 vols. Colombo: Government Press, 1896–1898.

Lefebvre, Henri. *The Production of Space*. Trans. Donald Nicholson-Smith. Oxford: Blackwell, 1991 [1974].

——. *The Urban Revolution*. Trans. Robert Bononno. Minneapolis: University of Minnesota Press, 2003 [1970].

——. *Writings on Cities*. Trans. Eleonore Kofman and Elizabeth Lebas. Cambridge: Blackwell, 1996.

Leopold, Aldo. *A Sand County Almanac, and Sketches Here and There*. New York: Oxford University Press, 1949.

Lévi-Strauss, Claude. *The Raw and the Cooked: Introduction to a Science of Mythology*. Vol. 1. Trans. John Weightman and Doreen Weightman. New York: Harper and Row, 1970 (1964).

——. "The Structural Study of Myth." *Journal of American Folklore* 68, no. 270 (1955): 428–44.

Lewis, J. P. "The Language of the Threshing-Floor." *Journal of the Ceylon Branch of the Royal Asiatic Society* 8, no. 29 (1884): 237–70.

Lincoln, Bruce. *Theorizing Myth: Narrative, Ideology, and Scholarship*. Chicago: University of Chicago Press, 1999.

Liyanaāracci, R. A., ed. *Alagiyavanna Mukaveṭi Tumāgē Sävul Saṅdēśaya: Sarala Siṅhala Artha Vigrahayen Saha Anvayen Yutu Nava Saṅskaraṇaya*. Colombo: Samayavardhana Pothala Samāgama, 2009.

Liyanagē, Bandula, ed. *Ruvan Kavi*. Kuruwita: Isuru Mudraṇa, 1995.

Lopez, Donald S., and Peggy McCracken. *In Search of the Christian Buddha: How an Asian Sage Became a Medieval Saint*. New York: Norton, 2014.

Ludowyk, E. F. C. *The Footprint of the Buddha*. London: George Allen and Unwin, 1958.

MacMillan, Allister. *Seaports of India and Ceylon: Historical Descriptive Commercial Industrial Facts, Figures, and Resources*. London: W. H. and L. Collingridge, 1928.

Mahinda Amugoḍa, Raṃjanī Dedduvakumāra. *Siripā Vanayē Yōgī Bhikṣuvak Samaṅga*. Maharagama: Katru Prakāśanayak, 2008.

Mahmood, Saba. *Religious Difference in a Secular Age: A Minority Report*. Princeton, NJ: Princeton University Press, 2016.

Maitreya, Vīdāgama Mahānētra Prasādamūla. *Purāṇa Samanala Hälla*. Colombo: Granthālokayantrālaya, 1902. Colombo National Museum Library 104/T14.

Majīt, Maṇippulavar Marutūr Ē. *Mattiya Kiḻakkil Iruntu Maṭṭakkaḷappu Varai*. Kalmunai: Marutūr Veḷiyīṭṭup Paṇimaṉai, 1995.

Malan, Solomon Caesar. *The Book of Adam and Eve*. London: Williams and Norgate, 1882.

Mandelbrot, Benoit B. *The Fractal Geometry of Nature*. New York: W. H. Freeman, 1983.

Manders, Neville. "Some Breeding Experiments on *Catopsilia Pyranthe* and Notes of the Migration of Butterflies in Ceylon." *Transactions of the Royal Entomological Society of London* 4 (1904): 701–8.

Mārambē, A. J. W., ed. *Tri Siṃhalē Kaḍaim Saha Vitti*. Mahanuvara: Laṃkāpradīpa Yantrālaya, 1926.

Marty, Martin E. "Pluralisms." *Annals of the American Academy of Political and Social Science* 612 (2007): 13–25.

Marzolph, Ulrich. "From Mecca to Mashhad: The Narrative of an Illustrated Shi'i Pilgrimage Scroll from the Qajar Period." *Muqarnas* 31 (2014): 207–42.

Masefield, Peter. *Divine Revelation in Pali Buddhism*. London: George Allen and Unwin, 1986.

Masuzawa, Tomoko. *The Invention of World Religions, or, How European Universalism Was Preserved in the Language of Pluralism*. Chicago: University of Chicago Press, 2005.

Mattsson, Eskil, Madelene Ostwald, S. P. Nissanka, and Buddhi Marambe. "Homegardens as a Multi-Functional Land-Use Strategy in Sri Lanka with Focus on Carbon Sequestration." *AMBIO* 42 (2013): 892–902.

Mattsson, Eskil, Madelene Ostwald, S. P. Nissanka, and D. K. N. G. Pushpakumara. "Quantification of Carbon Stock and Tree Diversity of Homegardens in a Dry Zone Area of Moneragala Distrcit, Sri Lanka." *Agroforest Systems* 89 (2015): 435–45.

Mauss, Marcel. "Techniques of the Body." In *Incorporations*, ed. Jonathan Crary and Sanford Kwinter, 455–77. New York: Zone, 1992.

Māyārañjan. *Piṭisara Minissu*. Colombo: Sūriya Prakāśakayō, 2015 (1966).

McCutcheon, Russell T. *Critics Not Caretakers: Redescribing the Public Study of Religion*. Albany: State University of New York Press, 2001.

McGilvray, Dennis B. *Crucible of Conflict: Tamil and Muslim Society on the East Coast of Sri Lanka*. Durham, NC: Duke University Press, 2008.

——. "Sri Lankan Muslims: Between Ethno-Nationalism and the Global *Ummah*." *Nations and Nationalism* 17, no. 1 (2011): 45–64.

McKinley, Alexander. "The Apotheosis of Emptiness: God Suniyan and the Soteriological Necessity of Negativity in Sinhala Buddhism." In *The Meaning and Power of Negativity*, ed. Ingolf U. Dalferth and Trevor W. Kimball, 341–59. Tübingen: Mohr Siebeck, 2021.

——. "Farming Songs from the Poet King: Translation and Explication of a Sinhala *Janakavi* Work." *Sri Lanka Journal of the Humanities* 41, no. 1–2 (2017): 64–117.

——. "Making Lanka the Tamil Way: A Temple History at the Crossroads of Landscapes and Watersheds." *South Asian History and Culture* 11, no. 3 (2020): 254–76.

——. "Merchants, Maidens, and Mohammedans: A History of Muslim Stereotypes in Sinhala Literature of Sri Lanka." *Journal of Asian Studies* 81 (2022): 523–40.

——. "Religious Innovation in the Pilgrimage Industry: Hindu Bodhisattva Worship and Tamil Buddhistness." In *Multi-Religiosity in Contemporary Sri Lanka: Innovation, Shared Spaces, Contestation*, ed. Mark P. Whitaker, Darini Rajasingham-Senanayake and Pathmanesan Sanmugeswaran, 113–25. New York: Routledge, 2022.

——. "The Spacing of Pilgrimage: Two Journeys to Sri Pada in Sinhala Verse." *SAGAR: A South Asia Research Journal* 25 (2017): 96–133.

McKinley, Alexander, and Merin Shobhana Xavier. "The Deconstruction of Dafther Jailani: Muslim and Buddhist Contests of Original History in Sri Lanka." *History of Religions* 62, no. 3 (2023): 254–83.

McPhee, John. *Basin and Range*. New York: Farrar, Straus, Giroux, 1981.

Meynard, C. Barbier de. "Le livre des routes et des provinces, par Ibn Khordadbeh." *Journal Asiatique* (January–February 1865): 1–527.

Mīdeṇiya, Piyasēna. *Samanala Katāvak*. Colombo: S. Goḍagē saha Sahōdarayō, 2013.

Miller, Konrad. *Mappae Arabicae*. Ed. Heinz Gaube. Beihefte zum Tübinger Atlas des Vonderen Orients. 2 vols. Wiesbaden: Dr. Ludwig Reichert Verlag, 1986 (1926–1931).

The Minor Anthologies of the Pāli Canon. Vol. 3: *Chronicle of Buddhas (Buddhavaṃsa) and Basket of Conduct (Cariyāpiṭaka)*. Trans. I. B. Horner. Bristol: Pali Text Society, 1975.

Modder, F. "Kurunegala Vistaraya; with Notes on Kurunegala, Ancient and Modern." *Journal of the Ceylon Branch of the Royal Asiatic Society* 13, no. 44 (1893): 35–57.

Mohan, R. Vasundhara. *Identity Crisis of Sri Lankan Muslims*. Delhi: Mittal Publications, 1987.

Monius, Anne E. *Imagining a Place for Buddhism: Literary Culture and Religious Community in Tamil-Speaking South India*. South Asian ed. New Delhi: Navayana, 2009 (2001).

Montgomery, James E. "Serendipity, Resistance, and Multivalency: Ibn Khurradādhbih and His *Kitāb Al-Masālik Wa-L-Mamālik*." In *On Fiction and Adab in Medieval Arabic Literature*, ed. Philip F. Kennedy, 177–232. Wiesbaden: Harrassowitz Verlag, 2005.

Morgan, Llewelyn. *The Buddhas of Bamiyan*. Cambridge, MA: Harvard University Press, 2012.

Morton, Timothy. *Dark Ecology: For a Logic of Future Coexistence*. New York: Columbia University Press, 2016.

——. *Ecology Without Nature: Rethinking Environmental Aesthetics*. Cambridge, MA: Harvard University Press, 2007.

Munasinghe, Tissa, and C. B. Dissanayake. "A Plate Tectonic Model for the Geologic Evolution of Sri Lanka." *Journal of the Geological Society of India* 23 (August 1982): 369–80.

Mustawfī, Ḥamd-allāh. *The Geographical Part of the Nuzhat-Al-Qulūb*. Trans. G. Le Strange. Leyden: E. J. Brill, 1919 (1340).

Nagarajan, Vijaya. *Feeding a Thousand Souls: Women, Ritual, and Ecology in India—an Exploration of the Kōlam*. New York: Oxford University Press, 2018.

Nākaliṅkapiḷḷai, C., ed. *Takṣiṇa Kailāca Purāṇam*. Jaffna: N. Kumāracuvāmi, 1928.

Namba, Miki. "Becoming a City: Infrastructural Fetishism and Scattered Urbanization in Vientiane, Laos." In *Infrastructures and Social Complexity: A Companion*, ed. Penny Harvey, Casper Brunn Jensen, and Atsuro Morita, 76–86. New York: Routledge, 2017.

Ñāṇamoli, Bhikkhu. *The Path of Discrimination (Paṭisambhidhāmagga)*. Oxford: Pali Text Society, 2014.

Ñāṇamoli, Bhikkhu, and Bhikkhu Bodhi. *The Middle Length Discourses of the Buddha: A Translation of the Majjhima Nikāya*. 4th ed. Somerville, MA: Wisdom, 2015.

Ñāṇavimala, Kiriällē. *Sabaragamuvē Päraṇi Liyavili*. Nugegoda: Mānavahitavādi Lēkhaka Parṣadaya, 2001 (1942).

——. *Saparagamu Darśana*. Ratnapura: Śāstrādaya Yantrālaya, 1967.

Nanayakkara, S. S. M. "Sri Pada: Sanctuary for All Faiths." *Sunday Observer*, August 27, 2000.

Naṭarācā, K. C., ed. *Tirikoṇācala Purāṇam*. Koḻumpu: Intucamaya Kalācāra Aluvalkar Tiṇaikkaḷam, 1997.

Naṭarācā, Vittuvāṉ F. X. C. *Īḻattut Tamiḻ Nūl Vālāṟu*. Koḻumpu: Aracu Veḷiyīṭu, 1970.

Navaratnam, C. S. *A Short History of Hinduism in Ceylon and Three Essays on the Tamils*. Jaffna: Sri Sanmuganatha Press, 1964.

Neelis, Jason. *Early Buddhist Transmission and Trade Networks: Mobility and Exchange Within and Beyond the Northwestern Borderlands of South Asia*. Leiden: Brill, 2011.

Neubert, Christopher. "Power, Everyday Control, and Emerging Resistance in Sri Lanka's Plantations." *Contemporary South Asia* (2015): 1–14.

Nianthi, Rekha. "Climate Change Adaptation and Agroforestry in Sri Lanka." In *Climate Change Adaptation and Disaster Risk Reduction: An Asian Perspective*, ed. Rajiv Shaw, Juan M. Pulhin, and Joy Jacqueline Pereira, 285–305. Bingley: Emerald, 2010.

Nissan, Elizabeth. "Polity and Pilgrimage Centres in Sri Lanka." *Man* 23, no. 2 (1988): 253–74.

Nūṟulhak, M. M. M. *Ciṟupāṉmaiyiṉar Cila Avatāṉaṅkaḷ*. Sainthamaruthu: Marutam Kalai Ilakkiya Vaṭṭam, 2002.

Obēsēkara, Gaṇanāth, ed. *Vanni Rājāvaliya*. Colombo: S. Goḍagē saha Sahōdarayō, 2005.

Obeyesekere, Gananath. "Between the Portuguese and the Nāyakas: The Many Faces of the Kandyan Kingdom, 1591–1765." In *Sri Lanka at the Crossroads of History*, ed. Zoltán Biedermann and Alan Strathern, 161–77. London: UCL Press, 2017.

——. *The Creation of the Hunter: The Vädda Presence in the Kandyan Kingdom: A Re-Examination*. Colombo: Sailfish, 2022.

——. *The Cult of the Goddess Pattini*. Chicago: University of Chicago Press, 1984.

——. *The Doomed King: A Requiem for Śri Vikrama Rājasinha*. Colombo: Sailfish, 2017.

——. "Religious Symbolism and Political Change in Ceylon." In *The Two Wheels of Dhamma: Essays on the Theravada Tradition in India and Ceylon*, ed. Gananath Obeyesekere, Frank Reynolds, and Bardwell L. Smith, 58–78. Chambersburg, PA: American Academy of Religion, 1972.

——. "The Ritual Drama of the Sanni Demons: Collective Representations of Disease in Ceylon." *Comparative Studies in Society and History* 11, no. 2 (1969): 174–216.

Ohnuma, Reiko. *Unfortunate Destiny: Animals in the Indian Buddhist Imagination*. New York: Oxford University Press, 2017.

Okumura, Shohaku. *The Mountains and Waters Sūtra: A Practitioner's Guide to Dōgen's "Sansuikyō."* Somerville, MA: Wisdom, 2018.

Osanai, Yasuhito, Krishnan Sajeev, Masaaki Owada, K. V. W. Kehelpannala, W. K. Bernard Prame, Nobuhiko Nakano, and Sarath Jayatileke. "Metamorphic Evolution of High-Pressure and Ultrahigh-Temperature Granulites from the Highland Complex, Sri Lanka." *Journal of Asian Earth Sciences* 28 (2006): 20–37.

Paññālōka, Deniyāyē, ed. *Prācīta Madhyama Vibhāgayaṭa Niyamita Samantakūṭavaṇṇanā*. Colombo: Samayavardhana Pothala Samāgama, 2001.

Paraṇavitāna, Rōhiṇi, ed. *Sītāvaka Haṭana*. Śrī Laṅkā Rajayē Mudraṇa Depārtamēnttuva: Madhyama Saṅskrutika Aramudala, 1999.

Paranavitana, S., and C. E. Godakumbara, eds. *Epigraphia Zeylanica: Being Lithic and Other Inscriptions of Ceylon*. Vol. 5, part 3. Ceylon: Government Press, 1965.

Paranavitana, Senarat. *The God of Adam's Peak*. Ascona: Artibus Asiae Publishers, 1958.

Parker, H. *Ancient Ceylon*. London: Luzac, 1909.

Patel, Roshni. "Releasing Boundaries, Relieving Suffering, Becoming Pained: An Engagement with Indian Buddhism and Martin Heidegger." *Philosophy East and West* 69, no. 4 (2019): 1053–75.

Pathmanathan, S. "The Munnesvaram Tamil Inscription of Parākramabāhu VI." *Journal of the Sri Lanka Branch of the Royal Asiatic Society* 18 (1974): 54–69.

——. "The Portuguese in Northeast Sri Lanka (1543–1658): An Assessment of Impressions Recorded in Tamil Chronicles and Poems." In *Re-Exploring the Links: History and Constructed Histories Between Portugal and Sri Lanka*, ed. Jorge Flores, 29–47. Wiesbaden: Harrassowitz Verlag, 2007.

Patiraāracci, Jayaratna. *Dakuṇu Budu Siripatula Pihiṭi Makkama Saha Rāvaṇa Rajugē Sellipi*. Boralesgamuwa: Udaya Gräfiks, 2005.

——. "Jana Kaviyā Duṭu Vam Siripādaya Saha Dakuṇu Siripādaya." *Budusaraṇa*, January 22, 2008.

——. "Ṭolamiṭa Anuva Makkama Kalā Oya Muhudu Sīmāvayi!" *Budusaraṇa*, July 10, 2008.

Perera, Arthur A. *Sinhalese Folklore Notes*. Bombay: British India Press, 1917.

Perērā, B. E. *Śrī Pāda Lāñchana: Samantakūṭa Parvataya Hā Divā Guhāva*. Nugegoda: Prasanta Mudraṇa, 1979.

Perērā, K. D. G. *Śrī Pāda Vandanā Gamana*. Sevyaśrī Yantrālaya: J. A. Guṇsēna, 1926. Colombo National Museum Library 104/K4.

Perera, K. R. *Samanaḷagamana Saha Śripādavandanāva*. Colombo: K. D. Siyadōris Appuhāmi, 1890.

Perēra, M. G. K. Jōn. *Śrī Pādavandanāgamana Nohot Perasirit Saha Dänsirit*. Aluthgama: I. D. Jōn Siññō, 1924. Colombo National Museum Library 104/C8.

Perera, Nihal. *People's Spaces: Coping, Familiarizing, Creating*. New York: Routledge, 2016.

Perera, Nimal, Nikos Kourampas, Ian A. Simpson, Siran U. Deraniyagala, David Bulbeck, Johan Kamminga, Jude Perera, Dorain Q. Fuller, Katherine Szabó, and Nuno V. Oliveira. "People of the Ancient Rainforest: Late Pleistocene Foragers at the Batadomba-Lena Rockshelter, Sri Lanka." *Journal of Human Evolution* 61 (2011): 254–69.

Perērā, Tiyaḍōr G. *Samanaḷa Sandeśaya*. Dharmavardhana Mudra Yantrālayē: Śrīmat Ārtar Älibänk Hävlok, 1895.

Perniola, V. *The Catholic Church in Sri Lanka: The Dutch Period.* Vol. 2, *1712–1746: Original Documents Translated Into English*. Dehiwala: Tisara Prakasakayo, 1983.

Peterson, Indira Viswanathan. *Poems to Śiva: The Hymns of the Tamil Saints*. Princeton, NJ: Princeton University Press, 1989.

Pfaffenberger, Bryan. "Serious Pilgrims and Frivolous Tourists: The Chimera of Tourism in the Pilgrimage of Sri Lanka." *Annals of Tourism Research* 10 (1983): 57–74.

Pieris, P. E. *Ceylon: The Portuguese Era, Being a History of the Island for the Period 1505–1658*. Vol. 1. Colombo: Colombo Apothecaries, 1913.

Pinhāmi, Gedara. *Dolahadeviyangē Kavipota Saha Dalumura Upata*. Mahanuvara: T. M. Migel Appu, 1900.

Ponnambalam, Satchi. *Sri Lanka: National Conflict and the Tamil Liberation Struggle*. London: Zed Books, 1983.

Ponsēkā, Don Kornēlis. *Sumaṇa Śaila Mārgā Laṅkāraya Hevat Sumanaselmagalakara*. Sarasavisaňdaräsa Mudrāyantra Śālāvē, 1891.

Povinelli, Elizabeth A. *Geontologies: A Requiem to Late Liberalism*. Durham, NC: Duke University Press, 2016.

Pragnaloka, H. U., ed. *Purāṇa Sivpada Saṃgrahava*. Colombo: Government Publications, 1952.

Pranāndu, M. S. *Samanala Hasuna*. Panadura: M. Jēsan Pranāndu, 1932. Colombo National Museum Library 104/Z2.

Prasad, Leela. *The Audacious Raconteur: Sovereignty and Storytelling in Colonial India*. Ithaca, NY: Cornell University Press, 2020.

——. "Co-Being, a Praxis of the Public: Lessons from Hindu Devotional (Bhakti) Narrative, Arendt, and Gandhi." *Journal of the American Academy of Religion* 85, no. 1 (2017): 199–223.

Pridham, Charles. *An Historical, Political, and Statistical Account of Ceylon and Its Dependencies*. 2 vols. London: T. and W. Boone, 1849.

Puṅcibaṇḍāra, Dehigama Paṇḍita Samarasiṅha. *Buduguṇa Kav Nohot Śrīpāda Vandanāva*. Henarathgoda: Siriyālōka Mudraṇālaya, 1922. Colombo National Museum Library 104/C8.

Queyroz, Ferñao de. *The Temporal and Spiritual Conquest of Ceylon*. Trans. S. G. Perera. 3 vols. Colombo: A. C. Richards, 1930.

Ṟahīm, Apturˌ. *Muslim Tamiḻp Pulavarkaḷ*. Chennai: Yuṉivarsal Papliṣars aṇṭ Puk Cellars, 1980 (1957).

Rahula, Maha Thero Sri. *Selalihini Sandesa*. Ed. K. W. De A. Wijesinghe. Colombo: Godage International Publishers, 2006 (1949).

Rajapaksa, Ranjith, and Lasantha Niroshan Perera. "Sri Pada Pilgrimage Will Continue: Prelate." *Daily Mirror*, March 17, 2020.

Rājapakṣa, Śrīyāṇi. *Sabaragamu Kumāra Samayama*. Colombo: S. Goḍagē saha Sahōdarayō, 2000.

Rājāvaliya. Trans. A. J. Suraweera. Ratmalana: Sarvodaya Vishva Lekha, 2000.

Ramaswamy, Sumathi. *The Lost Land of Lemuria: Fabulous Geographies, Catastrophic Histories.* Berkeley: University of California Press, 2004.

——. *Passions of the Tongue: Language Devotion in Tamil India, 1891–1970.* Berkeley: University of California Press, 1997.

Rambukwella, Harshana. *The Politics and Poetics of Authenticity: A Cultural Genealogy of Sinhala Nationalism.* London: UCL Press, 2018.

Ratnasēkara, Hēnepola G. K. *Sūvisi Vivaraṇa Śrī Pāda Vandanāva.* Maradana: Śrī Laṃkōdaya Yantrālaya, 1923. Colombo National Museum Library 104/B20.

The Reḥla of Ibn Baṭṭūṭa (India, Maldive Islands and Ceylon). Trans. Mahdi Husain. Baroda: Oriental Institute, 1953.

Rhys Davids, T. W., and William Stede, eds. *The Pali Text Society's Pali-English Dictionary.* London: Pali Text Society, 1921–1925.

Ricci, Ronit. *Banishment and Belonging: Exile and Diaspora in Sarandib, Lanka and Ceylon.* Cambridge: Cambridge University Press, 2019.

Richman, Paula. *Women, Branch Stories, and Religious Rhetoric in a Tamil Buddhist Text.* Syracuse, NY: Maxwell School of Citizenship and Public Affairs, Syracuse University, 1988.

Rocher, Ludo. *The Purāṇas.* Wiesbaden: Otto Harrassowitz, 1986.

Rockhill, W. W. "Notes of the Relations and Trade of China with the Eastern Archipelago and the Coast of the Indian Ocean During the Fourteenth Century." *T'oung Pao* 16, no. 3 (July 1915): 374–92.

Rogers, John D. "Religious Belief, Economic Interest and Social Policy: Temple Endowments in Sri Lanka During the Governorship of William Gregory, 1872–77." *Modern Asian Studies* 21, no. 2 (1987): 349–69.

Rost, Adolphus E. L. "Adam's Peak (Ceylon) in 1902." *Journal of the Royal Asiatic Society of Great Britain and Ireland* (1903): 655–57.

Rowell, George. "Ceylon's Kristallnacht: A Reassessment of the Pogrom of 1915." *Modern Asian Studies* 43, no. 3 (2009): 619–48.

Rudwick, Martin J. S. *Bursting the Limits of Time: The Reconstruction of Geohistory in the Age of Revolution.* Chicago: University of Chicago Press, 2005.

Rūpasiṃha, Karuṇādāsa. *Śrī Pāda Vandanā Sāhitya.* Colombo: Äs Goḍagē saha Sahōdarayō, 2013.

Ruschenberger, W. S. W. *Narrative of a Voyage Round the World, During the Years 1835, 36, and 37; Including a Narrative of an Embassy to the Sultan of Muscat and the King of Siam.* Vol. 1. London: Richard Bentley, 1838.

Russell, William Howard. *My Diary in India, in the Year 1858–9.* London: Routledge, Warne, and Routledge, 1860.

Ryan, Bryce. *Caste in Modern Ceylon: The Sinhalese System in Transition.* New Brunswick: Rutgers University Press, 1953.

Saddhāratna, Pūjya Kanattegoḍa. *Bududahama Hā Parisara Pavitratāva.* Divulapitiya: Sarasvatī Prakāśana, 2011.

Salā, G. M. *Samanala Gamanā Laṅkāraya.* Kegalle: Vidyākalpa Yantrālaya, 1924. Colombo National Museum Library 104/C8.

"Samanala and Its Shadow." *Cornhill Magazine* 6, no. 31 (January 1886): 44–53.

Samarasēkara, J. A. Sumanapāla. *Tovil: Devol Maḍuva Hā Aṭasanniya Piḷibaňda Samāja Vidyātmaka Vigrahayak.* Colombo: Guṇasēna, 1995.

Sandiford, M., R. Powell, S. F. Martin, and L. R. K. Perera. "Thermal and Baric Evolution of Garnet Granulites from Sri Lanka." *Journal of Metamorphic Geology* 6 (1988): 351–64.

Sannasgala, Puñcibaṇḍāra. *Siṃhala Sāhitya Vaṃśaya.* Colombo: Lēkhavus Mudraṇālaya, 1964. (1961).

Sawers, Simon, and Henry Marshall. *Recollections of a Journey from Kandy to Caltura, by Way of Adam's Peak, Made in the Year 1819.* Edinburgh: Royal College of Physicians of Edinburgh, 1823.

Schaefer, Donovan O. *Religious Affects: Animality, Evolution, and Power.* Durham, NC: Duke University Press, 2015.

Scherzer, Karl. *Narrative of the Circumnavigation of the Globe by the Austrian Frigate Novara, in the Years 1857, 1858, & 1859.* Vol. 1. London: Saunders, Otley, 1861.

Schonthal, Benjamin. "Buddhist Perspectives on Freedom of Religion and Belief." In *Routledge Handbook to Freedom of Religion and Belief,* ed. Silvio Ferrari, Mark Hill, Arif A. Jamal, and Rossella Bottoni, 73–87. New York: Routledge, 2020.

——. "Economies of Expert Religion in Sri Lanka." *Journal of Religious and Political Practice* 4, no. 1 (2018): 27–45.

——. "The Tolerations of Theravada Buddhism." In *Toleration in Comparative Perspective,* ed. Vicki A. Spencer, 179–96. Lanham, MD: Lexington Books, 2018.

Scott, David. "Dehistoricizing History." In *Unmaking the Nation: The Politics of Identity and History in Modern Sri Lanka,* ed. Pradeep Jeganathan and Qadri Ismail, 20–33. New York: SSA Sri Lanka, 2009 (1995).

Scott, David Allen. "The Iranian Face of Buddhism." *East and West* 40, no. 1/4 (December 1990): 43–77.

Seed, John, Joanna Macy, Pat Fleming, and Arne Naess. *Thinking Like a Mountain: Towards a Council of All Beings.* Philadelphia: New Society Publishers, 1988.

Senaratne, L. B. "Siri Pada Election: Kandy Lawyers to Lodge Protest." *Sunday Times,* December 4, 2011.

Sēnāsiṃha, Tilak. *Saman Deviyangē Aḍaviya (Śrīpāda Aḍaviyē Cārikā Saṭahan Peḷak).* Kudabollana: Udaya Prinṭars Änḍ Pabliṣars, 1997.

Senaveratna, John M. *Dictionary of Proverbs of the Sinhalese: Including Also Their Adages, Aphorisms, Apologues, Apothegms, Bywords, Dictums, Maxims, Mottoes, Precepts, Saws, and Sayings: Together with the Connected Myths, Legends, and Folk-Tales.* Colombo: Times of Ceylon, 1936.

Seneviratna, N. B. M., ed. *Siṃhala Kāvya Saṃgrahaya: Mātara Yugaya.* Colombo: Laṃkā Jātika Kautukāgāra Prakāśana, 1964.

Serres, Michel. *The Natural Contract.* Trans. Elizabeth MacArthur and William Paulson. Ann Arbor: University of Michigan Press, 1995.

——. *Religion: Rereading What Is Bound Together.* Trans. Malcolm DeBevoise. Stanford, CA: Stanford University Press, 2022.

Shafiq, Suhanna. *Seafarers of the Seven Seas: The Maritime Culture in the Kitāb 'ajā'ib Al-Hind (the Book of the Marvels of India) by Buzurg Ibn Shahriyār (D. 399/1009).* Islamkundliche Untersuchungen. Berlin: Klaus Schwarz Verlag, 2013.

Shahriyār, Buzurg ibn. *The Book of the Wonders of India: Mainland, Sea, and Islands.* Trans. G. S. P. Freeman-Grenville. London: East-West Publications, 1981.

Sharma, Mukul. *Green and Saffron: Hindu Nationalism and Indian Environmental Politics.* Ranikhet: Permanent Black, 2012.

Shryock, Andrew, Daniel Lord Smail, and Timothy K. Earle, eds. *Deep History: The Architecture of Past and Present.* Berkeley: University of California Press, 2011.

Shulman, David. *Tamil Temple Myths: Sacrifice and Divine Marriage in the South Indian Saiva Tradition.* Princeton, NJ: Princeton University Press, 1980.

Siebenga, Rianne. "Colonial India's 'Fanatical Fakirs' and Their Popular Representations." *History and Anthropology* 23, no. 4 (2012): 445–66.

Silva, Kalinga Tudor. "Gossip, Rumor, and Propaganda in Anti-Muslim Campaigns of the Bodu Bala Sena." In *Buddhist Extremists and Muslim Minorities: Religious Conflict in Contemporary Sri Lanka*, ed. John Clifford Holt, 119–39. New York: Oxford University Press, 2016.

Silvā, Yon Merañña Siman Hēvāgē Sālis. *Sirisaraṇabhivādanaya*. Grantha Prakāśayantrālayē, 1892.

Singh, Vikash. *Uprising of the Fools: Pilgrimage as Moral Protest in Contemporary India*. Stanford, CA: Stanford University Press, 2017.

Sinnatamby, J. R. *Ceylon in Ptolemy's Geography*. Colombo: Times of Ceylon, 1968.

Siripāla, Nōman. *Sabaragamu Janakaviyē Samāja Muhuṇuvara*. Nugegoda: Piyasiri Prinṭin Sisṭams, 1999.

Siriwardene, Serika. "Rethinking Religious Education." *Daily Mirror*, August 7, 2020.

Sivaraja Pillai, K. N. *Agastya in the Tamil Land*. Mylapore: University of Madras, 1930.

Sivaramakrishnan, K. "Ethics of Nature in Indian Environmental History." *Modern Asian Studies* 49, no. 4 (2015): 1261–310.

Sivasundaram, Sujit. *Islanded: Britain, Sri Lanka, and the Bounds of an Indian Ocean Colony*. Chicago: University of Chicago Press, 2013.

The Skanda Purāṇa. 20 vols. Delhi: Motilal Banarsidass, 1950–2003.

Skeen, William. *Adam's Peak: Legendary Traditional, and Historic Notices of the Samanala and Srí-Páda with a Descriptive Account of the Pilgrims' Route from Colombo to the Sacred Foot-Print*. Colombo: W. L. H. Skeen, 1870.

Skinner, Thomas. *Fifty Years in Ceylon*. London: W. H. Allen, 1891.

Smith, Jonathan Z. *Relating Religion: Essays in the Study of Religion*. Chicago: University of Chicago Press, 2004.

Somadasa, K. D., ed. *Catalogue of the Hugh Nevill Collection of Sinhalese Manuscripts in the British Library*. 7 vols. London: British Library, 1987–1995.

——. *Catalogue of the Sinhalese Manuscripts in the Library of the Wellcome Institute for the History of Medicine*. London: Wellcome Trust, 1996.

Sōmasiri, Ranmalī. "Kaḷugalen Kaḷa Doḷosmahēpahana Siripā Maḷuvaṭa Guvanin Genagiya Trāsajanaka Meheyuma." *Lakbima*, January 12, 2014, 16.

Sorkhabi, Rasoul. "Ananda K. Coomaraswamy: From Geology to *Philosophia Perennis*." *Current Science* 94, no. 3 (2008): 394–401.

Spencer, Jonathan, Jonathan Goodhand, Shahul Hasbullah, Bart Klem, Benedikt Korf, and Kalinga Tudor Silva. *Checkpoint, Temple, Church and Mosque: A Collaborative Ethnography of War and Peace*. London: Pluto Press, 2015.

Sponberg, Alan. "Green Buddhism and the Hierarchy of Compassion." In *Buddhism and Ecology: The Interconnection of Dharma and Deeds*, ed. Mary Evelyn Tucker and Duncan Ryūken Williams, 351–76. Cambridge, MA: Harvard University Press, 1997.

"Śrī Pādasthānayē Vihāra Maluva." *Savadeśa Mitrayā* Vesak Atirekaya (BE 2473): 58.

Śrī Pādavarṇanā Kāvyaya Hevat Śrīpāda Alaṅkāraya. D. P. D. Raṇatuṅga Appuhāmi, 1910. Colombo National Museum Library 104/C8.

Star, Susan Leigh. "The Ethnography of Infrastructure." *American Behavioral Scientist* 43, no. 3 (1999): 377–91.

Stern, S. M., Sophie Walzer, and Muḥammad ibn ʿAlī Ibn Bābawayh al-Qummī. *Three Unknown Buddhist Stories in an Arabic Version*. Columbia: University of South Carolina Press, 1971.

Still, John. *The Jungle Tide*. 3rd ed. Edinburgh: W. Blackwood and Sons, 1930.

——. "Notes on Adam's Peak and Some of the Paths in the Range." *Spolia Zeylanica* 5 (1908): 80–86.

Stone, Christopher D. *Should Trees Have Standing? Law, Morality, and the Environment*. 3rd ed. New York: Oxford University Press, 2010.

Stone, Michael. "The Death of Adam: An Armenian Adam Book." *Harvard Theological Review* 59, no. 3 (July 1966): 283–91.

Strathern, Alan. "Towards the Source-Criticism of Sitavaka-Period Heroic Literature, Part Two: The *Sitavaka Hatana*: Notes on a Grounded Text." *Sri Lanka Journal of the Humanities* 34, nos. 1–2 (2008): 45–72.

Subhāvikrama, Munidāsa. "Samanoḷa Mudunēdī." *Sarasavi Hañḍa* 1, no. 1 (March 1934): 6.

Subramanian, Samanth. *This Divided Island: Stories from the Sri Lankan War*. Haryana: Penguin India, 2014.

Sudhīra, Kaḍarodagama. *Saparagamu Paḷātē Diya Äli Puda Sirit Vimarśanaya (Ratnapura Distrikkaya Āśrayeni)*. Colombo: S. Godagē saha Sahōdarayō, 2005.

Sujāta, Talgaskandē. *Śrī Pāda Vandanā Atpota*. Ratnapura: Prinṭ Havus, n.d.

Suḷu Rājavaliya. Colombo: Ratna Pot Prakāśakayō, 2005.

Sundberg, Jeffrey, and Rolf Giebel. "The Life of the Tang Court Monk Vajrabodhi as Chronicled by Lü Xiang: South Indian and Śrī Laṅkān Antecedents to the Arrival of the Buddhist Vajrayāna in Eight-Century Java and China." *Pacific World* Third Series, no. 13 (Fall 2011): 129–222.

Sunil, Āriyaratna, ed. *Jōn Da Silvā Nurti Nāṭya Ekatuva*. Vol. 3. Colombo: S. Goḍagē saha Sahōdarayō, 2008.

Sūrasēna, A. G. *Paurāṇika Janapravāda Hā Janaśräti*. Thalawathugoda: Ḍī Sī Guṇasēkara, 2000. 1999.

Suraweera, A. V. *The Rājāvaliya: A Comprehensive Account of the Rulers of Sri Lanka, and the First Ever Translation of the Alakeśvara Yuddhaya*. Colombo: Vijitha Yapa Publications, 2014.

Swaris, Nalin. *The Buddha's Way to Human Liberation: A Socio-Historical Approach*. Nugegoda: Sarasavi Publishers, 2008 (1999).

Sykes, Jim. *The Musical Gift: Sonic Generosity in Post-War Sri Lanka*. New York: Oxford University Press, 2018.

Tambiah, Stanley J. *World Conqueror and World Renouncer: A Study of Buddhism and Polity in Thailand Against a Historical Background*. Cambridge: Cambridge University Press, 1976.

Taneja, Anand Vivek. *Jinnealogy: Time, Islam, and Ecological Thought in the Medieval Ruins of Delhi*. Stanford, CA: Stanford University Press, 2018.

Tennekoon, N. Serena. "Rituals of Development: The Accelerated Mahaväli Development Program of Sri Lanka." *American Ethnologist* 15, no. 2 (1988): 294–310.

Tennent, James Emerson. *Ceylon: An Account of the Island, Physical, Historical, and Topographical, with Notices of Its Natural History, Antiquities, and Productions*. 2 vols. London: Longman, Green, Longman, and Roberts, 1859.

Tezcan, Semih. *Das Uigurische Insadi-Sūtra*. Berlin: Akademie-Verlag, 1974.

Thambyahpillay, George. "Tropical Cyclones and the Climate of Ceylon." *University of Ceylon Review* 17, nos. 3–4 (1959): 137–80.

Thawfeeq, M. M. *Muslim Mosaics*. Colombo: Moors' Islamic Cultural Home, 1972.

——. "Muslim Saints and Shrines in Sri Lanka." In *The First Twenty One Years: Moors' Islamic Cultural Home, 1944–1965*, 39–41. Colombo: Moors' Islamic Cultural Home, 1965.

Thornton, John. *The English Pilot. The Third Book. Describing the Sea-Coasts, Capes, Headlands, Straits, Soundings, Sands, Shoals, Rocks, and Dangers. The Islands, Bays, Roads, Harbors and Ports in Oriental Navigation*. London: John How, 1703.

Tibbets, Gerald R. "The Beginnings of a Cartographic Tradition." In *The History of Cartography*, vol. 2, book 1, *Cartography in the Traditional Islamic and South Asian Societies*, ed. J. B. Harley and David Woodward, 90–107. Chicago: University of Chicago Press, 1992.

Tomalin, Emma. *Biodivinity and Biodiversity: The Limits to Religious Environmentalism*. Burlington: Ashgate, 2009.

Trainor, Kevin. "The Buddha's 'Cave of the Midday Rest' and Buddhist Relic Practices in Sri Lanka." *Material Religion* 9, no. 4 (2013): 516–21.

The Travels of Ibn Battūta A.D. 1325-1354. Trans. H. A. R. Gibb. Vol. 2. Cambridge: Hakluyt Society, 1962.

The Travels of Ibn Baṭṭūṭa A.D. 1325–1354. Trans. H. A. R. Gibb and C. F. Beckingham. Vol. 4. London: Hakluyt Society, 1994.

Tschacher, Torsten. "Can 'Om' Be an Islamic Term? Translations, Encounters, and Islamic Discourse in Vernacular South Asia." *South Asian History and Culture* 5, no. 2 (2014): 195–211.

——. "Drowning in the Ocean of Tamil: Islamic Texts and the Historiography of Tamil Literature." In *Literature and Nationalist Ideology: Writing Histories of Modern Indian Languages*, ed. Hans Harder, 51–83. New Delhi: Social Science Press, 2011.

Tsing, Anna Lowenhaupt. *The Mushroom at the End of the World: On the Possibility of Life in Capitalist Ruins*. Princeton, NJ: Princeton University Press, 2015.

Tuan, Yi-Fu. *Space and Place: The Perspective of Experience*. Minneapolis: University of Minnesota Press, 1977.

Turner, Victor. "The Center Out There: Pilgrim's Goal." *History of Religions* 12, no. 3 (1973): 191–230.

Udāris, T. H. *Śrīpāda Vandanāva Saha Gālu Kōralē Siṭa Yana Vandanākārayingē Gaman Vistaraya*. Ambalangoḍa: Vijaya Yantrālaya, 1923. Colombo National Museum Library 104/C8.

Uḍavatta, Amal. *Śrī Pāda Aḍaviya: Saṃskrutika Vividhatvaya Saha Jaiva Vividhatvaya*. Dankotuwa: Vāsana Pot Prakāśakayō, 2014.

Uisso, A. J. "Agroforestry Practices as an Option for Climate Change Adaptation: A Review." *Octa Journal of Environmental Research* 3, no. 3 (2015): 219–25.

Vajirabuddhi Himi, Maḍalagama. *Dēva Purāṇaya: Saman Deviňdu Hā Saman Devola*. Ed. Saviman Urugoḍawatta. Balangoda: Sunil Śānta Vīrasēkara, 2007.

Valgampaya, Mahathera Abhayaraja Pirivena. *Rājaratnākaraya (the Gem Mine of Kings)*. Trans. Kusuma Karunaratne. Colombo: Central Cultural Fund, 2008.

van der Leeuw, G. *Religion in Essence and Manifestation* Trans. J. E. Turner. 2 vols. New York: Cloister Library, Harper and Row, 1963 (1933).

van Gelder, Geert Jan. "To Eat or Not to Eat Elephant: A Travelling Story in Arabic and Persian Literature." *Bulletin of SOAS* 66, no. 3 (2003): 419–30.

van Sanden, J. C. *Sonahar: A Brief History of the Moors of Ceylon*. Colombo: Daily Mail Press, 1925.

Vásquez, Manuel A. *More than Belief: A Materialist Theory of Religion*. New York: Oxford University Press, 2011.

Vedeha Thera. *In Praise of Mount Samanta*. Trans. Ann Appleby Hazlewood. London: Pali Text Society, 1986.

Vellupillai, A. "Historical Evaluation of Kōnēcar Kalveṭṭu." In *Perspectives in Archaeology: Leelananda Prematilleke Festschrift*, ed. Sudharshan Seneviratne, 95–100. Peradeniya: University of Peradeniya, Department of Archaeology, 1990.

Vettasiṅha, D. P. *Śrīpādasthānayaṭa Hā Samandēvālavalaṭa Adhigruhita Siri Sumana Saman Deviyō*. Anula Yantralaya: H. D. D. Guṇasēkara, n.d.

Vijētuṅga, Navanäliye. *Śrī Pādasthānaya*. Navanagara: Dänuma Väḍuma Prakaśayō, 2014.

Vikramasiṅha, T. B. "Mahakaňdugala Matadī." *Siṅhala Kav Kiruḷa* 12, no. 3 (March 1934): 43.

Vimalakīrti, Dhammadinnācārya. *Saddharmaratnākaraya.* Ed. V. D. S. Guṇavardhana. Colombo: Samayavardhana Pothala Samāgama, 2001.

Vimalakīrti, Mädauyangoḍa. *Vimalakīrtigē Siṃhala Āṇḍuva.* Colombo: S. Goḍagē saha Sahōdarayō, 2001 (1955).

Vimalaratna, Mänävē. "Rāvaṇā Parapurē Säňgavuṇa Toraturu." *Divayina*, July 22, 2009.

Vīrasūriya, Guṇasiri Baṇḍā. *Jalaya Parisaraya Minisā Saha Budu Dahama.* Colombo: Āriya Prakāśakayō, 2013.

Vīratuṅga, Sumanā. *Kavi Situvili.* Colombo: Mavbima Kartru Maṇḍalaya, 2014.

Vitanage, P. W. "The Geology, Structure and Tectonics of Sri Lanka and South India." In *Recent Advances in the Geology of Sri Lanka: Proceedings of the Symposium on the Geology of Sri Lanka, Peradeniya, 1983.* Paris: CIFEG, 1985.

Vitarana, K. M. *Sri Pada: Adam's Peak, the Holy Mountain of Religious Amity and Miracles.* Nugegoda: Sarasavi Publishers, 2011.

Wadia, D. N. "The Ring of Waterfalls in Central Ceylon and Its Bearing on the Geological Structure and Earth Movements." *Spolia Zeylanica* 23, no. 1 (1941): 19–20.

Waldstein, Michael, and Frederik Wisse, eds. *The Apocryphon of John: A Synopsis of Nag Hammadi Codices Ii,1, Iii,1, and Iv,1 with Bg 8502,2.* Vol. 33. Leiden: E. J. Brill, 1995.

Walker, Mrs. Col. "Journal of an Ascent to the Summit of Adam's Peak." In *Companion to the Botanical Magazine*, ed. W. J. Hooker, 2–14. London: Samuel Curtis, 1835.

Wallace, Alfred Russel. *The Geographical Distribution of Animals: With a Study of the Relations of Living and Extinct Faunas as Elucidating the Past Changes of the Earth's Surface.* New York: Harper and Brothers, 1876.

Walleser, Max, and Herman Kopp, eds. *Manorathapūraṇī: Buddhaghosa's Commentary on the Aṅguttara-Nikāya.* Vol. 2. 2nd ed. London: Pali Text Society, 1967.

Walters, Jonathan S. "Buddhist History: The Sri Lankan Pāli Vaṃsas and Their Commentary." In *Querying the Medieval: Texts and the History of Practices in South Asia*, 99–164. New York: Oxford University Press, 2000.

——. "Lovely Lady Lanka: A Tenth-Century Description." *Sri Lanka Journal of the Humanities* 19, nos. 1–2 (1993): 45–56.

——. "Multireligion on the Bus: Beyond 'Influence' and 'Syncretism' in the Study of Religious Meetings." In *Unmaking the Nation: The Politics of Identity and History in Modern Sri Lanka*, ed. Pradeep Jeganathan and Qadri Ismail, 34–60. Colombo: Social Scientists' Association, 2009 (1995).

Walton, Jeremy F., and Neena Mahadev. "Religious Plurality, Interreligious Pluralism, and Spatialities of Religious Difference." *Religion and Society: Advances in Research* 10 (2019): 81–91.

Webb, James L. A. *Tropical Pioneers: Human Agency and Ecological Change in the Highlands of Sri Lanka, 1800–1900.* Athens: Ohio University Press, 2002.

Weerakoon, B. M. B., A. M. R. S. Bandara, and K. B. Ranawana. "Impact of Canopy Cover on Butterfly Abundance and Diversity in Intermediate Zone Forest of Sri Lanka." *Journal of Tropical Forestry and Environment* 5, no. 1 (2015): 41–46.

Westerhoff, Jan. *The Dispeller of Disputes: Nāgārjuna's Vigrahavyāvartanī.* New York: Oxford University Press, 2010.

White, David Gordon. *Myths of the Dog-Man.* Chicago: University of Chicago Press, 1991.

Whitmore, Luke. *Mountain, Water, Rock, God: Understanding Kedarnath in the Twenty-First Century.* Oakland: University of California Press, 2018.

Wickramasinghe, Anoja. "Conservation Innovations of Peripheral Communities: Case Study of Adam's Peak Wilderness." *Journal of the National Science Foundation of Sri Lanka* 31, nos. 1–2 (2003): 105–23.

——. *People and the Forest: Management of the Adam's Peak Wilderness.* Battaramulla: Sri Lanka Forest Department, 1995.

Wickremasinghe, Don Martino de Zilva, H. W. Codrington, and S. Paranavitana, eds. *Epigraphia Zeylanica: Being Lithic and Other Inscriptions of Ceylon.* 4 vols. London: Published for the Government of Ceylon by H. Frowde, 1904–1934.

Williams, C. B. "A Study of Butterfly Migration in South India and Ceylon, Based Largely on Records by Messrs. J. Evershed, E. E. Green, J. C. F. Fryer and W. Ormiston." *Transactions of the Royal Entomological Society of London* 75 (1927): 1–33.

Witharana, Bandura Dileepa. *Negotiating Power and Constructing the Nation: Engineering in Sri Lanka.* Colombo: Tambapanni Academic Publishers, 2022.

Wittgenstein, Ludwig. *On Certainty.* Ed. G. E. M. Anscombe and G. H. von Wright. Trans. Denis Paul and G. E. M. Anscombe. Oxford: Blackwell, 1969.

Witzel, E. J. Michael. *The Origins of the World's Mythologies.* New York: Oxford University Press, 2012.

Woodward, George Ratcliffe, and Harold Mattingly. *St. John Damascene: Barlaam and Ioasaph.* New York: Macmillan, 1914.

Wright, G. N. *A Guide to the Lakes of Killarney.* London: Baldwin, Cradock, and Joy, 1822.

Wright, John B. "Sri Pada: Sacred Pilgrimage Mountain of Sri Lanka." *Focus on Geography* 50, no. 2 (2007): 1–6.

Yusuf, Imtiyaz. "Muslim-Buddhist Relations Caught Between Nalanda and Pattani." In *Ethnic Conflict in Buddhist Societies in South and Southeast Asia*, ed. K. M. de Silva, 157–93. Colombo: International Centre for Ethnic Studies, 2015.

Zadeh, Travis E. *Mapping Frontiers Across Medieval Islam: Geography, Translation, and the 'Abbāsid Empire.* London: I. B. Tauris, 2011.

Zalasiewicz, Jan, Mike Walker, Phil Gibbard, and John Lowe. "When Did the Anthropocene Begin? A Mid-Twentieth Century Boundary Is Stratigraphically Optimal." *Quaternary International* 383 (2015): 196–203.

Zalasiewicz, Jan, Mark Williams, Richard Fortey, Alan Smith, Tiffany L. Barry, Angela L. Coe, Paul R. Brown, Peter F. Rawson, Andrew Gale, Philip Gibbard, John F. Gregory, Mark W. Hounslow, Andrew C. Kerr, Paul Pearson, Robert Knox, John Powell, Colin Waters, John Marshall, Michael Oates, and Philip Stone. "Stratigraphy of the Anthropocene." *Philosophical Transactions of the Royal Society* 369 (2011): 1036–55.

Index

GPSR Authorized Representative: Easy Access System Europe, Mustamäe tee 50, 10621 Tallinn, Estonia, gpsr.requests@easproject.com

www.ingramcontent.com/pod-product-compliance
Lightning Source LLC
Chambersburg PA
CBHW022136020426
42334CB00015B/917
9780231210614